DOGFIGHT

DOGFIGHT

THE TRANSATLANTIC
BATTLE OVER AIRBUS

Ian McIntyre

Westport, Connecticut
London

Library of Congress Cataloging-in-Publication Data

McIntyre, Ian.
    Dogfight : the transatlantic battle over Airbus / Ian McIntyre.
      p.   cm.
    Includes bibliographical references and index.
    ISBN 0-275-94278-3
    1. Airbus Industrie. 2. Aircraft industry—Europe. 3. Aircraft
industry—United States. 4. Competition, Unfair—Europe.
5. Industry and state—Europe.   I. Title.
    HD9711.E884A345 1992
    338.8'8729133349—dc20   92-168

British Library Cataloguing in Publication Data is available.

Library of Congress Catalog Card Number: 92-168
ISBN: 0-275-94278-3

First published in 1992

Praeger Publishers, 88 Post Road West, Westport, CT 06881
An imprint of Greenwood Publishing Group, Inc.

Printed in the United States of America

The paper used in this book complies with the
Permanent Paper Standard issued by the National
Information Standards Organization (Z39.48-1984).

10 9 8 7 6 5 4 3 2 1

To Rupert,

who never just stands there

"All systems either of preference or of restraint, therefore, being thus completely taken away, the obvious and simple system of Natural Liberty establishes itself of its own accord. Every man, as long as he does not violate the laws of Justice, is left perfectly free to pursue his own interest his own way, and to bring both his industry and capital into competition with those of any other man or order of men. The sovereign is completely discharged from a duty, in the attempting to perform which he must always be exposed to innumerable delusions, and for the proper performance of which no human wisdom or knowledge could ever be sufficient: the duty of superintending the industry of private people."

—Adam Smith, *Inquiry Into the Nature and Causes of the Wealth of Nations,* 1776.

Contents

Contents

Acknowledgments

During the writing of this book I incurred debts to a great many people in Airbus Industrie, Boeing and McDonnell Douglas. Without the help and advice I received in Toulouse, Seattle, Long Beach and St. Louis it would not have been possible to unravel the complexities of this tangled tale.

I am also indebted to a number of people in the companies that make up the Airbus consortium. I did not visit Spain, but I was greatly helped in my research by those I spoke to in Paris, Hamburg, London and Bristol.

It was important to have the perspective of the customers, which is to say of the airlines, and I learned a great deal from my visits to Lufthansa in Frankfurt, SAS in Stockholm, British Airways in London, American Airlines in Dallas and Northwest Airlines in Minneapolis. I am also grateful to the many officials who agreed to see me in Paris, Bonn, London, Brussels and Washington, and to members of the GATT secretariat in Geneva.

One or two of those I consulted wished to speak without attribution, but most are identified in the text with an indication of where and when the interviews were conducted.

There are four people to whom I am particularly indebted—Arthur Howes and David Velupillai of Airbus Industrie and Ray Waldmann and Kent McCormick of Boeing. They opened many doors, answered endless questions and dispensed generous hospitality.

I also wish to record my thanks to David Appia, Robert Atkins, MP, Barrie Austin, Thomas J. Bacher, Robert Baker, William Benke, Howard Berry, Jan Bevan, André Bloch, Borge Boeskov, Donald H. Charles, James F. Chorlton, David L. Clancy, Lawrence W. Clarkson, Philip Condit, Thomas R. Craig, Dorothy Dwoskin, Peter Ehrenwald, Jochen Eichen, Richard Gardner, S. Gillibrand, George Greenfield, Don Hanson, David Henderson, Gerald A. Hendin, Fred R. Howard, Christine Howarth, John Hunt, Charles W. Hutton, Klaus Kautzer-Schröder, Christian Klick, Tadatsuna Koda, Karyl H. Landes, Patrick Lefas, J.C. Longridge, Mrs. Paulette Lundgren, Jerry Martin, T. Craig Martin, Christian Masset, Alan

W. Muncaster, Geoffrey Norris, E. Paul Osborne, Jr., M.E. Oliveau, Jr., Dietmar Plath, Patrice Prévot, John Price, Fred Randall, Jean-Yves Richard, Tom Riedinger, Robert E. Robeson, Jr., Derek Ross, Miguel de Santiago-Juárez, Charles H. Slater, Tim Soane, Peter Sutherland, Peter Thaldorf, David C. Venz, Daniel Weygandt, John R. Wheeler, Clarence F. Wilde, Andrew Wilson, Jeremy M. Wooding, Ian Woodward, Andrew Wrathall, D. Scott Yohé.

My wife kept an eye on successive drafts and told me when she thought I was parting company with the general reader. I am also very grateful to George Fischer, who read the whole manuscript and offered valuable advice about structure and style.

Preface

One of the more boneless proposals to emerge from the European Parliament in Strasbourg in recent years was that the school curriculum should be enlarged to include something called Eurohistory. This emollient discipline, purged of nationalist bias, would rewrite the history of the old continent and broaden the mind of the rising generation.

In London, *The Times,* editorial tongue some way in cheek, offered silky support to the idea. "Scholars, after all, already recognise that the result of the Spanish Armada was a draw—with the Spaniards having to play against the wind. Trafalgar was a minor naval skirmish, named after a well-known square in central London, while French children know that Napoleon won Waterloo—then died while on a holiday island in the Atlantic."

This book is an account of a transatlantic quarrel. It is written by a Scotsman—an off-shore European of conservative disposition whose admiration of how they do things in America is almost as strong as his attachment to the way they look at things in Europe.

One of my favourite Europeans is Edmund Burke. He exaggerated, of course, as Irishmen do, and his judgment in 1790 that the glory of Europe was extinguished for ever has not worn particularly well. One of my favourite Americans is Ambrose Bierce, and while I have been writing I have had in mind his definition of prejudice as "a vagrant opinion without visible means of support."

Any nonvagrant opinion that appears in these pages without attribution is my own.

Prologue

"In the old days we used to crash a lot but when it was all over we nearly always just stood up, shook the wreckage off, and walked away."

Memory hold the door . . .

When he celebrated his hundredth birthday in 1988, the British pioneer aviator Sir Thomas Sopwith thought back not only to those early flying machines he had walked away from but also to the many thousands he had built. "In the first World War, when we thought up a new type, the thing was flying in six weeks. Now it's not flying in six years. It's all got so big, hasn't it?"[1]

Sir Thomas was right. Today, by any standard, the building of civil aircraft is an industry on a positively Brobdingnagian scale. It supplies the needs of upwards of 200 airlines. The three major manufacturers—two American and one European—disagree about many other things, but they are at one in forecasting an annual growth in passenger traffic of 5 percent or more between now and the early years of the next century and a requirement of at least 9,000 new aircraft to meet it. These figures apply only to aircraft with more than a hundred seats, and such toys do not come cheap. A journalist on a French paper amused himself a few years back by working out what else you could buy for the price of one A320 Airbus— 145 Rolls Royce Silver Shadows, 81 million second class tickets on the Paris Métro, 40,600 tonnes of potatoes, a holiday lasting 390 years at the Club Méditerranée in Martinique . . .

If the figure at which one plane sells is difficult to grasp, the size of the investment necessary to launch a new programme is even more mindboggling. A senior McDonnell Douglas executive, appearing before a House of Representatives' subcommittee in Washington in 1987, said that the cost of launching a new small commercial transport exceeded $3 billion, and that more than $5 billion would be required for a new, very large transport. "These numbers equal or exceed the net worth of McDonnell Douglas," he said.[2] Similarly, when Boeing did its sums during the early gestation period of what was to become the 747, it found itself looking at a figure that was several times the net value of the whole enterprise. The expression "betting the company" is very far from being a figure of speech. Small wonder that quite a few of the rather sober men who work for the company in the Pacific Northwest have a reputation for playing a mean game of poker.

It is not just the sums of money that are very big. Drive 30-odd miles north out of Seattle on Interstate Highway 5 and you come to Everett. This is where the Jumbo jets are assembled, and here the scale of the enterprise finds direct physical expression. This is the world's largest aircraft assembly plant.[3] You don't believe it? Speak nicely to Lew Zink, who is the senior manager, program management there, and he will take you on a guided tour that demonstrates it and zap you with a hail of statistics that proves it conclusively.

The building covers 62 acres. It measures 631 metres by 492 and is 37 metres high. At nine million cubic metres it is the largest building by volume in the world. Each set of doors is the size of an American football field, and devotees of the sport get an even bigger thrill when they hear that there is room inside to play 58 games simultaneously. Lew takes his visitors round in a sort of electric golf buggy. An assembly plant of that size is hard on shoe leather, and the workforce moves round it by bicycle, rather like postmen in rural England.

The industry has changed enormously in the past 45 years. At the end of the Second World War there were about two dozen companies that could turn out large commercial aircraft. Today, Boeing, McDonnell Douglas and Airbus divide the market between them. The individual European companies are appreciably smaller than their American counterparts— Aérospatiale, for instance, the French partner in the Airbus consortium, is only about a quarter as big as Boeing—although taken together, the four companies in the Airbus consortium have not lagged far behind the aggregated profit margins for Boeing and McDonnell Douglas in recent years.

There are marked differences in corporate character. McDonnell Douglas has existed in its present form only since 1967. John Newhouse, writing in the early 1980s, detected a view in the industry that "the people in St. Louis" and "the people in Long Beach" were separated by more than geography: "It seems that in 1967, Douglas, a family-controlled company weakened by poor management, was taken over by another family-controlled company, McDonnell—a more strongly and strictly managed operation, but one with little feel for the commercial side of the business. Neither company was to benefit from the merger; each has suffered from it."[4]

Airbus headquarters at Toulouse, on the other hand, seems to have functioned as a reasonably effective meltingpot for a varied mix of national ingredients (22 of them at the last count). In one or two cases, people on loan from the partner companies appear to have gone pretty sensationally native, in the way that United Nations staff sometimes do, but their enthusiasm has on the whole been successfully absorbed. Within a few years of the first programme's getting under way, a Franco-German class had been established at a local school, paid for by Deutsche Airbus and the West German government.

Boeing is something different again.Traditionally a very self-contained enterprise, 60 percent of its employees are concentrated in the Pacific Northwest, and the company has always favoured a policy of promoting its managers from within. That breeds a strong *esprit de corps,* but has sometimes been felt to carry with it a certain danger of insulation from the larger world.

He is 30 feet up in the trees on a ropes course, a grid of ropes, logs and cables that looks more like a prop for a Tarzan movie than a management tool. Mr. Thorsberg, public relations man for Pacific Gas and Electric Co., is helping Steven Krieger demonstrate the use of the ropes course, located in a wooded tract near suburban San Francisco, as "a metaphor for corporate risk taking."

That is not a passage from an unpublished novel by John Updike but an extract from an article in *The Wall Street Journal* about new techniques in management training. I would not expect to find too many executives from Boeing flying down to California to enrol in such courses, however. Men who spend their days making commercial aircraft and selling them on five continents are exposed to near-lethal doses of risk in the normal way of business. They would learn nothing up in the eucalyptus branches that they haven't known for a very long time.

In the United States, the business of making and selling aircraft has always been permeated with risk to a quite exceptional degree. This is not simply because very large sums of money are involved but because those sums are being ventured in a commercial environment made chronically unstable by changes in the conditions of the market, shifts in the competitive situation and advances in technology. Major swings in demand and production are the norm. For example, production of the Boeing 727 dropped from a peak of 160 planes in 1968 to 33 just three years later. It rose to 136 again in 1979, but was back down to 26 in 1982. The Douglas DC-9 varied even more dramatically—down to 44 planes in 1971 when three years previously it had stood at 203. The same pattern is apparent across the industry. In 1968, manufacturers in the United States and Europe between them produced 741 aircraft. Three years later the total had shrunk to 250.

Changing fuel prices also induce uncertainty. In the early 1980s, about 30 percent of an aircraft's operating costs were accounted for by fuel. Towards the end of the decade, that figure had been more than halved. More than half the cost of running an aircraft had become the cost of the finance that acquired it, so the most important factor in the sales battle was a low basic price, which meant that design and construction methods once again came under close scrutiny.

Aircraft manufacturers can never afford the luxury of waiting to see how things turn out. They are perpetually in the position of the master of an oil tanker in the English Channel—if you want to turn left into the Bay of Biscay, you must make up your mind as you pass Calais. Lead times in the aircraft industry are seldom less than five years, and if you're late, you're dead.

Risk is essentially what the quarrel between Uncle Sam and Airbus has been all about. Or more precisely, a perceived lack of it. The American complaint is that the European consortium has been feather-bedded; that because its members receive large sums of public money from their governments, there are certain types of risk to which they have not been exposed, and that this has given them an unfair commercial advantage. They feel that the U.S. manufacturers have been asked to play uphill and into the wind, and that big as they are, this is unfair.

There are, of course, other strands to the argument as well. The American case has been that Airbus has benefited from many other kinds of assistance besides launch aid—subsidies to counter exchange rate losses, guarantees for working capital loans, R&D programme assistance, regional development grants, manufacturing plant investments and cross-subsidization from military sales. The U.S. industry alleges that in order to justify launch aid requests, Airbus has consistently overestimated the market and its potential sales, lumping in with their firm sales the figures for options, which American manufacturers do not include in sales commitments.

Boeing and McDonnell Douglas have also complained that Airbus has enjoyed the advantage of a controlled home market, and that when they and Airbus have been in competition in France and Germany, the law of averages seems to have gone into suspense and Airbus has almost invariably carried the day. Outside what they regard as these captive markets, they claim that although Airbus has been in business since 1970, they still pursue a "market entry" pricing strategy, and that their planes have been consistently underpriced. McDonnell Douglas allege that Airbus aggressively pursued some of their launch customers for the MD-11, offering prices that fell below those of MD derivatives and dangling before airlines such inducements as the reimbursement of any penalties or legal costs incurred by breaking contracts with McDonnell Douglas.

American indignation has not been confined to what they regard as dirty tricks in the market place. They have also complained of government-to-government pressure and government inducements, which they believe to be in breach of the Civil Aircraft Agreement of the General Agreement on Tariffs and Trade (GATT). One instance frequently cited is of a case of attempted mayhem in Bangkok. Officials in the government of Prime

Minister Prem Tinsulalond who were contemplating cancelling an order for two A300s in favour of Boeing 767s were said to have been threatened by Airbus salesmen with cuts in European import quotas for tapioca. This might have slightly comic overtones of warfare in the nursery—except that tapioca happens to be Thailand's second most important export.

The European consortium's emphasis on new technology has also made the Americans hot under the collar. The contention here has been that Airbus has incorporated expensive technology in its aircraft in order to claim leadership, snug in the knowledge that the full cost of these new technologies would be borne not by the customer but by Airbus's government backers. Smarting under Airbus claims that the American industry benefits from government R&D, McDonnell Douglas and Boeing have felt that there has been insufficient acknowledgment of the European debt to U.S.-sponsored developments that have been placed in the public domain.

Airbus have not remained silent under this onslaught and have shown considerable inventiveness in marshalling spirited counterarguments. They have relied heavily on the assertion that the American pot is just as black as the European kettle. In the spring of 1988 they published figures that purported to show that in the previous ten years the U.S. government had provided something of the order of $23 billion to the American industry through what they described as governmental and quasigovernmental agencies, though there was a careful concession that this support was both direct and indirect.[5]

They claim that the purpose of this funding by the U.S. government is to maintain the dominant position that the American aerospace industry holds in world markets and assert that this aim was built into the legislation under which NASA was established. Apart from NASA, they identify the Department of Defense as the biggest source of funds, although they also point to the Federal Aviation Administration and the Department of Transportation. Another Airbus argument is that their competitors enjoy substantial tax benefits, although they fail to note that these advantages are available to American industry as a whole and are not specific to those companies active in civil aerospace.

A word that bobs up with great frequency in the Airbus saga is "transparency," crisply defined by an official in the British Department of Trade and Industry as "GATT-speak for knowing what the other chap is up to." Airbus have countered the American arguments by alleging that although a great deal of information on federal aeronautical support is publicly available in the United States, there are important limitations on access and a number of obstacles to determining the types and levels of government support. They have noted that some information is protected by considerations of national security, but have also recorded, rather plaintively, that "some data is not recorded in searchable data bases and research requires sifting by hand through hundreds of records."

The Airbus pamphleteers have sometimes got a bit bored with scientific method and enlivened their text with a dash of conspiracy theory: "To complicate matters further, government subsidies are often 'masked' to protect them from the vagaries of changing American political philosophies. Thus, funding can be hidden in the relative obscurity of a budget maze, or in a labyrinth of terms which have been created to politically justify funding of a subsidy nature . . . "

Most professionals fall into their own special forms of shorthand or jargon. People who work in the aerospace industry and enthusiasts for the splendid machines that they build tend to speak a language that is every bit as arcane as that of trainspotters, and when it is laced with the serial numbers used to designate aircraft or engines it can become well-nigh impenetrable. It seems sensible therefore to pause here and offer a lay guide to the product range of the three major manufacturers.

In the case of Airbus Industrie, there are six main aircraft types currently on offer. When the European consortium made its bid to enter the market, it decided to do so with a high-capacity, wide-bodied, medium-range airliner. It was called the A300. Launched in May 1969, it entered service with the airlines in 1974 and was the first of the twin-aisle twins, which is to say that the seats in the passenger cabin are divided by two aisles and that it has two engines. (Most of the American aircraft with which it was intended to compete had three engines, and therefore generally needed more fuel.)

It initially had a range of 1,500 nautical miles, but developments over the years increased this substantially. It can now operate in a range of from 3,000 to 4,250 nautical miles and can make long over-water flights—from Paris to Central Africa, say, or from New York to destinations well down into Latin America. The shortest scheduled hop for which it has been used is the link between Gassim and Riyadh, a mere 180 nautical miles (340 kilometres). It normally seats 260–270 passengers, but if a charter company really wanted to pack them in, it could take up to 345. The hold will take 22–23 LD3 containers (Airbus literature describes them as the most widely used, which is the case, although they are also the smallest).

This was followed nine years later by the A310, also twin-engined and twin-aisled, but approximately 20 percent smaller than the A300. It can seat between 220–280 passengers and has a proportionately smaller cargo capacity. Its takeoff weight is some 15 tonnes less than the A300's, and it can fly about 1,000 nautical miles further—Lufthansa, for instance, flies them from Frankfurt to Chicago, and Kenya Air between London and Mombasa.

The year 1988 saw the introduction of the third member of the Airbus family, the A320. This was smaller again, and with a maximum range of 3,000 nautical miles is intended for short- and medium-haul routes. With what is known in the argot of the industry as a typical volumetric payload—150 passengers and 8,400 lbs of cargo—a plane based at Dallas could cover most of Central and North America apart from Alaska and the extreme northwest of Canada. Unlike the two earlier Airbus planes, it has only one aisle. Airbus say that it burns less fuel than the Boeing 737 and 757 and substantially less than three planes in the McDonnell Douglas MD-80 range—the 82, the 87 and the 88. They make similar claims when the comparison is made on the basis of direct operating costs per seat.

These three planes, in their various versions, are the only Airbus aircraft at present in service, but two new models—two versions, in fact, of a single new programme that was given the go-ahead in the summer of 1987—are due for delivery towards the end of 1992. The two aircraft, the A330 and the A340, will have many features in common. The fuselage and the cockpit will be identical and they will have the same basic undercarriage. The overall design of the wings will vary only to the extent needed to accommodate the A340's additional engines and systems.

The A330, which will have two engines and carry 335 passengers, will have a range of 4,750 nautical miles and is aimed at regional routes. Airbus see it principally as a competitor for the older Douglas DC-10 and Lockheed 1011 and claim that it has advantages over both in terms of aircraft-mile and seat-mile costs. They also hope that it will make some inroads into Boeing 747 territory.

Airbus's main competitive thrust against the Jumbo, however, will be with the A340—"the logical companion and alternative to the 747," says the promotional literature in silky tones. It will have four engines, a maximum range of 7,550 nautical miles and a capacity of up to 295 passengers. As a long-haul aircraft designed with what are known as "long, thin" routes in mind, Airbus hope they can persuade airlines to buy it either as a replacement for 747 operations or as an addition to them. Airbus also point to the possibility of opening up certain new long-range point-to-point services, dangling before their airline customers what is enticingly described as "reduced revenue-dilution."

Airbus are quite clever at producing oblique knocking copy. There was a good example in the promotional literature about the A340 that they distributed at the 1988 Farnborough Air Show and that took a sly pot-shot at several targets simultaneously: "Replacing outsize jumbos with aircraft flying the 'lower-traffic city pairs' will ease crowding at major airports and enable airlines to take passengers where they want to go instead of squeezing them through congested 'hub' airports." There will, then, be five different planes by the end of 1992, and a further addition to the family two years later in the shape of the A321, a stretched derivative of the A320.

In talking about an aircraft family and stressing the advantages of commonality, Airbus are paying Boeing, the undisputed market leader, the sincerest form of flattery. Boeing entered the commercial jet business in

1952. It had been trying for some time to interest both the airlines and the military in a "paper" jet, but the response had been discouraging, and the then chairman of Boeing, Bill Allen, finally authorised the $16 million needed to build a company-funded prototype. The first sale—20 707s to Pan American—was made in 1955. It quickly introduced a shortened version, which became known as the 707/720, and the company was launched into the market strategy of developing families of aircraft that has paid such handsome dividends ever since.

The present-day Boeing family is less easy to describe than is the Airbus brood, because the process of evolving derivative types has been going on a good deal longer and has become that much more sophisticated in the process—it is really now a family of families. If one does it strictly by numbers and confines the arithmetic to basic planes, the total comes to a rather misleading five: the 737, the 747, the 757, the 767 and the 777.

Now that the 707 and 727 programmes have been wound down, the oldest member of the Boeing family is the 737, which first entered service in 1968. It was aimed at the low-capacity segment of the market, and it got off to rather a shaky start partly because it appeared more than two years after the Douglas Aircraft Company's DC-9. Derivatives multiplied over the years, however, and by the end of 1990, with 2,885 planes ordered, it had become the best-selling model in the history of commercial aircraft. The 737-400, which went into commercial service with Piedmont Airlines in September 1988, has a fuselage ten feet longer than earlier versions, allowing a passenger capacity of about 145. A smaller version, the 737-500, with a seating capacity of 108, was delivered to its first customer in 1990.

If the 737 is Boeing's best-selling plane, its best known is the 747. In the long-range high-volume market it has no real competitor. It was conceived at a high point in world travel growth, and there was a time when it looked as if it might break the company. "Boeing managers," one market analyst observed drily, "tend to invoke the 747 episode with all the didactic flavour of Maoists recalling the Long March." It survived to spawn a bewildering range of derivatives—all passenger, all cargo, short range, stretched upper deck—and airlines have been able to choose between some 20 different engine options. Northwest Airlines and the other customers who started taking delivery of the new 747-400 early in 1989 found themselves with a machine capable of providing nonstop service on such routes as Singapore–London and Los Angeles–Hong Kong.

Then there is the 757, a single-aisle aircraft with six seats abreast in coach class. It is designed to carry 186 passengers, but charter operators can shoehorn in as many as 239. Boeing had recognised the need for a successor to the 727 for short- and medium-range routes in the early 1970s, and the 757 was in effect an updated version of it—the same narrow body, a new wing, two engines instead of three. It has 50 more seats than does the 727, but this was achieved with the same direct operating costs—a crucial consideration since the escalation of fuel costs.

The launch customers, in August 1978, were Eastern Airlines and British Airways, and they took delivery four years later. Initially most of the other larger airlines held back, feeling that they were being offered mutton dressed as lamb. By the end of 1990, however, there had been a resurgence in orders, and sales had passed the 700 mark. There are now two derivatives. A dedicated cargo version called the Package Freighter is in service with a number of businesses that specialise in overnight delivery of small parcels, and the Combi version of the aircraft can be used exclusively for passengers or in a configuration that also allows substantial cargo space.

The 767 provides with the 757 something of a subgrouping within the family—the common flight decks and common type rating allow crews to fly either model, and common parts and systems offer savings both in spares and in training. Like the Airbus A310 it is wide bodied and double aisled and aimed at the short- and medium-range routes. In its extended range version it can cover distances of more than 6,000 nautical miles. The 767 was announced in 1978, only a few weeks before the 757, and it first went into service with United Airlines in 1982. The period of preparation before it was given the go ahead—about six years—had been unusually long, and it was the result of a collaborative effort with the Italians and the Japanese, who assumed a share of the risk and were associated in both the design and production effort. Initially it sold badly, but by the end of 1990 there had been more than 500 sales to 46 customers.

The Boeing range will be extended in 1995 with the introduction of the 777. Designed to fill the market niche between the 767 and the 747, it will be the company's first entirely new plane in a decade and the world's largest twin-jet. With an eye to congestion at airports, Boeing are offering as an option a feature that has been common on naval aircraft for decades—folding wing-tips that will reduce the span when the plane is on the ground and allow it to use existing gates and taxiway space.

The McDonnell Douglas product line is appreciably shorter. By the late 1980s they had in effect put all their commercial eggs into two baskets, the MD-80 and the MD-11, although each of these programmes had a fair claim to be regarded as a family in itself, and marketing discussions were in progress about a new derivative. To make sense of the history of the competition with Airbus, however, it is necessary to say something of the earlier DC-10 programme. This was the then still independent Douglas Aircraft Company's bid for a place in the market for commercial jumbo jets, and as things turned out it was also the last commercial transport programme initiated by the company before the 1967 merger with McDonnell.

The DC-10 first flew in 1970, two years after the maiden flight of the 747. It is roughly 80 percent the size of its Boeing rival—a double-aisle wide-bodied plane with a maximum passenger load of 400. To the untutored eye it is almost indistinguishable from the Lockheed Tristar. Both have three engines, one under each wing and the third mounted in the tail. There was scope for only one such plane to achieve profitability in the market, however. "The DC-10 took the lead in a crowded field of two where there would be no winner," a semiofficial history of McDonnell Douglas noted glumly in 1985.[6] The competition drove Lockheed out of the commercial aircraft business.

The DC-10, although plagued by a succession of crashes, continued in production until 1988, by which time civil and military sales totalled 446. (In the early 1980s, under the designation KC-10, the U.S. Air Force had adapted a convertible freighter version of the plane mainly to meet the aerial refuelling needs of its Strategic Air Command.) In the summer of 1991 it was still being operated by 47 airlines around the world. Finnair were using it on their Helsinki–Tokyo route, and at the other end of the scale KLM had it flying the 119 kilometres between Aruba and Curaçao in the West Indies. The company continued to flourish brave statistics ("As of July 1, 1988, DC-10s had transported more than 701 million passengers"), but the fact is it never achieved real commercial success.

McDonnell Douglas say in their promotional literature for the MD-80 that it has evolved from the most successful twin-jet in history. What this means is that although it has been marketed as a new programme since the early 1980s, it is in fact an extension of the old DC-9 programme, which had been conceived by Douglas before the merger and first flew in 1965. It had been the best-selling commercial jet in the company's history (976 of them were delivered), and at one stage was outselling the Boeing 737 by about two to one.

The MD-80, therefore, is in fact the DC-9 Super 80, which first flew in 1979 and was the first plane to be given the new MD designation (this in 1983). It has two engines, and comes in five different models: the MD-81, MD-82, MD-83, MD-87 and MD-88. The MD-87 is shorter than the rest and can carry 139 passengers. All the others can take up to 172. The range of the MD-87 is 2,487 nautical miles. The launch customers were Swissair and Austrian Airlines. The main assembly line is at Long Beach in California, but some have been assembled in the People's Republic of China and are flown there by both China Eastern and China Northern Airlines.

The successor to the DC-10 is the MD-11, which was launched in 1986. McDonnell Douglas describe the two programmes as a continuum and are looking for substantial economies from the maintenance of an uninterrupted tri-jet assembly line, the benefits of the DC-10's long learning curve translating directly into lower MD-11 costs. It competes head on with the Airbus A340. It is offered in four models—passenger, all freighter, convertible freighter and "combi"—and there are two lengths of fuselage. The range is 6,880 nautical miles (the extended range version will go about 1,000 nautical miles further) and in an all-economy configuration it will carry up to 405 passengers. First deliveries were in 1990, two years ahead of its Airbus rival. Like the much smaller Boeing 757, the freighter version is attractive to firms specialising in the express delivery of small packages—one such company, Federal Express of Memphis, Tennessee, was a launch customer.

The new derivatives occupying McDonnell Douglas's attention in the early 1990s were known as the MD-90 series. They are twin-engined models derived from the MD-80, and are to be powered by high-bypass ratio turbofan engines which it is claimed will reduce fuel consumption by anything between 25 and 40 percent. Made by International Aero Engines, they use jet turbines to power "propulsors", large, counterrotating fan systems with blades that are very broad and highly contoured. These move a much greater volume of air around the core of the engine than is drawn into it. Air taken into the engine is burned with fuel, and the energy of the exhaust powers the fan system. The bypass air, accelerated by the propulsor, does the work of propelling the aircraft with minimum fuel burned. The first in the series, the MD-90-30, is scheduled to make its first flight early in 1993, with initial deliveries towards the end of 1994. It will carry 153 passengers and have a range of 2,400 nautical miles (4,440 kilometres). Operation with full-passenger loads will be possible on runways as short as 5,000 feet (1,524 metres). A planned variant, the MD-90-50, which will increase the range to 3,100 nautical miles, will be offered a year later.

Such then are the aircraft that the airlines mainly use to shuttle us between neighbouring cities or transport us halfway round the globe. The controversy between the companies that make them and the governments that in varying degrees stand behind them has rumbled on since the late 1970s. It has been very much more than a spat between rival sales forces. The Americans have taken it extremely seriously, and so have the Europeans. Mogens Peter Carl, the Danish Eurocrat who led the European Community team in some of the earlier negotiations, rated it as the issue that had more potential to damage European-American relations than any other, and he did not exclude agriculture. "If it were to develop into a trade war," he said, "the consequences would be more serious than in any other trade conflict we have ever known. If the famous substance hit the fan, it would make a much bigger splash than soya beans." [7]

The conflict could also spill beyond the boundaries of trade. There are political implications and implications, even after the dissolution of the Soviet Union, for defence. Some of the issues are quite as emotive in the Old World as they are in the New. For some Europeans and for the French in particular, Airbus is a sort of Declaration of Independence in reverse. That was certainly how Airbus Industrie's first managing director, Bernard Lathière, saw it. "We are fighting for our children," he said in 1975, and it is unlikely he thought he was being melodramatic. "If we don't have a place in high technology in Europe we should be slaves to the Americans and our children will be slaves. We have to sell . . . We must fight, fight, fight and fight . . ."

Pinpointing the moment at which disputes begin is always arbitrary, particularly when the issues are complicated. To follow all the twists and turns of the Airbus story and to understand something of its origins, it is necessary to turn the page back more than quarter of a century to 1965.

NOTES

1. *Financial Times,* February 15, 1988.

2. Testimony of James E. Worsham before the Subcommittee on Commerce, Consumer Protection, and Competitiveness of the Committee on Energy and Commerce, House of Representatives, Washington, June 23, 1987.

3. It is unlikely that the Russian equivalent of *The Guinness Book of Records* would challenge this, although the aircraft industry in what used to be the Soviet Union is enormous, accounting for about 30 percent of world output. It was traditionally oriented towards the needs of the former eastern bloc rather than to western export markets. The authorities there have never been particularly forthcoming with information on such matters, but Western estimates put the number of aircraft produced in the last 30 years at about 4,000—rather less than half the American total.

4. John Newhouse, *The Sporty Game* (New York: Alfred A. Knopf, 1982).

5. *Government Funding of Boeing and McDonnell Douglas Civil Aircraft Programs* (Airbus Industrie, March 1988). See Chapter 8 for a discussion of this.

6. Bill Yenne, *McDonnell Douglas: A Tale of Two Giants* (New York: Crescent Books, 1985).

7. Interview in Brussels, June 1988.

DOGFIGHT

1

Believing the Impossible

"Why, sometimes I've believed as many as six impossible things before breakfast."

—Lewis Carroll, *Through the Looking Glass
and What Alice Found There*, 1871.

One impossible thing to believe in the 1960s, before or after breakfast, was that anyone could ever challenge the ascendancy of the powerful American companies that manufactured commercial aircraft. Their domestic market, which had expanded dramatically during the war, was huge, and at that time still regulated. They commanded more than 90 percent of world sales, and in the long-haul market enjoyed almost total dominance.

By the mid-1960s, their number had been reduced to three. Lockheed, based in Burbank, California, was a company widely admired for its engineering brilliance and innovative flair. John Newhouse, in his book *The Sporty Game*, quotes an investment bank aerospace analyst as saying, "If someone hired me to rebuild the Great Pyramid, I'd ask Lockheed to design it and Boeing to assemble it." Lockheed will figure only occasionally in this story, however, because by the time the European industry had established itself as a force to be reckoned with in the late 1970s, they were already finding the competition too bruising. The company was to withdraw from the U.S. civil airliner business once and for all in 1983, leaving the field to McDonnell Douglas and Boeing.

William E. Boeing, the founder of the company, was the son of a German-born father and a Viennese mother. The family had large holdings in iron ore and timber in Minnesota, and the young Boeing enjoyed financial independence from an early age. He studied engineering at Yale and then, at the age of 22, he moved west and acquired timber interests of his own. That was in 1903. Flying was in its infancy, and Boeing was soon caught up in the general enthusiasm for the dangerous new game.

He formed his first company during the First World War and built planes in Seattle, mainly for the U.S. Navy, but it was not until ten years after the war that he went public. Boeing Airplane & Transport Corporation stock first went on the market on November 1, 1928, and sold quickly. Shortly afterwards Boeing became the chairman of a new corporation that drew in a number of other companies, including Pratt & Whitney, who made the Wasp motors, the Hamilton Propellor Company and Pacific Air Transport. It built aircraft, ran an airline, carried the mails. It was called the United Aircraft and Transport Corporation, and it was the biggest organisation of its kind in the United States. Six years later, in response to antitrust legislation, it was dissolved and the board of the newly independent Boeing Airplane Company held its first meeting on September 26, 1934.

It is not always remembered that Boeing's preeminence in the commercial aircraft market is of comparitively recent date. Between the middle 1930s and the late 1950s the dominant players were Douglas and Lockheed. In 1958, the U.S. airlines between them were operating 1946 aircraft. Of that total 998 had been built by Douglas and 261 by Lockheed. Of the remaining 687, Boeing had built only 32.

That was all changed in a few short years by one bold throw. The British de Havilland Comet, the world's first commercial jet transport, had first flown in 1949 and had gone into service three years later. It soon showed itself prone to metal fatigue, however, and in 1954, after a series of crashes, it had been grounded. The Douglas DC-7 had come into service with American Airlines only a year earlier. When work had begun on it, Douglas had made a judgement that jets were not yet economical enough, and decided to stay with the tried technology of the piston engine. Boeing saw its opportunity. There were many technological uncertainties, and they were also to some extent gambling on the market, but on this occasion good nerves paid big dividends.

Their delivery to PanAm in 1958 of six B-707s was a decisive date in the history of the company's fortunes. The transaction was also the occasion of one of the industry's more celebrated wagers. The boss of PanAm bet the boss of Boeing that they couldn't deliver ahead of schedule, and backed his judgement to the tune of $25,000 a month on each plane. Boeing won, as it happened, though there are those in Seattle who suspect it cost them dear in productivity payments.

In the middle 1960s Boeing once again showed its predilection for living dangerously when it ventured $750 million on the 747—a sum not far short of the net worth of the company at the time. Mass travel was expanding rapidly, and many airports were approaching the limit of their capacity. The aim was to design a plane that would combine high performance with low seat/mile costs. It was to be oversized at introduction, and become a "market fit" only some four years after coming into service.

It was not an entirely novel inititiative, certainly, because the same philosophy had informed both the DC-8 and the 707, but in the case of the Jumbo the gamble was incomparably greater. Not only would its success depend on the development of a new and untried engine, but if delivery schedules were to be met, everything that was critical to the project—not only engine development but also aircraft design and factory construction—would have to be embarked on simultaneously. Boeing also had to give its mind, before the actual go-ahead, to the small matter of rebuilding the entire production and management control systems of the company.

There are few points of similarity between Boeing and its main American competitor. McDonnell Douglas make much of the origins of their founders—"James Smith McDonnell and Donald Wills Douglas were as Scottish a pair of Scotsmen as America ever produced," says one of their promotional booklets. There is an artist's impression of the two men in a recent company history, and both sport ties in a rough approximation of the tartan of their respective clans.[1]

They were a remarkable pair, although apart from their Scottish ancestry they had very little in common. "Mr. Mac," as McDonnell was invariably called, had been born in Denver in 1899, four years before the first flight of the Wright Brothers at Kitty Hawk. He studied physics at Princeton, but that did not preclude a keen interest in animism and the spirit world, which is why in later years his planes were given names like Goblin, Banshee and Voodoo. He was, in fact, keen to go to England to work for the Society for Psychical Research, but his father opposed the idea. Instead he went to the Massachussets Institute of Technology and took a master's degree in aeronautical engineering, but it was 14 years and a dozen or more jobs later that he finally set up in business on his own account. The McDonnell Aircraft Company was established just three months before the outbreak of the Second World War. It operated out of a rented office at Lambert Field near St. Louis, and had a staff of one.

Ol' Mac was a self-confident man, which was just as well. The achievement of his company's first year is recorded laconically as "zero sales, zero backlog and negative earnings." During the war, the company was mainly a subcontractor for the likes of Boeing and Douglas. The latter built more than 30,000 aircraft and by 1945 had made more than $1 billion. McDonnell made only a fraction of that amount and had designed only two aircraft of his own.

When war broke out, Douglas was already the General Motors of American aviation. Donald Douglas, Sr., also an MIT graduate, had been chief engineer of the U.S Army Signal Corps.and had set up his own business in 1920 at the rear of a barber shop in downtown Los Angeles. He was a man of solitary habit who liked to play the bagpipes (the two sometimes go together). He lived in a large Spanish-style house near Santa Monica, owned a yacht called *Endymion* and was partial to chocolate ice-cream sundaes. He transacted a good deal of the company's business by himself on the telephone, and at the outbreak of war had his furniture put into storage in Salt Lake City in case there were Japanese bombing raids.

The Douglas clan motto is *"Jamais arrière" ("Never behind"),* but in the late 1950s and early 1960s the company was no longer living up to it. Donald Douglas, Jr., had become president in 1957, and his management style did not go down well. The company lost ten of its vice-presidents within a period of three years. They totally failed to anticipate the important role the jet engine was going to play in civil aircraft and lost the lead to Boeing. They attempted to make up lost ground with the DC-8, but the development costs pushed the company into the red. Between 1957 and 1961 the plane took only 47 orders, a period in which Boeing sales totalled 172.

By the mid-1960s it looked as if the tables had been turned. In 1965 the DC-9, a new short-range jet, went into airline service two months ahead of schedule. More than 200 orders had been placed, and within a year the total was well above the 400 mark. Boeing, its 737 still two years away, was caught unawares.

The jubilation at Long Beach was shortlived, however. The very success of the DC-9 programme had within it the seeds of failure. Rapid expansion severely strained the company's reserves. It also quickly emerged that one reason for the aircraft's popularity with the airlines was that it had been underpriced. The war in Vietnam had caused the economy to expand, and there was a shortage of labour. The war also forced up the price of engines and of components supplied by subcontractors. Late deliveries led to late payments. The company had counted on a loss of $750,000 on each of the first 20 or so aircraft, but this figure rose to $1.25 million.

In the spring of 1966 the company's stock stood at $112, and it turned in a healthy first-quarter profit of $4 million. Investors were ceasing to be impressed, however. The company had made a stick for its own back by a radical change in its formerly conservative accounting practices. When the old man was in charge, development costs had been written off as they occurred. Some years after his son took over, they began to appear in the accounts as an asset under deferred charges—writing off, in other words, was postponed until the aircraft had begun to sell. The banks were unsympathetic, and by October the company's stock had plummeted to $30.

Without an immediate cash injection of $400 million, the company would not be able to meet its commitments. The money was not forthcoming, and in December 1966, merger proposals were invited. Lockheed and Chrysler were not interested. Those who were included General Dynamics, North American Aviation and McDonnell. North American, based, like Douglas, in Southern California, seemed a good bet, but couldn't come up with the money. Old Mac could, and without having to borrow. He had, what's more, suggested a merger some four years previously. Three months later, at the age of 68, he became the chairman and chief executive officer of what was now to be known as the McDonnell Douglas Corporation.

* * * * *

Nationally, the mid-1960s were troubled years for the United States. The two years and ten months of the Kennedy presidency had come to an end in 1963, and Lyndon Johnson was in the White House. On the world stage, it was a period in which the international power of the United States had been reestablished and deployed on a scale without precedent since the end of the war. Zbigniew Brzezinski saw it in retrospect as "the highwater mark of the progressive post–World War II expansion of a worldwide U.S. presence,"[2] and in 1965 Robert McNamara estimated the military preponderance of the United States over the Soviet Union to be of the order of three or four to one. At the beginning of 1965, the United States had started to bomb North Vietnam, and by the end of the year the number of American troops committed in the field was approaching 200,000.

At home, there were civil rights marches, urban riots and campus disorders, although it was also a period of economic growth and falling levels of unemployment. It was a time, too, when foreign trade was beginning to play an increasingly important part in the national economy, even though exports were still a fairly marginal element in the gross national product. The Kennedy Round of the General Agreement on Tariffs and Trade, which lasted from 1963 to 1967, represented for the United States an economic initiative with a political objective. "Our efforts to promote the strength and unity of the West are thus directly related to the strength and unity of Atlantic trade policies," the president had said when he presented his Trade Expansion Act to Congress in January 1962.

Twenty years after the end of the Second World War, Europe was still labouring. The political scene in France was dominated by one man in a way that it had not been since the death of Napoleon. In the course of 1965 General de Gaulle variously suggested the reform of the United Nations and a return to the gold standard. President Johnson took issue with him on the first, and the American Treasury Department scoffed at the second as "a retreat to 1931." The French also got a fair way up American noses by more than once joining with the Soviet Union in a call for a settlement in Vietnam, and by making it plain that they would not support the United States if a spread of hostilities brought them into conflict with China.

During the summer, France was also considerably at odds with her Common Market partners, particularly over the extent and timing of the Community's plans for agriculture, and boycotted a number of meetings. None of this had any effect on her currency reserves, which rose healthily, and in July she rejected an American proposal for a world conference to discuss possible reforms to the international monetary system.

In September, de Gaulle stepped up his attacks on the Common Market, and announced for good measure that France would leave NATO by 1969. In November he let it be known that he would stand for a second seven-year presidential term, but he failed to win the necessary majority in the first round. This meant that he must submit himself to the will of the electorate a second time. The general was not amused, either by this gesture of *lèse-majesté* or by the puny majority that they grudgingly afforded him a fortnight later.

Across the Rhine, it was only ten years since the most powerful industrial nation in Western Europe had regained her national sovereignty. After 1945 there was no German state. All authority had passed to the occupying military powers, and initially the primary concern of all four allies had been to destroy Germany's political and economic potential to wage war.

Later there had been differences about what form a new constitution should take. The United Kingdom had favoured a centralised structure along British lines, with a parliamentary rather than a presidential system. The French preference had been for decentralisation, which they saw as potentially less threatening. The United States had argued the case for a federal system as the one that would least threaten a private market economy. The Americans had in general shown themselves less hesitant than either the French or the British in transferring rights and responsibilities to the German authorities, although they sometimes seemed puzzled by the slowness of transplanted American values to take root in the new garden of German democracy.

The received view that the economy was rebuilt from absolutely nothing is something of an exaggeration. The general level of fixed capital was certainly reduced—wartime air-raids, the dismantling of industry after the war and a certain amount of old-fashioned plunder saw to that—and there were substantial losses through reparations, but industrial capacity was still greater in 1948 than it had been in 1936, and West Germany inherited both a larger and more modern capital stock from the war than has been allowed in some of the more enthusiastic accounts of the German *Wirtschaftswunder.*[3]

It had been official policy to reduce the power of the state in the management of the economy. The man most closely associated with that policy was Ludwig Erhardt, who served first as economics minister and then, less successfully, as chancellor, and in a book published in the 1950s he had explained its rationale:

More perhaps than any other economy the German one has had to experience the economic and supra-economic consequences of an economic and trading policy subjected to the extremes of nationalism, autarky and government control. We have learnt the lesson; and if the basic principles of a liberal economic policy are championed in the following pages with a vigour possibly startling to foreign readers, the reason must be sought in the special circumstances of our recent history.[4]

From the early 1950s, the German economy had grown steadily and at a faster rate than that of its main Western competitors. Between 1950 and 1965, for instance, real per capita national product rose by an average of 5.6 percent a year, which was twice the equivalent rate in the United Kingdom, Sweden and the United States. Germany's recovery had been export-led, and the boom in world trade induced by the Korean War, and in particular the demand for capital goods, had been of major importance.

Unlike most of her competitors, Germany was not committed to military production, and was therefore able to attract an increasing proportion of that increased demand. She also derived great benefit from the steady flow of skilled manpower from the East. One German economic writer claims that this transfer of "human capital" was equivalent to some DM 30 billion in the 1950s alone, a figure greater than the contribution made to German reconstruction by the European Recovery Programme.[3] The number of people employed in agriculture (over 5 million in 1950) had been almost halved by 1965, and this too represented an injection of strength into the labour market.

The doctrine of economic liberalism, however, did little to blunt the traditionally strong instinct in Germany to industrial collaboration. Andrew Shonfield, writing in 1965, took the view that in its fiscal practice Germany was much closer to France than to Britain. Subsidies, cheap loans provided by the state and discriminating tax allowances were all, he said, used with an abandon that could only be acceptable in a society where the average citizen expected the state to choose its favourites and to intervene on their behalf.[5]

What emerged most clearly from a comparison with the United Kingdom was an enormously greater German propensity to use public finance to discriminate in industry and trade. Measured in terms of the impact on the budget, the total German bill for fiscal discrimination amounted to almost a quarter of all central government budgetary expenditure, compared with less than a tenth in Britain.

Britain in the mid-1960s found herself in a less happy state. The protracted agony of the pound sterling lasted from the arrival in power of the Labour government towards the end of 1964 until the Basle agreement four years later. In 1965 Winston Churchill died, providing newspapers with a rare occasion to use phrases like "the end of an era" without being accused of journalese. The new government announced that it would buy American built military transport planes and scrap a $560 million project to develop its own. They also said they were going to nationalise the steel industry. Roy Jenkins, the minister of aviation, told the House of Commons that the prototype of Concorde was expected to make its first flight as early as 1968, and the country decided to go metric in weights and measures.

The Beatles were included in the Honours List and became Members of the Order of the British Empire. Sir Alec Douglas-Home resigned as leader of the Conservative Party and was succeeded by Edward Heath and the leaders of 21 trade unions protested at the appointment of an American as managing director of the Ford Motor Company. A clothing manufacturer presented a civil servant in the north of England with a new pair of woollen trousers. He had worn his old pair, of the same make, for thirty-one years, keeping them in shape with frequent dry cleaning and occasional alterations. The colony of Rhodesia made a unilateral declaration of independence, and Britain seized her funds and sent warplanes to neighbouring Zambia.

Shortly after Labour had come to power it had appointed a Committee of Inquiry into the Aircraft Industry. The chairman was Lord Plowden, who immediately after the war had been chief executive of the Aircraft Supply Council. From 1947 to 1953 he had been chief planning officer at the Treasury and in the late 1950s he had chaired a Committee of Enquiry into Treasury control of public expenditure.

The membership was a typical trawl of the great and the good—the chairman of the Atomic Energy Authority (a job Plowden himself had also done some years previously), a senior Bank of England official, an industrialist, an admiral, a member of parliament from each of the two major parties and, inevitably, a trade union official. Their report, presented to Parliament towards the end of 1965, is important documentary evidence of the condition the aircraft industry found itself in in the mid-1960s. What is also remarkable, reading it a quarter of a century later, is how clearly some of the seeds of future conflict between Europe and the United States can be identified.[6]

Britain had not developed or manufactured transport aircraft during the war but had relied on her American allies, and when the war was over and the United States reverted to making civil versions, they soon dominated the field. The main strength of the American industry lay in the inherent cost advantage derived from domestic sales—at that time it sold nine aircraft at home for every one it sold abroad. The equivalent French ratio was two to one, which obviously made her much more vulnerable to the ups and downs of the export market. Even so, the export sales of the United States were eight times those of France and three or four times those of the United Kingdom.

The committee also remarked on American success in achieving early delivery dates, noting that they regularly developed and cleared an aircraft for service in a year less than it took a British manufacturer. "This ability to overtake a competitor after he has committed himself to an enterprise," said the report in its careful mandarin prose, "has proved a formidable advantage." It sounds like a restrained early version of the definition of a Hungarian as a man who goes into a swing door behind you and comes out in front.

American salesmanship was also acknowledged to be superior— thorough, aggressive and ready to respond to consumer demand. British sales teams were felt to be at a disadvantage because the specification for an aircraft had frequently been tailored to the wishes of a particular operator, reducing the prospects of subsequent sales overseas.

By the time Plowden was sitting, only 8 of the 36 different types of British aircraft built since the war had achieved combined home and export sales of more than 100. Much of the industry's capital was obtained by borrowing. In 1961, for instance, 47 percent of the physical assets was financed in this way, compared with only 4 percent for industry as a whole. Profitability was in decline, too. In 1951, profits expressed as a percentage of capital employed had stood at just under 23 percent. By 1964, the figure was down to 6.3 percent.

This catalogue of inadequacy made it necessary to consider why it was thought desirable to have an aircraft industry at all, and Plowden passed in fairly predictable review the various defence and foreign policy considerations that arose, the benefits or side-effects of technology, the impact on the balance of payments. He also paused over a less tangible aspect of the matter, which he described as a social contribution, and at this point the report took on a tone of diffidence that was characteristically English:

It is difficult to know how much importance to attach to it. One tends to underrate or overrate it, according to one's preconceptions and prejudices. We refer to the part played by the aircraft industry in the nation's view of itself. The traditions of the industry, especially its role in the last war; the penetration of scientific frontiers that it involves; the tangible way in which it spreads the nation's name across the world; and, quite simply, the inherent glamour of aeroplanes: all these combine to make the industry a symbol of Britain's aspirations. In a period when she has lost many such symbols, this fact cannot be dismissed out of hand.

Having permitted themselves that one note of subdued lyricism, the committee remembered that they were spending taxpayers' money and passed briskly to their conclusions. "There is no predestined place for an aircraft industry in Britain. The economic justification for the industry receiving more Government support than other industries must rest on whether it provides particular benefits to the country . . . The present degree of support is already higher than these benefits justify."

They saw no realistic prospect of achieving anything jointly with the United States. "We believe that the future for the industry lies in a recognition of some overwhelming economic realities on the one hand and an imaginative and wholehearted collaboration with Europe on the other." The aim should be a European industry capable of producing aircraft fully competitive with those from the United States.

They also recommended that the government should acquire a financial stake in the airframe companies. Only Aubrey Jones, the Conservative MP and former minister of supply, dissented. He did not believe that the acquisition of a share in ownership would cause the industry to adopt a more commercial attitude. It would be seen as a rescue operation—the second in only a few years. In his view it would be an inauspicious start to what should be a new attempt to inculcate into the industry a sense of financial discipline.

A government holding would also increase the pressure to keep capacity in being and to find projects to fit the capacity rather than adjust the capacity to more realistic projects. The proposal was, he said, a recipe for speculation with the taxpayer's money to an extreme degree. Aubrey Jones was one of those unlucky politicians whose opinions become the orthodoxy of the next generation. He found no support for them among his colleagues on the committee, a majority of them holding to their view that more than half of the equity should be in government hands. Jones had to content himself with penning a note of reservation which was printed at the end of the report.

The committee did, in fact have some quite severe things to say about the use of public money, noting sternly that in the 20 years since the war the government had contributed more than £88 million and recovered only £25 million. They were also clear about the difficulties of withdrawing support once commercial returns had begun to appear: "the world is full of large and lusty industries still clad in their government-issue swaddling clothes." They saw no alternative, however, to substantial continuing injections of funds, urging only that the manufacturers should be pressed to contribute at least 50 percent of the launch costs of civil ventures.

In one respect it was a bad moment to be advocating further measures of collaboration. The commercial risks entailed in Concord (still at that time in Britain spelt without its final placatory *e*) were so great that the manufacturers had not been willing to make any contribution to the development costs. The cancellation of extravagant "prestige projects" had been one of the planks in the Labour Party's general election platform the previous year. By 1964, the cost of building the two prototypes, originally put at £150 million, had risen to £380 million. Changed days from the war, when the production cost of a Spitfire, £10,000, was the same as the prime minister's salary.

The Labour government soon discovered that they had no room for manœuvre, however. Roy Jenkins, the minister of aviation, had discussions with the French in October 1964 and discovered that they were unwilling not only to cancel the programme but even to review it. Nor was that all, as Harold Wilson was later glumly to record in his memoirs:

The Concorde arrangement was not a commercial agreement which could have allowed the two parties to break off the programme when costs escalated or commercial prospects grew dim. It was the subject of an international treaty, registered at the United Nations and subject to all the procedures of the International Court at the Hague. Had we unilaterally denounced the treaty, we were told, we could have been taken to the International Court, where there would have been little doubt that it would have found against us. This would have meant that the French could then have gone ahead with the project no matter what the cost, giving us no benefit either from the research or the ultimate product. But the Court would almost certainly have ruled that we should be mulcted for half the cost. Faced with this situation, we had little alternative but to go on.[7]

Lord Plowden's committee had done their homework rather better than the Labour Party, and in the course of their inquiries had visited both Paris and Bonn. The degree of wartime damage in Germany had provided an enormous stimulus to economic reconstruction, but until 1955 the Federal Republic had not been permitted to build aircraft, and the industry there was still relatively small, with a workforce of about 30,000, and no particular expectation of growing. Most of her equipment was of American design, much of it manufactured under licence, and the Lufthansa fleet was largely of American origin. Plowden had formed the view that the Germans were eager to collaborate, but only in projects that they could be in on from the start. Another interesting point they had picked up was that Germany was keen for the basis of cooperation to be as broad as possible— to include countries like Italy and the Netherlands, for instance.

In Paris, Lord Plowden's colleagues had liked what they saw: "The Committee gained the impression that the French are particularly good at making quick decisions on aeronautical matters and putting them into effect promptly. Industry and Government seem to work closely together." Measured by manpower, the French industry was only a third the size of the British, although it achieved half the output. The two industries seemed to the committee to be reasonably complementary in capacity and evenly matched in competence. Concord apart, France was already a partner in several of the 28 collaborative projects Britain was then engaged in. They were listed in Appendix L to the report—3 production agreements, 23 Research & Development agreements and 2 described as "projects under discussion."

One of these was still not much more than a gleam in the eye of a few enthusiasts, and the name it went by was propped up by inverted commas, as if to emphasise its speculative and fluid nature: "Airbus."

NOTES

1. Yenne, *op. cit.*
2. "How the Cold War was played," *Foreign Affairs* (October 1971).
3. W. Abelhauser, *Wirtschaftsgeschichte der Bundesrepublik Deutschland, 1945-80* (Frankfurt am Main: Suhrkamp Verlag, 1983).
4. *Germany's Comeback in the World Market* (London: Allen and Unwin, 1954).

5. Andrew Shonfield, *Modern Capitalism. The Changing Balance of Public and Private Power* (London: Royal Institute of International Affairs/Oxford University Press, 1965).

6. *Report of the Committee of Enquiry into the Arcraft Industry appointed by the Minister of Aviation under the Chairmanship of Lord Plowden, 1964-65* (London: Her Majesty's Stationery Office, Cmnd. 2853, December 1965).

7. Harold Wilson, *The Labour Government 1964-70. A personal record* (London: Weidenfeld and Nicolson and Michael Joseph, 1971).

2

A Certain Idea of France

"Toute ma vie, je me suis fait une certaine idée de la France . . . "

—Charles de Gaulle, *Mémoires de guerre,* 1954-59.

The memoirs of the general do not simply paint the man. Like everything he wrote, they are also a powerful if exaggerated portrait of the character and personality of the French nation. Airbus may be a four-country consortium, but there is no question about which of them has been its driving force. To understand what makes it tick, it is necessary to understand the French—their pride, their rigour and precision of mind, their prickliness, their anxious concern for the integrity of the language, their tenacity; necessary above all to understand the peculiar intensity with which they invest their view of France's place in the world.

The Oxford historian Theodore Zeldin says that de Gaulle loved France but not the French. "How can you be expected to govern a country that has two hundred and forty-six kinds of cheese?" he used to ask sardonically. He was certainly never at any pains to conceal his views about the Anglo-Saxons, as he always called them. He was sorry, he said on one occasion, to see the English moving closer to the Americans. They were in danger of becoming their commercial travellers.[1]

To the Americans themselves, his attitude was one of condescension. His old comrade in arms, General Eisenhower, paid a state visit to France in September 1959. "He was just as I had known and esteemed him when he commanded the allied forces during the war," de Gaulle wrote in his memoirs, but then he added, characteristically, "No doubt he shares the rather elementary conviction which animates the American people about the primordial mission they believe Providence has laid on the United States and about the primacy they believe they enjoy by right."[2]

The United States bulked large in French thinking in the years when the Airbus venture was taking shape. The year 1967, for instance, saw the publication of Jean-Jacques Servan-Schreiber's book, *The American Challenge.*[3] Its theme was the weakness and disarray of postwar Europe and the dangers for it of American economic penetration. Unless Europe made a sufficiently vigorous and coherent response to this challenge, it would become subservient—a colony, a satellite, an annexe of the United States. Cairo and Venice, he wrote, had been able to retain their sociocultural characteristics during centuries of economic decadence. Europe would not have this consolation. It was not so much a book as a piece of extended colour-supplement journalism, but it appealed to the latent anti-Americanism of the chattering classes and sold well on both sides of the Atlantic.

The following year, Servan-Schreiber was invited to write the foreword to a more interesting book published in Germany that explored some of the same preoccupations. The author was someone who was to play a prominent part in the Airbus story as it unfolded, and who at that time was a member of the federal government—Franz-Josef Strauss. One of his chapters was concerned with the gap in science and technology between Europe and the United States, and he quoted approvingly the ironic formula of a Dutch academic :

Let the U.S. Federal Government be done away with; let the USA be divided into its constituent States and let steps be taken to ensure that each has its own separate taxation system, currency, banking and insurance laws as well as customs regulations. Let the American minorities be settled in as many separate linguistic areas as possible—fifteen at the very least—and let there be in each such area at least one competing minority language, necessitating the maintenance of a bilingual school system. And do not let us forget to introduce some forty or fifty different systems of patent regulations. When all this has been done, the technological gap between the United States and Europe will soon begin to shrink.[4]

To the extent that they thought about them at all, the British took a much more relaxed view of their kissing cousins across the Atlantic. Although most people would have been hard put to define it with any precision, there was a general assumption that something called "the special relationship" did in fact still exist, that it was, as the authors of *1066, And All That* would have said, "a good thing" and that Britain and the United States were divided by nothing more serious than a common tongue.

The aircraft manufacturers in Britain had liked what Plowden had to say less than the government did, and they were also aware that the ruling Labour Party viewed them with less than total enthusiasm—Roy Jenkins had said the industry had been featherbedded for too long and was in for a "few shocks." Nobody in the industry doubted, however, that with rising costs and restricted national markets, cooperation would increasingly be the order of the day. British membership of the Common Market was also very much on the agenda, and there was an awareness that the United Kingdom's attitude to collaborative ventures would be read by her neighbours as a gauge of her political commitment.

As the institutions of the new Community slowly took shape in the early 1960s, there was a general assumption that there would be a substantial increase in traffic between its capital cities. A plethora of studies all pointed in the same direction—there was a need for a high-capacity/low-cost aircraft to fly short- and medium-haul routes. The first concrete proposal for a medium-range aircraft with 250 seats had come in 1963, only a few months after the signing of the Concorde agreement. It came from Joseph Roos, the director-general of Air France, who had in mind routes like Paris-London and Paris-Amsterdam.

Two Franco-British groups had in fact come out with preliminary designs for an "airbus" while the Plowden committee was deliberating, and there had been associated political initiatives. Jenkins, who was on the European wing of his party, had arranged a number of meetings with the French, and in May 1965 had announced the constitution of a joint working party.

At the 1965 Paris air show the prospects for cooperation were enlarged by informal meetings between representatives of German and French companies. In July, seven West German companies came together to form the Airbus Study Group (Studiengruppe Airbus), and later in the year the French government made money available for work to be continued by the three French firms engaged in design research.

The prospective customers—the airlines—experienced their usual difficulties in agreeing about what would meet their requirements, either as to size of aircraft or type of engine—put ten airlines round a table and they will come up with eleven different versions of what constitutes the ideal specification. There was now real interest, however, and a lot of enthusiasm was generated by a symposium organised in London in October 1965 by British European Airways. All the principal European carriers attended—Aer Lingus, Air France, Alitalia, Finnair, KLM, Lufthansa, Sabena, SAS, Swissair and TAP—and their number was matched by the manufacturers—Bréguet, Dassault, Nord, Sud, Dornier, Heinkel, Fokker, Fiat, BAC and Hawker Siddeley. The engine makers were represented by SNECMA, Rolls Royce and Bristol Siddeley, and there were observers present from the French and British governments.

In November a Franco-British working party, established to see whether the airlines' widely differing requirements could be reconciled, produced a specification for a plane that would seat 200–225 passengers. It was to have a range of 810 nautical miles and direct operating costs 30 percent lower than those of the Boeing 727-100. It was to be powered by two engines—British RB-178s from Rolls Royce or American JT9Ds from Pratt & Whitney. The evidence of a willingness to cooperate on the part of the two governments had its effect on the various manufacturers, and informal grouping began to take shape. Bréguet, Nord Aviation and Hawker

Siddeley drew together, and Sud Aviation and the British Aircraft Corporation, who were already partners in Concorde, began to consider whether they could not work together in this new area, too.

The Germans were also making their dispositions. In December 1965 they replaced their study group with a more formal structure—Arbeitsgemeinschaft Airbus. This was originally composed of Dornier, Hamburger Flugzeugbau, Messerschmitt-Bölkow and Siebel, and they were later joined by VFW. Germany was not yet greatly involved politically, but was an alert spectator as the political pace quickened. In February 1966 the British aviation minister (Fred Mulley had now taken over from Roy Jenkins) was in Paris for talks with Edgard Pisani, his French opposite number. Over lunch at the British Embassy they agreed on the need for a speedy decision. Pisani, in his report to the French Cabinet, said that a joint venture of the type envisaged could reduce operating costs by up to 30 percent, and stressed that it was an economic proposition.[5]

In these early months of 1966, engineers from Bréguet, Nord and Hawker Siddeley were busy evaluating five different projects which had emerged from independent studies within their companies. Hawker Siddeley had always been notably francophile, and Henri Ziegler, who was running Bréguet at the time and was later to become an important figure in the Airbus story, had long been convinced of the necessity for collaboration on a European scale.

Ziegler was a former pilot who had spent much of the war in England as chief of staff of the Free French and had many friends in the British aeronautical industry. Back in the French Air Ministry just before the war ended, he had been sent on a mission to the United States and the United Kingdom and returned convinced that no European power had the economic or financial resources to go it alone. "L'avenir de notre industrie aéronautique repose donc sur la coopération européenne," he wrote in his report. This was not at all the language that the Gallic cock wanted to hear in the heady months that followed the liberation. Ziegler was summoned to the office of the minister—Charles Tillon, a Communist whom de Gaulle had appointed to his first cabinet—and told that he was a traitor. Not surprisingly, he left the ministry a few months later. After a spell in charge of Air France, he moved into politics. In the mid-1950s Jacques Chaban-Delmas, an old friend from wartime days, became Pierre Mendès-France's minister of transport and asked Ziegler to run his office for him. He had been at Bréguet since 1956.

The Bréguet-Nord-Hawker Siddeley grouping settled on the project known as the HBN-100, and the details were made public at that year's Hanover Air Show. They reckoned that it could be ready for service in the spring of 1972, that it would seat 225 passengers and that its operating costs would be 21 percent better than those of the Boeing 727-100. This figure was 9 percent less than had been called for in the specification. The higher figure could be achieved by building a version with a longer fuselage that would carry an additional 36 passengers.

Sud Aviation and Dassault came up with a set of proposals that was very similar. There was little to choose between the two projects on grounds of technical merit. Eventually, the HBN-100 was preferred, although Paris now nominated Sud Aviation to be the French partner in the enterprise. The two governments invited West Germany to join them, and the Arbeitsgemeinschaft Airbus was designated as the German partner. By the spring of 1966 a Hawker Siddeley team from Hatfield in Hertfordshire and a group from Sud Aviation had got down to work together. (Henri Ziegler was appointed to run Sud Aviation shortly after this). Although the emerging consortium had its eye on the shorter and denser routes, the announcement on April 13th of the details of Boeing's 747 Jumbo jet provided a powerful competitive stimulus. Nor had the European partners closed all other options—a group of executives from Nord Aviation was in Seattle in July for talks about possible collaborative ventures, and Boeing, having sunk most of what they had in the 747, were not uninterested.

By July, however, a more detailed specification had been agreed, and within three months there was a design proposal to which all three contractors subscribed. The seating capacity had gone up to between 225 and 250 seats and the plane had now come to be known as the A300. The first formal company meeting at Board level took place in September 1966.

One of those who was present remembers that not everyone was exactly bowled over by the name "Airbus." The term was not new, as it happened—it had been used on a couple of occasions in the United States in the 1930s. Did it, to European ears, have a slightly plebeian connotation? Perhaps some recalled from their English schooldays those curious lines of verse by A. D. Godley, a former public orator at Oxford :

> *What is this that roareth thus?*
> *Can it be a Motor Bus?*
> *Yes, the smell and hideous hum*
> *Indicat Motorem Bum . . .*
> *Domine, defende nos*
> *Contra hos Motores Bos!*

None of this meant a great deal to French members of the board and in Germany, as is well known, the buses are not only clean and comfortable but also run on time. Next item of business. The following month a formal request was lodged with the three governments for approval—and for money.

Although things were coming together well on the industrial front, it was becoming clear that there were a number of issues on which the three governments were not of a mind. Britain, for instance, wanted Rolls Royce to build the engines, whereas the French and the Germans favoured Pratt & Whitney and wanted to go for the JT9D.

There was also more than one view over whether the contractors should make a contribution to the launch costs, and on whether a firm commitment to buy should be required of Air France, Lufthansa and British European Airways. (The British national carrier, always less amenable than its French and German counterparts, had made itself extremely unpopular only a month previously by announcing that it wanted to place a big order with Boeing—18 727-200s and 23 737-200s. Fred Mulley rapped them over the knuckles with an instruction that they must do their duty and "buy British.")

The first ministerial meeting was held in Paris on May 9, 1967, and the portfolios of the middle-rank ministers dispatched to attend it give some indication of how the respective governments saw the enterprise. In swinging London, only two and a half years had passed since Harold Wilson had come to power promising to plunge Britain into the "white heat of the technological revolution." The choice made itself—John Stonehouse, the Labour Government's minister of state for technology. No great hesitations, either, from those who had worked Europe's postwar "economic miracle,"—Johann Schollhorn, from Bonn, was state secretary at the West German Ministry of Economics. Their Gaullist hosts in Paris saw things rather differently. They knew that the matter in hand had quite as much to do with national prestige as with technology or economics. Diplomatic elbow work of that kind is the prerogative of the Quai d'Orsay. The home team fielded André Bettencourt, minister of state for foreign affairs.

The document to which they put their signatures committed the three governments "to proceed rapidly with a joint project definition study of the best aircraft capable of being built around two such engines"—the Rolls Royce RB-207, that is to say. Airframe research and development was agreed at £190 million. Germany was to pay 25 percent, France and Britain 37.5 percent each. Research and development costs for the Rolls Royce engine were put at £60 million, with Britain meeting 75 percent and the remaining 25 percent to be divided equally between France and Germany. The ministers accepted a market estimate of 250 aircraft, but agreed that they would look to the three national airlines to do their duty in that regard.[6]

The ministers met again in July 1967. There was one change of cast, the French seat at the table now being taken by Jean Chamant, the minister of transport. At the end of the month there was an announcement in the House of Commons that agreement had been reached to proceed immediately with the first stage of the joint development of a European short-medium range airbus. John Stonehouse told MPs that it would be powered by two Rolls Royce RB-207 engines, and that work on them would be undertaken jointly by Rolls Royce, SNECMA and MAN. The aircraft would be designed jointly by Sud Aviation, Hawker Siddeley and the German Arbeitsgemeinschaft. The cost of developing the airframe had been got down to £130 million, and this was to be more or less equally shared.[7]

Britain, therefore, had won the argument about how the aircraft was to be powered and was to have responsibility for directing the engine work. The *quid pro quo* was that design leadership on the airframe went to Sud Aviation, although there was a rather pompous sentence in Stonehouse's statement that indicated that the British had not yielded on this point with a particularly good grace: "We have emphasised during these talks that the British aircraft industry is not only outstanding in the field of aero-engine design, but also in airframe design, and we would expect, in the event of any future joint civil project being developed with Europe, that design lead to come to us."

The Conservative opposition spokesman, Robert Carr, wanted to know about safeguards against unilateral withdrawal, and asked whether the government would publish the agreement, as his party had done in the case of Concord (still at this stage in Britain spelt *a l'anglaise*). No, said the minister. Nor was he to be drawn on when assurances from airlines would have to be converted into firm orders. A joint company was to be formed to promote the sale of the aircraft, and some calculations had been done about market share, though Stonehouse did not say by whom, describing it only as "an expert assessment." There would, he said, be a requirement for 1,000 aircraft by 1985, of which something like 400–450 would be bought in the United States and 300–350 in Europe. "We would hope to achieve sales for the European airbus of approximately 300 aircraft out of the total of 1,000."

In July 1967 Roger Béteille had been brought in to coordinate the various study projects. Béteille had been an engineer first with Sud-Est and then with Sud Aviation, and had worked with de Havilland at the time of the Comet. When he paid his first visit to Hawker Siddeley at Hatfield the following month, he judged the prospects for collaboration to be good. He was firmly of the view that the plane must be built to suit the customer and not just to please the engineers—one of the factors that had been the undoing of the Caravelle, a project with which he had also been closely associated. He was strongly influenced by the ideas of Frank Kolk, the Technical Director of American Airlines in Dallas. It was he who had first made a wide-body proposal to the American manufacturers, and he had let Béteille see his specifications.

When the formal Memorandum of Understanding was signed in September at Lancaster House in London, it was stated that the design would be completed in a year and that the in-service date would be the spring of 1973. The go-ahead on the building of a prototype was to be subject to a condition, and it can be seen now to contain the seeds of future controversy with the consortium's American competitors—construction would only proceed if the three national airlines between them had by that time ordered 75 aircraft. It was a condition made at the insistence of the

United Kingdom.

The minister had managed to work into one of his parliamentary answers some carefully prepared noises about "the beginning of a new era in cooperation in European aircraft production," but of course the British government was playing for much more than a successful outcome to an exercise in industrial collaboration. Only two months previously, in Paris, General de Gaulle had given one of his elaborately theatrical press conferences. *"Chers amis,"* he had begun, "I am going to answer your question about Britain and the Common Market. Of course, I am not going to prejudice what the negotiations, if they take place—I repeat, if they take place—would be about . . ." One British newspaper called it "the velvet veto." Before the year was out, the velvet was stripped away, and for the second time in four years, the general pronounced an emphatic "non."

He did so only a couple of weeks before Concorde was rolled out, and one of those present was the British minister of technology, who in those days still called himself Anthony Wedgwood Benn. Mr Benn, a diarist of heroic application, could never be accused of setting out deliberately to amuse, but his entry for that day is richly entertaining: "In Toulouse for the roll-out of Concorde. I made a little speech. I didn't speak in French, but I did say that as a tribute to this occasion we would now in future have a British Concorde which would be spelt with an 'e.' There was great cheering. I said, 'That is "e" for excellence, "E" for England and "e" for "entente concordiale."' This went down very well."

It went down less well back at the ranch, where some popular newspapers, eager to demonstrate that the French did not have a monopoly of chauvinism, represented the gesture as a capitulation to de Gaulle. Benn also, inevitably, had a disgruntled letter from a man living north of the border. "I live in Scotland, and you talk about 'E' for England, but part of it is made in Scotland." This small-minded son of Caledonia got an accommodating reply, but Benn let off steam in his diary—"I wrote back and said that it was also 'E' for 'Ecosse'—and I might have added 'e' for extravagance and 'e' for escalation as well!"[8]

Bill Gunston, the author of a 1988 book on Airbus, lays much of the blame for the political difficulties it encountered at Mr. Benn's door. He says that Benn had an antipathy to what he called "technomania," and that the A300B was singled out for particular dislike because it was a collaborative project with Europe. He records that Benn told him in an interview "I cannot see one factor in its favour. We have proved unable to cancel Concorde, but I am determined we shall have no more costly and pointless projects like this, where we are not even masters in our own house."[9] Certainly, there is a degree of irony in the fact that the Wilson government, with all its flatulent rhetoric about technology, should prove so hostile to the aircraft industry. It is also the case that Benn was on the anti-European wing of the Labour Party, though a lack of enthusiasm for

Airbus was far from being a sign of eccentricity in that first Wilson administration.

In February 1968, Stonehouse, Benn's deputy, confirmed to the House of Commons that the plane was likely to enter service early in 1973. There was a possibility that an American airbus might come into service a year earlier, but as it would have a longer range, it was not seen as a competitor. He said that work was going well, and that the next stage would be the submission of detailed reports by the companies at the end of April. Asked which airlines had expressed interest, the minister gave a stolid nonanswer: "British European Airways, Air France and Lufthansa are cooperating in the preparation and evaluation of the aircraft's specification. Interest in the aircraft has been expressed by many airlines, both inside and outside Europe." He confirmed that it was the government's position that work would not go forward until 75 firm orders had been placed.[10]

Professional people always work better across frontiers than politicians do. Bill Gunston tells a good story from those days about an early test of the collaborative will of the partners. An elderly German said at a meeting that he was not happy about the fatigue life of the wing. The leader of the wing design team was called Jock Macadam, and on asking his neighbour who the German was, was told, "That is the great Dr. Willy Messerschmitt." Macadam stood up. "Herr Messerschmitt," he said, "I believe the fatigue life of the Bf 109 was about 50 hours—provided it didn't meet a Spitfire!"

Further away from the drawing board, however, the camaraderie engendered by a sense of common purpose was less in evidence. The British government had not been alone in having something bigger than Airbus in its sights. Rolls Royce's beady corporate eye had been on the American market, and they had gone bald-headed for the contract to supply their new, bigger RB-211 engine to Lockheed for the L-1011. In March 1968 they landed it—to the displeasure of the French, who felt that an American involvement on that scale must necessarily divert their attention from Airbus.

Assiduous French readers of Hansard might also reasonably have had doubts about the degree of commitment of the British government. Towards the end of June, John Stonehouse once again faced questions about Airbus in the Commons, and the tone of his answers was rather different from before. "We are very hopeful that it will be built," he said, "but we have always made clear that this is not a political project; it is a commercial one."[11]

The minister then went on to make clear that as a commercial project, it was now a good deal less attractive than it had been. "Engine launching costs are now estimated by Rolls-Royce at something over £70 million for a 54,000 lb thrust engine as against the earlier figure of £62 million for a 47,500 lb thrust engine. Airframe launching costs are estimated by Sud Aviation as at least £215 million as against the earlier figure of £130 million." These new figures, he said, which took into account the effects of devaluation, represented an increase of nearly 50 percent, although they were subject to further negotiation and had not yet been officially endorsed. He might have added that not a single order had been received.

French and German supporters of Airbus would have been even more dismayed if they had been able to eavesdrop on the discussions of the British Cabinet a month later. Under the Thirty Year Rule the official papers will not be available until the late 1990s, but Richard Crossman, who at the time was lord president of the council and leader of the House of Commons, dictated for posterity even more relentlessly than did Benn, and his diary entry for July 22 contains the following:

After that we turned our attention to the joint plan for a European airbus which is being built to beat the American airbus. Again there seemed to be a repetition of past mistakes. The price was escalating once again, particularly of the airframe. Tony Crosland made the very modest suggestion that we should defer a final decision for five months and go on paying till then.[12] The Chancellor wanted to cut the project now and it was fairly obvious that he was mainly concerned that if we postpone the decision on this we shall find it more difficult to cancel Concorde in December. But I've got a feeling the French won't allow us to cancel Concorde anyway and we must be content to cancel the airbus by itself.[13]

Crossman was not to know it, but at that particular juncture the Airbus project did not have all that many political friends on the other side of the channel, either. In July, shortly after Couve de Murville had replaced Pompidou as prime minister, Ziegler was asked to take on Sud Aviation with a brief to get the Concorde programme back on course. He reminded his prospective employers that he had been against the project and said that the programme they should really be giving their minds to was Airbus, only to be told that the government had decided to abandon the project.

There were a number of reasons for French political disenchantment. Orders had been slow in coming. The airlines seemed to feel that the aircraft that was emerging was too spartan—minimal galley provision, no individual lighting or ventilation. One of the people the French academic Pierre Muller spoke to when he was writing his study of Airbus described it witheringly as a sort of "down-market Air Inter."[14] Doubts about its commercial credibility had also been fed by the appearance of a new prospect called Mercure. It was not directly competitive with the Airbus, but a short-haul aircraft with 150 seats from the glamorous Dassault stable would have had considerable allure, even if Marcel Dassault had not gone the rounds of the ministries in his Rolls Royce, lobbying all his highly placed chums and dangling before them the beguiling idea of a successor to the Caravelle. It was only after Ziegler had played the unemployment card ("30,000 workers out of a job if you abandon Airbus") that the government changed its mind, and the project was given a six-month reprieve.

Ziegler became chairman of Sud on July 31, 1968, just as Paris was emptying for the holidays. Crosland's "very modest suggestion" was in fact adopted, and the manufacturers were asked to work on a revised design that would reduce both development and operating costs. By the beginning of 1969, that design was well advanced, though there was still uncertainty about whether Rolls Royce was going to produce an engine that met the consortium's requirements. Roger Béteille, by this time formally the director of the Airbus programme, was making confident claims for it, saying that it set entirely new standards, and made "no technical or economic concessions to political expediency," but it was plain that the interest of the British government was ebbing fast.

Early in February, the British prime minister, Harold Wilson, visited Bonn for what had become an annual exchange with the German chancellor, and technological cooperation figured prominently on the agenda. Dr. Kiesinger tackled his guest on Airbus, but the response was lukewarm. Later, in his memoirs, Wilson wrote that the discussions on technological cooperation were the most constructive part of the visit,[15] but at a press conference before returning to London, he spoke about collaboration in aerospace as "a desert track littered with the whitening bones of abortive joint projects mostly undertaken at high cost."[16] The Germans and the French became increasingly restive, and in March 1969 announced that they would fund the building of a prototype "with or without the participation of the UK."

They did not have long to wait for confirmation of what they had suspected. On April 16, the British minister of technology reported to the House of Commons on the latest ministerial meeting to discuss the economic and commercial prospects of the project and the terms of the financial assistance requested by the firms. "I had to make it clear," he said, "that Her Majesty's Government were not yet satisfied with all aspects of the project, in particular with the market and economic prospects, development costs and recovery, and the lack of a firm commitment to a European engine." (He meant British, but European sounded more high-minded.) "The French and German Governments are, however, satisfied with the general outline of the present proposals, and for the time being will pursue the project on a bilateral basis, while keeping us fully informed."[17]

That was the meat of the statement, but by way of ballast, Benn added a homiletic flourish or two. "In my judgement the greatest political disaster would be if we were to abandon economic criteria in the investment of public money in advanced technology . . . Nothing could be more fatal to European collaboration than for the British Government to be ready to finance anything that was international and advanced regardless of its prospects."

The wording of the announcement was curious, seeming as it did to suggest that the decision might be less than final, but the French and the Germans were in no doubt that Britain was pulling out and confirmed their intention of pressing on alone with the signature of a formal agreement at the end of May.

Hawker Siddeley, who had done most of the design work on the wing, were in a dilemma. Manufacture was going to be more expensive than for any wing ever previously made in Britain, calling for an investment in plant and equipment of the order of £35 million. If they were to stay in, these sums would now have to be found entirely from their own resources. Their board took the view that in this new situation the completion of finished wings was financially beyond them, but they were keen to retain their association with the project, and proposed that they should finance 40 percent of the cost of developing the wing from their own resources, which would represent about 7.5 percent of the development cost of the whole aircraft. Hawker Siddeley had already tested the wing and were tooled up for manufacture. If they dropped out, a whole year's development work would be lost.

The solution lay in Bonn—the first of a number of occasions on which the Germans were to pull the consortium's chestnuts out of the fire. In some respects, obviously, the British withdrawal suited Germany well enough. There was some political advantage. The exclusive nature of the industrial partnership with the French would lend further momentum to the process of reconciliation symbolised by the 1963 treaty. More concretely, they would now be on an equal footing with the French, and their push to get back on terms in the civil aircraft market would be both strengthened and accelerated. There is evidence that during the previous autumn and winter, when the French had been wavering, the Germans had been fairly blunt about where *they* stood. One of Muller's informants, an official from the French Ministry of Defence, had been present at a Franco-German meeting of ministers. The French produced an equivocally worded draft communiqué that made it plain that they were prepared to see the project sink quietly beneath the waves—"On enterrait l'affaire . . . on noyait l'Airbus."[18] The German minister handed it back and uttered four words: "Kein Airbus, Kein Communiqué!" [19]

What happened was that Karl Schiller, the SPD finance minister in the grand coalition, and Franz-Josef Strauss, who was defence minister at the time, gave their backing to the idea that West Germany should not only match the French contribution but also find the 60 percent of the development cost of the wing that Hawker Siddeley were not able to meet. In effect it meant that Hawker Siddeley got an injection of DM 250 million, and in July 1969 the British company signed fixed-price contracts with Sud Aviation and Deutsche Airbus to supply the main structural wing boxes for the prototypes. (A very sound business decision, as it turned out, because the contracts turned out to be lucrative.)

This meant, however, that responsibility for the secondary structure and the movable surfaces of the wing went elsewhere (to Germany, naturally enough), though Hawker retained an option on all future wingsets and were left with some responsibility for the design and further development of the wing. In essence, the British firm had become a subcontractor, although it also had to make a contribution to the sales and support costs of the enterprise—activities in which it would have no say.

There was a certain urgency in both France and Germany to get the matter settled—in France because of the referendum that was looming, in Germany because elections were due in September. The agreement between the two countries was concluded in four sessions. Because of the substantial differences between the French and German industries and the ways in which they were financed, the negotiations were complex. They were spread over six weeks, and both sides expressed themselves as highly satisfied. "You have found the philosopher's stone," one of the German negotiators said admiringly to a French colleague.

Two features of the agreement were of particular importance. The first was that technical and commercial decisions should be taken by those in industry and not those in government—this a notable departure from the Concorde precedent. The second was that the enterprise should be recognised as a partnership of equals. There was also a clause in Article 6 of the agreement that stipulated that in the event of withdrawal, a partner would be obliged to meet its financial commitments.

The agreement was signed on May 29, 1969, at the Paris Air Show. Karl Schiller signed for the Federal Republic and Jean Chamant, the transport minister, for France, and the text was initialled by Bernhardt Weinhardt for Deutsche Airbus and by Henri Ziegler for Sud Aviation. Late in the day, somebody had the delicate idea of adding a few Union Jacks to the display of flags—Hawker Siddeley was still on board, after all, even if Great Britain was not.

It was the last aeronautical initiative of the de Gaulle era. "The Captains and the Kings depart . . . " In mid-June, Georges Pompidou succeeded to the presidency and the general retired to Colombey-les-deux-Eglises for the last time. As a result of the September elections in Germany, Willy Brandt came to power. Franz-Josef Strauss became president of Airbus shortly afterwards.

As a consequence of the British withdrawal, there was a drain of expertise from the United Kingdom to France and Germany and a rapid growth in the equipment and accessory industries in those countries. It was an unimpressive performance by the Wilson government. Opportunism and incoherence seldom combine attractively, and in this case there was a measure of fecklessness, too. The government had committed itself to meeting 70 peercent of the launch cost of the RB-211 engine, and yet the Ministry of Technology did not see a full text of the contract with Lockheed until six months after it had been signed.

The following year they were turned out of office by the Conservatives. The Germans were still wistful about British membership, and the new

Heath administration was promptly invited to rejoin. The fly was cast with some cunning, because the invitation was accompanied by an offer of financial assistance from the West German government to build a version of the RB-211 for use on the A300B.

Early in December 1970, however, the new minister of aviation supply, Frederick Corfield, announced that the government had decided not to accept. If Britain took part in the airframe part of the project alone, the initial cost to the government would be of the order of £30 million. If in addition the RB-211-61 engine were launched for the aircraft, it would rise to £100 million, and that took no account of further costs likely to be incurred during the production phase. Corfield announced at the same time that no government money would be forthcoming either for the Rolls Royce engine or for the British Aircraft Corporation's BAC 311. Together they would have cost £144 million. The government was already committed to launch aid to the tune of £88 million in that year and felt that this represented a sufficient call on the public purse.[20]

A couple of weeks later, on December 18, 1970, Airbus Industrie was formally constituted as a *groupement d'intérêt économique* under French law.

NOTES

1. "Je suis mélancolique de voir l'Angleterre se diriger vers les Etats-Unis, car elle risque de se comporter comme leur commis voyageur." Press conference at the Elysée Palace, May 16, 1967. Quoted in J-R Tournoux, *Le mois de mai du Général* (Paris: Plon, 1969).

2. "Sans doute partage-t-il la conviction, quelque peu élémentaire, qui anime le people américain sur la mission primordiale qui incomberait aux Etats-Unis comme par décret de la Providence et sur la prépondérance qui leur reviendrait de droit." *Mémoires d'espoir: Le Renouveau, 1958-62* (Paris: Plon, 1970).

3. *Le défi americain* (Paris: Denoel, 1967).

4. *Challenge and Response. A Programme for Europe* (London: Weidenfeld and Nicolson, 1969). Originally published as *Herausforderung und Antwort: Ein Programm für Europa* (Stuttgart: Seewald Vorlag, 1968).

5. *Le Monde,* February 19,1966: "Le ministre a insisté sur le caractère rentable de cet investissement."

6. House of Commons *Hansard,* June 6, 1967.

7. *Ibid.,* July 26, 1967.

8. Tony Benn, *Diaries,* Vol. 1: *Out of the Wilderness, 1963-67* (London: Hutchinson, 1987).

9. Bill Gunston, *Airbus, The European Triumph* (London: Osprey Publishing Company, 1988).

10. House of Commons *Hansard,* February 12, 1968.

11. *Ibid.,* June 24, 1968

12. At that time president of the Board of Trade.

13. Richard Crossman, *The Diaries of a Cabinet Minister,* Vol. 3 (London: Hamish

Hamilton and Jonathan Cape, 1977).

14. "C'était de l'Air Inter détérioré." Pierre Muller, *Airbus. Du référentiel de l'arsenal au référentiel de marché* (Saint-Martin-d'Hères: CERAT, 1988).

15. Wilson, *op. cit.*

16. *Financial Times,* February 14, 1969.

17. House of Commons *Hansard,* April 16, 1969

18. "They were burying the issue . . . Airbus was being drowned"—i.e., barely got a mention.

19. Muller, *op. cit.*

20. House of Commons *Hansard,* December 2, 1970.

3

The Unwanted Mousetrap

"If a man write a better book, preach a better sermon, or make a better mousetrap than his neighbor, though he build his house in the woods, the world will make a beaten path to his door."

—Ralph Waldo Emerson, 1803-1882.

Twenty orders to show for ten years of effort. Throughout much of the 1970s, it must often have seemed to the mixed bag of nationalities who worked for Airbus that the woods in which they had chosen to build their particular house were impenetrably deep.

To begin with, that house was a small suite of offices at 160, avenue de Versailles in Paris, but everyone was clear from the start that their location in the French capital would be only temporary. Once the enterprise got into its stride, it would be important to be close to the sharp end—or at least one of the sharp ends. Frankfurt, Paris, Geneva and Zurich were all passed in review. Finally, proximity to an existing assembly line, thoughts about the climate (an important consideration for test flights) and the price of property all began to point insistently in one direction, and that direction was south.

Toulouse, the old capital of Languedoc, is the fourth city of France. It is known as "la ville rose," a not very precise reference to the colour of the brickwork in the old quarters of the town. *Michelin* gives the eleventh century Basilica of St. Sernin three stars, which is only reasonable, because it is not only the largest but also the most perfect Romanesque building in France. In ancient times the town was famed for a sacred pool into which pilgrims threw coins and other offerings, though to see that as a metaphor for the subsequent relationship between Airbus and the European taxpayer would be one part fanciful and three parts malicious.

It was in Toulouse in 1764 that Adam Smith, who was travelling as tutor to the Duke of Buccleuch, began to pass the time by writing *Wealth of*

Nations, a book whose arguments have not been much regarded in the economic pursuits for which the town has subsequently become best known. Henry James, that great student of contrasts between things American and European, passed this way, too, but did not find much to detain him: "The oddity is that the place should be both animated and dull. A big, brown-skinned population, clattering about in a flat tortuous town, which produces nothing whatever that I can discover."[1]

If James had travelled only a few years later, the beginnings of Toulouse's long connection with aviation might have been forced on his attention. The first heavier-than-air, steam-powered machine was designed and built there in 1890, and subsequently a factory was established to build planes for the French Air Force in the First World War. Later it became the home of Sud Aviation, which built France's first passenger jet, the Caravelle, and which was the French partner in Concorde. When it joined forces with Nord Aviation in 1970 to become Aérospatiale, the result was not only the biggest aerospace concern in France but also one of the five or six largest industrial enterprises in the country.

Once it was agreed that Toulouse was to be the centre for the final assembly of Airbus, it clearly made a great deal of sense that the headquarters of the consortium should be sited there too. The decision was made early in 1972. Airbus Industrie's austere and functional building began to rise just across the way from Aérospatiale, close to the airport at Blagnac, and the move took place in 1974.

When those responsible for an enterprise look back on its early struggles, events often take on a patina of coherence and order that was not apparent in the reality of the time. In a speech to the Wing's Club of New York City in 1986, Jean Pierson, who had succeeded to the top job at Airbus the previous year, rehearsed the authorised version of the history of those pioneering days:

We Europeans have a long history of technical innovations in the field of powered flight, inventions that made Man's dream of flying possible . . . However, we were not able to translate our technical success into commercial success. By the 1960s, Europe was purchasing 25% of the world's airplanes, but could claim less than 2% of the manufacturing business. By this time, Europeans had recognised that their industrial future lay not in the production of cheeses or perfumes, but rather in the manufacture of high technology products such as civil aircraft.[2]

This realisation, Pierson said, required an abrupt shift in philosophy, and a recognition that the industrial future of the continent demanded cooperation. Europe's collective experience had taught it two important lessons. The first was that industrial success could not be achieved through a system of management by committee. The second was that the direct involvement of government agencies in day-to-day project management inhibits productivity. Both those lessons must have been engraved on his heart. He had, after all, been production general manager for Concorde at the age of 28.

The shadow of that earlier, more grandiose collaboration never entirely disappeared. It certainly slowed the Airbus programme by several years. Concorde might be costing the French and British taxpayer an arm and a leg, but it was undoubtedly glamorous; Airbus suffered from the comparison, and was seen as something of an ugly duckling. Even in the 1980s, at the time when the Conservative government in Britain was giving rather grudging consideration to the funding of the A330/340 Airbus programme, the memory had not faded: "We don't want another Concorde," said Margaret Thatcher in her best no-nonsense manner.

In some ways, it had always been an improbable collaboration:

The British wavered when the French were steadfast. The British constantly wanted to cancel the project, to whittle down its expense, to scale down its vision. The French, it is argued, were more confident, willing to indulge in extravagance so that greatness could be achieved. The British were confined to commerce, the French were meeting their destiny. The overall image is one of contest more than cooperation, with each country reverting to cultural type.[3]

That is an account not of how it was, but of how received opinion held it to be, and yet there is only a touch of caricature in the contrasting stereotypes of the two government machines that came unenthusiastically together to make it possible—the French, driven by thrusting, rational technocrats, brought up in the centralising Jacobin tradition, the British by well-educated generalists, unashamed of their devotion to the cult of the amateur, never overimpressed by expertise or by men who speak foreign languages too well, not unhappy when thought to be muddling through.

If there were four specific occasions when Britain wanted to pull out, there were at least three when the French wanted to do the same, although rather inefficiently the two sides never contrived to think the thought simultaneously. The 1962 treaty—ten short paragraphs, one and a half pages of typescript—had been submitted to neither parliament for ratification. There were no reliable estimates of cost. There was not even a mechanism for withdrawal—this at the insistence of the British side, although the Treasury had objected: a rare instance of a British departmental minister getting his way in the face of Treasury opposition. Possibly the minister in question, Julian Amery, was helped a little by the fact that the then prime minister, Harold Macmillan, was his father-in-law.

All in all, the Concorde saga was rich in lessons of how not to do things. Raymond Nivet, who was deputy director of technical development at Air France, described the extended development and cost escalation of the project as an exercise in industrial existentialism. The contracts were drawn up on a cost-plus basis. There was no incentive to control expenditure. To be part of the project was, as Feldman says, to have access to almost unlimited funds, to enjoy substantial prestige and to experience the excitement and challenge of new technology. To work on Concorde was to know what things were like for Adam before Eve developed a taste for apples.

By the end of 1978, and taking no account of research, the British and French governments had each spent ten times the 1960 estimates. Nor did the end of production mean the end of expenditure. British Airways, committed to the maintenance of the planes in operation, had set up a complete stock of parts at each Concorde station. In 1976, the stock at Washington, D.C., was worth $2.2 million, and there were similar establishments in Bahrain and at Dallas, New York, Rio, Dakar and Caracas.

There was no attempt at recovering any of the investment in research or development. The manufacturing costs were to be recovered (without interest) by setting the unit cost against the projected construction of 150 aircraft. Even then, the price bore a closer relationship to the price of a 747 Jumbo jet (at that time something less than $30 million) than to any reasonable approximation of what it had cost to get Concorde off the assembly line.

The governments could not say they had not been warned. Air France had refused to take part in the plane's development, but as early as 1963 it was directed to buy it because of what the French Ministry of Transport described as its "national importance." When British Airways was asked by the British Department of Trade for its views on the plane's prospects, the reply was unequivocal: "The conditions and assumptions necessary for profitable Concorde services are not those on which a commercial management could prudently plan its future operations."[4]

When Concorde went into service in 1976, British Airways owned five of them and had won access only to Bahrain. The French, with four planes, had access to Rio and Caracas. The French president and the British prime minister both pressed the U.S. president to permit landing in New York. The French appeared to think that the White House could dictate access to U.S. airports, and this failure to appreciate the federal nature of the United States generated a good deal of ill feeling between Washington and Paris. Feldman quotes the contemptuous comment of a senior official in the French Ministry of Transport and Civil Aviation some years later: "Any bunch of hippies plus lawyers could be stronger than the signature of Uncle Sam himself on any air transport agreement."

By 1978, when production ceased, it had cost $4.28 billion to build two prototypes and fourteen commercial aircraft. Each Concorde therefore cost $267 million. The first one was sold for $31.2 million, the last for $80 million. This improbable genetic cross between an albatross and a white elephant never had a single willing customer, and was, in effect, given away.

Strong political currents tugged at the project in both countries, the Right concerned as often as not with prestige, the Left with jobs—when the Labour Party in Britain was fingering the axe in 1964, the mention of major factory closures by the manufacturers was enough to bring the unions out against cancellation. Socialist rhetoric would normally label such a project élitist and exclusive: Feldman notes the irony of left-wing support for major public expenditure on it. In Concorde's declining years, two of its most prominent champions were the Communist leader Georges Marchais in France and the left-wing Labour politician Tony Benn in Britain. Benn's position was no doubt a highly principled one, although it is a foolish politician who disregards all considerations of pragmatism, and he did number several thousand of the Concorde workforce among his Bristol constituents . . .

It is difficult to quarrel with Feldman's judgement on the enterprise, severe as it is: "For both the French and the British, Concorde produced a common U.S. villain and no native heroes. It proved that Britain and France were capable of great joint achievement (they did build and fly Concorde), and of great collaborative folly. They could equal each other's genius, creativity, inefficiency, incompetence, tragedy, and waste."

It is not all that surprising that when they found themselves working in close proximity at Toulouse, relations between the Concorde and Airbus teams were not always of the best. Airbus people tended to see Concorde people as indulged perfectionists; Concorde veterans looked down on the Airbus camp as a very mixed bunch who had little experience and even less chance of getting their programme off the ground.

Initial scepticism about the prospects of Airbus ever becoming more than a "paper" plane was not confined to the grandees of Concorde. "The French and the Germans will never work together," people said. "This camel of an aircraft will never fly." The first customer was Air France, who signed a letter of intent for six A300B2s on September 3, 1970, but that particular decision to buy could hardly be said to have been based on an unfettered commercial judgement.

Another factor making for uncertainty was that in the early years the enthusiasm of politicians for the project was distinctly muted. No real measure of political support emerged in France until 1971–72, on the eve of the first launch. The only credible demonstration of political will had come from Germany, from Franz-Josef Strauss and Karl Schiller. Without their intervention in 1969, when they were both ministers in the grand coalition, Airbus would have been stillborn. It was they who had found the money to make it possible.

Airlines traditionally have a preference for the tried and the familiar. With the lives of so many passengers in their hands that is understandable. That alone does not entirely explain their reluctance to do business with the newcomer in the first ten years of its existence, however, and in its efforts to get a toehold in the American market, it was undoubtedly the case that

Airbus Industrie initially had to carry the burden of Europe's past reputation, which was for poor quality and indifferent maintenance. "U.S. carriers wouldn't touch European airliners with a ten-foot pole," one analyst said.

It is also the case that good ideas cannot exist in a vacuum. It's no use being right at the wrong moment; timing is even more important for aircraft builders than for people who do things on a more modest scale. Deciding when to take your courage in your hands with a new product is a bit like surfing. Launch yourself at the right instant and you are carried further up the beach than anyone else. Misjudge it by only a little and you end up sitting in the undertow examining your bruises. In taking on the Americans, Airbus was pitting itself against some very expert surfers, and there was a good deal of scepticism in the late 1960s and early 1970s about whether it would succeed in the attempt.

The need for a smaller sized wide-bodied aircraft that could be used in domestic services had been spotted in the mid-1960s on both sides of the Atlantic, but the Americans got in first, and in early 1968 McDonnell Douglas launched the DC-10 and Lockheed launched the L-1011 Tristar, each with a capacity of 300–350. Airbus, recognising that the competition had a two-year start, decided that discretion was the better part of valour and head-on competition with the Americans was averted by scaling the capacity of the A300 down to 250. With its shorter range (3,000 nautical miles as opposed to 4,500) and lower price (at $24 million about $6 million cheaper than the American planes), the A300 turned out in the long run to be better sized in a number of markets, and production of the Tristar was eventually closed down. As traffic growth gradually improved during the 1970s, therefore, it turned out to have been a prudent decision, although Airbus had to wait for several anxious years for the satisfaction of knowing that.

The first enlargement of the consortium was not long in coming. Negotiations with the Spanish manufacturer Construcciones Aeronauticas S.A. (CASA), began in the autumn of 1971. Agreement was reached that a condition of entry would be the purchase by Iberia, the Spanish state airline, of thirty A300Bs. Iberia did not take all that kindly to having their arm twisted, however, and their negotiators showed themselves to be resourceful. At one point the word was put about that they were contemplating buying the Tupolev 144 from the USSR, who were said to be offering a deal at 3 percent over 20 years. Finally, in January 1972, CASA signed a contract to buy four Airbuses with an option on eight more, and took a 4.2 percent share in the consortium.

Total development costs for the A300 programme were initially set at 2.3 billion French francs (at 1968 prices), and these were to be met by government loans and by the sale of the three prototype aircraft that were to be used for test flights. France and Germany would pay the lion's share of this (42 percent each) and the Spanish government 2 percent. Hawker Siddeley's private contribution came out at 7.4 percent of the total and the remaining 6.6 percent was to be met by the government of the Netherlands, which had opted to remain as a sponsor even though Fokker, who were originally to have been a risk-bearing partner, finally decided to take up only associate membership.

The development phase involved manufacturers in six different countries—France, Germany, Spain, the Netherlands, The United Kingdom and the United States—and each of them assumed design and development responsibility for those parts of the aircraft it would eventually produce. Decisions about who should do what were influenced partly by the share of the risk that had been assumed by the country in question, partly by the experience and capacity of the manufacturers.

Deutsche Airbus, for example, was assigned responsibility for the forward and rear fuselage, the upper centre fuselage and the vertical tail surfaces. Hawker Siddeley, the acknowledged leader in aerodynamics, took on the design of the wings. Aérospatiale, in many ways the company with the widest range of experience of civil aircraft among the original partners, was to design and build the nose section, including the flight deck, the lower part of the centre fuselage (the critical stress section which houses the landing gear) and the engine pylons. The engines themselves were to be made by General Electric. Of the smaller companies, Fokker's expertise was to be enlisted to manufacture all the ailerons and flaps and CASA was to produce the horizontal tail surfaces.

The break-even point for the A300 programme was estimated at 360 planes, and the remuneration of the risk-sharing partners was calculated accordingly. Because associated members bore no risk, their contracts were for shorter production runs (typically of up to 100 aircraft), after which they were subject to renegotiation. The normal arrangement with subcontractors was for even shorter runs. They were mainly concerned with the supply of components such as landing gear and with various types of specialized equipment, and negotiated contracts for each particular order.

As things turned out, rather more than 40 percent of the production costs for this first programme was incurred in France. The figure for Germany was 28 percent, and the next largest the United States—this because of the engines. The French share was as big as it was for a number of reasons—the fact that the final assembly line was in Toulouse, the advanced state of the component and equipment business in France and the participation of the French company SNECMA in the manufacture of the engine. An analysis of production costs by category showed that Airbus Industrie's financial costs and overheads accounted for 9 percent of the total.[5]

The setting of the break-even point for the A300/A310 programme at 360 was optimistic, and imposed a substantial financial burden. That figure would in any case have covered only the government loans that had been received, with no allowance for the contribution made by the partners or any profit margin. Economies associated with the learning curve are of particular importance in aircraft manufacture, and it was only after production had passed the 100 mark that the deficit run up through average cost pricing would begin to decrease. Bill Gunston quotes some interesting figure offered by MBB. When the first A300B1 was being built, 340,000 man-hours were required for the fuselage sections. By the time they had got to the seventy-fifth aircraft, the figure had dropped to 85,000 and it eventually settled at 43,000.[6]

There was also a considerable timelag between ordering up materials for manufacture and receiving payment—possibly a year or more. If production was running at the rate of three planes a month, the bridging of this gap incurred a revolving debt of several billion francs. In the event, the break-even point was to recede steadily. By 1982, Airbus's own estimate was that for the A300/310 programme it lay somewhere between 850 and 900.[7]

A third factor was that in pursuit of Airbus Industrie's market entry strategy, the selling price of the A300 was initially pitched low. This meant that by the time the hundredth plane was produced, the programme was in the red to the tune of 10–15 billion francs. The servicing of a debt of this order was quite beyond the capacity of the members of the consortium, and there was nothing for it but to seek government guarantees for the large sums that it became necessary to raise in the money markets.

From the start, the Airbus objective was to achieve a European lead in the twin-jet sector. The strategy was to go for strong initial market penetration and to aim for commercial viability by a sustained rate of sales over a longer period of time. Even before work started on building the prototype, the consortium had hoisted aboard one of the keys to Boeing's success, and there were plans for a family of derivatives to suit different market requirements. The shortage of orders in the early years was also a strong incentive to Airbus to keep the design flexible, particularly in the matter of exploiting the capacity for greater range, and there were considerable modifications over the years to the length of the fuselage. The underlying design premise, however, was to be commonality, and all of its twin-aisle planes were to be derivatives of the original A300. This was used as a basic design, and as time went on, alternative models would be derived by adding or subtracting length on its various sections.

The A300 prototype lifted off the runway at Toulouse on October 28, 1972, 33 days ahead of the date stipulated by the contract with the partner governments. The certification programme was carried out by four prototypes in 1,580 hours of flying. The first production plane flew on April 15,1974, and the inaugural Air France flight between Paris and London followed on May 23, carrying 225 economy passengers and 25 in the first class.

FAA certification followed a week later, but there was little initial interest from the American airlines. In these early years, the U.S. market was still regulated. If an airline's costs increased, it usually sought—and got—permission to raise its fares. There was no particular incentive to consider any new products that might be on offer from Europe. For most airlines, the choice offered by Lockheed, Boeing and McDonnell Douglas seemed adequate.

Airbus thought they had won a toe-hold in the Latin American market in 1973. TransBrasil was on the point of signing a contract for two Airbuses, but the Export-Import Bank declined to finance the transaction, even though the American element in the plane represented something over 20 percent. The Airbus version of what happened next is that Boeing got wind of a deal that Crédit Lyonnais and the Dresdner Bank had managed to put together and moved with their legendary speed around the corridors of Washington. The U.S. government certainly intervened to block the export of the necessary currency, giving as a reason the high level of Brazilian indebtedness to American banks.

Another tale that Airbus like to tell is of the occasion early in 1974 when they competed with the major American manufacturers for an order from South African Airways. Sealed bids were invited, and the contenders were asked to include an assessment of what they thought their competitors had to offer. There are no prizes for modesty on such occasions, and each company naturally voted itself into first place, which didn't get the South Africans much further forward. One of the Airbus salesmen, who happened to be British, made a suggestion. Why not weight the marking by taking into account what the competitors thought of each other? It was a cunning throw, and not for the last time, Airbus was able to exploit the intense rivalry of the Americans. Each had been so intent on inflicting injury on their compatriot that Airbus stood demurely in second place on both of their lists.

McDonnell Douglas liked the outcome even less than Lockheed or Boeing did, and stayed in town to argue the toss. They deployed every argument in the book. Airbus was an unknown quantity, untried and untested; they, by contrast, had a distinguished record, with a reputation for all-round technical superiority and safety. They were still there on March 3, but on that Sunday afternoon there was suddenly nothing further to discuss. Shortly after taking off from Orly Airport a plane belonging to Turkish Airlines crashed in the Forest of Ermenonville to the north of Paris. It was the worst disaster in aviation history—346 people died. The aircraft was a Douglas DC-10.

Airbus had most feared competition from a new model from Boeing, but the 767 was not in the event to get the go-ahead until 1978. Head-on rivalry did not become a reality until almost ten years after the launch of the first

Airbus. The European consortium paid a lot of attention from the start to the cargo and military potential of their planes. Airbus Industrie offered a dual-role tanker-transport to the Luftwaffe as early as February 1973, but there was no response.

Orders in the middle 1970s came in a painfully slow trickle, and some of them were never taken up. A particular disappointment was Iberia's cancellation, in October 1974, of its order for four aircraft, invoking a clause that allowed it to do so if Airbus did not have 50 orders in the book by a certain date. Once again, there were dark mutterings from Airbus about a commando from the Boeing Department of Dirty Tricks having been seen in town.

Lufthansa was also showing some reluctance to acknowledge where its duty lay, and during April 1975 displayed what Airbus thought was an unseemly interest in a similar clause in its contract. Their reasons, however, were far from frivolous. One was the existence of common maintenance agreements between two groups of European airlines that had the same sort of aircraft in their fleets. With a new airframe and new engines, the Airbus would incur additional maintenance costs, offsetting the benefits of the lower operating costs that were claimed for it. The new flight deck would also mean pilot training courses, and that could delay the date of full certification.

The cancellation of the Spanish order had been a blow, especially as Spain was a member of the consortium, but it was softened before the end of the year by a sale to South Korea, which mopped up the planes that were to have gone to Iberia. It was an important transaction in a number of ways. It was the first deal in which aircraft were not sold but leased. It was also the first with a non-European customer. The importance of the Asian market increased greatly in the 1970s, rising from 11 percent to 22 percent of the world market in the course of the decade. The sale marked the beginning of something that was later to be of major importance to Airbus—the opening up of what was known as the Silk Route.

Early in 1975 Henri Ziegler had retired and he was succeeded by Bernard Lathière, like his predecessor an Aérospatiale nominee. The new broom made a bold public commitment at his inaugural press conference to build 54 aircraft, though orders stood only at 20. It was plain, however, that relations between the partners in the consortium were not of the most cordial, because Lathière also told the press that he regretted that his sales teams found themselves up against not only American diplomatic resistance but that of British embassies, too.

Sales remained sluggish. Demand never came anywhere near the four a month for which the Toulouse assembly line was equipped. Yet the Airbus team seems to have been remarkably unaffected by the setbacks and disappointments of those early years. The impression one has talking to some of the old hands is that it was an epoch not only of enthusiasm but also of high spirits. The customers didn't for quite a few years buy the planes in any numbers, but they were struck by the exuberant morale of the men who were trying to sell them. "We were a bunch of people somewhere between cowboys and sharpshooters," said Pierre Pailleret, Airbus's senior vice-president of marketing until he left to join the Compagnie Financière de Suez. "We had no limos, made our own coffee, occasionally typed our own letters. We were working 18 hours a day. We were doing things that sounded crazy to European industry, like trying to sell planes to U.S. airlines. A lot of people thought that idea was just ridiculous."[8]

Certainly, to take a noncertificated prototype on a world sales tour as they did in the autumn of 1973 argued a certain buoyancy. One of the capitals visited was Delhi, and their visit there had a sequel that showed that feelings of European solidarity were stronger in some areas than in others.

Copies of two letters found their way to Toulouse. The first was from the French ambassador in New Delhi. He was loud in his praises for the Airbus initiative. The Indians had been delighted, and so had he. He had one small observation to make. At the reception he had given at his embassy, it had seemed to him that the Airbus team contained rather more Germans than Frenchmen. Perhaps on a future occasion a little care might be taken to see that an appropriate numerical balance was achieved . . .

The second letter was from the ambassador of the Federal German Republic to his political masters in Bonn. It was couched in very similar terms—except that it had seemed to him that the French had outnumbered the Germans . . . Perhaps that marked a modest advance in the evolution of diplomatic method. It was only a century or two, after all, since differences over precedence at the Court of St. James had the French and Spanish ambassadors overturning each others' coaches in the streets of London.

A year or so later, Delhi was also the setting for a demonstration of the verve with which Airbus pursued the prospect of a sale. The story goes that the consortium had secured a firm commitment from Air India for the purchase of three aircraft, but that Boeing bustled back into the fray with an offer of six 737s for the same price. Bernard Lathière, who had succeeded Henri Ziegler only a month previously, flew into Delhi and pulled out all the stops.

First of all he announced to Major P. C. Lal, the director-general of Air India, that it was his birthday. His forty-sixth. He was very glad, he said, that the imperatives of business allowed him to celebrate it in the land of his birth. (He had indeed been born in Calcutta. His father had worked there for Michelin.) Then, with a nicely judged sense of theatre, Lathière took out his wallet and produced his trump card. It was a faded snapshot of Mahatma Gandhi. He and his parents had travelled with him on the same boat to Europe. The photo showed the Mahatma at his spinning wheel. The small figure standing beside him was the future boss of Airbus, aged three and a half.

That evening, in a Delhi restaurant, Major Lal joined in the celebrations—*Happy Birthday, dear Bernard* . . . History does not record whether the singing was accompanied by the sound of violins, but the men from Boeing at a nearby table must have been wondering what the French word was for schmalz. There are many ways of selling aircraft.

* * * * *

If things were bad for Airbus in the early-middle 1970s, life was not exactly a bowl of cherries for the American manufacturers. They might be big, but they were not immune from the operation either of world economic forces or Murphy's Law. Boeing had particularly severe problems with the 747. When the programme had been launched, U.S. domestic traffic was increasing at an annual rate of 15 percent, and international trends looked even more promising. "Makers of passenger airplanes and their customers," wrote John Newhouse, "saw themselves as standing at the gates of El Dorado."[9]

In the event, the growth in passenger traffic between 1969 and 1975 turned out to be something under 4 percent a year. At first the 747 had sold like hot-cakes, and the purpose-built Everett plant had been working at full capacity. Then there came a period of three years in which not a single order was taken, and production dropped from seven planes a month to less than two. Boeing laid off some 60 percent of its workforce, and as they are the largest employers in the State of Washington, the effect on the local economy was catastrophic. If it hadn't been for the continued success of the 727, the company might well have gone under. Things only really began to pick up in 1977, the first year in which orders got back to their 1967 level.

McDonnell Douglas was having difficulties of a different kind. In 1972, the rear cargo door of an American Airlines DC-10 had blown out over Windsor, Ontario, but the pilot had managed to get the plane down safely at Detroit. Two years later, in the Ermenonville disaster, the locking system of the cargo door failed, and the decompression that resulted was so violent that the control cables of the aircraft were severed as it was still climbing through 13,000 feet. Five years after that there was another major disaster involving a DC-10. This time, the plane's certificate of airworthiness was withdrawn by the FAA, and the entire DC-10 fleet was grounded.

Once again, it was an aircraft belonging to American Airlines that was involved. Taking off for Chicago for Los Angeles, it had reached a height of only 300 feet when the port engine was torn off, ripping away the hydraulic cables that run along the leading edge of the wing. The flight deck warning lights failed, the plane rolled over, crashed to the ground and exploded on impact, killing all 273 people on board.

The enquiry established that the crash was caused by metal fatigue, and found fault with the airline's maintenance routines. The DC-10 itself was given a clean bill of health, but the damage to the reputation of the company was severe. It also turned "Mr. Mac" against the idea of a new plane. There had long been plans within the Douglas part of the merged company to build a DC-11, a twin-aisle plane with about the same number of seats as the Boeing 757. Associates urged him to give it the go-ahead, asserting that it would "fill a hole in the market." "Why should I fall into it?" he countered sardonically.

The fall of Saigon at the end of April 1975 had signalled the end of the war in Vietnam and led to a sharp decline in military orders. It was the beginning of another serious recession in the American aircraft industry. That was a source of no consolation to the struggling consortium on the other side of the Atlantic. 1976, in particular, was a year that Airbus Industrie would choose not to live through a second time. Total sales for the 12-month period amounted to precisely one aircraft. The only glimmer of light during the year came when Franz-Josef Strauss handed over its first Airbus to Lufthansa, and was able to point out that it was the first European aircraft bought by Germans since 1945.

World economic recession and the unprecedented rise in oil prices were to thrust not just Airbus but the entire industry into deep crisis. There were differences among the partners about how to respond. The German view was that there should be a cutback on investment and that the production rate of two planes a month should be reduced. The Airbus management in Toulouse disagreed, partly because the complexity of the production system they had evolved made a sudden reduction of the programme extremely difficult, partly because they believed that when the outlook improved, they would be well placed to take advantage of it. It was the German view that prevailed, however, and production was wound down to one a month.

It was two years since the A300's entry into commercial service, seven years since the programme had been launched. The Airbus management decided it was time to review those lean years and consider whether future prospects might be fatter. As Lathière and his colleagues embarked on their strategic study, the order book did not make reassuring reading—34 firm orders, 23 options. The early and middle 1970s had been a pretty disastrous period for the airlines. In 1974–75, for example, Air France had incurred a deficit of $200 million, and the balance sheets of many of the American airlines showed a high degree of financial leverage—TWA and PanAm both had a debt-to-equity ratio of 4 to 1. Plans for fleet expansion had been drastically curtailed, and the sort of financial terms the airlines clamoured for made seasoned salesmen want to go and lie down in darkened rooms.

There were 21 A300s in service with eight airlines. They had clocked up more than 30,000 flying hours without any difficulties to speak of. The record of on-time departures (fifteen minutes either side of scheduled takeoff) was good—at 97 percent a couple of percentage points better than the 747's, though it was debatable whether that was to compare like with like. All aircraft so far delivered had weighed between 350 and 1,000 kilos less than specified, and this found a small but important reflection in the figures for fuel consumption, which were 0.5 percent lower than Airbus had claimed in its sales literature. Valuable structural reinforcements had also been carried out. The A300 was consequently able to carry more fuel, and its standard range had been increased by about a quarter.

Three basic models were being offered. The short-range A300B2 had 250 seats and a range of about 2,400 nautical miles. The medium-range B4 carried the same number of passengers but could fly almost half as far again. The newly introduced B4-FC had the same range as the B2 and could carry 40 tonnes of cargo. In the first seven months of 1976 the rate of production had almost doubled, and it was expected to average just under two aircraft a month during 1977.

The Airbus range was in competition not just with existing older jets, but with a number of "paper" planes that were beginning to figure in the sales campaigns of their American competitors. McDonnell Douglas and Boeing were able to advance very seductive arguments. Older models could be offered at extremely competitive prices because of the length of time they had been in production and because to airlines that were already operating similar aircraft the introductory costs were negligible. This allowed American salesmen to say, "Look, take this tried and tested model to tide you over. Then in a year or so you can modernise your fleet with planes of our new generation, and we will buy the dependable old ones back as part of the deal."

It was a highly effective pitch. In 1976, against Airbus's one new sale of a B2/B4, Boeing raked in orders for 114 of the 727-200s, 87 of them between May and November. For the industry in general, the crisis was clearly passing, but Airbus's luck stubbornly refused to turn. The tally of "whitetails" (unsold aircraft) on the tarmac at Toulouse rose to 16.

Relations between the French and their semidetached associates across the English Channel were not of the best, either. Aérospatiale was being run at the time by General Jacques Mitterand, the brother of the future French president, and he had said in April that he found the British so negative that for future collaboration they would have to look to the United States. It certainly looked by the end of the year as if they would have to look to somebody.

It was not only in European minds, however, that thoughts about cooperation and partnership were beginning to run. During those confused middle years of the 1970s the intensity of the search for firm ground and new alliances was reminiscent of the mad round of European diplomacy in an earlier age, and there were players on both sides of the Atlantic. Long heads at Boeing knew that economic disarray could well have political consequences, and their concern was not to be excluded from the European market by any trend towards protectionism. They suggested an investment of risk capital in their projected 7X7 programme to firms in both Italy and

Japan and had talks with Aérospatiale about the joint development of a new supercritical wing.

McDonnell Douglas had their wits about them, too. The French company Dassault announced in August 1976 that they had reached an agreement in principle for the production of a twin-engine 175-seater—reenter the Mercure. Aérospatiale was to take a 40 percent share in the joint venture, a group of unnamed European partners would do the same, and McDonnell Douglas would have 15 percent. Dassault itself would have only a 5 percent share in the project, but would retain design responsibility. The hope was that with the help of their American partner they could do good business in the United States market, and there was talk of selling upwards of 800 planes by 1990.

There was plainly a French strategy of trying to minimise potential competition to Airbus, and they were not alone in Europe in seeing the various American initiatives to make cooperative arrangements as attempts to pick off individual Airbus partners. Airbus Industrie itself, judging that attack was the best form of defence, was in there pitching with the best of them. They had talks with both McDonnell Douglas and Boeing, and to the latter they boldly proposed the merging of the B10 and 7X7 designs. It is not known whether Miss Bardot was consulted, but wits in Toulouse had soon christened the project the BB.

These conversations were not in all respects exchanges between equals. Lew Bogdan has a story about an occasion when Boeing and Airbus had agreed that they would each come to a meeting equipped with a number of marketing scenarios. The Airbus side strained every nerve, chewed their pencils through the night and were hugely pleased with themselves to come up with 16. The Boeing team had turned the assignment over to their computers, and arrived in Toulouse with 16,000.[10]

As Britain edged warily towards Europe, all three major American manufacturers were sniffing vigorously round the United Kingdom industry, and they were not only looking for ways of reducing their investment costs. Boeing in particular were keenly interested in blunting the growing British interest in going back into the European consortium, and were pressing the various elements of the United Kingdom industry very hard to join in the development and production of the new 757 programme.

There is something for everybody in what we have to offer, said the siren voices from Seattle. For Rolls Royce, the launch engine—a derivative of the RB-211 giving 30,000 lbs. of thrust; for British Airways, the smaller 150-seat aircraft it so badly needed on its low-density routes; for British Aerospace, once it emerged from its parliamentary chrysalis, a major share in the design and manufacture of the new 757 series, including the wing, tail section and landing gear—in all, something more than a third of the total airframe costs.

If 1976 had been a dismal year for Airbus on the sales front, 1977 started no better. They had been in negotiation for some months with Western Airlines, and their hopes had been rising, with talk of Western being interested in as many as ten aircraft. Then things went wrong. The French authorities released a Palestine Liberation Organisation terrorist, there was a violent outburst of anti-French feeling and at the end of January, it was announced that the order was to be split between DC-10s from McDonnell Douglas and 727s from Boeing.

In April, however, Thai International placed an order for four planes, and a month later it was announced that Eastern Airlines of Miami was going to lease four planes for a period of six months. After the Western deal had fallen through, the Airbus management in Toulouse had decided that they must have a higher profile in the United States. They set up an office in New York and they persuaded George Warde, a former president of American Airlines, to run it for them. Warde had only been installed a matter of weeks when he was asked to go and make a presentation to the top management of Eastern Airlines.

Eastern's president was the former astronaut Frank Borman, and Warde managed to persuade him and his colleagues that the A300 was well worth looking at. What they needed convincing about was the quality of after-sale service and support that Airbus was able to offer. Provided the test period was satisfactory—and Eastern proposed to try out the planes on the Florida to New York and Montreal routes in winter, which would involve considerable variations in temperature—there was the prospect of a substantial sale. "Fly before buy" as it became known was an untried financing technique for the aviation industry, but Airbus jumped at it. The airline had to lay out some $7 million to train flight crews, but Airbus agreed to carry the costs of maintenance and of U.S. certification.

Before the summer was out there was another breakthrough in the Middle East when Egyptair followed the Eastern example and also entered into a leasing arrangement. There were probably not many Airbus salesmen who remembered that it was after the Battle of Egypt that Churchill spoke about the end of the beginning, but spirits began to lift a little in Toulouse.

The following April they positively soared. The Eastern trial period had been a success. Fuel consumption had been 3 percent less than Airbus had promised. Borman took the plunge and started negotiating a massive order worth $778 million—23 of the A300B4s, options on a further 9 and 25 of the new B10 version of the plane that was planned.

For Airbus, it was far from plain sailing. The undercarriage of the A300 was built in such a way that the concentrated weight of the aircraft would exert unacceptable stress on certain parts of the runway at New York's La Guardia airport, and this put a question mark over whether Eastern would be granted landing rights. Some reinforcement work was carried out, a way was found of modifying the landing gear and certain taxiing procedures were agreed.

That was the easy part. The crucial question was how the planes were going to be paid for. Eastern did not have a great deal of elbow room. For the past ten years it had barely washed its face and it was in debt to the tune of $1.3 billion. George Warde and Roger Béteille managed to come up with a package that was as inventive as it was controversial. $552 million came in external loans arranged by the Bank of America at a fixed rate of 3.5 percent over 15 years—this at a time when the normal 15-year rate was 8.9 percent. Crédit Lyonnais and Dresdner Bank advanced $250 million in the form of export credits at the same rate and on the same conditions as the Export-Import Bank—at 8.25 percent over 10 years. Airbus Industrie itself underwrote $96 million in bonds at variable interest and General Electric, who were to supply the engines, did the same to the tune of $45 million.

A clause was inserted in the contract to compensate Eastern for the difference in operating costs between the B4 and the smaller B10, which was the aircraft they would ideally have liked. Frank Borman had driven a remarkable bargain. He had originally asked Airbus to take his Tristars off his hands and told them for good measure that what he really wanted was a plane with only 170 seats. Very well, said Roger Béteille—pay us for the use of 170 seats, and then if you find yourself using more, you can pay us more.

Eastern did not believe in spoiling the ship for a halfpennyworth of tar. They laid out an additional $6 million on the construction of a maintenance and repair hangar at Miami, complete with a spare parts store, and launched a big advertising campaign to introduce what they called the *Whisper Liner.*

The American competition was not best pleased, particularly by the leasing arrangement, although the idea was not entirely new in the United States—Airbus, indeed, claimed that Boeing had made a similar arrangement over some hydrofoil ferry boats a few years previously. The operating cost support clause also got up the nose of the industry and of some politicians. Representative Charles Vanik, a member of the powerful Ways and Means Committee of the House of Representatives said that the Eastern sale focussed attention on "the serious question of unfair trade practices and excessive export subsidies," and a unit of the committee announced hearings to examine what was described as the "financial gimmickry" that attended the transaction.

Airbus parried the demands that came from American manufacturers for protection from European imports by pointing out that almost a quarter of the A300 was of American manufacture, and George Warde reverted to the theme that the whole of the U.S. aerospace industry was heavily subsidised by the U.S. government. But he probably wished that Frank Borman had reflected a little before addressing his assembled staff: "If you don't kiss the French flag every time you see it, at least salute it," he told them. "The export financing on our Airbus deal subsidized this airline by more than $100 million."[11]

"In baiting a mouse-trap with cheese, always leave room for the mouse," wrote Saki. The Eastern mouse was a very big one indeed. Perhaps the woods in which Airbus had built its house were not quite so impenetrable as they had thought. It was beginning to look as if they were going to sell a few mousetraps after all. It also looked as if things were going to get rough.

NOTES

1. *A Little Tour in France* (Boston: Houghton Mifflin and Co., 1884).

2. *The Right to Exist,* April 23, 1986.

3. Elliot J. Feldman, *Concorde and Dissent. Explaining high technology project failures in Britain and France* (Cambridge: Cambridge University Press, 1985).

4. *Concorde Appraisal* (London: British Airways, April 9, 1974).

5. *Airbus Industrie* (Fontainebleau: INSEAD, The Europeans Institute of Business Administration, 1980).

6. Gunston, *op. cit.*

7. Chris Bulloch, Udo Phillip and Bron Rek, "West German Aerospace: Deutsche Airbus to Play New Role" *Interavia,* April 1982.

8. *Time Magazine,* August 3, 1987.

9. Newhouse, *op. cit.*

10. Lew Bogdan, *L'Epopée du Ciel Clair* (Paris: Hachette, 1988).

11. *Business Week,* January 11, 1982.

4

Perfidious Albion's Second Thoughts

"'Tis safest in matrimony to begin with a little aversion."

—Richard Brinsley Sheridan, *The Rivals,* 1775

A Gallup pollster working the streets of London with a questionnaire about Airbus would have an unrewarding time. People do not talk about it in pubs or make jokes about it on television chat shows. It has never been an issue at an election. It receives only occasional attention in Parliament, as often as not at the prompting of a politician who has an interest because there is an aerospace factory in his constituency, and when the 30-year rule permits the scrutiny of Cabinet papers for the last quarter century, references to it there are likely to be sparse.

James Callaghan, who was prime minister when Britain went back into the consortium, did not give it very much space in his memoirs. When the research for this book was in train he had been out of active politics for some years, speaking only occasionally in the House of Lords. He had also been ill, and was cutting down on his commitments. He had, however, talked at length to John Newhouse when he was at work on *The Sporty Game* in the early 1980s. "I gave him a great deal of assistance in the material that he used in connection with Airbus," he wrote, "and I do not think I could add to it in conversation. Indeed my recollection is certainly less clear than it was then." He added that he considered the book "very good and accurate."[1]

Newhouse certainly seems to have relied heavily on Callaghan's memory for his account, though it is not clear how much he aimed off for the tendency most politicians have to award themselves immodestly high marks—"On this occasion," he quotes the former prime minister as saying, "unlike many others in politics, I feel that we got it just right—that we were wholly successful." This suggests that the British had a clear and coherent objective that they achieved in an orderly fashion to the plaudits of the crowd. Things were in fact a little messier than that. They were also more complicated, because there were pressing decisions to be made in the United Kingdom in the course of 1978 not only about aircraft manufacture but also about government involvement in the development of new engines and the purchase of new planes by Britain's state-owned airline. The issues sprawled untidily over domestic politics and foreign affairs.

Airbus had never entirely disappeared from British calculations in the years since she had left the consortium. In 1972, for instance, when the then aerospace minister, Michael Heseltine, announced that the government was prepared to advance 75 percent of the development cost of the Rolls Royce RB-211 engine programme, he pointed to the possible use of the RB-211-24 in versions of the A300B Airbus. The French, he said, had been told that Britain was very willing to consider specific proposals for suitable applications. "In doing so I explained to M. Galley (the French transport minister) my view that for the future it will be essential for European countries to develop a more coordinated procurement policy for aircraft and a more integrated manufacturing capability. I have made clear my readiness to enter into discussions of these wider issues at any time with the French and other European Governments."[2]

Talks between the French and British began in earnest in May 1976, and a month later, the British secretary of state for industry told Parliament that the U.K. industry was engaged in discussions with the existing Airbus partners about derivatives and the possibilities for United Kingdom participation. "The Government," he continued, in the unlovely language of written parliamentary answers, "are doing all they can to facilitate these discussions and have indicated to all concerned that they will look seriously and sympathetically at any properly supported proposals which might be put forward by the United Kingdom industry for participation, subject to being satisfied as to their economic viability and to the constraints on public expenditure."[3] Much virtue in "if."

In fact the two sides were very far apart. The talks had been between Lord Beswick, a former Labour minister who was now BAe's chairman, and General Jacques Mitterand, brother of the future French president and president of Aérospatiale. The former had flown a kite about some form of British participation in the A310 project outside the ambit of Airbus. The French were indignant at what they saw as a typically absurd suggestion by the Anglo-Saxons. An appropriate figure for the U.K. share of the launch costs of the A310 would be £60-100 million, and that was that. They also made it clear that they thought the British should pay a sizeable "reentry fee" if they wanted to be members of the club again—a figure of £100—200 million was mentioned as a contribution to what the A300B had so far cost. The British thought this a steep price to pay, and felt that when people slid down learning curves they should do so at their own expense. There was another obstacle. The French were insistent that British Airways should place a substantial Airbus order, and they would never understand in a thousand years why such a small matter could not be arranged by one quick phone call from 10, Downing Street.

Late in 1977, the French president was in England for two days and there were talks at Chequers, the official country home of the prime minister. Politically, relations between the two countries were not of the best. The question of Airbus came up, though according to Sir Nicholas Henderson, who was the British ambassador in Paris at the time, the discussion was brief and inconclusive.[4]

Two months later, there was a meeting between Giscard d'Estaing and the German chancellor. The French, partly because they were eager to find markets for the CFM-56 engine, were urging a start on a new programme for an aircraft with 150 seats as well as a derivative of the A300. The Germans, who very sensibly paid a lot of attention to the advice of Reinhardt Abraham of Lufthansa, did not rate the commercial prospects of the 150-seater highly and had no great enthusiasm for the idea of financing a completely new programme. The prospect of having the British back in as partners began to acquire increased appeal in Bonn.

Engines also bulked large in the domestic argument in Britain. Rolls Royce, its nightmares of the early 1970s fading, once again had its eyes on the United States. If the company could get its engines on the proposed Boeing 757, which it was known that both British Airways and Eastern Airlines were looking at, that would do a lot to get them back on terms with their American competitors. That put two out of Britain's three major players—all of them nationalised—in the pro-American, anti-Airbus camp.

For the biggest of the three, however—British Aerospace—the choice was less clear. They, too, were being wooed by Boeing, and the prospect of building the wing for the 757 was in some ways a beguiling one. The U.S. market was huge. So was Boeing—and efficient into the bargain; perhaps some of that would rub off onto the British workforce. The company, however, was not convinced that Boeing was offering a true partnership— "we were supposed to do all the clever bits and take on all the risk," one official said.[5]

Discussions on how BAe might be involved had gone on throughout 1977. The formal offer of participation that Boeing made in February 1978 specified that there should be a fixed-price agreement. British Aerospace should not exceed Boeing's own estimated in-house costs, apart from a reasonable allowance for profit and inflation. Rolls Royce urged them to accept, and the scheme also had the support of the chairman of Britain's National Enterprise Board, Sir Leslie Murphy. It would mean 14,000 jobs for Rolls Royce and 9,000 for British Aerospace—more than could be expected from any European alternative—and it would give the United Kingdom responsibility for more than 50 percent of the project.

British Aerospace held back. Boeing was determined to retain control over marketing and sales, and the British company felt that to retain its own commercial expertise and its contacts with its existing customers, it must have some share in those functions. Boeing responded with the offer of some final assembly work and a share in flight testing, but also said they wanted an answer by May 15. They did not get it. What British Aerospace was really worried about was production costs—the gap that yawned between them and Seattle was of the order of 30 percent.

Looking back on the episode ten years later, the man who was running Boeing Commercial at the time, Tex Bouillioun, shook his head regretfully. "They thought we didn't want them as partners? But we were going to put in all the wing tooling." Bouillioun had no doubt about the main reason: "The fact is they didn't think they could go down the learning curve. We thought they could—even to this day I feel they could. But they couldn't agree to the number of man-hours. We didn't care about the price—but we did want a commitment to build them in a certain number of man hours, and to do it in dollars."[6]

Someone who would have been happy for BAe to enter the Boeing embrace was Howard Davies, a Treasury official at the time, later the controller of the Audit Commission in the United Kingdom and director-general of the Confederation of British Industry. "As things turned out, we'd have made out like bandits on dollar prices from 1979 to 1981–2," he said.[7] "Everyone said if Boeing insists on a dollar price for this we've absolutely had it, and it didn't occur to people that we could get productivity improvements in excess of the Americans, which of course we've now had for a decade. It was a pessimistic mind-set that people had in relation to our competitiveness *vis-à-vis* the Americans. First of all, if we got locked into some deal, we were children in relation to Boeing, so we'd get screwed. Secondly, with the dollar, we wouldn't be able to match their competitiveness and productivity, and then they'd junk us in the end anyway. Whereas the Europeans love us terribly and will always keep us in business . . . Ha ha!"

The Treasury was traditionally against such involvements as Airbus. Sir Douglas Wass, who was the permanent under-secretary at the time, and therefore Davies's boss, recalls that they opposed it not just on straightforward financial/economic grounds, but also because there had been a whole catalogue of public-sector investments of one sort or another that had gone wrong. "We costed it, scrutinised the assumptions about the volume of sales, the price that could be obtained and so on, and concluded that it was a rather dubious investment. We felt that our minority holding wouldn't give us the sort of freedom we thought we ought to have to abandon the project if it got out of hand. It seemed to us that we'd be locked into a gung-ho European enterprise, and that quite the best course would be to stay out and let British Airways buy in the best market—which was Boeing."[7]

The Cabinet seems at first to have inclined to the Treasury position, although there was more than one view. "The entire affair was too sensitive to be handled in the normal fashion," writes John Newhouse. "Callaghan decided to deal with it personally." That is to find drama where none existed. There was nothing remotely unusual about the way the matter was dealt with. All that happened was that a Cabinet committee was formed—a perfectly normal procedure: a dozen or more exist at any given time. Nor is it of particular significance that the prime minister sat in the chair—his predecessors had frequently done the same, and so would his successors.

The committee—its members included Denis Healey, the chancellor of the Exchequer—met eight times in the course of 1978. It was shadowed by another committee composed of officials—again, an entirely normal Whitehall procedure. Their job was to do the detailed work, and the chairman was Sir Kenneth Berrill. He was at that time the head of the Central Policy Review Staff, the government think tank located in the Cabinet Office and working directly to the prime minister. During the Heath administration in the early 1970s he had been chief economic adviser to the Treasury: "The Six Day War, the oil-price hike and the three-day week: if you like tight-rope walking, try being an economic adviser when that sort of combination hits you—there's nothing in your statistics to tell you what's happening."[8] Just the man, clearly, to pursue the grand arcanum that was Airbus.

Berrill says that for a long time Callaghan was extremely reluctant to take sides on the issue—"He really wanted to get a much better feel for the economics of the thing." He adds that at first he himself was genuinely agnostic. "I suppose the basic problem was that it was very difficult to get the data. It's difficult enough with someone like Boeing, but when you get a thing like Airbus, it's deeply impenetrable. I could see the argument for the strength of Boeing. I could see the argument which said 'Let's all face in the same direction.' I could see the argument that this was just somebody who was frightened of the real world and tough competition—British Aerospace just wanting to be protected by Daddy, as it were, and getting the government to subsidise it to join Airbus—I could see all those arguments."

Not all those who entered the debate took it as axiomatic that the other parties were acting in good faith. At various times both the Department of Industry and the Foreign Office maintained that Boeing did not really have any intention of building the 757, and that it was purely a spoiling operation. Berrill set off on a round of visits to see and hear for himself. He went to Toulouse to see Airbus, he spoke to Boeing and McDonnell Douglas. "Boeing clearly didn't want us to join Airbus, and gave a good impression that they were offering an attractive joint venture. But the marketing people at Airbus had some very good studies of trends in the market, too, showing the extent to which Third World buyers were showing an interest in what they had to offer."

He went the rounds at home, too—Rolls Royce, British Airways, British

Aerospace. "Rolls Royce had never sold any engines for Airbus. They hadn't even tried, because to be able to put a Rolls Royce engine into the Airbus, you would have had to have a special pylon into which it would fit, and that meant a fair bit of investment in R&D. So they were basically competing with General Electric and Pratt & Whitney to put their engines onto American airframes. So far as British Airways was concerned, their strategy was to reduce the number of types of plane they had in their fleet, which was large, and to concentrate on Boeing. They definitely did not want to buy Airbus. And the unions in both Rolls Royce and British Airways fully supported their managements."

"When you looked at British Aerospace, the picture was rather different. They knew they couldn't build a plane themselves—if McDonnell Douglas were apprehensive about going it alone, there weren't even the beginnings of a chance for them. The question was, if they had to have a partner, who should it be? Lockheed were not really in the game. McDonnell Douglas talked, of course. There's an enormous amount of talk in the aircraft industry—they're the greatest talkers I know. They'll talk you up a new plane and give you a diagram and a flying piece of cardboard in about three days. But you have to take more salt with it than almost any other thing I've ever been engaged in. Boeing, on the other hand, were extremely keen, but what scared British Aerospace was that after a short time they might become a very junior partner, that they would be just an assembly plant and would not have any design capability of their own."

The company's heart wasn't in it. That much was plain even to members of the official committee like Howard Davies who wished that it had been. "For outsiders, people making the decisions at a political level, that was a major factor, the feeling that they would be pushing the company into something it didn't want to do. And having just set it up, and created all that agony and *angst*—and this is a very interesting example of how you have less control over a nationalised industry than you have over something else—they felt they couldn't then impose a decision on it. That was a very important psychological factor, I think." Certainly, when the nationalisation legislation had been going through Parliament, Labour spokesmen, harried by their Conservative opponents, had asserted that the company would be free to make its own commercial judgements.

Sir Douglas Wass's recollection is that the then chancellor of the exchequer, Denis Healey, did not interest himself greatly in the issue. "He had a lot of other things on his mind. If he'd been interested it would have cropped up at my weekly meeting. We used to have a sort of dustbin session for an hour every Friday morning. We'd pick up all the things that were on his mind and on my mind that hadn't gone forward in the ordinary course of business, and we swept into that hour a host of issues—I don't remember Airbus ever coming up. If he had been really worried about it, it would have done, I think." Sir Kenneth Berrill's recollection bears this out. "They didn't ask to put somebody senior on the negotiating team with the French and the Germans, and if they had been really concerned, they would. Basically speaking if the Treasury and the Chancellor says I want my chap there, he always goes."

So the man who rode point for the Treasury was Howard Davies, who from 1977 to 1979 was the principal in the Treasury for both civil and military aerospace. Trivial details lodge incongruously in the mind. Airbus Industrie's Roger Béteille, he recalls, performed smoothly—and always wore a white tie. More generally, he remembers the meetings he had to attend as "the worst sort of Eurocracy." "I've always been fundamentally opposed to the Common Market, and therefore to this project as well. You felt as if you were engaged in an elaborate bout of shadow boxing, and as if the real decisions were being taken elsewhere."

That does not seem to have taken the edge off Davies's relish for the fray. "We fought a lengthy Whitehall battle in which the main players were the Foreign Office, the Ministry of Defence, who were always a bit of a wild card, and the Department of Trade and Industry—they were very suspicious, too, because they'd been once bitten, but we always felt in the Treasury they would eventually come down on the side of the company. There was also a feeling that the Foreign Office would sell out anything in order to be friends with Europe—the sort of Anglo-French relationship which was a kind of 'pieces of eight' cry of the FO. Nobody in the Treasury could ever understand what return we'd had for all the money we had spent on Anglo-French relations. All we got was more abuse from the French and more hassle over the Common Market agricultural policy."

That the strongest arguments for going down the Airbus road were deployed by the Foreign Office is scarcely surprising. Europe was very much their *métier,* and they were becoming increasingly concerned at what they saw as the emerging Franco-German ascendancy within the Community. From Paris, they were urged on by Sir Nicholas Henderson, the British ambassador. He saw it as a choice between continued industrial collaboration with the Europeans and becoming hewers of wood and drawers of water for Boeing—a phrase he used more than once in his telegrams and despatches.

From the summer of 1978 onwards he was diligent in promoting the case for Britain's reentry—so much so, he recalls, that he was more than once ticked off by the prime minister, who thought him overzealous— "London tended to think that I was saying we should go in at any price."[9] He brought Sir Kenneth Keith of Rolls Royce and General Mitterand together over lunch at the embassy (though Keith, he remembers, declined to meet the head of SNECMA, the French engine manufacturers who had close ties with Rolls's U.S. rivals, General Electric). Henderson also went the rounds of the French industry and was assiduous in keeping both the Quai d'Orsay and the French president's office up to date on the shifts in the British position.

Berrill, as an old Treasury hand, was in no doubt about the strength of feeling of those who were against the European venture. "The general view of those who opposed it was that Airbus was a financial sump of unknown depth. The only guaranteed winner was Boeing. And he conceded that the Concorde saga may have played a role. "Certainly there's hardly a civil servant of that generation who hasn't had the Concorde file across his desk, looked at it, put his hand over his eyes and thought 'God!'"

He had just such a man on his committee in the person of Howard Davies. "I remember when I first went to the Treasury—you know the way you get shown the Crown jewels and told the jokes of every job you take over—my predecessor brought out this dog-eared document, which he was clearly very proud of, and it was a list of orders for Concorde. It went up to plane number 364 which was designated to Aerolineas Argentinas or somebody, and they'd all signed up, and they'd all paid. It was all official stuff—and it was all nonsense."

Davies's membership of the intergovernmental committee on Concorde clearly coloured his attitude to Airbus:

That was no fun—at that point real wreckage. The decision not to build any more was being made, there were acrimonious debates on cost-sharing and everybody knew that we were going to have to write off billions of pounds. Essentially the attitude of my superiors was "don't let the bastards spend a penny." Concorde, for example, had no delegated authority at all. The Ministry of Defence normally operated under delegated authority whereby it could spend 10 million quid without asking the Treasury, but the Concorde programme couldn't buy a pencil. There was that level of distrust. I mean, some people in the Treasury thought that these people were criminals. The Treasury tends to take a moralistic view about these things. They had come along and said it would cost x, and it cost ten times x. And they should be in jail, let alone being congratulated for technological advances.

"I remember something Denis Healey said to me," Davies said. "'The civil aviation projects are always justified on the grounds that unless you waste this money now you won't be able to waste any more money in the future, and therefore they are all to be regarded with the deepest possible suspicion'." Healey had had a lot to be suspicious—and cynical—about in his time as chancellor: it was only a year previously that the United Kingdom had had to be substantially bailed out by the International Monetary Fund. "It did seem," Davies said, "as though maybe somebody else should carry out this global public service that Airbus was performing, and not the Treasury, which was having to cut capital spending on things like hospitals and roads. Every possible infrastructural investment in the UK was being chopped. If you look back at the figures, 1977–78 was when capital spending collapsed, and we've never really recovered in this country. That's why the roads are the way they are, that was the absolutely major cut-back at that period. And therefore any penny that was spent on a project like Airbus had to justify itself against this background."

There was one person who did not share the general Foreign Office enthusiasm for Airbus, and it was an exception of some importance. The British ambassador in Washington at the time was Peter Jay. Jay was not a career diplomat. After Oxford, he had served briefly in the Treasury before entering journalism. He was a former economics editor for *The Times*, and he had fronted a rather high-minded television programme that sought to correct what he and his editor described as "the bias against understanding" in current affairs broadcasting. He was the quintessential coming man—a 1977 profile in one of the colour supplements had carried the title "The Cleverest Young Man in England?" He was the son of Douglas Jay, a former Labour cabinet minister. More importantly he was the son-in-law of the prime minister, a fact that had made for some controversy when he was plucked out of Fleet Street by the then foreign secretary, David Owen, and sent to Washington.

Jay was quite often in London during this time, and in June 1978 Callaghan was persuaded to make a visit to the United States, principally to meet some of the leading figures in the U.S. industry. Berrill went with him. They had dinner with the top people of both McDonnell Douglas and Boeing, and lunched with Frank Borman of Eastern Airlines. Borman was not only considering the 757, but had also just completed his "fly before buy" experiment with four Airbuses, and the British were eager to pick his brains. This seems to have been the most successful encounter of the trip.

The British prime minister does not seem to have been entirely at his ease with the Boeing top brass, and is supposed to have said that they treated him like the leader of an underdeveloped country.[5] That would be surprising. Possibly Callaghan, not the most secure of men, simply misinterpreted the air of high-octane confidence that Boeing people undoubtedly exude. He seems to have got on rather better with the more wishy-washy McDonnell Douglas people who sat at the British ambassador's table the following evening, but the discussion about some sort of collaborative arrangement involving the French and the Germans as well as British Aerospace was inconclusive.

The British were not weighing these complex choices in some sort of leisurely and pressure-free vacuum. While the prime minister and his party were in Washington, the French transport minister, Joël le Theule, had repeated that the United Kingdom's readmission to the club depended on British Airway's ability to see where its European duty lay. If the Airbus enterprise was to retain its momentum, decisions could not be endlessly delayed. The French president and German chancellor issued a reminder of that by announcing in July that the A310 would go ahead with or without the United Kingdom, and at a meeting in Munich, representatives of Aérospatiale, MBB, CASA and Fokker signed an agreement to launch the B10 version of the A300.

Berrill detected differences of attitude between the French and the

Germans. "The Germans were extremely keen that we should come in, partly because they had a very considerable respect for the technical capabilities of British Aerospace in making wings, but also for financial reasons, so that we could share the mounting cost of the Airbus operation." Howard Davies confirmed that the Germans had solid economic reasons for wishing to see the consortium enlarged: "There were all these private deals—we were told, for instance, that because of the way in which the dollar had moved, the Germans had agreed effectively to fund a third of the cost of every Airbus sold. But that was not a public deal and nobody would tell us what it was."

German official thinking was not necessarily in harmony with the views of the industry. If France and Germany were to soldier on by themselves, there would no longer be any question, now that Hawker Siddeley had been absorbed into the nationalised British Aerospace, of the wing for a new programme being subcontracted to the United Kingdom. The Germans might display a generous regard for British expertise, but that did not erase the memory of their own achievements. A patent for a variable sweep wing had, after all, been granted to Messerschmidt in 1941; the oblique wing was originally conceived by Vogt at Blohm and Voss in 1943. For a few months in 1978, there were aeronautical engineers in the most talented nation in Europe who dreamed old dreams . . .

So far as the French were concerned, Berrill formed the impression that they "rather doubted our long-term commitment." That was to put it mildly. A headline in the French aerospace weekly *Air & Cosmos* caught the generally liverish tone of the French press, which tends to be well briefed on such occasions—"L'industrie aérospatiale britannique veut manger à tous les râteliers." (A *râtelier* is the wall rack that holds hay above a stall in a stable, and the expression carries a suggestion not only of greed but of a certain lack of scruple.)

Coming from the French, who had always (very sensibly) put their own national interest first, this was rather rich. Aérospatiale might have a solid bourgeois marriage in Toulouse, but it was, after all, only two years since the company had been trying all it knew to form *liaisons* in both Long Beach and Seattle. And yet their mistrust of perfidious Albion is entirely understandable. Rolls Royce had been the villain of an earlier piece, and that had not been forgotten. One senior French official said they wanted the British back in—"but not as wreckers." "I think Giscard was very doubtful," Nicholas Henderson said. "The Quai d'Orsay and the French Transport Ministry were both in favour, but my impression was that the President thought we were playing a dirty game—having done so before. I mean, it was just like the first time round with the Channel Tunnel. We got so far, and then we pulled out."

From where Henderson sat, it was very much a matter between the French and the British—"Schmidt had left the hand entirely to Giscard to play." The Foreign Office was getting similar feedback from Germany—a despatch from Bonn characterised Schmidt's support for the British position as "not robust." Before the game was over, however, Schmidt did intervene. He and Callaghan had known each other over the years on the European Socialist circuit, and the German chancellor put it to the British prime minister that a "European gesture" by the United Kingdom would not be out of place. Schmidt, who knew that human nature was fairly evenly distributed between nationalities, also pointed out that if the British came back on board, French influence over European civil aerospace policy would not exactly be increased . . .

The final negotiations were held in the Ministry of Transport in Paris, and Berrill led the British delegation. "The French chap in the chair was in a sense my equivalent, he was from the Elysée, but in fact he was very new to Paris, and I think only a few weeks before he had been down building submarines in Toulon. I'm sure he was a brilliant engineer, but he wasn't a civil servant—he had to be in the chair because of protocol. You could see that their regular civil servants—the people from the Treasury, but more particularly from the Ministry of Transport—were not at all happy at the position."

There is some evidence that things were not all sweetness and light on the British side either. "Berrill was deeply suspicious of the Ministry of Defence boffins," Howard Davies told me, "and I always felt that the Foreign Office people got up his nose." This may have had something to do with the way that Foreign Office people traditionally view those less fortunate mortals who serve in home departments of the Civil Service, and which is not unlike the attitude of a cavalryman to the infantry. It is not clear how much the presence of an outsider in the driving seat was appreciated. "He *was* there an awful lot," Nicholas Henderson said, gazing diplomatically into the middle distance. "I did think it rather odd that someone from the Cabinet Office should be the ultimate negotiator." Although his view of the issue prevailed, it was not a period that Henderson subsequently remembered with much pleasure—"It was a pretty nasty business, really." Berrill, on the other hand, looks back on it with some zest—"It was an enjoyable, interesting episode, partly I suppose because it was more down at the coal-face of negotiation than most of the job I was doing."

Howard Davies expresses his views with a trenchancy that is uncommon among his former colleagues in Whitehall, and obviously most admires those who do the same. "Ken Berrill was a consummate committee chairman in Whitehall terms. He was absolutely perfect at it—as long as nobody asked him what he thought." Somebody quite important *did* want to know what he thought, however. Berrill and his colleagues produced a number of papers that were broadly agreed between officials and then went to the Cabinet Committee, but it was also part of his brief as head of the think tank to produce private briefing papers for the prime minister.

"It wasn't so far as I was concerned absolutely open and shut," Berrill said, ten years after the event. "It depended to a very large extent on the judgement of something inherently uncertain, which was the future of Airbus as compared with Boeing. That was jolly difficult, so that it was never more than a balance of probabilities. I suppose I had come to the view that if we were to continue with British Aerospace as someone in the airframe manufacturing business on a significant scale, then it had to be on a joint-venture basis. There were really only two practical joint-venture options—one was to go in with the biggest in the world as a very small fish, the other was to join something fairly new, inevitably uncertain, and with some of the inherent problems of joint management. The Boeing option was not unattractive—and it was safe, even if it would have meant losing our design skills. But we had become, for good or ill, a part of the European Community, and it seemed to me that we had to do a number of things to make that market work. Airbus was something that looked like a reasonably successful collaborative EEC effort, and there weren't many of those."

The advice he offered did not command the support of every member of his committee. "When it finally came to the crunch and it was to go to the Cabinet," Howard Davies said, "I can remember writing what in Treasury terms was a purple-prose minute—quite over the top. Denis Healey said he agreed with it and off he went, but we lost. I talked to Healey about it alone on quite a few occasions, but there were no very major meetings in the Treasury. He was quite convinced that he should argue strenuously against joining Airbus Industrie, but he also thought that he would lose. And it wasn't the kind of issue on which the Chancellor, who had been fighting terrible battles with the Cabinet over public spending and interest rates, would want to dig in. So my information was that he did argue his case strenuously, he said 'I don't like this, I think it will cost us a lot of money, I think the American route would be better,' but he did not, if you like, play his joker in the way a Chancellor can and say, 'Look, this is a Chancellorial issue, and I'm not having it'."

This was early in August. The Cabinet also gave the nod to British Airway's purchase of the 757. It was, indeed, inconceivable that they should do anything else. It was more than ten years since an airline had been directed to "buy British." Finally, on August 31, there was an official announcement that British Aerospace would rejoin Airbus, that British Airways was getting its 757s, and that they would be powered by the RB211-235 engine—which Rolls Royce would get government money to develop.

The French did not immediately run up the Union Jack on top of the Arc de Triomphe. They had maintained to the last their insistence on an order from British Airways as a condition of entry, though the Germans had supported them only half-heartedly in this, and the announcement about the order for 19 of the 757s, which they regarded as a competitor to the A310, poured grains of salt into the wound. At this point Freddie Laker, the ebullient boss of the privately owned Laker Airways, popped up through a trap and announced that he would like to buy ten Airbuses, and this mollified the French somewhat, though the British government had no hand in it. The British government also told the French—rather fatuously—that if British Airways ever saw a place for the Airbus in its fleet, the government would expect it to choose the A 310, though they wisely did not enlarge on how they would achieve this.

Most of the pieces were now in place. By mid-October, Callaghan was able to tell his Cabinet colleagues that the French would no longer press the British Airways point. The three governments announced that they were in accord on October 24, and industrial agreement on the launch of the A310 was reached in late November. When he spoke to John Newhouse some years later, however, Callaghan emphasised that in his view, Airbus had been only part of the jigsaw, and not the most important one. "Rolls Royce was the national asset we had to preserve," he said, "which meant that establishing it in the U.S. market was the central consideration."[5]

Berrill remembered it later as just one issue among a great many others, and not one that took up an inordinate amount of his time—"There were some weeks when I was doing nothing else because I was on the road somewhere, but broadly speaking, if you take a six-month period, I suppose I may have spent about 10 percent of my time on it. I mean, at any one time, there are hundreds and hundreds of issues flowing past on the conveyor belt, and the think tank got involved in a surprising number of them."

He also says that he has no idea whether it was he who swayed the prime minister. "I'm not trying to be modest, but I do think it's just historically wrong to say 'X advised this, or Y advised that'—I really do. These matters are messy, and I'm almost never sure when the balance of one person's argument has been decisive. You must remember—and if you don't remember, you soon find it out the hard way in the Cabinet Office—that a Prime Minister gets a vast amount of information and advice from here, there and everywhere. As an official, you only see what is going to your Minister or to your Prime Minister through official channels—you don't see a hell of a lot of the other stuff, and what finally makes a Prime Minister come down on one side or the other, who knows?"

Details of the industrial agreement were given to the House of Commons on November 6 by Gerald Kaufman, the minister of state at the Department of Industry. British Aerospace was to become a full member of the consortium from January 1, 1979. It was to have a share of 20 percent. The company was to be accorded "representation appropriate to a major member" on the supervisory board of Airbus Industrie, and major decisions of the board would from then on need a majority of at leat 80 percent (it had previously been 75 percent).

British Aerospace would continue to participate in the A300B2/B4 programme, would have a substantial share in the new A310 derivative programme, and would be entitled to a share (also described as "substantial") in future Airbus programmes. All the parties undertook not to participate in projects competing with present or future Airbus Industrie programmes, except with the agreement of the others.

That much had been agreed in August. In subsequent discussions, it had been agreed that the position on voting rights outlined above should apply to all future Airbus programmes, to the A310 programme and to questions relating to that programme and to the B2/B4 programme. The French rearguard action had produced one important concession, however. The 75 percent majority rule was to continue to apply in any decision relating to the B2/B4 programme where those aircraft were in competition with aircraft fitted with British (i.e., Rolls Royce) engines, and this would continue either until 150 B2/B4s had been delivered, or until August 1, 1981. If, however, Airbus Industrie were to receive a letter of intent to purchase from British Airways, the French and German partners would immediately agree to a change to the 80 percent majority figure.

There was a passage for domestic consumption. "British Aerospace considers that joining Airbus Industrie will make a significant contribution to stabilising employment levels in the corporation and should help to safeguard several thousand jobs." There was also a line about membership of Airbus making it easier for BAe to get a better balance between military and civil programmes.

It only remained for Mr. Kaufman, like a waiter in a discreet hotel, to present the reckoning. The company estimated that it would require additional investment of some £250 million at 1978 prices by 1983 (inflation was rising ominously at this time). "To assist the corporation I propose, subject to the approval of Parliament, to make available to BAe up to £50 million under the Aircraft and Shipbuilding Industries Act of 1977." (This was the piece of legislation under which British Aerospace had been nationalised the previous year.) He reminded the House that in the past few months, the government had taken a series of decisions affecting the future operations not only of British Aerospace but also of British Airways and Rolls Royce, and that all these corporations had to work in a highly competitive environment. "It is the policy of the Government," he concluded, "that they should be supported as far as possible in the decisions which they take on commercial grounds."

The Labour administration was rather pleased with itself. Christmas was approaching, and it is a rare politician who is unwilling to be cast as Santa Claus, with something in his sack for everybody. The Treasury apart, the Whitehall machine felt pretty satisfied, too. French officials conceded that they had been bested in the negotiations, something that had not happened very often under the Fifth Republic. The "presidentialization" of foreign policy that was such a marked feature of the de Gaulle years had continued under his successors.[10] De Gaulle and Adenauer had established a special relationship, a tradition that Giscard and Helmut Schmidt revived, but the high profile that Giscard adopted in this particular instance, partly no doubt in response to the prominent role Callaghan was playing on the British side, seems in the event to have worked against the French interest.

So the Brits were back. One or two small points still required clarification, however. Cranley Onslow, a member of the Conservative opposition, homed in on one of them in the House of Commons at the end of November: "What guarantees have been given to BAe about the availability of public funds to meet the negative cash flow involved in participation in the European Airbus project?"

Hansard for November 27 records that Les Huckfield, a junior minister, responded at some length, but the words that his civil servants had drafted for him read like a less than complete answer to Mr Onslow's question. After that, it was not posed again with any great insistence for the best part of ten years. When it did resurface, in the late 1980s, it was at the instance of British Aerospace. The company had by then been denationalised and become accountable to those awkward people known as shareholders.

NOTES

1. Letter to author, October 1988.
2. House of Commons *Hansard,* August 7, 1972.
3. *Ibid.,* June 18, 1976.
4. Interview in London, January 1989.
5. Newhouse, *op. cit.*
6. Interview in Seattle, January 1989.
7. Interview in London, May 1988.
8. Interview in London, September 1988.
9. Interview in London, January 1989.
10. See "The Diplomacy of as Self-Assured Middle Power" by Michael Harrison, in *National Negotiating Styles,* ed. by Hans Binnendijk (Washington: U.S. Department of State Foreign Service Institute, 1987).

5

Let's Get Organised

"Probable impossibilities are to be preferred to improbable possibilities."

—Aristotle, *Poetics.*

The question is, which of Aristotle's two categories does Airbus Industrie fall into? Sitting in his office near Toulouse Airport one summer afternoon in 1988, Adam Brown, then Airbus Industrie's vice-president, strategy, paused in mid-sentence and gave his attention to a Super Guppy that had just taken off outside. "I always say that you can take a model of that plane, put it in a wind tunnel and in about five minutes you can prove it can't fly," he said. "Similarly, if you take the organisation of Airbus and put it to the London Business School, in about five minutes you can prove it can't possibly work."[1]

The decision to constitute Airbus Industrie as a *groupement d'intérêt économique* (GIE) under French law was not uncontroversial, and at an industry level appears initially to have found more favour with the Germans than with the French. In the very early days, most of the work, both in Paris and Toulouse, went forward under the umbrella of Aérospatiale. The Germans quickly made it plain that they had no intention of playing second fiddle, however. The British withdrawal had put them on a equal footing with the French—indeed, the fact that they had picked up the Hawker Siddeley tab even gave them a certain edge. Realism dictated that they should acknowledge France's technological leadership, but they saw that as distinct from the question of where the programme should be headed strategically. It therefore became an aim of German policy to find some institutional method of keeping the function of industrial coordination separate from the direction of the programme in a broader sense.

This meant a good deal of argument and a lot of hard bargaining, both about how the work was to be divided and about what sort of formal organisational structure was required, and it was the best part of 18 months before there was a substantial measure of agreement. Pierre Muller, in his excellent and Cartesian study, analyses the Franco-German differences of the day very acutely.[2] The French were minimalists. The Germans, on the other hand, saw in a strong central framework the best guarantee that their influence over the programme would not be diluted. Although (because a GIE is a French juridical structure) the outcome had the appearance of a victory for France, it was in reality a solution that best served Germany's interests.

Muller also points out that the decision to constitute the enterprise as a GIE effectively buried the idea that one of the partners in a cooperative venture must necessarily exercise industrial leadership, a concept that had bedevilled many previous collaborative experiments, and most notably Concorde.The result was that some of the French engineers in Toulouse saw the agreement with the Germans as just about the most outrageous thing that had happened since the capitulation of France in 1940.

The issue of test flights was a particular flash-point. Muller recounts a conversation with a German source who recalled that he had spent two days arguing with the man who at the time was in charge of test flights for Sud Aviation. This, he insisted, was a task that could only be carried out by Frenchmen licensed by the appropriate authority—those were the rules. When the German pointed out that he could produce some of his compatriots who held this precise qualification (they had been engaged on the Franco-German Transall programme) he was told that in case of emergencies, everybody on board should speak the same language, and that it was self-evident which that language should be . . .

France fell a second time. Airbus acquired its own test-flight setup, and the members of it travelled on a variety of passports and spoke to each other in what Muller's informant described as "aeronautical Anglo-American"—"or rather 'Boeing slang,' a language spoken by a half-civilised tribe from the north-west coast of the United States."

Writing in 1987, Heribert Florsdorff, the German engineer who was Airbus Industrie's number 2, said that the idea of a limited liability company had originally had some appeal, but it had been felt that in a high-risk, capitally-intensive enterprise, limited liability might prove a handicap when trying to sell in markets beyond the supporting countries. A detailed account of the nature of a *groupement d'intérêt économique* occurs in a private-placement memorandum prepared in 1985 by Lehman Brothers when they were arranging loan participations in a leveraged leasing transaction for eight A300B4 Airbuses. The information came largely from Airbus Industrie sources, and offers a useful insight into what they saw as the advantages it offered over a more traditional structure.

A *groupement d'intérêt économique* is a legal entity made possible by Ordonnance No. 67–821 of the French Republic enacted on September 23, 1967. It had been felt in France in the 1960s that the legislation governing the formation and operation of commercial companies was unduly restrictive; the GIE was specifically aimed at making it easier to set up cooperative ventures. Article 3 of the ordinance endows a GIE with full corporate personality and legal capacity but offers substantial flexibility in matters of organisation and administration.

So far as Airbus's American competitors are concerned, it is a device calculated to engender incomprehension and suspicion in roughly equal degree. Articles 1 and 2 provide that a GIE does not itself give rise to the making and division of profit, which is a profoundly un-American activity for a start. It is, however, "intended to enable its members to avail themselves of all means to develop and improve their own economic activity and to improve or increase the results of such activity." By this point, the worst fears of the men in Brooks Brothers suits and button-down collars are thoroughly roused. They are too polite to say anything, but they're thinking hard, and if a cartoon bubble formed above their heads, the words could well be along the lines of those that Stanley Baldwin lifted from Rudyard Kipling in the 1930s: "Power without responsibility—the prerogative of the harlot throughout the ages."

A GIE may be formed with or without share capital. Airbus Industrie has none, although it has entered into borrowing agreements with banks. In 1984, for example, under a revolving acceptance facility, the company raised £35 million on the London market through S. G. Warburg and Banque Paribas. It has borrowed from Chase Manhattan and the U.S. Export-Import Bank to finance the purchase of one of its Super Guppies and from Citibank to finance engine purchases. On another occasion it went to the Midland Bank and to Barclays to finance aircraft wings.

It is managed by one or more directors nominated by the members in a general meeting. Article 9 stipulates that in dealing with third parties, a director binds the GIE by any act within its corporate objectives and that any limitiation of a director's power is invalid against third parties. Its accounts are subject to external audit, but not to any form of compulsory publication or general disclosure to third parties. This privileged status continued even after 1985, when the rules governing all regular French companies, public or private, were revised and the publication of annual financial statements was made a legal requirement.

It was, of course, this freedom from disclosure that was to be the cause of much of the exasperation subsequently felt on the American side. When challenged on this point, Airbus officials tend to explain soothingly that the accounts of a GIE can be thought of as a sort of internal ledger in which there is a record of its revenues and expenses and of its transactions with its members. They also assert that its financial status is reflected in the accounts of the individual members of the consortium, but that, as will emerge later, is a dim reflection in a very dark glass.

One feature of the GIE that is claimed to be particularly appropriate in dealing with products of high unit cost like aircraft is that the members are responsible for its debts jointly and severally. Creditors are therefore able to take action against an individual member if they have failed to get payment from the GIE itself. (No such case has ever arisen, but this could in theory make membership of the GIE unattractively risky to a partner who had only a small share—Spain with her 4.2 percent, for instance. A member with only a small percentage could be liable for the whole amount due to a third party, and would then have to turn to its partners to recover their share of such a liability in proportion to their respective participation.)

A new member assumes liability not only for future debts but also for any that already exist, and a member that formally withdraws remains liable for any debts existing on the effective date of its withdrawal. Tax returns are submitted to the French authorities as would be the case with a normal commercial company. Its results, however, whether profit or loss, are viewed for tax purposes as taxable income in the hands of the members, and are taxed in the same way as the rest of the member's taxable income.

Article 5 of the company's charter states that it was formed for the period of time necessary for the fulfilment of its objectives and these are defined in Article 3—to assume and continue all the design leadership and coordination of the work relating to specified projects and derivatives. This is held to include design, development, certification, manufacture, marketing, product support, maintenance of airworthiness and all related activity. There is provision for new members to be admitted (and for membership rights to be adjusted accordingly), but only with the unanimous consent of existing members. Unanimity is equally a requirement for the assignation of membership rights to third parties or other members. It is also specified in the charter that except by way of such assignment, no member may withdraw before the company has achieved its objectives and performed all its obligations. As will emerge later, this "till death us do part" clause is taken extremely seriously by the member companies.

The most influential of those member companies is Aérospatiale—this because of the size of its stake in the enterprise, its role as the final assembler and the importance within Airbus of its personnel. It came into being at the beginning of 1970 through the merger of three other companies (Sud Aviation, Nord Aviation and SEREB), a fact still reflected in its widely dispersed locations—the aircraft division alone has four plants in different parts of the country. It is France's largest aerospace manufacturer and its fifteenth-largest industrial group.

It is a 'national company'—in 1990 slightly more than 93 percent of its share capital was held directly by the French state, the remainder indirectly by a body called SOGEPA (Société de Gestion des Participations Aéronautiques), a holding company that handles government investments in aerospace ventures. It is heavily dependent on state aid and government contracts—in 1988, for instance, it received a total of FF 5.4 billion in reimbursable advances, capital infusions and contracts for R&D, a figure equivalent to between 15 percent and 20 percent of its sales revenues. It employs more than 33,000 people, of whom more than 14,000 work on the Airbus programmes.

As well as civil and military aircraft, the company builds helicopters, tactical and strategic missiles and space systems. It is, however, not big enough to mount very large projects from its own resources, and this is one of the reasons it has joined a substantial number of international consortia—including Airbus, it is currently involved in ten European cooperative ventures. It has sizeable holdings in eleven commercial subsidiaries around the world. It also has a range of manufacturing subsidiaries, and a minority shareholding in a number of foreign aerospace companies, including MBB in Germany.

Its 37.9 percent stake in Airbus Industrie makes Aérospatiale one of the consortium's two major shareholders. (The German stake is the same.) It has two functions. It supplies components and it assembles the aircraft from the parts contributed by other members and by third-party suppliers. This takes place at Toulouse. For the A300/310, Aérospatiale builds the wing carry-through structure, the main landing gear well and the cockpit. For the A320, it produces the fuselage front section, the cabin floor, the nose gear well and the upper fuselage panels, and it will do much the same for the A330/340.

The company's performance is characterised by high fixed costs, due in the main to high wages and to French social policies that make it difficult to adjust workforce levels. This in turn means that it is not easy to adjust production levels in response to a variation in demand, and one effect of this is a tendency to price aggressively to maintain sales volume. The 1990 accounts disclosed that for the fiscal year 1989 the board had set a net dividend of 0.54 francs per share, along with a tax credit of 0.27 francs. There had previously been a period of ten years when no dividend was paid, all earnings being retained by the company. Given that the company looks to the state as stockholder, as financier in the civil area and as customer in the military, the payment of a dividend is in any event something of a circular transaction.

CASA (Construcciones Aeronauticas, S.A.), is Spain's biggest aerospace manufacturer and Airbus Industrie's smallest partner, holding only 4.2 percent of the consortium's shares; 88 percent of CASA's own shares are owned by the state holding company, Instituto Nacional de Industria (INI). The company was formed in 1923 to build aircraft for the Spanish Air Force, and has a long history of building under licence to foreign manufacturers. It has seven plants and employs about 10,000 people. Spain's domestic base is too small to support its growing aerospace industry, and the company has accordingly entered into a wide range of collaborative programmes, including two with manufacturers in Indonesia.

It also does a lot of maintenance and modernisation work for the Spanish military, for Iberia, Spain's national airline and for the U.S. Air Force in Europe. The work it does for Airbus includes the production of horizontal stabilisers, various doors for the wide-bodied models of Airbus and a section of the fuselage for the A320.

Since the middle 1980s, CASA has been beset with difficulties. It plunged into the red in 1986, and a year later INI removed its chairman. His successor did not immediately fare much better, and in 1987 the company recorded pre-tax losses of Pta. 14.2 billion, the worst in its history. Consultants were called in, and their report identified undercapitalisation, low productivity and what was described as "an irrational excess of programmes." One of them is the STOL C-212 Aviocar, which a 1988 *Financial Times* Aerospace supplement described as having "a lot of the romance of the old DC-3 and, arguably, an equivalent amount of its obsolescence."[3]

A four-year "viability plan" was announced at the beginning of 1988 by the new chairman, Javier Alvarez Vara. The obstacles in the way of a return to profitability by the early 1990s were formidable. According to the labour union, the Union General de Trabajadores, there was "an absolute lack of motivation" among the workforce. Absenteeism in some plants was well over 10 percent. They also said that work on virtually all the company's collaborative programmes, including Airbus, was behind schedule, and that delays on the production line had caused McDonnell Douglas to withdraw some Pta. 2 billion–worth of business.[3]

The West German Airbus connection calls to mind a remark made some years ago by Alan Greenspan, the U.S. Federal Reserve chairman—"I guess I should warn you, if I turn out to be particularly clear, you've probably misunderstood what I said." Airbus activity in the Federal Republic predates the formation of Airbus Industrie by about three years, Deutsche Airbus GmbH having been set up as a limited liability management company by five German aircraft manufacturers in 1967. From 1969 on, the industry went through a series of mergers and consolidations, and out of this MBB (Messerschmidt-Bölkow-Blohm GmbH) eventually emerged as West Germany's largest aerospace group, with Deutsche Airbus as a wholly owned, limited-liability subsidiary, an arrangement designed to isolate the Airbus programme financially from MBB's other operations and to make it easier for the government to supervise the administration of state aid.

The German industry was hampered over the years by a relatively small home market, restrictions on military exports and the high cost of developing new products. Like its partners in the consortium, therefore, MBB has been heavily dependent on its membership of programmes like Airbus. It is a partner with Aeritalia and British Aerospace in Panavia, the Tornado military aircraft venture, and is also involved in Euromissile and the development of the Fokker 100.

Some years ago, *The Economist* described the ownership of the company as "a mixed bag of shareholders which rarely share the same views about where the company should go next."[4] The "mixed bag" includes the *Länder* of Bavaria, Hamburg and Bremen, firms like Bosch and Siemens and a number of financial institutions. One measure frequently applied to companies in the United States is what is known as asset leverage. This is calculated by dividing total assets by total shareholders' equity and is the most general measure of a company's debt structure. A comparison of MBB's financial statements for 1982–86 with those of McDonnell Douglas and Boeing showed that by U.S. standards, the German company was two and three times more highly leveraged.

MBB has enjoyed a reputation as one of the most technologically advanced companies in the former Federal Republic. It produces much the same range of aerospace products as Aérospatiale, but has also diversified into such fields as biotechnology and industrial electronics. It has some claim to be the least enthusiastic of the Airbus partners, and has more than once had to have its arm twisted by the government. It supplies fuselage sections, fins, rudders, flap tracks and interior furnishings for the A300 and the A310, which represents about 34 percent of the production of these aircraft. Its share in the A320 was reduced to about 30 percent.

British Aerospace, with a 20 percent share, is the smallest shareholder among the three major Airbus partners. It is also the largest defence conglomerate in the Western world outside the United States; in 1990, about a fifth of its 127,000 labour force were employed in commercial aircraft and sales totalled £10.5 million. Its manufacturing plants are small compared with those of its competitors in the United States, and are scattered throughout the United Kingdom, a reflection of the fragmented nature of the British industry before and after the Second World War. It came into being only in 1977, with the merging of the British Aircraft Corporation, Hawker Siddeley and Scottish Aviation. Initially it was nationalised, and the government continued to hold 48.43 percent of its shares until 1985. The company was then privatised, although the government held on to one "golden share"; this was to ensure that the provisions in the company's articles of association that restricted the foreign ownership of shares could not be changed without the government's consent.

The return to the private sector had a tonic effect on its management, and in 1987 the company achieved a 45 percent increase in revenues over the previous year. In spite of this it showed the highest financial loss since it was formed, largely because the Civil Aircraft Division continued to limp behind the others (military, weapons and electronic systems, space and communications). The civil division produces three types of commuter aircraft, but a significant part of its activity, accounting for some 30 percent of its civil aircraft revenues, is Airbus related. In 1987 BAe bought

Royal Ordnance, which makes explosives and rocket propellants, an acquisition that increased its dependence on the Ministry of Defence from 40 percent to 50 percent.[5] In 1988 it raised some eyebrows in the City of London when it diversified into motor car manufacture by the purchase of the Rover Company; the word *synergy* was heard a good deal, and it is possible that some of those who used it actually understood what it meant. Later it also went into property development and construction.

In 1991, British Aerospace experienced a dramatic reversal in its fortunes—in the first six months of the year its net debt increased from £808 million to £1.5 billion. In September the group announced a sharp fall in profits and launched its first rights issue since privatisation. This was felt to have been clumsily handled, and after strong pressure from non executive directors and City institutions, the chairman stepped down. The approval of the rights issue did not altogether scotch speculation about a break up bid, and there were reports that some of the group's biggest shareholders wished to explore proposals from European defence groups interested in buying a stake and spinning off some of its businesses.[6]

Like its partners in the Airbus consortium, BAe has a wide range of association with other collaborative programmes, though it shows a greater tendency than the others to undertake joint ventures with U.S. companies. Its debt/equity ratio has generally compared favourably with that of Aérospatiale and MBB, although it has been weaker than that of its U.S. competitors.

The British industry had traditionally been strong in wing technology, and Hawker Siddeley, as has been seen, supplied large parts of the wing for the original A300. For all later models, British Aerospace supplied the entire wing boxes. A member's work share (what it does as a subcontractor) can differ from its equity share from programme to programme. While BAe's work share for the A300 and A310 was close to its shareholding of 20 percent, its share on the A320 and A330/340 is nearer to 25 percent.

Slowly, from the early 1970s on, an intricate web of relationships was spun between Airbus Industrie, its partners, its sponsors and its subcontractors. The essence of the system was that Airbus Industrie subcontracted both development and manufacturing to the partner companies, to certain companies who enjoyed associate status and to a number of other specialist subcontractors. In June 1971 the relationship between the companies and their governments and the terms on which development was to take place were elaborated in a "Convention Cadre." This stipulated that each of the member countries would enter into a national financing agreement with its manufacturing company, and that each of the companies would in turn enter into an industrial agreement with Airbus Industrie.

Airbus Industrie itself operated essentially as a management company, responsible to the partners for resolving problems that related to the total programme, but under these industrial agreements it kept a number of activities firmly in its own hands. In the field of research and development, this included the conceptual design of new products and the supervision of design and development. Marketing was of central importance. Market studies, aircraft sales and financing and contract administration were all retained in Toulouse, as were advertising and public relations. It was also judged that certain important functions relating to production were best performed from the centre. Engine procurement fell into this category, and so did flight testing and aircraft certification. Certain operations in the technical area were also retained, such as the publication of technical materials and spare parts and maintenance support.

As Airbus Industrie was situated from 1974 on just across the way from Aérospatiale's assembly facility at Toulouse, much of this made a great deal of sense. Criticism has been voiced over the years, however, both by partners and by member governments, that the system carries within it a tendency to overmanagement; that the nature of the partnership not only adds a tier to the management structure of the consortium but also that the costs of the corporate bureaucracy that had emerged at Toulouse (and which are of course passed on to the members) are too high.

One indisputable advantage was that Airbus Industrie was the single point of contact for the customer, a lesson learned by not following the Concorde example. It was not the only one. At one time, for instance, there had been an official instruction on the Concorde project that a document written in English had no force until it had been translated into French by an official translator. Felix Kracht, Airbus's director of production in the early days, made it plain soon after his arrival from Germany that while any language was acceptable for paper coming into Toulouse, anything going out would be written in English.[7]

Under its charter, the consortium has one director, known as the "administrateur-gérant," the rough equivalent of a president and chief executive officer in the United States or a managing director in the United Kingdom. For a time the first incumbent, Henri Ziegler, wore two hats and also ran Aérospatiale, but the undesirability of this economical arrangement was fairly soon recognised. Both the Germans and the British have grumbled a bit over the years at the apparently divine right of the French to the top job, but without success.

Since 1985, it has been filled by the substantial figure of Jean Pierson. Pierson is the son of an army officer and was born at Bizerta in Tunisia in 1940. A product of the *Ecole Nationale Supérieure de l'Aéronautique et de l'Espace,* he joined Sud Aviation as an engineer in the production department in 1963. He finds his relaxation on the tennis court and in the opera house, and within the company he appears to have not one nickname but two—Sitting Bull and the Pyrenees Bear. His management style tends to be gruff, and he has a reputation for being a good butcher when the need arises, and just occasionally when it doesn't. He has certainly made his presence felt. In his first two years with the company he presided over the sale of more planes than all his predecessors put together. He also revamped the marketing operation in the United States, shrewdly replacing European salesmen with Americans. Until the reforms introduced in the spring of 1989, his management team consisted of an executive vice-president and general manager and a clutch of vice-presidents who each had a specific responsibility—marketing, technical, industrial, finance and administration, flight and support.

The administrateur-gérant is appointed by the members in a general meeting for a period of five years, and is formally responsible to a Supervisory Board. Until the 1989 changes, this was an unwieldy body that was 17 strong—6 each nominated by Aérospatiale and Deutsche Airbus, 4 by the United Kingdom, 1 by Spain. From the very beginning until his death in 1988, the Supervisory Board was presided over by Franz-Josef Strauss, the leader of the Bavarian CSU. Although over the years it has made common cause with the the CDU on the federal stage, it has always been more nationalistically minded, and under Strauss's leadership their policies tended to find more emotional and demagogic expression than those of Christian Democrats in the other *Länder*.

It is almost impossible to exaggerate the importance of Strauss to Airbus in its formative years. From the day that he was appointed chairman, he poured his political energies into the work of the consortium. It was a vehicle marvellously suited to his talents—in some ways a glittering compensation for the federal chancellorship that always eluded his grasp. He had for many years been a thorn in the flesh of Bonn governments, not excluding those of which he was a member. The Airbus connection increased his nuisance value geometrically, and he loved it.

Hartmut Medhorn, MBB's executive vice-president, expressed a high regard for his knowledge of the industry and was somewhat in awe of his ability to pick up the telephone and get himself into the presence of the Mitterands and the Thatchers and the Gorbachevs of this world at a couple of days notice. Most of all he admired him for his capacity to bring a fist down on the table and bulldoze something through. "Our systems are too democratic. We talk and we talk and we talk and we talk. We never decide." (He was speaking a few months before Strauss died.) "And you find always a group of parliamentarians behind you, some of them for, some of them against. You need at times a voice who will say, 'Bullshit, we go.' And for this Strauss is a very good man. He says 'go,' and even if he makes mistakes now and again, it doesn't matter. Basically he's a 'go' man, and that's good."[8]

Strauss relished the scope the chairmanship afforded him to flex his muscles on a larger stage, and the Airbus order book owed quite a lot to his robust diplomacy. His competitors at Boeing recognised a heavyweight when they saw one. "We thought we had airplanes sold to Turkey on one occasion," said Bob Perdue, one of Boeing's sales vice-Presidents at the time, "but Strauss paid a state visit in an A310 and promptly whipped our ass."[9]

Under the former dispensation, the Supervisory Board met three or four times a year. It decided broad lines of policy, approved the accounts and authorised the launch of new programmes. Minutes of the deliberations and decisions of this body are not made public, and an account of its proceedings by Sir Raymond Lygo, British Aerospace's former managing director, suggests that is perhaps just as well: "You had all the hangers-on and the lesser nodders and the yes-men, and it was an enormous gathering, at which Strauss would appear and put his head down and lecture us all on European collaboration. After we'd had half an hour of that we got down to the agenda—everything was being translated into four different languages—it was a most *extraordinary* performance".[10]

Sir Raymond was quick to concede, however, that the death of Strauss was very serious for Airbus. "It's a very big hole. He was an enormous supporter of the aviation industry. I don't know what the political outturn is going to be in Germany, but it's going to be considerable, because he was a power in the land. And as far as Airbus is concerned, it's difficult to think of anybody who could strut about the world stage as that man did."

After the launch of a programme, the company must allocate research and development activities. Development and other nonrecurring costs— engineering, tooling—are negotiated with the members, and allowance is made for a margin of profit. A portion of the price agreed for nonrecurring costs is recovered by the members with each shipset delivered. Production work also has to be allocated, and the members quite often in their turn subcontract. Complete subassemblies are manufactured in each of the four partner companies and are then flown to Toulouse for final assembly, Airbus Industrie taking title from the member companies when the subassemblies are *en route* to France.

Airbus Industrie's manufacturing methods differ strikingly from those of their American competitors. Although Boeing purchases parts and components from subcontractors around the world, the assembly work on its family of jetliners is essentially carried out in and around Seattle. Each Airbus partner, on the other hand, completes its portion of the package to the most advanced stage of completion, and delivers large components already equipped with wiring and tubing, functionally tested, and ready for final assembly. This means that final assembly takes up only 5–6 percent of total assembly manhours.

The two systems could not be more different. Whereas, for instance, Boeing wings are built and installed at the same facility, Airbus wings are begun in England, finished in Germany and fastened to the plane in France. Again, Boeing brings components together to be assembled into body sections at one site. Airbus, on the other hand, has two partners build the major body sections at four factories in two countries. Another major difference occurs in the procedures for installing interiors. Boeing does this at the site where the aircraft is built. Airbus interiors are installed by MBB in Hamburg, so the plane must be flown a distance of 900 miles each way, which is not cheap.

Enter the Super Guppy. Anyone clapping eyes on one of these extraordinary machines for the first time might well echo the words of the American music critic when he first encountered the Beatles—"I see it, but I don't believe it." They had originally been put together in the early 1960s to meet the needs of NASA in getting the hardware for the Saturn space programme from California to Cape Canaveral. A former Boeing test pilot called Jack Conroy had the idea of cannibalising old Boeing Stratocruisers and C97s. He bought a dozen of them for the price of the scrap metal. "It's a guppy," said a bystander when he saw the rather improbable result, and the name stuck.

The guppy—*Lebistes Reticulatus*, if we're going to be scientific about it—is a small, tubby, rather cheerful looking fish with a domed head. It comes from the West Indies and takes its name from the Reverend. R. J. L. Guppy, a Trinidad clergyman who sent the first recorded specimen to the British Museum in the nineteenth century. The first airborne version, nicknamed the Pregnant Guppy, first took to the skies in September 1962, powered by old Pratt engines, which had also been bought as scrap. It was not a commercial success, but Conroy was not a man to give up, and three years later he produced the Super Guppy, which NASA eventually bought. When Felix Kracht first saw them the biggest version had an interior diameter of 18 feet. "Make it 25 feet," said Kracht, "and I'll place an order." Which he did—at $17 million a throw and without any sort of authority from anyone in Europe. Old Airbus hands tell the story with a hint of nostalgia and concede that a latter-day Kracht might just pick up the phone to Toulouse before closing the deal.

Le Bourget–Hamburg–St. Nazaire–Nantes–Toulouse–Lemwerder–Manchester–Lille–Madrid—the fleet is worked hard, each plane flying 1,200 hours or so a year. The whole of the front swings open and the huge sections of wing or fuselage disappear inside, much as Jonah was engorged by the whale. The Guppies are obviously of crucial importance to the Airbus operation. Airbus claim that with no component out of the production process for more than 48 hours, "in-pipeline" stocks are cut to a minimum. There is also a marked reduction in transit damage—in both Europe and America, components shipped by rail have been known to attract the attentions of amateur marksmen at the side of the track. All this represents a saving of tens of thousands of dollars in the production of each aircraft. It would no doubt be cheaper by rail, but the Channel Tunnel isn't open for business yet, and the European rail systems have too many narrow tunnels and low bridges. Back in the early 1970s, the very first Guppy arrived two months too late to transport the parts for the first Airbus, so they had to go by sea to Bordeaux and then on to Toulouse by road, a hair-raising epic that old hands like to retell but have no desire to relive.

Airbus makes much of this dispersed system of production and distribution, although as in so much of its promotional material the tone adopted by its copywriters is that of Little Jack Horner—"A totally new system of cooperation on a basis of full equality, which also takes full advantage of the competitive spirit and proven expertise of each member of the partnership . . . Rationalised facilities ensure minimum production costs and maximum efficiency . . . The unique Airbus system brings the work to the workers . . . "[11]

Not everyone involved in the enterprise shares the enthusiasm of their colleagues in Toulouse. Sir Raymond Lygo of British Aerospace was particularly outspoken. "It's impossible to explain Airbus to anybody who has any rational thought processes. You have to recognise that some of the partners regard it as an act of social engineering." Sir Raymond cited as an example the experience of his company when BAe rejoined the consortium and the wings were transferred to the United Kingdom. "Our share was then about 16 percent of the total, and of course a wing is not a very profitable thing to make—it doesn't need spares, because it doesn't wear out. That wing was to be equipped, however, in Bremen. So it was going to be built in Chester, it was then going to be flown to Bremen, where it was equipped, it goes down and is fitted onto an Airbus, and you may think that's the end of the story, but it isn't, because it flies back to MBB to be fitted out, and it then comes back to Toulouse for final test before delivery. Now if you look at a bar chart of the time that takes it is horrendous, and compared with the Boeing time (and time is money) it doesn't make sense."

When the A320 came along, British Aerospace managed to persuade Airbus Industrie and their partners that the wings should be equipped in the country where they were built, and the company set up a big wing-equipping facility at Bristol. "The wing-boxes are made at Chester, they're moved to Bristol where they're equipped with all the bits and pieces, and then they're taken to Toulouse and bolted onto the aeroplane. The rest of the nonsense still goes on, but at least we'd cut that bit out."

When the allocation of work for the A330/340 programme came to be discussed, British Aerospace argued that the procedure agreed for the A320 should be continued. "The Germans said that they would never accept this—never. It had to go to Bremen, otherwise there would be massive unemployment there. So I said, 'I'm sorry about that, but that can't be price competitive. How can it be, with your labour rates, and with the time involved and all the rest of it?' So a study was carried out by Airbus Industrie of the comparative cost of doing it in both places. And can you believe it? They came out even. And therefore the work went to Bremen. And when I asked my government to support me in opposing this, I was told, 'We do not wish to have a row with the Germans on this issue'."

The British have not been alone in their criticisms of the system. German voices have also been heard, though the complaints they voice are rather different. Pierre Muller quotes one of the people he spoke to (his text clothes them all in prudent anonymity) as saying that when Roger Béteille and Felix Kracht were setting things up in the early 1970s they didn't think they needed more than about 40 people.[2] The staff at Toulouse now numbers about 1,250. In 1986, 23 percent of them were seconded from Aérospatiale, 21 percent from Deutsche Airbus, 8 percent from British Aerospace and the rest were employed directly by the GIE. If those in North America and elsewhere are included, the figure is closer to 2,000.

That sort of thing will have a familiar ring to anyone who has ever worked in a large organisation, public or private, whose activities have expanded over the years. It is a commonplace that bodies who are spending other people's money or passing on their costs tend to have a more Rolls Royce view of their staffing requirements than those in the private sector. Titles can of course be deceptive, but the organisation chart at Toulouse does seem to provide a generous allowance of chiefs for the number of indians they have about the place—Jean Pierson and his chief operating officer are supported by the efforts of seven senior vice-presidents, two vice-presidents and two directors.

A more substantial complaint from the partners concerns Airbus Industrie's conduct of commercial negotiations. Muller again quotes a German source: "Airbus Industrie is the sole point of contact with the customer. If they say, 'We've got a contract, but only on such and such a condition,' the partners have no choice—they have no means of forming a judgement." It is widely believed that Airbus Industrie do not pay sufficient attention to production costs and that this leads them to make overgenerous concessions on price. Another common complaint in the German industry is that Airbus Industrie are too accommodating towards the airlines in such matters as cabin configuration or the siting of the galleys.

What this all boils down to is a feeling that Airbus Industrie has got too big for its boots. There are many in the partner companies who see it essentially as a sales organisation and who resent what they see as their own relative exclusion from the making of important decisions. It is not always easy, however, to see that some of the solutions canvassed by the companies would actually have much effect on the matters they complain of. The way of doing business that has evolved around Airbus bristles with difficulties not because the people involved are obtuse or incompetent but because of the very nature of the enterprise. If Dr. Johnson were still with us, he might have rephrased one of his most celebrated pronouncements: "A woman's preaching is like a dog walking on his hinder legs. It is not done well; but you are surprised to find it done at all."

In any situation calling for speed of response, Airbus is clearly severely handicapped. For Jean Pierson and his colleagues getting any sort of initiative up and running is like the start of a horse race in slow motion. It is not only that the four governments and partners frequently pull in different directions but also that domestically the companies must all operate in different political climates. Full equality and dispersal of effort are all very well, but Airbus Industrie and the companies lack any integrated structure and do not enjoy any of the benefits that some sort of hierarchical relationship would confer.

There are elements of paradox in the position of the companies, because they are at one and the same time partners and subcontractors. They are represented, as shareholders, on the Supervisory Board, and yet in their capacity as contractors they are subject to decisions made by that same corporate entity. Each partner is therefore selling to Airbus Industrie those parts that were allocated to him when the work was originally divided up and at a price agreed at that time. Adam Brown gave an engaging thumbnail sketch of the mechanics of the process: "It's a multilateral negotiation—everybody together in the same room. Allocation of work share comes first, and then the transfer prices are negotiated in open court. It's called the liars' club." Since 1978, all such internal transactions have been in dollars. In one way this clearly introduces an element of stability into the system. Equally, however, if the partner fails to hold his costs down or if the dollar moves against him, he is going to find himself in difficulties.

Obviously, therefore, each of the partners, wearing his subcontracting hat, will tend to pitch his prices as high as possible. This however, is not at all in his corporate interest as a member of the consortium and positively against the interest both of his fellow partners and of the Airbus system viewed as a whole. It is a very unusual way to run a railroad—and it is made even more so by the fact that as well as being partners in Airbus, the companies are competitors in a number of other areas.

Towards the end of 1987, the relevant ministers commissioned a study of the working of the Airbus system. Each of them nominated a member, and the press, in an access of originality, dubbed them the Four Wise Men. Their report, and the changes that flowed from it, are the subject of a later chapter.

NOTES

1. Interview in Toulouse, June 1988.
2. Muller, *op. cit.*
3. *Financial Times,* September 1, 1988.
3. *Financial Times,* September 1, 1988.
4. *The Economist,* November 21, 1987.
5. *Financial Times,* April 4, 1987.
6. *ibid.,* October 3, 1991.

7. Bogdan, *op. cit.*
8. Interview in Hamburg, July 1988.
9. Interview in Seattle, February 1988.
10. Interview in London, October 1988.
11. *The Airbus Builders,* May 1985. By the early 1990s, it was plain that the Super Guppy fleet would have to be replaced—the aircraft had an average age of 40 and were becoming increasingly difficult to maintain. Airbus decided in September 1991 to build a modified version of the A300-600R, nicknamed the Dolphin. It was hoped that other operators might eventually be interested in it for the carriage of outsize cargo— preliminary studies suggested it would be able to carry the first stage of the Ariane 5 rocket, for example.

6

Challenge and Response

"A horse never runs so fast as when he has other horses to catch up and outpace."

—Ovid, *Ars Amatoria,* early first century.

Selling an Airbus or a Jumbo jet is a bit more complicated than persuading someone to buy a Mercedes or a Pontiac. It takes a bit longer, too. The market price of a commercial aircraft is the figure at which it is competitive against another model. It also has a cost price—which combines the launch or development costs and the recurring costs incurred by each aircraft as it is produced. If, within the anticipated market share, these two figures can be brought within shouting distance of each other, then you are in business. If, on the other hand, your cost targets and the number of planes delivered go adrift, then you are in trouble. Or rather you should be, if you are subject to the traditional commercial disciplines.

This is all a bit theological to the people at the sharp end whose business it is sew up the deal so that their boss and the head of the airline can pose for photographs with champagne glasses in their hands. A sales campaign can last three months or it can last three years. Accounts of why they went the way they did by those involved are not always models of objectivity, but only those of a utopian cast of mind look for identical descriptions of the Battle of the Somme in German and French history books. Such accounts can also be incomplete, because commercial sensitivity can attach to sales tactics just as much as to price.

Some years ago, when he was Airbus Industrie's general sales manager, Arthur Howes took an English reporter extensively into his confidence about one particular campaign in which he and Airbus had come out on top.[1] He was not the first to discover that phrases like "off the record" are sometimes rather poetically interpreted by the Torquemadas of investigative journalism. He remembers feeling rather pale about the gills when he saw the article in print, but he lived to tell the tale—and to sell more Airbuses.

The campaign in question began in the early 1980s when British Caledonian, later swallowed up by British Airways, was still an independent airline and felt that the time had come to replace its fleet of BAC-111s. B Cal's only concessions to sentiment were an occasional burst of bagpipe music and the pretty tartans worn by its stewardesses, and even those had a shrewdly calculated commercial value. They were in reality as hard-nosed as all airlines have to be to stay in business. Arthur Howes managed to get in and make his first pitch slightly ahead of everybody else, but he knew that the Americans were going to be very hard to beat.

McDonnell Douglas had a stretched version of the DC-9 to offer. That did not seem to him to be particularly formidable competition. Boeing, on the other hand, had their 737-300, not only a well-established product but also one of exactly the size British Caledonian were in the market for. What Arthur Howes had in his briefcase was some very attractive literature about the A320. What he had on his mind, however, was that no amount of sales patter about new technology could disguise two big drawbacks. The first was that it was a bigger plane than B Cal were looking for. The second was that it still existed only on paper, and that he couldn't offer delivery before the late 1980s.

British Caledonian's head office was at Gatwick Airport in Sussex, and they used to recommend their passengers to stay at their own Copthorne Hotel just down the road. Arthur Howes booked himself in and settled into a routine that was to keep him in the Sussex countryside for the best part of three years. His wife and children stayed put in the French countryside near Toulouse and saw him sometimes on the weekends.

The particular importance of the deal for Airbus lay in the fact that they were still at that time looking for launch customers for the A320. Airbus were sensitive to the charge that the governments of the consortium partners were not above leaning on national airlines like Lufthansa and Air France to "buy European." A sale to a company like B Cal, known to be nobody's poodle, would be an important victory for them politically as well as commercially.

Howes made it his business to cultivate people in five of British Caledonian's directorates—corporate planning, engineering, special projects, flight operations and marketing. The men from Boeing were never far away, and the airline played the rivals off against each other. "It's like the economics of the *souk*," a director of B Cal was reported as saying cheerfully, "except that the manufacturers are pricing in the dark." Howes identified a ploy that he described as the "nausea factor"—wait till one side thinks it's doing well, and then make its stomach churn by indicating that things are in fact running in the opposition's favour.

Throughout 1982 and 1983 Boeing did seem to be gaining the upper hand and a recommendation went to the B Cal board to buy the 737. Business goes on late in the bazaar, however, and no great degree of confidentiality seems to have attached to the recommendation. Arthur Howes bounced back and laid before B Cal something called a Launch Customer Incentive. Airbus now offered to meet the cost of having the old BAC-111s "hush-kitted" (trade jargon for modifying them to meet new, more-stringent noise requirements) and proposed an arrangement of Byzantine complexity by which a consortium of banks would then buy some of the planes and lease them back to the airline until the A320s were ready. Airbus also dangled one or two substantial fringe inducements like free pilot training and the establishment at Gatwick of free field service support.

In August 1983 Howes made what he thought was a final presentation in the B Cal boardroom. He felt he had done well, but it seemed he had not done well enough—word trickled through to him that B Cal's finance director had flown off to Seattle. Eventually, however, after Airbus had offered further assurances about operating costs and profitability, the champagne was opened and Airbus and British Caledonian signed a memorandum of understanding—less than a contract, more than a gentleman's agreement.

The contract was to be signed in January 1984. There was still a lot of work to do. Arthur Howes is very fond of skiing. What better place for the two sides to conclude their business than the fashionable resort of Mégève in Haute Savoie? The best laid schemes . . . They were not, as things turned out, much seen on the slopes. Although British Caledonian were important, Airbus had an even more important customer, and that was Air France, the national airline of a major partner in the consortium. They were going to buy the A320 to replace their fleet of Boeing 727s. What had emerged was that their load factor requirement was different from B Cal's, and this called for six additional seats. Arthur Howes knew that if that was what Air France needed, that was the way it was going to be. His skiing plans were in ruins and his deal was in jeopardy.

His recollection is that they got onto the *piste* once in five days. But the deal was signed. It occured to Airbus that there was one last thing they could offer the airline, and that was the ability to fly the plane on some of their longer charter routes, something which the existing specification did not allow without a stop for fuel. If B Cal would buy the extra seats, Airbus engineers would modify the design and fit an extra fuel tank— which they did, at a cost of almost half a million dollars a throw. Arthur Howes packed up his skis and headed south to Toulouse . . .

But that is to anticipate, and we must return for a time to the chronology of the Airbus story in the late 1970s. In the summer of 1979 an American academic called Joseph Monsen, who ran the Graduate School of Business Administration at the University of Washington in Seattle, attended a dinner for the British ambassador to the United States, Peter Jay. One of his fellow guests was Thomas J. Bacher, at that time Boeing's hawkish director of international business. They found they had a lot to talk about, and a few days later he received a letter from Monsen. It had, he said, been a pleasure to meet him—"and to find someone at Boeing who is deeply aware of the problems of competition from nationalised European firms." Monsen enclosed a couple of articles he had recently written on state-owned firms and suggested that Bacher might like to pass them around—"since I found in talking with a number of your colleagues at Boeing that they seldom read *The Harvard Business Review*—indeed seemingly specialising in inter-office memos . . . "

There is a school of thought that maintains that both the industry and the administration in the United States were slow to wake up to the challenge of Airbus—that for too long they viewed it with lazy indulgence as no more than a flea on an elephant's leg with rape in its mind. This is not in fact an interpretation that has much to sustain it.

The Tokyo Round of the General Agreement on Tariffs and Trade (GATT) had been in train since 1973. It had been the most comprehensive and far-reaching since the inception of GATT more than thirty years previously. The Trade Act of 1974, which authorised United States participation in the Round, had also set up a number of so-called Industry Sector Advisory Committees (29 of them in all) as a channel for the views of the private sector.

There was one on Aerospace Equipment. It had 17 members, mainly appointed on the recommendation of the industry's trade associations, and the chairman was George C. Prill, president of Lockheed International. In the early stages, ISAC 24, as it was called, had only part-time members. The feeling grew among them, however, that the administration's trade negotiators were not all that well attuned to the concerns of the industry, and Prill eventually left Lockheed and assumed the chairmanship on a full-time basis. The committee held discussions from time to time with industry officials in Europe and Canada and Japan and generally kept its ear close to the ground. By the middle of 1978 it had been borne in on the U.S. administration that there were problems in the civil aircraft sector that the trade package emerging from the Multilateral Trade Negotiations would do little to solve. ISAC lobbied skilfully, and a reference to trade in commercial aircraft found its way into the communiqué of the Bonn Economic Summit attended by heads of government that July.

The major trading partners of the United States were willing to make substantial cuts in their tariffs for civil aircraft, and in some cases these had already been suspended. The commitments they were prepared to make on nontariff barriers seemed much less satisfactory, however—it was clear, for instance, that the proposed Government Procurement Code was not going to apply to purchases by national airlines, and that there was therefore little prospect of greater discipline in the matter of inducements. The U.S. government accordingly took the initiative in seeking a special trade agreement for the civil aircraft sector—something that would go further than the across-the-board measures of liberalisation emerging from the negotiation.

There was a clear basis for negotiation. The Europeans were eager for the elimination of U.S. duties on aircraft, engines and components. The American interest lay in the lowering of nontariff barriers to trade by establishing that the basic rule of the game should be commercial competition. The negotiation was concluded and the deed was done. There were a number of respects in which the agreement fell short of the objectives that the ISAC had originally urged on the government, but it was, the committee declared, "an excellent first step in removing tariff and nontariff barriers that affect the free and fair trade of aircraft world-wide."

The European side had certainly got what it wanted, but the removal of duties in the U.S. did not immediately do a great deal for Airbus, and it looked for some time as if the sale to Eastern had been something of a false dawn. By early 1978, however, there was a steady flow of orders from elsewhere, and in that year they extended their Asian base with sales in Iran, the Philippines, Pakistan, Malaysia and Indonesia. In 1979, Airbus sold more wide-bodied aircraft than any American company and expanded into Latin America with a sale to Cruzeiro and Australia (TAA). On April 18, at the Savoy Hotel in London, a contract was signed with Laker Airways, a British independent airline, and that took the number of entries in the Airbus order book past 300, a higher figure than had ever been reached for a European aircraft since the jet age began. Two years later, when Freddie Laker eventually took delivery of the first plane, Bernard Lathière marked the occasion with a stylish PR gesture. Inside the Airbus there was a small present for Lady Laker—an Austin Metro car.

Airbus had had some early successes in the Far East, and their strategy was to build on this and acquire a chain of customers stretching from there back towards Europe—the so-called Silk Route. Third World airlines tend to be small, and therefore buy only a few aircraft at a time, but the rule of thumb in the industry is that one sale can quite well guarantee two more. Equally, the loss of one sale can very easily have a 20-year impact on an entire regional market. Switching from one type of aircraft to another can be an expensive business. Crew retraining and the purchase of new maintenance equipment could add anything between 10 and 20 percent to the price. The manufacturers are always eager to exploit the possibility of selling to airlines in neighbouring countries, who can then take advantage of each other's maintenance services and spare parts stores and achieve substantial savings. Airbus had made an A300 sale to Egypt in 1979, and in 1980 they scored a spectacular hat trick in the Middle East with successful campaigns in Kuwait, the Lebanon and Saudi Arabia, a victory in each case over Boeing, who were offering the 767.

Increasingly from the late 1970s onwards there were American allegations that sales competitions were being influenced by extrinsic considerations. There was certainly a strong whiff of politics surrounding all three Middle Eastern sales. The French president, Valéry Giscard d'Estaing, for example, had been on a visit to the region in the spring of 1980. He made a number of strongly pro-Arab speeches, urging Israeli withdrawal from the occupied territories and asserting the Palestinian right of self-determination. While he was in Kuwait, he signed a big contract for the construction of a chemical fertiliser plant. He also happened to be there on the day that the UN Security Council passed a resolution deploring Israel's policy of installing settlements in the territories and calling for them to be removed. The vote had been unanimous, but two days later the United States government enraged the Arab world by changing its mind.

The contest in Kuwait between Airbus and Boeing had been closely fought. There was little to choose between the two aircraft on offer, and when it came to a vote at a board meeting of Kuwait Airways a couple of months later, the majority favoured the 767. That was only a recommendation, however. The government, with whom the decision lay, disregarded it. Their decision was made known in Paris at the end of June by Bernard Lathière and the strongly pro-Palestinian Kuwaiti finance minister, and the word was put about that the French had a better understanding of the situation in the Middle East than did the Americans. The decision therefore was undoubtedly political, though it was more a case of a sales campaign having been caught up in politics than of a specific intervention by a politician in a particular campaign.

A few months later, Middle East Airlines in Beirut were also moving towards a decision, and they announced that they were going to proceed in a rather unusual way. They did so because some years previously, when they had been interested in some 747s, the man who was then their number 2, Asad Nasr, had come into possession of a sizeable sum of money in circumstances that caused questions to be asked. Some called it a consideration, others a commission. Those who were uncharitable or simply knew how business was conducted east of Suez used a word that was shorter and began with an earlier letter of the alphabet. Asad Nasr did not deny receiving the money, but was hurt at the suggestion that he had kept it for himself. It had, he explained, been shared out among those who laboured alongside him in the MEA vineyard. The board, charmed by this explanation, not only accepted that he was a pioneer in industrial partnership and profit sharing but also welcomed him as their chairman when there was next a vacancy. They felt that evil tongues should not be encouraged, however, and that was why sealed bids seemed a prudent idea on this occasion.

The envelopes were opened on November 24, and the sale went to Airbus. Few things in the Middle East are entirely straightforward, however. It had not just been a matter of choosing the lowest price. Boeing were later told that each of their planes had been loaded with a penalty of

$2.6 million. The race had, in fact, been an undeclared handicap. No explanations were forthcoming about how the stewards had hit on that particular figure, but Boeing were given to understand that it had to do with a lack of commonality. MEA had formed the view that no other airline in that part of the world was going to buy the 767, and the $2.6 million represented their estimate of what it would cost them to be excluded from such things as the trade in spare parts at remote airports. The explanation did not make Boeing feel much better. John Newhouse says that one of them described it to him as "the new law of maximum misery."[2]

The Saudi decision had in fact been arrived at a couple of months earlier, but it was not announced until December 18, doing great things for the reputation of Père Noël in Toulouse. There were suggestions at the time that Boeing, inhibited by the spate of corruption scandals in the late 1970s, had for once played its hand with less than customary skill, exerting itself less than it might have done to cultivate the powerful Saudi royal family.

Boeing had not been first in line, but all the American manufacturers had undoubtedly undergone a severe buffeting and they had all also subsequently experienced the reforming zeal of the Carter administration. The company that had come closest to the flame was Lockheed, and the disclosures of the late 1970s tarnished many reputations far beyond the shores of the United States.

In a book about the Lockheed affair, published in 1978, an English writer quotes Pooh-Bah from *The Mikado* as a chapter heading: "I don't say that all these distinguished people couldn't be squared; but it is right to tell you that they wouldn't be sufficiently degraded in their own estimation unless they were insulted with a very considerable bribe."[3] Some of the action would certainly not have been out of place in the *kabuki* theatre—indeed a piece about a group of *samurai* involved in bribery found its way into the repertory.

One of the actors in the real-life drama was Yoshio Kodama, a man of the extreme right with a reputation as a powerful political broker. He used to receive currency from Lockheed in wooden packing cases and stack them in his cellar—in all he got about $7 million. Bundles of receipts later came to light which read, "I received One Hundred Peanuts." A peanut was a million yen, and a record with the title "I also would like peanuts" got into the pop charts. More seriously, there was much anxious questioning about the health of Japanese democracy: a former prime minister found himself in court on bribery charges, and diplomatic relations between Japan and the United States came under quite severe strain.

Lockheed had also been active in Europe over many years. Boulton says that as early as 1958, the Grand Hotel in Bonn was so full of Lockheed lobbyists and salesmen that it was known to German Air Ministry officials as the *Lockheedshof,* and it was to emerge in the proceedings of the Church Committee in the 1970s that the company had enjoyed especially close relations with the West German defence minister, who at the time was Franz-Josef Strauss.

Much of the activity of the Lockheed men was directed towards selling the Starfighter, which was to become uphill work, because by 1965 there was a Starfighter write-off every ten days, and by 1975 there had been 174 crashes. The plane became known in the Luftwaffe as the "Flying Coffin," and numbers of black jokes went the rounds. "What is an optimist?" "An optimist is a Starfighter pilot who gives up smoking because he is afraid of dying of lung cancer."

In the summer of 1976 it emerged that all the files concerned with the German purchase of the F-104G from Lockheed were missing from the Defence Ministry in Bonn, but in the light of the testimony given to the Church Committee by a former Lockheed employee, that is not altogether surprising. Ernest F. Hauser had been a military intelligence officer in Germany after the war and had become friendly with Strauss, who was then working as a translator with the occupying forces. Later, Strauss used his influence to get him placed in the Lockheed office in Koblenz, which was where the Starfighter deal was being handled. He had an official title, but his main function seems to have been as a go-between with Strauss.

Hauser's story was that when the Starfighter contract was signed in 1959, Robert Gross, who was then Lockheed's chairman and chief executive officer, came to an understanding with Strauss (referred to in the Lockheed code-book as "Halibut") that a percentage of the sale price of each plane would be paid into the funds of Strauss's CSU party in Bavaria. These "commissions," Hauser said, were to be paid not only on sales but also on the hundreds of equipment change proposals that formed part of the contract and on any subsequent contracts under which West Germany might establish its own production line and build the Starfighter under licence.

Hauser estimated that something like $10 million flowed into the coffers of the CSU as a result of this "gentleman's agreement." At that time it was permissible under German law for political parties to accept donations from business concerns provided they were not intended as bribes. The most explosive part of Hauser's evidence related to a diary note he had made in July 1962. The implication of this was that Lockheed had secured German agreement to profitable equipment change proposals by bribery, and that these had contributed to the plane's disastrous crash record. Hauser's evidence was given in closed session. The diary was examined by staffers of the Church Committee and leaked to *The Wall Street Journal.* Both thought it authentic.

Lockheed's buccaneering and openhanded ways were to cause embarrassment elsewhere in Europe, too. Prince Bernhard of the

Netherlands was a director of several hundred companies, including KLM, and was well known for the energy with which he travelled the world drumming up business for Dutch industry. What was less well known was how spectacularly he was rewarded for these activities. Sometime in 1960, for instance, the idea was mooted that he should be presented with a Jetstar, a new executive plane that had recently come off the Lockheed assembly line. When Fokker got in first with one of their Friendships, the prince, a parody of a latter-day Pooh-Bah, indicated that he would not be offended by some alternative token of Lockheed's esteem and goodwill. $1 million changed hands—roughly the price of a Jetstar.

L'appétit vient en mangeant . . . In September 1974, Bernhard wrote to Lockheed suggesting that their commission arrangement should be updated. Times were hard, even for people who fared richly in palaces. A sum in the region of $6 million was mentioned. Lockheed apparently didn't have that much in the petty cash just then and demurred, and this earned them a second letter from the Princely Promoter, as he was sometimes called. The tone was rather pained. He reminded them of the way he had exerted himself over the years "to turn things in the right direction and to prevent wrong decisions influenced by political considerations"—a decision to purchase from Britain or France, that's to say. The devotion of the House of Orange to the European ideal was obviously susceptible of some flexibility in interpretation.

When all this came out later, Lockheed told the Church Committee that the payments they had made to the Dutch Queen's consort were not for services rendered but had as their aim "to create a favourable climate for Lockheed products in the Netherlands." Eventually, in the Netherlands, Bernhard had to face the music. The Commissie van Drie, which looked into the affair, did not accept his version of events. The presiding judge, who was the Netherlands member of the European Court of Justice, concluded that Bernhard's denials that he had ever received money from Lockheed "cannot be reconciled with established facts." The commission, in its findings, noted drily that its enquiries had been "repeatedly hampered by His Royal Highness's poor memory," and found that he had shown himself "open to dishonourable requests and offers." He had, they concluded, "allowed himself to be tempted to take initiatives which were completely unacceptable and which were bound to place himself and the Netherlands' procurement policy in the eyes of others in a dubious light."

One way and another, Lockheed seemed to have been trying to buy its way out of trouble since the 1960s. Robert McNamara, President Kennedy's secretary of defence, had been appalled by the high costs of the procurement arrangements he had inherited and set about changing the rules. The first test of the new system he put in place came in 1965 when the Pentagon invited tenders for the first wide-bodied Jumbo. The requirement was for a transporter that could carry the military equipment—including tanks and helicopters—of an entire army division.

The Pentagon's own estimate of what it would cost to produce the required number of planes was $2.2 billion. "Contract nourishment" was out, total package bids were in. Boeing named a figure of $2.3 billion, Douglas thought it could do it for $2 billion. Lockheed underbid them both with $1.9 billion—and had the ill-luck to win the contract.

Boeing converted its efforts to a commercial application and got down to work on what was to become the 747. Lockheed, lumbered with a fixed-price contract for the C-5A Galaxy, was also soon slogging it out with Douglas in a segment of the wide-body market that one model would have satisfied. The Pentagon relented a little. It agreed to make progress payments before the completion of the stage at which profits were properly due, a procedure that called for a certain amount of creative accounting.

A civilian working on cost control in the Air Force Department smelled a rat, and when nobody would pay attention, he tipped off Senator William Proxmire, who opened congressional hearings to investigate the charges. A departmental manager at Lockheed realised that something fishy was going on, too, but was sacked for his pains. Later, reinstated at a lower level, he was summoned by the director of manufacturing and asked if he knew what had happened to the civil servant who had tipped off Proxmire. "When I said I did not, Mr. Frech said that Mr. Fitzgerald was now the Chief Shithouse Inspector for the Civil Service . . . "[4]

By the end of 1969, Lockheed had been obliged to write off $290 million and reported a loss for the year of $32 million. By the end of 1970, the company had overdrafts totalling $350 million. It was reprieved by the collapse of Rolls Royce. Heath's United Kingdom offered Nixon's United States a deal—they would bail Rolls Royce out to the tune of $240 million, which would enable them to complete the RB-211 engine. The *quid pro quo* was that the United States should guarantee the future of Tristar so that there would be wings to hang the engines on. The American banks came up with a further $250 million, but here too there was a condition— that Congress itself should take on to guarantee the company's survival. The House of Representatives gave the idea grudging approval—by a margin of three votes—at the end of July. Three days later, the Senate endorsed the idea even more grumpily. The voting was 49 to 48.

Senator Church was a Democrat from Idaho, and the committee that bore his name was strictly speaking the Subcommittee on Multinational Relations of the Senate Committee on Foreign Relations. Its hearings had begun with disclosures about interventions by ITT in Chile, and by May 1975 had moved on to public hearings on the activities of some of the big oil companies. The committee first turned its attention to aerospace early in June. Church, from the chair, said that competition in the industry was out of control, but he was not referring only to America. "If the NATO alliance is not to be ruptured by greed run amok," he said, "the United States should press for fundamental reforms in Western military sales practices."

Competition in the Senate was pretty hot, too. Church was not at all pleased when at the end of August, Senator Proxmire tried to get in on the act with hearings of his Senate Banking Committee. It was before this committee that Dan Haughton, then Lockheed's chief executive officer, was asked whether "questionable payments," a phrase that Lockheed had acknowledged using, meant the same as bribes, and his reply went straight into the anthologies. "My counsel says he'd prefer to characterise it as a kick-back, but, you know, if you want to call it bribes, I guess it's all right."

Church pronounced again in September. "The bribes and the pay-offs associated with doing business abroad represent a pattern of crookedness that would make, in terms of its scope and magnitude, crookedness in politics look like a Sunday school picnic by comparison . . . " As the hearings ran on into 1976, however, the senator's resolve to expose wrongdoing seemed to weaken. He was a presidential hopeful. A certain backlash against investigative journalists and investigative politicians had begun to be apparent, and it looked as if this might damage his chances.

He did not back off for long, however. An intervention by Henry Kissinger saw to that. The secretary of state had become concerned by the effect the hearings were having on the reputation of the United States. He accordingly wrote to the attorney-general asking for a protective order to prevent further disclosures. They could, he said, have "grave consequences for significant foreign-relations interests of the United States." The Washington District Court obliged, and that galvanised Church into renewed activity. A British television company also now took an interest. They flew Hauser to London, and over the next few days, extracts from a long interview with Church's star witness were seen round the world.

Such were some of the extraordinary events that in the words of one observer turned the United States in the mid-1970s into one vast confessional. Boeing announced that over a five-year period it had disbursed $70 million in commissions on foreign sales, although it stressed that there had been no violations of the law in the countries in which the payments were made. Lockheed did in the end admit to violations. There were no prosecutions, but the company paid a fine of $647,000. McDonnell Douglas, on the other hand, had the book thrown at them. The company and four of its senior officials, including Ol' Mac's son, were indicted on a whole range of fraud and conspiracy charges, and it was only in 1981, after a good deal of plea bargaining, that matters were settled. The government dropped the criminal charges against the officials, and the company pleaded guilty and paid fines of $1.2 million.

There had been corrupt practices legislation in the United States since the Pendleton Act of 1883, although initially it had been aimed at injecting an element of equal opportunity and fairness into domestic campaigns and elections. It had proved to be ineffective and unenforceable. Evasion and subterfuge proved easy, with companies making contributions through their employees or their employees' families. When the Carter administration decided to legislate against corrupt practices abroad, it was done economically by amending the Securities Exchange Act of 1934, which had made it unlawful for an issuer of securities to make certain payments to foreign officials and also required the maintenance of accurate records.

It became known as the Foreign Corrupt Practices Act of 1977, and it was widely drawn. First of all it became unlawful to pay a foreign official with a view to influencing him in his official capacity—and that included a decision to *fail* to perform his official functions. It further became unlawful to induce such an official to use his influence with a foreign government "or instrumentality thereof" (a nationalised airline, for instance) in order to obtain or retain business. The same provisions applied to foreign political parties or anyone working for them. Individuals convicted under the act could be fined up to $10,000 or sent to prison for five years, or both, and it was specified that companies might not pay fines for their employees. Companies could be fined up to $1 million. The legislation also provided that if the attorney-general had reason to believe that an offence was about to be committed, he might bring an action in an appropriate district court and obtain an injunction or restraining order.

Little cause for surprise, therefore, if for a year or two after these traumatic events, the American aircraft manufacturers occasionally played the game with less assurance than they had done before. Europe had looked on while the industry in the United States battled through its own private Watergate and did not entirely believe what it saw. It certainly could not have happened in France. Indeed the whole chapter offers a striking illustration of the profound difference in relations between government and business in the two countries. Mention government involvement to a businessman in the United States and he conjures up a picture of control, regulation or "bureaucratic interference." A Frenchman, on the other hand, would immediately understand you to be talking about assistance and promotion.

The promotion of exports, indeed, had been explicitly identified as a policy priority in the Seventh French Economic Plan of 1974, and was cited as the main remedy for a worsening trade deficit.[5] The armaments industry had always been one of France's most successful exporters, third only to the United States and the USSR. France was America's leading non-Communist competitor in sales of military aircraft in the Third World, with a market share perhaps two-thirds that of the United States. There had been a sustained drive over many years to increase arms sales to the Arab countries, and especially those such as Iran, Iraq and Saudia Arabia that were members of OPEC. Although France had a nuclear energy programme, it had become obvious to her in the aftermath of the oil price shock in the early 1970s that she could not expect to enjoy anything approaching energy independence. She therefore had to diversify her sources of energy imports and increase her exports to pay for them.

The commercial strategy that was mapped out in the middle 1970s also resulted in radical changes in the pattern of French exports. Between 1973 and 1978, her total exports increased by 116 percent. Those to industrialised countries went up by 99 percent. The figure for developing countries as a whole was 171 percent. To countries in the Middle East that were not oil producers, the figure was 149 percent. To oil exporting countries, however, the figure *averaged* 259 percent: the rise in Nigeria's case was 676 percent and in the case of Saudi Arabia 1466 percent.[6] This shift was partly achieved by financial incentives at home, but the government also exerted itself politically and diplomatically with offers of military and technical assistance, the disbursement of aid and support for foreign policy positions.

France's export incentives were of two kinds—those that were tax-related and those that were not. Non-tax incentives included official credit assistance, insurance guarantees and cash grants. The tax-related variety related to French income tax practices and to the remission of indirect taxes on goods destined for export. Part of her success in selling to Third World countries, particularly to former French colonies, lay in the substantial volume of development assistance she has been prepared to extend to them. In the early 1970s, her official aid disbursements grew more rapidly than those of any other country apart from Japan.

France also led the field in the volume of technical assistance offered to developing countries. The OECD's 1978 Review of Development Assistance, for instance, showed that France was providing between two and three times as many technical assistants as were the United States. When Giscard d'Estaing went on a five-day visit to the Ivory Coast early in 1978, one of the items on the agenda was the purchase of radio and TV networks from France. The contracts under negotiation were valued at FF 6 billion. The French government had agreed to finance 1.5 billion of this, and to provide technical assistance in the shape of 2,000 technicians.

Morocco provides another good example of coherent and aggressive targeting. French aid increased in 1978 by 15 percent to FF 15 billion, of which FF 270 million was in the form of long-term low-interest loans and FF 580 million in the form of export credit insurance. The loans helped to pay for a cement works in Casablanca, the extension of an oil refinery, the construction of a weaving mill and the development of sugar factories and chemical works.[7] Nor was France's political support for Morocco's claim to the Western Sahara purely a manifestation of altruism.

The fortunes of Airbus cannot therefore be viewed in isolation. France and Airbus are not one and the same, but the French role in the consortium had always been a dominant one, and to some extent the successes of those years may be seen as part of a more general pattern of displacement of

American exports. It was achieved in spite of France's high rate of inflation and the appreciation of the French franc against the dollar. It was apparent in the Third World generally, in a number of OPEC countries like Iraq and Nigeria and Saudi Arabia and in certain of the more advanced countries of the developing world—Brazil, Mexico, Argentina—which were not oil-rich. The American industry began to realise that to have a good product that was competitively priced got them only as far as first base and that the mere matching of export credits and insurance guarantees was, like patriotism, no longer enough.

The American industry also felt that the administration had been slow to take the threat posed by Airbus seriously. There is a revealing accounts of how Boeing saw the competitive situation at the time in a report which the company sent to the Department of Justice in Washington early in 1982. "Even the highest government officials seem to view us as impervious to competition," it said complainingly in the introduction. "Unfortunately, these are judgements made while looking in the rear-view mirror. What we would like to accomplish through this report is to tilt the gaze of the Department of Justice away from the rear-view mirror and on to the road ahead."[8]

In Airbus, Boeing saw itself as dealing with a new kind of competitive adversary. "The Airbus Consortium is not constrained by the rules of American business ethics, business incentives, or the U.S. Department of Justice." It drew the department's attention to the importance of exports, both for itself and for the country. Although at that time U.S. aerospace companies accounted for only 2 percent of GNP, they constituted 11 percent of America's exports of manufactured goods. Boeing itself was the nation's largest exporter, and was at that time selling about 60 percent of its production abroad.

The particular importance of exports to the U.S. manufacturers was that while they traditionally relied on large initial orders for new generations of aircraft from domestic airlines, the balance shifted as each aircraft programme matured. In its first ten years, for instance, just over half of all 747 orders had come from U.S. carriers. In the most recent five-year period, 89 percent of all 747 orders had been for export. If that large export base were to be eroded, the scope for economies of scale would be reduced and with it the prospects of reducing manufacturing costs.

The company voiced its concern about the role of the government. Not only did it offer less support than was available to the European consortium—it also, by its policies, placed impediments in the way of the sale of aircraft abroad. Export controls were a particularly sore point, because a number of established customers had been denied licences for follow-up orders. The company believed that the government's policy of using trade restrictions in civil aircraft as a gesture to symbolise foreign policy disapproval was a boomerang, because it encouraged others—

Kuwait, for example—to play the same game.

There were also marked differences between the industry and the administration on the role of the Export-Import Bank. The bank, an independent government agency, had been incorporated by Congress in 1934 for the purpose of promoting exports. The authorising legislation required that it operate as a self-sustaining institution and provided an initial capitalisation of $1 billion. Its activities are covered by the unified federal budget, which is to say that in effect the Congress establishes a ceiling on the level of activity for which it is authorised to borrow funds to cover its loans.

It was common ground between the industry and the administration that the bank's role in subsidised financing should ultimately be reduced, but they agreed on little else. The administration wanted to see an early reduction in the budget; the industry thought that during the transitional period there was a case for increasing it. The administration wanted to tighten the definition of eligible products; the industry's position was that it should be broadened. The administration favoured a policy of discouraging direct credits and guarantees; the industry, while not against an eventual shift to guarantees only, wanted to see the bank aggressively matching the competition from abroad and providing access to private capital markets for all manufacturers.

In April 1978, in what was seen at the time as a direct response to the Eastern sale, John Moore, the director of the Export-Import Bank had announced that they were going to be more flexible in their financing of foreign sales, and were introducing what were described as a number of "exceptional measures" that would benefit developing countries. Four years later, the bank appeared to be going through a period of retrenchment. Its total loan authorisations had been declining in real terms, and U.S. export support programmes lagged substantially behind those of France and the United Kingdom (though not of West Germany).

The manufacturers believed that they were in a period when the depressed state of airline earnings made a strong Export-Import Bank particularly important. Earnings were low partly because of world economic conditions, partly because of the disruption occasioned by the recent deregulation legislation. There had been a proliferation of route awards, new airlines had sprung up like mushrooms after rain and there had been a rash of totally unrealistic fare discounts. As the manufacturers saw it, this increased the vulnerability of the airlines to foreign economic initiatives tied to sales campaigns. Unless they could rely on matching support from the Export-Import Bank, they would be fighting Airbus with one hand tied behind their backs.

Boeing itemised four recent campaigns in which they felt the bank had let them down. In Nigeria and Canada they had failed to match the competitive financing proposals made by the European export credit agencies. In Malta they had not felt able to respond when the Europeans had extended their offer, and there had been a similar failure to deliver in Singapore. The result was an estimated initial loss of more than $800 million on 757 and 767 sales and anything up to $1 billion in follow-on orders. They were critical of a perceived tendency on the part of the bank to vacillate on financing commitments to sales that had already been made, calculating that this could put in jeopardy a sum approaching $1.6 billion.

Boeing was also restive at what it described as ambiguities in the interpretation of the Foreign Corrupt Practices Act and believed that Airbus had been able to capitalise on the constraints this legislation had placed on U.S. manufacturers. In common with its American competitors, Boeing had tightened up its rules on the engagement of sales consultants. The procedure they now followed required them to communicate the name of anyone they were considering as a consultant to the airline in question and also, if the airline was state-controlled, to the appropriate government ministry. They also required that the prospective consultant should be checked out by the U.S. Embassy. This all took time, did not always result in particularly good appointments and invariably meant that they were left at the post by Airbus, who were not encumbered by any such restrictions.

American salesmen, regardless of their company, still found themselves bobbing in the backwash of the Lockheed investigations. Airline executives in some countries had been approached, through the local embassy, by U.S. officials who wanted to know things about their dealings with Boeing. They had felt harrassed by this and in some cases had expressed reluctance to continue sales discussions. Airbus offered an easy escape from such embarrassment. The chief executive of one Middle Eastern airline had said that he would only do further business with them "if Boeing could get a letter from the U.S. Justice Department stating that 'Boeing is clean'."

In three recent sales competitions—those in Egypt, the Lebanon and India—Boeing felt they had suffered from campaigns in the local media that had resurrected accounts of U.S. government investigations involving the airlines in question. They thought they saw the hand of Airbus in this particular piece of psychological warfare, and took it that the intention was to unsettle the people in the airlines who would be taking the decisions this time around.

They also reported on a new feature in a number of recent campaigns, which was that the airline opened the proceedings by seeking an assurance from Boeing that they were not employing a consultant. They presumed that Airbus were being asked to jump through the same hoop, but they believed that the Europeans had found a sneaky way of doing so with impunity. A consultant *had* been retained in the Airbus interest, but he had been employed by an agency of the French government . . . Boeing believed that such consultants were being paid something like 10–12 percent of the price of the aircraft. In the case of an A300 that would amount to some $6 million, which in the American book was distinctly over the odds.

Both sides have their favourite stories, although they do not always tell them on oath. Airbus, for instance, allege that McDonnell Douglas, hearing that the Yugoslavs had no dollars to pay for DC-9s, agree to take ham instead, and that as a result the canteens in every McDonnell Douglas factory from California to Missouri served Yugoslav ham three or four times a week for years on end.

Although much of the evidence in this area is necessarily anecdotal, there are one or two episodes that have been documented, and they make intriguing reading. One such concerns a deal with Thai International in the early 1980s. Lew Bogdan, who appears to have had his information only from Airbus sources, tells the story as follows. In February 1981, Thai International ordered two A300-600s. Because General Electric were behind schedule with the CF6-80-C1 engine, however, Airbus had to inform the company that they were not going to be able to meet the agreed delivery date. They proposed instead fitting Pratt & Whitney engines, which would allow delivery in June 1984. In September 1982, the airline told Toulouse that they were cancelling the order. The reason turned out to be that Boeing had offered long-range 767s, and the airline, subject to government approval, had accepted. Bogdan then concludes the story rather economically by saying that after seven months of further negotiation, which he describes as rough and occasionally humiliating ('âpres et parfois humiliantes'), Ranjit Jayarathman, who was Airbus's general sales manager at the time, managed to swing things back their way, even persuading the Thais to accept a delivery date as late as September 1985.

The files of the airline disclose a little more of the detail, however, and a letter from Jayarathman to the airline's president, Air Chief Marshal Bancha Sukhanusat, makes it fairly easy to understand why it was not too painful for them to change their mind a second time. It consists of three short paragraphs and comes briskly to the point: "Further to THAI decision to pursue acquisition of the B767 aircraft we believe it our obligation to THAI as a valued A300B4 aircraft customer to ensure THAI is protected in the event of failure in finalising its B767 definitive Purchase Agreement." In the second paragraph, Airbus extends the terms and conditions of their own proposals by a further month. The third paragraph reads: "In addition and as an incentive to THAI to review/reverse its present decision in favor of Airbus we offer THAI a price discount of U.S. Dollars Ten Million on each of the four A300 or A310 (2 firms 2 options) order."

Another entertaining example of Airbus enterprise and flexibility is to be found in the archives of the Ministry of Tourism and Civil Aviation in Cairo. It takes the form of a letter to the minister, written on October 27, 1983 by Airbus's area sales manager, who at the time was a Frenchman called Gourceaud, and it sets out his confirmation of what had passed at a meeting in the minister's office two days previously. The Egyptians had accepted in principle an offer made by Boeing, and Monsieur Gourceaud deploys his powers of persuasion over two and a half pages in an effort to get them to change their minds.

He reminds the minister that when they had initially rejected the idea of buying the A310-200, Airbus had offered in its place the A310-300. "Jointly with this offer we gave EGYPTAIR three aircraft type A 300-B4 fitted out in the same configuration of [sic] their present Airbuses, to be added to their fleet and used free of charge for a period extending from May 1984 until delivery of the new A310-300 aircraft." He assures the minister that these planes are capable of covering all the routes in the Egyptair network. This, he says, could be achieved with a high degree of efficiency, at the cost of one technical stop at Kano, in northern Nigeria, on the route between Cairo and Ghana. "Our company is prepared to bear the landing fees involved." It looks as if the Airbus team might have had some reservations about that particular part of the package, because they round it off with a throwaway line that would have gone down big in Seattle: "Alternatively, we offered EGYPTAIR verbally, in lieu of the three A300-B4s, a used Boeing 747/100 to be owned by them free of charge, should they wish to acquire such an aircraft."

Monsieur Gourceaud is now fully into his stride. He points out the increase in cash flow that would result from his proposal, and draws the minister's attention to the excessive charges and fees the Egyptians would incur if they had dealings with the American Export-Import Bank—a difference, he said, that would amount to about 2 percent of the price of each aircraft. The American plane, moreover, was only of U.S. manufacture as to 70 percent. This would force Egypt onto the free money market in search of the remaining 30 percent. There they would have to contend with a floating rate of interest, and he reminds the minister (perhaps with a slight lack of delicacy) that an Egyptian loan would have to be serviced at a rate of 14 percent . . .

Gourceaud slips with Gallic felicity into his coda: "Your Excellency, we are confident that the economic studies and the cash flow analysis will prove that our offer provides a lighter burden on the Egyptian economy and cover [sic] the requirements of Egyptair in full—a target that all the competent organisations of the Egyptian Arab Republic are seeking."

Boeing were busy with economic studies and cash flow analyses at about this time, too, but with a view to proving something rather different. Lacking the hard evidence about the scale of subsidy to Airbus that published figures would provide, they addressed themselves with characteristic thoroughness to devising a methodology that would allow them to come up with fairly accurate estimates. They began by defining the cash flow profile for a typical American programme, and this was then adjusted to take account of what was known about the Airbus programme in such matters as phasing, quantities produced and the like. The current and projected deficit cash flow, which could only be covered by government subsidy, could then be quantified.

In one such analysis which they sent to the deputy U.S. trade representative in late 1983, Boeing enumerated some of the fundamental economic considerations that informed their calculations:

• The production of commercial aircraft calls for a very large initial investment for development and an extended development lead time. Nonrecurring costs—design, development, tooling and certification—amounted in 1982 to something of the order of $1.5 billion. Recurring costs incurred before the delivery of the first plane would be about as much again.

• Recurring costs are subject to what is known in the jargon of the industry as the improvement curve phenomenon—the high initial labor costs diminish progressively with units produced because the repetitiveness of operations leads to efficiencies.

• All this means that it takes a long time and a substantial volume of production before the initial development investment is amortized.

• Production volume limits the number of producers that can be profitably sustained by the market. Only about half of the U.S. programs to date had been profitable. Most European programs had been failures, largely because of an inadequate volume of production.

At that time a typical American programme of the size of the Airbus A300 would involve a development period of about four years. If 700 planes were delivered over a ten-year period, the programme would incur a negative cash flow of about $3 billion, and could expect to break even some 12 years after the go-ahead. Initial sales for the A300 had been very low, however, with only 57 planes delivered in the first five years. It was also the case that the A300 had taken five years to develop rather than four. If publicised sales expectations were to be realised, the delivery of 700 aircraft would take 16 years. A programme stretched out to that extent would reduce production rates and cause the cash-flow situation to deteriorate still further, and the position would be additionally aggravated by model improvement costs—an additional $250 million in nonrecurring costs had already been reported for an upgraded version of the plane known as the A300-600.

Boeing also took account of European production costs, which was something they did not have to guess at—they did, after all, have several hundred subcontractors there. They reckoned that their hypothetical U.S. programme would have swallowed up some $6 billion over an 18-year period, and that there would be no realistic prospect of a break-even point ever being reached. (They had confirmation of this only a few months later from an impeccable source. Visiting Seattle in April 1984, Michel Lagorce, the deputy director of Civil Aeronautics Programmes in the French Civil

Aviation Authority, told Boeing officials in a moment of candour that the break-even point for the A300 and A310 programmes was now "infinity.")

Boeing's calculation was that at a conservative estimate Airbus had by that date been subsidised to the tune of more than $6 billion. Spread over 700 aircraft (a sales assumption they regarded as highly optimistic), that worked out at a discount of about $8.5 million per plane, or approximately 15 percent of the "sticker" price. The conclusion was that if the A300 had been a private programme, it would have been abandoned—which was precisely what had recently happened to the Lockheed 1011, although its deliveries had equalled those of the A300 and the A310 combined.

Over the years, the Airbus camp have forged an ingenious armoury of weapons to defend themselves against the charges made by the Americans. Their corporate nerves are good, and they have quite often taken their cue from what Marshal Foch said at the second Battle of the Marne—"Mon centre cède, ma droite recule, situation excéllente. J'attaque!" Sometimes they simply pick up the hand grenade and lob it back over the parapet—Herr Strauss' remarks about predatory pricing by Boeing at the Paris Air Show in 1987 were a good example.

There is, however, one defence that Airbus has never adopted, and the omission is curious. They are skilled at deflecting American charges, fertile in counterclaims of their own, eloquent in four languages about there being no case to answer. The only thing they have never done is demonstrate conclusively that this is so by opening up the books and letting the figures speak for themselves.

NOTES

1. Tom Mangold, "The Dealmaker," *Airport* (March 1985).

2. Newhouse, *op. cit.*

3. David Boulton, *The Lockheed Papers* (London: Jonathan Cape, 1978).

4. Evidence to the Proxmire Subcommittee on Priorities and Economy in Government of the Joint Economic Committee, September 29, 1971.

5. See Lawrence G. Franko and Sherry Stephenson, *French Export Behavior in Third World Markets* (Washington D.C.: The Centre for Strategic and International Studies, Georgetown University, 1980).

6. International Monetary Fund, *Annual,* 1971–79.

7. Economist Intelligence Unit, *Quarterly Economic Review, no. 2, 1977, and no. 2, 1978.*

8. *The Changing Character of the Commercial Airplane Marketplace. Airbus vs Boeing. The Government Support Factor.* January 1982.

7

The Public Trough

State aid to industry is a very old story indeed. It is also convoluted, and anyone hoping to buttress an argument by pointing to patterns of consistency in national policy should tread with care—unless, that is, he is fortunate enough to be a Frenchman.

The history of state subsidy in France is a venerable one, going back at least to the reign of Louis XIV. Adam Smith dismissed Colbert, the Sun King's controller-general of finance, as "a laborious and plodding man of business," but he plodded to some effect, using state money to acquire the Gobelin factory and to cut the Languedoc canal. Later, as minister for the navy, he built up the merchant marine. Premiums were allowed on ships built at home and a duty imposed on those brought from abroad, and there was a rapid increase in overseas trade. Colbert's regulations put anyone guilty of faulty workmanship in the pillory. The importance of quality was paramount. Competitiveness in price was a lesser matter. Small cause for surprise, therefore, if a certain *insouciance* in the matter of controlling costs remains characteristic of the French attitude to some aspects of economic activity today.

Not that protectionist sentiment in France has always gone unchallenged. The economist Frédéric Bastiat, for instance, carried on a vigorous propaganda for free trade in the first half of the nineteenth century, producing a flow of engaging pamphlets and essays demonstrating the connection between socialism and protection. His *Sophismes Economiques*, published in 1845, contains his splendid mock "Petition from the Candlemakers of France to the Chamber of Deputies":

Gentlemen—We are suffering from the intolerable competition of a foreign rival, placed, it would seem, in a condition so far superior to ours for the production of light that he absolutely inundates our national market with it at a price fabulously reduced . . . This rival, who is no other than the sun, wages war to the knife against us, and we suspect that he has been raised up by *perfidious Albion* . . . We pray that it may please you to make a law ordering the closing up of all windows, skylights, dormers, shutters and blinds—in short of all openings, holes, chinks, clefts and fissures through which the light of the sun can penetrate houses, to the injury of the flourishing trade with which we flatter ourselves we have endowed our country. . .

It is instructive to set that text against another, written half a century earlier and with no ironic intention:

The undertakers of a new manufacture have to contend, not only with the natural disadvantages of a new undertaking, but with the gratuities and remunerations which other governments bestow. To be enabled to contend with success, it is evident that the interference and aid of their own governments are indispensible.

The source of that is the Report on the Subject of Manufactures written for the House of Representatives in 1790 by Alexander Hamilton, whom Washington had appointed as his first secretary of the treasury. He had, he said, applied his attention to the subject "at as early a period as his other duties would permit." (He was busy, among other things, reestablishing the financial credit of the new nation, inventing a system of coinage and elaborating a scheme for a central bank. Not for nothing was his mother a Huguenot and his father a Scot.)

The report ran counter to the strong predilection for private economic enterprise in America and marks an early revolt against the free trade doctrines of Adam Smith. There was nothing apologetic about Hamilton's advocacy of collectively organised economic effort. He recognised that the measures he proposed might well require "the incitement and patronage of government." At first they were adopted only in part, but the War of 1812 demonstrated their attractions, and thereafter they furnished the pattern for a century of national legislation. The line is still strongly visible in the middle decades of the century. "We hold it to be wisest," said the legislative address of the Whig Party of New York State in 1838, " . . . to apply the means of the state boldly and liberally to aid those great public works of railroads and canals which are beyond the means of unassisted private enterprise."[1]

In this century, aviation attracted subsidy from the first on both sides of the Atlantic, although initially it was air transport rather than civil aircraft manufacture that was the beneficiary. In Europe, keen rivalry developed between Paris and London, but without government backing the British commercial pioneers soon went under and the French were left in control of the cross-channel routes. This produced considerable uproar in Britain, and from the early 1920s a measure of support was introduced. For a short time in 1922, for instance, when three commercial companies were operating between England and the continent, the British government provided half the fleet of each company on a hire-purchase basis and offered in addition a subsidy based partly on the load carried and partly on the gross earnings of the company. The arrangement soon proved to be both impracticable and wasteful.

The French were also characteristically quick to recognise the wider possibilities, seeing very clearly the advantages of rapid communication with their colonies in Asia and Africa, and a costly and ambitious programme of financial assistance was in place as early as 1919. It might have been thought that the empire had much to gain, too, but the British muddled their way well into the 1920s before setting up Imperial Airways in 1924 with a £1 million subsidy spread over ten years. The United States made a slower entry into commercial aviation, but there too the government saw a role for itself, and when Pan American Airways opened its transpacific service from San Francisco to China, it was made possible in large measure by a policy of generous subsidy.

When he published his magisterial survey in 1965, Andrew Shonfield's judgement was that historically, American capitalism in its formative period had been much readier to accept intervention by public authority than, say, British capitalism. "There were many elements in the early New Deal which pointed, at a time when few of the European politicians of either the Right or the Left were ready for it, in the direction which much of Western Europe has taken since the war."[2] It is easy to forget that the American attachment to free trade is essentially a modern phenomenon.

For several decades the economic direction that much of Western Europe took after the second World War was of only spasmodic interest to the United States. By the late 1970s, however, one or two American academics had begun to draw attention to what they saw as a new wave of public ownership in European industry. The first thing they tended to notice was the large amount of red ink in these companies' annual reports. They also observed, however, that poor economic performance in the public sector was not, as the mythology had it, a purely British phenomenon, but was just as common in Germany and France and Scandinavia.[3] Some of these nationalisations were to rescue industries that were ailing or in decline. Some of them, at least in theory, were temporary, aimed at counteracting the effects of the recession induced by the oil crisis of 1973. Capitalism's traditional response, the shakeout (what Joseph Schumpeter called capitalism's process of "creative destruction"), was ignored.

Something that American observers found especially baffling was the fact that this new wave of nationalisation was by no means exclusively the work of the political left. When, for instance, Margaret Thatcher, in the early days of her leadership of the Conservatives in Britain, criticized the Labour Party for its support of "lame ducks." James Callaghan, the Labour prime minister of the day, was able to remind her blandly that it was her predecessor Edward Heath who had nationalised Rolls Royce in 1972. Americans were similarly nonplussed by the performance of the nonsocialist government that came to power in Sweden in 1976, and which within a few years had brought into public ownership the steel industry, the shipyards and a number of textile and clothing companies.

Some enterprises passed into public ownership through a process of diversification—what the chairman of the French Senate's finance commission called "creeping nationalisation." The number of state-owned companies declined, but the number of their subsidiaries increased. Renault was a good example, diversifying into agricultural machinery, machine tools and agricultural products, with subsidiaries in Austria, Mexico, Portugal and Rumania.

Finally, there was increased government involvement in various types of enterprise that carried high risk in the marketplace. One beneficiary of this particular form of largesse was the former General Motors executive John DeLorean, who set up in business in Northern Ireland backed by £52 million of public money, a sizeable tranche of it in the form of outright grants from the United Kingdom government. It had, it seemed, been a close-run thing between Belfast and Puerto Rico. Later, when they got to know a little more about the colourful DeLorean, thoughtful British taxpayers reflected that there were some contests in which the smart thing to do was come in second.

The prospect of someone thriving without making profits is one that excites particular indignation in the American breast. Airbus is by no means the first instance of it. In the late 1970s, for instance, the U.S. Treasury Department produced figures to show that on the West Coast, British steel was underselling Japanese steel.[4] The British Steel Corporation was in those days still nationalised and had not yet benefited from the ministrations of Ian McGregor. Its production facilities were elderly, and it was widely regarded as overstaffed and inefficient. As it had also in the previous year incurred losses of several hundred million pounds, it was not clear how it was able to undersell the Japanese companies, whose efficiency was a byword. The American conclusion was that British Steel was in the business of keeping people in jobs rather than operating profitably. And the view of a private company not in a position to thrust its hand into the public pocket in this way would be that it was faced with an unfair competitive threat.[5]

The French are never to be outdone by the Anglo-Saxons, however. Renault, the First Lady of European public enterprise, has never turned in much in the way of profit. Olivier Giscard d'Estaing, the brother of the former French president, had some fun with the figures a few years ago and came up with a sardonic little statistic—over a period of five years in the 1970s Renault's main competitor, Peugeot, paid slightly more in taxes than the state-owned firm received in subsidies.[6] Laurence Sterne was right. They order this matter better in France . . .

* * * * *

So much by way of historical sugar on the pill. The rest of this chapter is not going to be easy. Those made queasy by figures and attempts to explore their significance should perhaps move on, although the figures in question are fairly central to an understanding of this particular story and cannot sensibly be relegated to an appendix. An examination of Airbus without an examination of its finances would be Hamlet without the Prince.

For a variety of reasons, some of them more reputable than others, the financial traces of Airbus are marvellously well covered, and investigating the facts of the matter is a bit like peeling an onion. As a *groupement d'intérêt économique* Airbus Industrie is under no legal obligation to publish its accounts, although when questions have been asked, its executives and those of the partners have frequently suggested that the information is in the public domain and accessible to those resourceful enough to ferret it out.

Barbara Kracht, for instance, Airbus Industrie's public relations manager, told an International Air Transport Association conference in Spain in the summer of 1987, "All the Airbus accounts are included and published in the balance sheets of our partner companies, as part of their Aircraft Division accounts."[7] A few months later, with what sounded like a trace of tetchiness, Sir Raymond Lygo, then British Aerospace's chief executive, made a similar assertion: "I get slightly irritated when people like Boeing, who are sloshing around in their monopolistic profits, actually start to criticise us . . . We have nothing to defend and nothing to hide. We can't hide anything. We're a public company."[8] There were those who remained politely sceptical. "Its transactions are supposed to show up in its four owners' books", a writer in *The Economist* noted drily, "but Sherlock Holmes could not detect them there."[9]

If Holmes and Watson were to rise the challenge, they might make a start with the annual reports of Aérospatiale, which usually appear in May. They are glossy affairs, with the text in both French and English, and they are also, as required by French law, published in the *Journal Officiel*.

In the Report for 1985, a note headed "Summary of Significant Accounting Principles and Methods" contained the following lapidary passage: "In accordance with the general rule, exchange rate differences arising on payment of payables and receivables in foreign currencies are recorded in income except for foreign currency transactions with the Airbus Industrie Consortium. These transactions are recorded in the Consortium's current account at the rates of exchange in effect at the transaction date. No exchange differences are recorded because the partnership current account, which represents Aérospatiale's entire interests in the net assets of the consortium (comprising fixed assets, inventories and receivables), is not available." The notes to the financial statements in subsequent years read almost identically, except that this reference to Airbus is omitted.

A further reference to Airbus occurs in that part of the accounts dealing with receivables and payables:

Accounts receivable (and payable) in foreign currencies are converted into French francs in accordance with the methods prescribed by the French Accounting Plan, except for the receivable from the Airbus Industrie Consortium, denominated in dollars and converted according to the rule specified in *1 B 6. This receivable from the GIE Airbus Industrie Consortium has no fixed maturity but is due as and when the Consortium receives payment from its customers. This being the case, the outstanding amount, included under "other operating receivables" has been spread between maturities of up to 1 year and over 1 year, in accordance with the projected inflow of cash resulting from the present state of the Consortium's order book.

Two other entries in the Notes to the Financial Statements, both relating to amortization, merit attention. The first discloses that research and development costs covered by advances that are repayable in the event of the success of the project are written off over a period "which may exceed five years." The second states that tooling for series production and industrialisation costs are written off against the sales of the aircraft series in accordance with a schedule determined on a case-by-case basis at the beginning of the marketing phase of each programme.

The section headed "Analysis of accruals and transactions with related companies" might seem at first to hold out some promise, until one reads in an explanatory note that related companies are those entities whose financial statements are consolidated with those of Aérospatiale. As these turn out to include eight companies which are fully consolidated and four consortia, including Airbus, which are consolidated on a pro-rata basis, the hope of any illumination which is to any degree specific fades rather rapidly.

Page 13 starts well. There is a table of subsidiaries and affiliates, which lists percentage shareholdings, stockholders' equity and results for the year. The questing eye travels eagerly down the columns, but is rewarded at the end only by another explanatory note: "The above list comprises only those subsidiaries and affiliates of significant importance to Aérospatiale which are included in the consolidated financial statements. The secrecy requirements imposed by the agreements between the partners preclude the disclosure of detailed informations concerning the consortiums."

None of this is to suggest any impropriety on the part of Aérospatiale. The specific accounting practices to be followed by the industry are set out in detail in the *Guide Comptable des Industries Aéronautiques et Spatiales,* and Aérospatiale's compliance with these is impeccable. *Glasnost* is no doubt a many-splendoured thing, but it is difficult to avoid the conclusion that so far as the affairs of Airbus are concerned, the general intention here is to conceal rather than to disclose.

The publications of the British partner in Airbus yield nothing to Aérospatiale's in glossiness, although they are presented in more insular fashion in only one language. Through the annual reports and accounts of British Aerospace for the years since the United Kingdom rejoined the Airbus project, there runs a clear thread of preoccupation with its financial impact on the company's affairs.

In his review of 1982, for instance, the chairman, Sir Austin Pearce, noted that by the end of the year the effect of the worldwide recession was being fully felt in the aerospace industry. Airlines were reporting serious losses and deferring or cancelling orders for aircraft. "The Board has decided it would be prudent to make an exceptional provision of £100 million to cover possible lower realisations and delayed sales that may occur for both our products and those of Airbus Industrie, including the recourse cost of sale finance packages. As a result of this, we show a loss after tax of £23.1 million."

Sir Austin reminded shareholders that the company had invested heavily in both the A300 and the A310. "Both these aircraft are excellent products, but we have to sell more in future years to ensure our income remunerates the investment already made . . . When the next Airbus model goes into production we want to maintain our 20 percent share of the workload, but to do this we need as an interim measure Government launch aid."

Two years later, Sir Austin was able to report that although pricing remained difficult, sales were showing an improvement at the larger end of the civil aircraft market. The signing by PanAm of a letter of intent involving 91 aircraft had obviously boosted morale. A comparative look at the military and civil sides of the business is eloquent of the impact of Airbus programmes on the profitability of the company, however. The turnover in military aircraft and support services during the year had been £995 million, and this had yielded a healthy trading profit of £114.3 million. For civil aircraft (which included Airbus) turnover had been £572 million, but this had resulted in a trading profit of only £7.5 million.

Relations with the government get a mention once again, and although the expression of concern is delicately coded, the words give the impression of a slight corporate frown conveying something between preoccupation and apprehension: "The UK Government is involved with us in Airbus Industrie and we trust that the Government is both flexible and adaptable enough to ensure that we, the British partner, are not disadvantaged relative to the other partners, or to the international competition."

By 1985 the frown lines are a little less pronounced. Airbus had taken orders totalling some $4 billion for 92 aircraft as against 35 the previous year. This was the highest level yet reached in one year and allowed them to claim that they had outsold Boeing by more than two to one in the world market for wide-bodied twin-jets. A more confident note is struck—the section about the consortium is headed "Partners in Airbus success." An analysis of the trading profit, however, shows that the success was distinctly relative, and that the civil side was still enjoying a piggy-back ride. Military aircraft and support services made a profit of £136.4 million out of a total of £180.1 million, civil aircraft were responsible for a loss of £4.9 million. The worry lines are still visible: "we wish to see further progress in ensuring that new orders will result in sustainable future profits."

1986 was an important date in the British Aerospace calendar because it was its first full year as a fully privatised company. Freed from what he called the restrictions of a government bureaucratic machine, Sir Austin Pearce, a man noted for his mildness, gave expression to his relief in language that bordered on the acerbic: "I know many government officials," he wrote, "and usually they are very nice people with a job to do, but they cannot be expected to be responsible or accountable for business decisions." Airbus had had an outstandingly successful year, winning 80 orders worth $3 billion, but B. E. Friend, the company's finance director, had to report yet another difficult year for civil aircraft, which had turned in a loss of £8 million at the trading level. "Competition for orders resulted in keen selling prices that are too low to produce profits and the strengthening of sterling against the U.S. dollar has had an adverse effect on margins."

Indeed, the sight of the company's preliminary results for 1986 had prompted one firm of London analysts to advise their clients to sell. At a time of strong demand for new aircraft, Airbus, in spite of having got its stock of whitetails down to three, seemed to be losing out overall to Boeing and McDonnell Douglas. Although the A310 had done better than the Boeing 767 during the year, Airbus was falling down on meeting the short-term demands of the airlines, mainly through its inability to offer the A320 for service earlier than 1988. Orders for aircraft in the 150-seat segment had increased sharply; taking 1984 and 1985 together, Airbus had captured only 8 percent of the segment, as against 32 percent for McDonnell Douglas and almost 60 percent for Boeing. Not only that, but if by 1992 the new propfan engines were to produce their widely anticipated fuel savings, the A320 would stand in some danger of being technically leap-frogged. New engines did not seem to figure in Airbus thinking till about the turn of the century.[10]

Up to 1987, anyone beachcombing his way through the reports and accounts of Aérospatiale and British Aerospace in search of financial disclosures about Airbus would have found the pickings pretty meagre. There was not in truth a great deal between them—the impression of greater openness given by the British company was largely illusory. In

September of that year, however, the British company's newly appointed chairman, Roland Smith, presented his first half-year report, and it immediately became clear that things were going to be rather different.

"What would we do without Professor Roland Smith?", wrote Lord Bruce-Gardyne, one of Mrs. Thatcher's Treasury Ministers before returning to journalism :

No decently equipped modern boardroom is complete without him . . . The taxpayers of Britain have reason to be grateful to him. For he has bravely contrived to twitch a corner of the seven veils which shield the finances of the Airbus Industrie consortium from the prying eyes of us compulsory investors . . . Gratitude is also due to BAe for the assurance that, whatever the other participants may say, it will have no truck with any future deals to give Airbuses out to prospective customers with solid gold tea-sets to tempt their jaded appetites.[11]

What had caught Lord Bruce-Gardyne's eye was a passage in the report that disclosed that in the first six months of the year, British Aerospace had set aside some £25 million in respect of present and prospective losses on the wings it was building for the A320. There was more of the same when the Annual Report and Accounts for 1987 were published a few months later.

As in the case of Aérospatiale, the course is plentifully supplied with water jumps that have names like "Consolidation," and the only free-standing figures relating specifically to Airbus are those for work in progress and participation. What leaps off the page, however, is a passage in the chairman's statement: "The implications of decisions taken in earlier years by the Company, with the support of HM Government, in the development of the Airbus consortium, are now coming through in the Company's accounts. Consequently, your Board is seeking to achieve fundamental changes in the Airbus structure *and financing arrangements*" (my italics). The words are discreet, but the tone signalled a determination on the part of the new management to distance itself from certain actions of its predecessors.

Professor Smith (later Sir Roland) was a large, bluff man who used to be a full-time professor of marketing at the University of Manchester Institute of Science and Technology. Twenty years previously he had begun to combine his academic work with a certain amount of company doctoring, and in 1980 he took over the chairmanship of the House of Fraser, the group that owned Harrods. His Lancastrian syntax and vowel sounds remained totally unsmoothed by all this boardroom exposure, and the impact of his northern directness was evident in the report.[12]

He spelled out the company's exposure to currency movements in a dollar-based industry. Much of British Aerospace's manufacturing cost was in sterling, and the time cycle for the ultimate delivery of products extended over several years. This made currency hedging especially difficult to manage and covering forward at acceptable rates very difficult

To cover anticipated trading losses on orders and assumed sales of civil aircraft, the company had decided to make an exceptional provision of £320 million, and Professor Smith disclosed that the amount included in that provision for Airbus was of the order of £180 million.

If British Aerospace and Aérospatiale appear parsimonious in making available financial data about their Airbus involvement, their accounts are positive mines of information in comparison with those of the German partner in the consortium. When the American arm of Coopers and Lybrand, the international accountancy firm, conducted a review of the public financial record of the Airbus enterprise early in 1988, they spoke of an almost complete masking of financial information so far as West German participation was concerned and expressed the view that this resulted from the way that MBB's Airbus activities were structured.[13]

Messerschmitt-Bölkow-Blohm had a fully owned subsidiary, Deutsche Airbus, which was interposed between itself and Airbus Industrie as the direct German participant in the consortium. DA, like MBB, was registered under federal German commercial law as a GmbH—a private corporation, that is to say, with limited liability.[14] Only if a GmbH is of a certain size is it obliged to publish financial statements, and MBB does. Deutsche Airbus, however, published no financial information of any sort, and its affairs were specifically excluded from the consolidated accounts of MBB.

Deutsche Airbus was not a manufacturing company. Coopers and Lybrand speculated in their report that this meant that MBB or one or more of its manufacturing subsidiaries served as the primary contractor or supplier to DA, and Hartmut Mehdorn, MBB's executive vice-president, confirmed that this was the case.[15] It followed from this that Deutsche Airbus sales were indirectly reflected in MBB's income statement. MBB's profit and loss account, however, is not broken down on the basis of particular programmes, or even on a product-line basis. This is in marked contrast to American accounting practice. The annual reports of both McDonnell Douglas and Boeing, for instance, provide a great deal of information on a product-line basis, and details of profit and loss on commercial aircraft are separated out from information on other business activities.

Because Deutsche Airbus's activities did not figure in MBB's consolidated accounts, there was no means of knowing anything about the results of its participation in the consortium. Nor did the MBB accounts show the results of its investment in DA. The only mention of DA in MBB's 1986 Annual Report, for instance, is an item headed "German Companies not included in the Consolidated Financial Statement," and this refers to an investment of DM 150 million in DA, a figure that was increased to DM 450 million the following year. It is reasonable to suppose, however, that MBB had to cover any losses not taken care of by the German government directly, and this would explain the substantial sum set aside over the years for risks and losses in its balance sheet—a figure of DM 2.6 billion as of December 31,1986. No indication was given of how much of this sum related to Airbus, but Hartmut Mehdorn said that this would account for almost all of it, apart from perhaps 15 percent relating to the helicopter side of the business.[15]

Coopers and Lybrand formed the view that there was some mechanism by which German government support was channelled directly to Deutsche Airbus. Although a totally owned subsidiary, however, its accounts were not consolidated in those of the parent company, and this means in effect that it acted as a screen between MBB and the consortium. Their conclusion was that Deutsche Airbus constituted "a fully obscured 'black box' which allowed MBB and the German government to deal with Airbus financially as they see fit."[13]

The Spanish participation in Airbus is not of enormous significance, CASA having a holding of only 4.2 percent. Slightly ironically, perhaps, an entry in the accounts of much the most junior partner offers almost more illumination than the statements of the other three combined. CASA's annual report for 1985 showed that the company's share of Airbus Industrie losses for the preceding year amounted to $16.8 million dollars. As Spanish participation in the enterprise is 4.2 percent, it takes only modest mathematical ability to calculate that Airbus Industrie's total loss in that year was of the order of $400 million, and that, on the basis of the 48 planes delivered during the year, translates into a loss of $8.3 million on each aircraft.

Coopers and Lybrand's concluded that there was insufficient information to piece together even a partial picture of Airbus enterprise performance. The financial statements of a public company would normally give enough information to permit an analyst to form a view about the company's performance, even if they did not provide specific detail on, say, a particular aircraft series. Details of sales revenue and operating profit by product line, for example, such as the major American manufacturers provide, offer an indication of whether variation in profitability is due to changes in the volume of sales or in the margin of profit. So far as Airbus is concerned, details concerning such matters as sales, the cost of inputs, depreciation and provisions, interest charges and extraordinary items are all effectively concealed from public scrutiny.

The existence and scale of government support would also normally find a reflection in a company's financial statements. Loans or advances and infusions of equity would appear on the balance sheet, and operating grants and other forms of continuing funding would appear in the income statement. While the accounts of a GIE must be submitted to external audit, there is no obligation to publish them or disclose them to third parties, and Airbus accordingly—and understandably—does not do so. A picture of the extent and nature of government aid is therefore mainly to be pieced together by sifting through government budget reports and by trying to evaluate the flood of news releases and articles in the press. There is more than one standard of reliability; such information as there is is often fragmentary, and disinformation is not always to be excluded.

French government support comes in the form of advances that are repayable out of the proceeds of sales. These reimbursable advances are regarded as the norm. Responding, for instance, to a 1985 report on Aérospatiale by the Cour des Comptes, the highest level of audit of public finances in France, the secretary of state in the ministry responsible for transport declared that the company could not by itself be expected to assume the considerable risks associated with the launch of new programmes. "The Company must continue to receive State aid. In civil aviation, that takes the form of reimbursable advances."[16]

The minister of finance, in his response, made it clear that he saw no distinction between such advances and infusions of equity capital, although there was an indication that he did not regard these arrangements as set in concrete for all time: "It should not be abnormal for part of the cost of development to be assumed by the industrialist" (Aérospatiale, that is to say). Indeed, he said, it was a major goal, though a distant one, that the company should be able to generate sufficient profit to finance the development of its products from its own resources.[16]

He was clearly taking a fairly long view. During the fiscal year 1987, the government accorded the company new capital funding of FF 1.25 billion, the first half of a contribution that would increase the shareholders' equity substantially. (At the end of 1986, it had stood at FF 3.14 billion.) This new injection was not associated with any particular programme and was in addition to the programme-specific reimbursable advances. Paid in during the first weeks of 1988, it was used to improve the working capital position and reduce the debt level.[17] The matter was not tested, but in the light of their countervailing duty legislation, the United States were inclined to view this as a subsidy.

Figures given in the French Finance Bill for 1988 showed that cumulative state disbursements to Aérospatiale up to the end of 1987 totalled FF 10.76 billion. Of this FF 686 million had gone to the ATR 42 regional transport programme and FF 402 million on four helicopter programmes. The remainder—FF 9.67 billion—had gone to Airbus: FF 6.2 billion for the A300 and A310, FF 3.3 billion for the A320 and FF 105 million for the A330/340.

The standard formula for these advances has been that repayment is related to the number of aircraft sold. Interest is payable at a rate equivalent only to inflation. In effect, therefore, much of the commercial risk attaching to the transaction is transferred to the government. So far as the A330/340 is concerned, the terms for the repayment of the principal are that payments, at present value, will be spread in direct relationship to sales of the first 600 planes. The state will also receive 1.5 percent of sales, but this will be paid only after the principal has been repaid in full. If the programme is a commercial failure, the 1.5 percent will not be payable, which suggests that in those circumstances repayment of the principal would also be waived.[18] When the 600 sales level will be reached is anybody's guess. There are optimists who believe it could be before the end of this century.

It is not known whether Aérospatiale has ever paid a dividend to the government. The cumulative balance owed to the state by Aérospatiale at the end of 1986 amounted to some FF 7.7 billion, which was equivalent to 45 percent of the company's total funding and 54 percent of its borrowing. In recent years, repayments have averaged rather less than FF 300 million a year. At that rate, and leaving aside any new advances, the balance outstanding would take 26 years to repay. Notes to the company's accounts indicate, however, that a faster rate is envisaged, and this would mean a repayment schedule extending over 16 years.

In the summer of 1986, evidence emerged that the French government would not protest too much if volunteers stepped forward to share the honour of replenishing the Airbus coffers. When the A320 project had been launched in 1984, they had agreed to find three-quarters of Aérospatiale's share of the development costs, but subsequently the French Treasury asked Aérospatiale and Banque Paribas to put their heads together. After a year of discussions they came up with a scheme under which a syndicate of twelve French banks (most of them nationalised) would lend Aérospatiale 380 million francs. So long as no deliveries were made, the company would not pay interest, although it would be added to the capital. Each time a delivery was made, a fixed sum would be levied on the selling price, and this would go to the banks to repay the accumulated interest and, eventually, the capital.

Repayment would begin in the second quarter of 1988. If the 120 or so orders in the Airbus book at the time of the deal were met on time, the loan would be repaid in full three years later. If there were delays to the A320 programme, the term of the loan would be extended, although the banks agreed—most unusually—that no interest would be payable after June 30, 1993. A despatch from the U.S. embassy in Paris described the transaction as an example of French government "off-budget financing." Jean Picq, Aérospatiale's director of finance, was understandably pleased. "This initiative sets a happy precedent," he said cheerfully. Bankers are discreet men, and whether they thought Picq had found altogether the *mot juste* did not become known. They had done their duty, though—to France, if not to their shareholders.

One or two voices have been heard in the French National Assembly in recent years urging that the financing requirements of Aérospatiale should be subject to more-orthodox commercial disciplines.[18] They can hardly yet be said to constitute a tide of opinion, but it is worthy of note that whereas the government originally agreed to meet 75 percent of the development costs of the A320, its contribution to the A330/340 programme has been fixed at 60 percent of the projected costs. The 1988 figures for repayable advances were FF 658 million for the A320 and FF 368 million for the A330/340. In 1989 and beyond, payments for the A320 were due to dip down to FF 154 million, although that takes no account of the possibility of a second production line or a stretched version of the aircraft. The amount so far committed for the same period to the A330/340 stands at FF 4.38 billion.

When the United Kingdom rejoined the consortium in the late 1970s the price exacted was an "admission fee" of £50 million and an additional £25 million in respect of work-in-progress. Reports of how much of this was found by the government vary from £70 million to £25 million.[19]

For the A320 programme, the British government provided a loan for launch aid of £250 million. This was to cover all nonrecurring costs for the period 1984–88. British Aerospace had to repay £50 million of this between 1990 and 1992, and pay a levy on sales aimed at recovering the amount advanced in launch aid and giving the government a return on its investment. No details of the levy payments have been made public, although it is believed to be on an escalating scale over time, as was the case with earlier programmes. The launch aid is not carried on the liability side of BAe's balance sheet as a loan from the British government, but is incorporated on the asset side as a reduction to inventories. The company was expected to provide £200 million from its own resources for initial wing production costs.[20]

So far as the A330/340 programme was concerned, the government contributed launch aid to the tune of £450 million, well short of the £750 million that the company requested. As with the A320 programme, the launch aid was "front-end loaded" and was expected to cover BAe's cash flow requirements until 1990.[20] In contrast to the A320 programme, there was no requirement for a fixed repayment, which is to say that reimbursement is contingent on sales. A note accompanying the 1990 accounts disclosed that the sums that the government had agreed to provide to the group in launch aid for Airbus projects totalled £700 million, of which £50 million was repayable by 1992.

Asked to say where the main thrust of support for Airbus came from in Europe, most Americans would identify the French as the villains of the piece. In many ways, and certainly politically, they would be right; indeed the French would be offended if it were not thought to be so. When it comes to the extent of financial support, however, they must cede first place to their neighbours across the Rhine. Every schoolboy knows that the former Federal Republic was the European exemplar of free-market economics and that ideas about hand-outs of public money were anathema—and every schoolboy has been misinformed.

By the standards prevailing in the rest of Western Europe, the Bonn government subsidises industry generally on a scale that is quite staggering. In 1986, for instance, agriculture received DM 21 billion, the mining industry DM 8 billion, the railways DM 3.3 billion. This might make aerospace, with a mere DM 0.5 billion, seem like the runt of the litter that had found it difficult to get near the trough at all. The fact is, however, that the amounts of public money made available to the Airbus partners in France and the United Kingdom pale into insignificance when compared with the sums handed out by the West German government to MBB.

Known government support in Germany has taken the form of loans and loan guarantees to Deutsche Airbus, unkindly described by *The Economist* as "a company with a messy coexistence between brilliant but difficult ideas men and stuffy officials bent on getting their next chunk of government aid."[21] The stuffy officials seem to have done pretty well. In late 1987, MBB itself put the total amount that the government had shelled out at DM 10.8 billion,[22] a figure remarkably close to the DM 11.1 billion that Coopers and Lybrand were to come up with a few months later.[13] In the MBB account, DM 6.8 billion was described as being for reimbursable development costs, and the same publication put their requirements between then and 1991 at a further DM 6.7 billion.

If the German government's contribution to keeping Airbus afloat has been greater than that of either France or the United Kingdom, it is also a contribution about which it is much more difficult to piece together precise information. The accounts of Deutsche Airbus are not published and they are not consolidated in the financial statements of the parent company, and no amount of scrabbling through government budget data and the specialist press can yield a complete picture.[23]

What can be said with reasonable certainty is that by the end of 1986, Deutsche Airbus had got through DM 2.7 billion of the DM 3.1 billion made available to it in government loan guarantees. These were originally scheduled to be repaid from the proceeds of sales by 1994. The government also provided a direct loan of DM 2.4 billion to support research and development. That represented 90 percent of the total development costs of the A300/310, and was reported to cover "everything except a production line."[24] This amount was originally thought to be sufficient to cover almost all of MBB's negative cash flows during the development period and the first several years of production. The loan was to be be repaid from DA profits, but could be cancelled by the government.

Then in June 1987, the government agreed that between 1988 and 1994 it would provide DM 1.9 billion to retire its original guarantees. According to the 1988 Annual Report on Economic Development in the Federal Republic, this was to be repaid "subject to sales."[25] It was widely regarded as a wiping of the slate to attract investors to Deutsche Airbus.

So far as the A320 is concerned, the government agreed to meet 90 percent of the development costs with repayable loans totalling DM 1.5 billion ($580 million). These were to be repaid at the rate of $1 million per plane for the first 600 sold. If fewer than that number were sold, the full amount of the loan would not be repaid. This followed the pattern of the A300/310. It was reported in July 1983 that similar payments on loans for that programme had been suspended because of insufficient financial returns from sales. It was also believed in Washington that the German government had said it was willing to provide assistance in financing serial production.[26]

For the A330/340 programme, repayable development grants totalling DM 3 billion are being provided between 1988 and 1996.This represents 90 percent of the anticipated development cost. Details of repayment terms have not been made public, but if past experience is anything to go on, it seems reasonable to suppose that some will be repaid from the proceeds of sales and that the remainder will then be cancelled by the government.

Specific programmes apart, a report in 1987 in one of the best-informed of the aerospace magazines said that between 1975 and 1982 the West German government had also provided Deutsche Airbus with DM 682 million in nonrepayable production subsidies, and that an additional DM 440 million had been made available to subsidise loans to prospective Airbus buyers.[27] There was no indication, as this book went to press, that the absorption of MBB by Daimler-Benz described in a later chapter had resulted in any increase in financial transparency.

Information on the operations of CASA, the Spanish member of the consortium, is also extremely difficult to come by, although as was mentioned earlier, the company's financial statements have occasionally thrown more light on its participation in Airbus than was perhaps intended. The 1985 accounts, for example, show an extraordinary cost item which reads, "Redemption of Airbus losses, financial year 1984—Pts 2,851 million." This is offset by an equivalent income item: "Contribution from Spanish government for redemption of Airbus Industrie losses, year 1984." Again, under the entry "Other debtors—public entities," the 1985 Balance Sheet shows a receivable of Pta. 8.9 billion, and a footnote reads "The losses of AI are guaranteed by the Spanish State, through I.N.I." In a second item, "Debtors—customers—Airbus Industrie c/c" the Balance Sheet shows balances of Pts 567.8 million and Pts 3,320.9 million respectively for 1985 and 1986. It was by translating these items into dollars and extrapolating on the basis of CASA's 4.2 percent share in the consortium that Coopers and Lybrand made the calculations referred to earlier in this chapter about how much Airbus Industrie as a whole had lost in that year.

Whether this degree of disclosure was intentional is not known. At all events, the cat was bundled quickly back into the bag. No such exercise in transparency has found a place in the accounts for any year since then.

NOTES

1. Quoted by Lee Benson, *The Concept of Jacksonian Democracy*(Princeton: Princeton University Press,1961).

2. Andrew Shonfield, *Modern Capitalism: The Changing Balance of Public and Private Power* (Oxford: Oxford University Press, 1965).

3. Kenneth D. Walters and R. Joseph Monsen, "The Nationalised Firm: The Politicians' Free Lunch?" *The Columbia Journal of World Business*(Spring 1977).

4. *Oversight of the Antidumping Act of 1921.* Hearings before the Subcommittee on Trade of the Committee on Ways and Means, U.S. House of Representatives, Ninety-fifth Congress, November 8, 1977.

5. Kenneth D. Walters and R. Joseph Monsen, "State-owned business abroad: new competitive threat." *Harvard Business Review*(March-April 1979).

6. Olivier Giscard d'Estaing, *Le Social-Capitalisme*(Paris: Fayard, 1977).

7. International Air Transport Association Public Relations Conference, Barcelona, June 15–16, 1987.

8. *Financial Times,* November 12, 1987.

9. *The Economist,* January 30, 1988.

10. Capel-Cure Myers, *Engineering Research bulletin to clients,* April 22, 1986.

11. *The Sunday Telegraph,* September 13, 1987.

12. The professor was not particularly popular with his colleagues, but his authority was to remain unchallenged until 1991, when a boardroom battle forced him out.

13. *The Airbus Enterprise: A Review of the Public Record,* March 1988.

14. Gesellschaft mit beschränkte Haftung.

15. Interview in Hamburg, July 5, 1988.

16. Cour des Comptes: *Rapport au Président de la République suivi des réponses des administrations,* 1985, Chapter 2, SSI; *réponse du Sécretaire d'Etat,* section III; *réponse du Ministre de l'economie, des Finances et du Budget,* paragraphs 3 and 7.

17. Aérospatiale *Annual Report,* 1987.

18. *Rapport, loi des finances, 1988,* annexe no. 23.

19. Keith Hayward, *International Collaboration in Civil Aerospace* (London: Francis Pinter, 1986).

20. *Flight International,* May 5, 1984.

21. *The Economist,* November 21, 1987.

22. *Flugzeugbau ohne Staat?*MBB, Hamburg, 1987.

23. MBB itself, however, did announce in the summer of 1987 that cumulative DA losses exceeded DM 2 billion, including DM 400 in 1986. *Süddeutsche Zeitung,* July 22, 1987.

24. *Flight,* May 5, 1984.

25.*Jahresgutachten 1987/88 des Sachverständigenrates zur Begutachtung der gesamtwirtschaftlichen Entwicklung,* para. 415, November 24, 1987.

26. U.S. Department of Commerce document dated February 27, 1984.

27. *Aviation Week & Space Technology,* February 9, 1987.

8

The Kettle and
the Earthen Pot

"Blunderbuss. A short gun with a large bore, firing many balls or slugs, and capable of doing execution within a limited range without exact aim. (Now superseded, in civilized countries, by other fire-arms.)"

—*Oxford English Dictionary.*

It is necessary to pause over the countercharges that Airbus level at their American competitors and at the U.S. administration. A document that they published in March 1988 was, they claim, the result of two years work by a firm of economists in Boston, lawyers in Washington, Wall Street analysts and a country-wide network of aviation consultants.[1]

It certainly reads like the work of many hands, but the considerable mass of material thrown up in the course of their researches has not been ordered with any degree of rigour. Nor does the methodology of the document inspire a great deal of confidence. The executive summary distinguishes between direct and indirect support, but the introductory chapter concludes by indicating that the distinction will not be observed in the discussion that is to follow—"In simple terms," it says cheerfully, "whether direct or indirect, it's all money." Airbus have shown some sophistication over the years in their choice of weapons; why they should decide in the spring of 1988 to fall back on the blunderbuss was not altogether clear.

The main thrust of the Airbus argument is that the civil aircraft industry in the United States is only part of the larger domestic aerospace industry, and that the linkage that they posit with the manufacture and sale of military aircraft has been vital to the wellbeing of the industry as a whole, the relative stability of military revenues helping to cushion the manufacturers against the cyclical nature of the business on the civil side.

In a way, this is to do little more than state the obvious. Defence business manifestly benefits all commercial aircraft manufacturers whether they are

American or European. When they touch on the cyclical nature of the business, however, Airbus are playing with a boomerang. Boeing, for instance, readily concede that the diversified nature of their operation makes it possible for employees to transfer between commercial aircraft and other operating companies. But they also point out that their employment figures have always been closely tied to the general economic conditions of the day. The severity of the recession in the late 1960s and early 1970s compelled them to lay off a large proportion of their workforce. This is quite unlike the situation of the Airbus partners, where access to public funds and a very different labour philosophy allow them to maintain employment at stable levels, regardless of the current demand for aircraft. American manufacturers have never enjoyed the luxury of being able to produce aircraft "for inventory."

The Airbus document begins with the assertion that in the period 1978–88, the U.S. government provided sums of the order of $23 billion in what are described as "direct and indirect financial support of a subsidy nature" to Boeing and McDonnell Douglas. The significance of that figure, they argue, is that in the same period, Boeing's net earnings totalled $4.6 billion and McDonnell Douglas's $2.4 billion. The conclusion drawn is that without federal aid neither company would have shown a profit, and both might well have gone under.[2]

Airbus claim that just over 45 percent of their $23 billion figure— $10.49 billion—is accounted for by R&D awards from the U.S. Department of Defense for aircraft and electronics and communications equipment, and that another 20 percent goes on what they describe as DOD profit subsidies. They acknowledge in a footnote that this second figure is an estimate, arrived at by taking 5 percent of the total turnover of the department for the period in question.

That the U.S. government pays contractors for specific goods and services purchased to meet its military requirements is not in dispute. Contracts to McDonnell Douglas and Boeing in the years covered by the Airbus review included the development of the AV-8 Harrier, electronic countermeasures and ammunition feed systems for the F-15 fighter and AWACS communications equipment for the E-3A, which is a Boeing 707 modified for military missions. It is not easy to see what impact any of these might have on commercial aircraft programmes. The Airbus document quotes from a 1985 Report of the National Research Council that says that "historically, civil aeronautics development was triggered by military advancements." It neglects to add, however, that the report also says: "In more recent years, a reverse situation has become common, with the results of civil research or component design subsequently being used for military purposes."[3]

The Airbus figure for what they call profit subsidies seems open to objection on two scores. They quote the contention of an industrial analyst that high profits and federal research support in the development and sale of military aircraft "have comprised an important government subsidy to the development and manufacture of new commercial designs,"[4] but do not offer the reader the means of forming an independent judgement on the matter. This could have been done by providing some details of aerospace company profits. These are published annually by the Aerospace Industries Association, and show that over the past two decades they have averaged 3.57 percent of sales and 4.2 percent of assets, figures substantially below those for American manufacturing industry as a whole.

There is a more fundamental objection, however, which is that the contract price figures that Airbus list in their table include both cost *and profit;* by then including a separate line for profit *from the same contracts,* they are in fact counting the profit twice, which makes nonsense of their own arithmetic and the case it supports. It must also surely have been known to those who assisted Airbus in their research that the Department of Defense has stringent procurement regulations aimed at preventing artificially high profit margins.

Airbus seem further to overlook the fact that Defense Department procedures require a strict separation between cost allocation and accounting on the military and commercial sides, a requirement scrutinised with some rigour by the U.S. government audit authorities. As these worthies additionally have Congress breathing down their necks, the scope for misdemeanour is not large. If violations do occur, there are both administrative and criminal sanctions to hand.

Cases in which the companies are able to apply government funded technology to commercial products are few and far between. Where they do arise, the department recoups the cost on a *pro rata* basis. This recoupment procedure, which has been in operation since the late 1960s, currently recovers approximately $300 million a year. DOD officials point out, a shade acerbically, that this figure would have been higher if recovery had not been waived in cases where military equipment was purchased by NATO allies, some of whom are partners in the Airbus consortium . . .

The smallest item in the Airbus catalogue of subsidy funding was in some ways the one that caused most indignation in the United States—a figure for $600 million under the U.S. government's Independent Research and Development Program. This is a Program that allows the DOD access to technical research and development that is being financed by the commercial companies. The companies meet the cost of their R&D work, and the government recognises only the militarily relevant part of that cost as an allowable overhead charge. Airbus again concede that they are offering an estimate, but enter a figure of $440 million for Boeing and $160 million for McDonnell Douglas.

Airbus had found its ammunition in a dissertation written at the Massachussets Institute of Technology:

This undirected R&D is considered to be a part of each contractor's legitimate overhead . . . IR&D covers company-directed research and development not required in support of a specific product or contract; it is treated as overhead on production contracts by DoD. The program is controversial since it represents government-funded R&D that is conducted outside of the normal R&D review and approval system.[5]

The policies and procedures relating to the IR&D Program are, in fact, published in the U.S. government procurement regulations.The administration concedes that the specific subject matter of some projects may be protected for reasons of national security or to safeguard legitimate proprietary requirements, but insists that the manner in which the program operates is open to public scrutiny. The Department of Defense rejected what Airbus has to say about Independent Research and Development as a misrepresentation: "It is actually a device to limit payments to contractors for their independent defense-related research. DOD currently reimburses contractors for only about half of such R&D costs."[6]

Airbus further argue that the use of government-owned production facilities and equipment, often free of charge, keep down the costs of the American manufacturers. "As far as is known," the report says, "no remuneration is made to DOD for the free lending facilities it provides, albeit directly, under DOD contracts awarded." Again, the Airbus researchers' desire to know does not appear to have been especially ardent. McDonnell Douglas pointed out that more than 99.9 percent of the facilities of their commercial company, Douglas, are either privately owned or commercially leased. Boeing, whose backroom boys plainly relish this sort of challenge, came up with an even more mind-blowing statistic. Their operations in the United States occupy more than 45 million square feet of property. Of this, three-tenths of one per cent is government owned, and the facilities that make up this fraction are at remote sites that have been used exclusively for government military contract work.

In this part of their case as elsewhere, Airbus appear to have been slipshod in the selection and use of their supporting evidence. One of the books they cite, for instance, is *Aircraft Industry Dynamics: An Analysis of Competition, Capital and Labor,* by Jordan Bluestone and others. It was published in 1981. The data it marshals to support the contention that the U.S. industry utilises government facilities free of charge was assembled in 1968 and refers to events that took place in the 1950s and 1960s. The book acknowledges, what's more, that the practice of allowing industry to use government facilities came to an end in 1957. In fact the facilities referred to had been standing idle, and their use by contractors represented an economy by the government, which got off with lower capital costs than it would have done if the military hardware in question had been produced in commercially owned premises.

The passages in the Airbus Report that dwell on the adaptation of World

War II and postwar military technology to American jetliners touched a particularly raw nerve in the United States. There is a tart line in the Boeing response that observes that the advances in technology made in those years were intended to defend not only America but Europe and other areas of the world "first against Axis aggression and subsequently the threat of Soviet expansion—not to finance the development of DC-8s or 707s."[7] And there is a telling passage from an article by Dr. Malcolm Currie, the former U.S. under secretary of defense for research and engineering:

An effective modern system of defense could not exist without such vital assets as aircraft, jet engines, radars, lasers, semiconductors, and microcircuits. Yet none of these technologies originated as a military requirement or specification . . . The original ideas were conceived and the initial explorations carried out largely independent of specific military input, by industrial and academic researchers, as projects for the advancement of science or as initiatives designed to secure competitive advantage through innovation.[8]

Airbus's free-wheeling way with source material is again apparent when the report attempts to demonstrate that the military business of the members of the consortium amount to only one-fifth of that of Boeing and McDonnell Douglas. It does this, however, by comparing only the *domestic* sales of military aircraft. When exports are taken into account, a dramatically different picture emerges. Aérospatiale, for instance, exports almost 70 percent of its missile sales; over 70 percent of MBB's sales are in military products; British Aerospace exports 90 percent of its military and civil aircraft, and its military aircraft programmes are half as big again as its civil programmes. Boeing calculate that between 1980 and 1985, on an apples-for-apples basis, Airbus consortium military sales were 20 percent higher than those of McDonnell Douglas and twice as great as their own.[7]

Elsewhere in the Airbus document, the argument being pursued is buttressed by the assertion that between 1977 and 1985, Boeing and McDonnell Douglas were both in the first five of the list of Department of Defense contractors. This is not untrue. It would have rounded the truth out a little, however, to have added that in the fiscal year 1987, Boeing had dropped to ninth position. The figures were available several weeks before the Airbus publication appeared.[9] Their omission does not seem to be attributable to sloppiness, because they are employed (though for a different purpose) elsewhere in the document.

Boeing, as it happens, received rather less than half the amount that went to McDonnell Douglas in defence contracts in that year, with Lockheed, General Motors (the parent company of Hughes Aircraft) and General Electric all getting more. The commercial arm of the company is not, in fact, a major government contractor, and recovers directly only a small part of its overheads through government contracts. Research and Development expenditure concerned with the development of a commercial aircraft is not allowable as an overhead charge under government contracts. Boeing point out, rather drily, that the law is specific, and the government auditors alert. A manufacturer who was found to be charging the government with overheads not related to contract work would be liable to criminal proceedings.

Airbus represents the most critical objective of federal funding as the maintenance of the dominant position enjoyed in world markets by the American manufacturers. Their research team has burrowed deep into the archives in search of chapter and verse. The National Aeronautics and Space Act of 1958, which was the legislation that established NASA, yielded a line about the preservation of the role of the United States as a leader in aeronautical and space science, and NASA's Annual Report for 1986 was found to contain an incriminating sentence about the aggressive pursuit of technological opportunities. A quotation is by definition something presented out of context, but in the crowded pages of this document it is almost impossible to form a view about what force these snippets lend to the argument that is being advanced. The trees crowd relentlessly in, and the wood is not easy to see.

Compared with the major role they allocate to the Department of Defense in their account of U.S. government funding for civil aircraft programmes, Airbus give NASA a relatively modest walking-on part— $2.6 billion to McDonnell Douglas and Boeing over ten years, or about a quarter of the DOD figure. Even so, NASA described this as a gross misrepresentation.[6] It could be that Airbus misread the relevant statistics. They show NASA's expenditure over ten years on aerospace products as $58.9 billion, but NASA say that such a figure can be arrived at only by including awards made for major space system development. Their total *aeronautics* budget for the period in question was in reality less than $3 billion, and the true figure for their aeronautics contracts to Boeing and McDonnell Douglas was only $148 million—a sum, that is to say, eighteen times less than the one quoted by Airbus.

The Americans also took issue with Airbus over their assertion that some NASA-funded technology is not released outside the U.S. for two years, thus depriving foreign manufacturers of equal access. There had certainly at one time been a feeling in the United States that the dissemination of technology was a one-way street in Europe's favour, and a two-year restriction had been adopted by NASA in an attempt to obtain reciprocal treatment from European governments. In the event, it had rarely been used—the restriction had been applied to less than one-fiftieth of one percent of all NASA-controlled documents. Indeed, in a number of cases, (a point that some Americans are relaxed enough to enjoy making) NASA-funded research results had been used by Airbus before they had been taken up by the U.S. industry—research on digital cockpit systems, laminar flow control and E-3 engine technology had all, for instance, found an application in the Airbus A320.

There was one assertion in the Airbus Report that was the cause of some hilarity in the United States, and that was that the National Aerospace Plane Program (NASP) was a civil aircraft project. NASP is officially described by NASA as a technology development program. The object of the exercise had been described several years previously by Stanley A. Tremaine of the U.S. Air Force Systems Command. It was, he said, to build a military flying machine that would be able to "insert itself into the upper reaches of the atmosphere and the lower regions of space and go around the planet in 90 minutes. We're not looking for a cargo machine. We're looking for a killer Air Force weapon system that can go out and get the enemy."[10] The technology for a flight research vehicle designed to attain hypersonic speeds of about 25 times the speed of sound clearly does not have much application to commercial transports, which is why some 80 percent of the funding for it is being found by various Department of Defense agencies. Airbus was felt to have made rather a fool of itself.[11]

The American manufacturers, then, rejected the suggestion that the Departments of Defense and NASA subsidize their commercial development. The amounts recovered from the Defense Department for costs incurred in company-funded R&D programmes are small—in the case of Boeing, something of the order of 3 percent of their total commercial R&D costs over the past ten or twelve years. The U.S. companies also denied another Airbus charge, which is that that they have access to Department of Transportation funds for the design and development of commercial aircraft. It is the case that the Department's Federal Aviation Administration runs programmes in air traffic control and safety, but these benefit airlines and manufacturers generally, both American and foreign.

Airbus make much of the benefits that they say accrue to American aircraft manufacturers from the provisions of the U.S. tax code. Since 1971, U.S. companies had been able to take advantage of the so-called DISC system (Domestic International Sales Corporation). This had been introduced as a counter to the favourable tax treatment of exports by countries that taxed companies only on income earned in the domestic market: a waiver of value added tax (VAT) on exported items gave foreign exporters a substantial advantage over American firms. There were complaints that DISC violated the General Agreement on Tariffs and Trade. The U.S. administration insisted that it was entitled to place its exporters on an equal footing with their foreign competitors, but replaced DISC in 1984 by a Foreign Sales Corporation Law (FSC) shorn of the provisions that had been held to be objectionable in DISC. This brought American arrangements into line with the provisions in place in most European countries.

Airbus also allege in their report that various other allowable deductions, credits and tax schemes enable the U.S. industry to minimize or even completely avoid tax liability. They make particular play with what is known as the completed contract method of accounting (CCMA), by which taxes on long-term transactions become payable only on completion of the contract. With aircraft sales contracts extending up to ten years, this is plainly a highly attractive proposition, even though tax law changes in 1986 and 1987 substantially reduced the amounts that might be deferred. Airbus quote figures to demonstrate that over a five-year period up to 1986, McDonnell Douglas and Boeing took advantage of this method to obtain tax benefits of more than $1 billion. The source of the figures, however, is Boeing and McDonnell Douglas's own annual reports. The unremarkable fact of the matter is that these provisions are available to all American companies, regardless of what they produce or supply—the question of special benefits to aircraft manufacturers simply does not arise.

Yet again, in this section of the report, Airbus damages their case by getting their sums badly wrong. They quote a publication by a stockbroker as authority for claiming that Boeing had received $2.61 billion in ITC and CCMA tax subsidies.[12] They appear to have arrived at this by extracting figures from Shearson Lehman and combining the deferred tax liability at the end of 1985 with the projected tax liability at the end of 1988—which resulted in a doubling of the actual amount.

Like CCMA, investment tax credits and depreciation deductions are available to all U.S. companies and apply to assets regardless of where they were manufactured.[13] A U.S. domestic airline therefore enjoys no advantage by buying American. Eastern Airlines and PanAm both derived benefit from the prevailing U.S. investment tax provisions when they decided to buy and lease from Airbus.

The Airbus Report concludes its section on the tax benefits available to its American competitors with the bold assertion that apart from the normal deductions for R&D expenses, there were no equivalent tax benefits in any of the Airbus Industrie partner countries. That was a claim that invited some scrutiny, and it was Airbus's bad luck that it received just that from the United States arm of Coopers and Lybrand, the international firm of chartered accountants.[14]

Tax devices designed to stimulate the domestic economy are a common feature of most of the western industrialized democracies, and the American view that the range of assistance on offer in western Europe is if anything more extensive and more generous than that provided in the United States received powerful confirmation from the Coopers and Lybrand study:

European countries have a tradition of fine-tuning their national and regional economies by offering businesses both tax and non-tax incentives to stimulate particular sectors of industry or commerce, to promote exports, to reduce unemployment and to improve the economies of depressed regions. France, Germany and the United Kingdom, the major participants in the Airbus enterprise, each have extensive lists of advantages which businesses may claim for themselves if, for example, they install a manufacturing plant in a depressed former coal mining area; . . . or if they expand their R&D effort; or if an envisaged investment will create new jobs. All three countries also offer their exporters considerable help in the form of credit insurance and in the financing of export related investments and cash flow needs—generally at advantageous or subsidised rates of interest.

Coopers itemised a range of specific tax and other incentives available in each of the three countries. France offered accelerated depreciation for investment in fixed assets and R&D—up to 50 percent in the first year; deferral of tax for investments in foreign subsidiaries; exemption from business tax for investments in depressed areas. Other carrots included grants for job creation, low-interest loans from regional and municipal authorities for investment in industrial buildings and tax holidays for investment in certain Free Enterprise Zones.

In West Germany, accelerated depreciation of up to 40 percent was allowed for movable assets and of 15 percent on R&D-related buildings. Capital investment incentives took the form of a cash grant of 8.7 percent of the cost of capital goods purchased for the purpose of setting up or expanding manufacturing operations. In the United Kingdom, generous capital (i.e., depreciation) allowances were available—an initial 75 percent for buildings in general, but 100 percent if they were located in certain enterprise zones or were used for scientific research. Businesses within designated Enterprise Zones qualified for property tax exemptions. Nontax incentives included regional cash grants of up to 22 percent of the cost of certain building costs.

Forms of assistance for exporters were broadly similar in all three countries, and especially generous in France. Exchange rate guarantees were available, offering 100 percent insurance against the risk of fluctuation in non-European currencies and of fluctuations in excess of 2.25 percent in European currencies. Credit insurance covered 80–90 percent of export receivables and protected manufacturers against losses from sudden interruption or cancellation of contracts. Prospecting and exhibition insurance was also available.

The Airbus Report has all the apparatus of scholarly research—the 33 pages of text are embellished with tables, graphs and 112 footnote references. More than 30 of these are drawn from one source—a doctoral dissertation by an MIT postgraduate student entitled *Federal Investment in Aeronautical R&D: Analyzing the NASA Experience.*[5] The author, John S.Langford, has read the report, and was not exactly flattered at the use to which his efforts had been put:

References to my thesis are made with the allegation that I conclude that each step of the R&D process is a "subsidy." This is grossly misleading. The thesis does not conclude that these are subsidies . . . I do not endorse either the methodology or the conclusions of the

Airbus Report, and I feel that it misrepresents my own work . . . [15]

The report was not greatly admired in Europe, either. Mogens Peter Carl, the senior European Community official who led the EEC team in many of the negotiations with the United States, was diplomatic about it— "Airbus are under the impression that their study of indirect support provides them with an extraordinary amount of protection against the U.S. activity in this area—I don't want to comment on that."[16] Paul Lawrance, on the other hand, the most senior official in the British Department of Trade and Industry with day-to-day responsibility for Airbus issues, was less delicate, and characterised it as "meaningless."[17]

It no doubt seemed a good idea at the time. Its authors say rather plaintively that some of the material they wished to lay their hands on was not recorded in searchable data bases, and that they had to sift hundreds of records by hand. Whatever the reasons, it has to be said that the result reads more like the jottings of an idiot savant than a serious piece of research.

Most damaging of all was the suspicion that those clever chaps in Toulouse had been reading Sir Philip Sidney's *Arcadia* and come across his description of the cuttlefish: "The fish called sepia, which being in the net, castes a blacke inke about itselfe, that in the darkenesse thereof it may scape."

NOTES

1. *Government Funding of Boeing and McDonnell Douglas Civil Aircraft Programs,* March 14, 1988.

2. Airbus soon decided that their $23 billion figure was too conservative. When I spoke to Colm Mannin, Airbus Industrie's senior counsel, in Toulouse, in June 1988, he told me it shold be just over $33 billion.

3. Frederick Seitz, *The Competitive Status of the U.S. Civil Aviation Manufacturing Industry* (Washington: National Academy Press, 1985).

4. R. R. Nelson, *Government and Technical Progress: A Cross-Industry Analysis* (New York: Pergamon Press, 1982).

5. John S. Langford, *Federal Investment in Aeronautical R&D: Analyzing the NASA Experience* (Cambridge, Mass.: MIT Press, 1987).

6. *U.S. Government Interagency Background Fact Sheet,* (Washington: April 7, 1988).

7. *An Assessment of the Airbus Industry Report, Allegations of U.S. Government Subsidies to Boeing and McDonnell Douglas* (Seattle: Boeing Commercial Airplanes, October 1988).

8. *Armed Forces Journal International,* September 1986.

9. *The Wall Street Journal,* February 22, 1988.

10. *Air Force* magazine (June 1984).

11. *NASA Response to April 7 Airbus Industrie Press Release,* May 13, 1988.

12. Shearson Lehman, *Equity Research Industry Comment,* May 16, 1986.

13. The investment tax credit scheme was designed to encourage investment in capital assets. It has been enacted and repealed on a number of ocasions, and at the time the Airbus Report appeared in March 1988 was not available to American business.

14. *Tax and Non-Tax Incentives Available in the Countries Participating in the Airbus Enterprise,* May 5, 1988.

15. Quoted in *An Assessment of the Airbus Industry Report.*

16. Interview in Brussels, July 1, 1988.

17. Interview in London, August 24, 1988.

9

Pizzazz in the
Market Place

"You must stir it and stump it,
And blow your own trumpet
Or trust me, you haven't a chance."

—W.S. Gilbert, *Ruddigore,* 1887.

Nobody seems to have much idea of where the word *pizzazz* comes from. "Probably echoic of exuberant cry," says Webster tentatively. Gilbert would not have heard it in Victorian London, although he clearly knew exactly what it was. He would at all events have been gratified by the wholeheartedness with which Airbus have followed his advice.

The impression conveyed by a lot of Airbus promotional material is of a plucky little consortium fighting its way onto the scene late in the day and against enormous odds—and in that there is a fair measure of truth. It is then further suggested that they found the field in the possession of a couple of dowdy provincial ladies from Seattle and St. Louis and that for the past 20 years they have been teaching these old dears how to suck eggs—and in that there are substantial elements of fantasy.

The emphasis on being first in the field has been relentless. "The Airbus builders pioneered the peaceful use of the gas turbine, with the world's first turbo-propelled airliner, the first pure-jet transport and the first turboshaft-powered helicopter. The world's only successful supersonic airliner is also a product of the Airbus builders . . . "[1]

That comes from a 1985 publication, and it reads like the work of someone on Madison Avenue who came back after a good lunch and whiled away what was left of the afternoon rifling a dictionary of quotations. Milton, Ruskin and Blake are all called in aid to embellish various chapter headings, and Tennyson gets two bites at the cherry *(Argosies of magic sails,/Pilots of the purple twilight . . .).* French literature is represented by du Bellay, one of the most celebrated of the Pléiade poets (they get the quotation from him slightly wrong, as it happens—careless when the client has his head office in Toulouse). The selection is not confined to living languages, either. Lucretius gets a look-in, and so does Vegetius, who as all potential Airbus customers would remember, wrote a treatise on military affairs in the 4th century A.D.—"a confused and unscientific compilation," says the *Encyclopedia Britannica,* "which has to be used with caution."

Boeing are rather different. Their style calls to mind the sort of advertisement favoured by the Jack Daniel's Distillery, makers of sour mash whiskey at Lynchburg, Tennessee. An employee sits on a barrel reading the *Moore County News.* "Normally we don't make the paper much," says the caption. "You see, we've been mellowing whiskey here since 1866. And according to the editor, there's no news in that any more." The Boeing tone of voice is much the same: relaxed, almost lazily self-assured, a slight suggestion of straw in the hair—and, of course, highly deceptive, because hayseeds don't come to dominate the market in the way that Boeing have now done for so many years.

Even in the other camp, their reputation stands very high. Bob McKinlay, for many years British Aerospace's "Mr Airbus," was quite ungrudging in his appreciation: "Boeing is clearly the standard in our business. We don't see as much of them as we used to before we became so competitive, but we rate them very highly. They have a very, very wide product range, they are very market-oriented, the airplanes are good. Their production efficiency is high. In fact, if Boeing are doing it and there's no other reason, then we will copy it to just try and improve ourselves. McDonnell Douglas are not in the same league as Boeing. McDonnell Douglas are surprisingly old-fashioned."[2]

For many decades now Boeing have maintained their monotonously high standards of aircraft manufacture and until not so long ago never saw much cause to be remotely assertive about the level and range of their capabilities. Technical developments were not thought to be of great public interest, and it was not their style to offer self-congratulatory running commentaries on their product-development activities. Possibly that is what suggested to Airbus what their strategy should be, because it has been a consistent thrust of their publicity and promotion material to acquire for the consortium an image of technological superiority: "At Airbus Industrie headquarters in Toulouse there is an army of earnest young men whose job descriptions include the words 'sales technology.' Their forte is not the technology of marketing, but the *marketing of technology.* For in Airbus experience, 'technology sells airliners'."[3]

It is only comparatively recently that the Americans have begun to give their mind seriously to this aspect of the competition with Airbus. In their view Airbus consistently claim the most they can with occasional sorties across what Boeing rather delicately describe as "the boundary of unreasonableness."[4] Most of the claims made are qualitative, but a benefit or advantage is implied. The issue is often inconsequential, but has a good ring to it. Boeing identify a technique of bombardment about technology-driven benefits rather than specific hard arguments.

Another Airbus technique that Boeing realised was going down well with airlines was that while stopping short of saying that they had invented or created a particular piece of technology, they laid claim to it by asserting either that they had been the first to employ it or that their application of it was more extensive than that of their American competitors. In this area, Boeing reckon to be the better students of Aesop and are often content to play the tortoise. They know better than most that the first use of a new technology is not always the best use, and cite the embarrassment caused by what they saw as Airbus's premature attempt to commit the V2500 Superfan engine to delivery dates and sales for the A340.

Boeing point out that it is seldom possible for any one company or research team to lay proprietary claim to a particular technology. Many of the new technologies employed by airframe manufacturers, whether in Europe or the United States, comes to them through suppliers or industrial research. In terms of cost and reliability, their evolution is uneven. Decisions about when they are mature enough for commercial application rest on careful monitoring and call for fine judgements. Seattle clearly view the Toulouse performance in this area with some distaste: "The first application of a technology, if not fully satisfying the appropriate stringent criteria, may not be proof of either wisdom or leadership."[4]

The debate about the respective merits of all-new-technology jets versus derivative jets is a complex one and is conducted on a number of levels.There is some evidence that Airbus have modified their posture in the last few years. A brochure about the A330/340 programme begins on a note of bluff reassurance: "Perhaps it is as well to start by dispelling a myth. Aircraft manufacturers do not use technology for technology's sake. Nor is there any advantage in being able to tell a potential airline 'my aircraft is more advanced than theirs'."[5]

That all sounds pretty uncontroversial. The only thing is that if such a myth has had currency, it has been very largely of Airbus's own making. Their Product Line Review of May 1988, for instance, said, "The A320 is the only all-new commercial jetliner in production anywhere in the Western World. It incorporates such a range of major advances in its aerodynamic, structural and avionics design, in its flight deck and in its payload accommodations that it will, at a stroke, render obsolete all previous aircraft in its category."

If Airbus believe that, they do not carry all the members of the consortium with them. When I quoted the passage to Bob McKinlay of British Aerospace, he laughed. "It was a marketeer who wrote that," he said. "The A320 is simply a good modern aeroplane. It uses less fuel than its competitors, it is more comfortable because the cabin is wider, it has systems which are easier to operate and easier to maintain. It has all the good features that you would expect in today's washing machine as opposed to the washing machine of ten years ago. Render obsolete? No, rubbish."[2]

The central claim advanced for the A320 when it entered service in 1988 was that it was the world's first fly-by-wire airliner. This means that almost all its flight control surfaces are electrically, rather than mechanically, signalled. This saves weight by reducing the number of mechanical parts—rods, bellcranks, pulleys and the like—and also means that less maintenance is required. Airbus also claimed substantial improvements in handling qualities, and offered a homely comparison with driving a stage-coach—the coach driver shouts a command and the horses take care of the road, the A320 pilot makes a control input and the aircraft takes care of the flight path. The layman may glaze over rather quickly if exposed to more than a little explanation of such things as pitch-rate feedback and the rudder authority of the yaw damper, but the general effect is reassuring, which was no doubt the intention.

Boeing are nothing if not thorough. Once they have decided to subject the claims of a competitor to critical scrutiny, nothing gets overlooked. Vacuum lavatory systems, for instance. These were originally developed commercially in Europe for use on ships and in apartment blocks. Waste is transported from individual lavatories to central storage tanks. In aircraft such systems offer a number of obvious advantages—smaller diameter waste pipes can be used, single-point ground servicing becomes possible and sanitation arrangements on board are generally much improved.

The research that adapted the technology for use in aircraft was initiated by Boeing in the early 1970s. Lavatory arrangements in the Old World have long been the object of suspicion by Americans, and they are not going to stand for sneaky suggestions that this might be an area where the French of all people have their noses in front. The company's guidance to its men in the field manages to sound sniffy and lordly at the same time: "Boeing pioneered the development and application of vacuum lavatory systems for commercial airplane use. Since Boeing has sold the rights to their system, other airplane manufacturers have purchased such systems, and are flying with Boeing-developed technology".[4] In big things and small, homework always pays. Airbus, with its taste for literary allusion, should have seen that one coming. Emerson, after all, touched prophetically on the issue in his journals more than 150 years ago: "People who wash much have a high mind about it, and talk down to those who wash little."

Airbus make large claims for the work they have done in improving the working environment of the pilots on the flight deck—what the Americans sometimes call human factors. McDonnell Douglas did little ergonomic work on the DC-9, and not a great deal more on the MD-80 and MD-88, although work on the MD-11 indicates a determination to narrow this particular gap. Boeing first began to pay serious attention to ergonomic considerations with the 737 programme and have done a great deal more on the 757/767 and the 747-400. They do however concede that this is an area of aircraft design that got its first significant publicity from Airbus.

Airbus claim that the flight deck they designed for the A310 was accepted as "one generation ahead," though they don't say by whom. The Americans have less of an opinion of it; they say it has poor instruments and general lighting and more switches, lights and indicators than any other two-crew and most three-crew planes. However that may be, Airbus commissioned an ergonomic study based on the A310 flight-deck from the Porsche Industrial Design Bureau (because their own design was so bad, say the Americans unkindly). "The result," say Airbus, "translated into industrial terms by experts in the physical relationship between man and machine in a dynamic environment, is a new world for the flight crew."[6]

Porsche were asked to concentrate on four aspects of flight deck design—fail-safe devices, crew comfort, workload reduction and improved visibility. To a layman, the result is both handsome and comfortable. The verdict of *Aviation Week,* when they published a pilot report in 1987, was that Airbus had made a success of matching human engineering and pilot workload with aircraft performance and that the A320 was enjoyable to fly. The test pilot's first impression was of an uncluttered work area with few controls and monitoring instruments. The cockpit area was wide, and the pilot seats easy to get into—this partly because of the absence of a central control column. He found the seats comfortable and the visibility excellent—he could, for instance, in the left seat see the left wingtip without much effort. "A pilot flying the A320 in normal commercial operations will have difficulty returning to another transport aircraft with less advanced technology," he concluded, "because of the aircraft's ease of operation and splendid instrument panel."[7]

Lighting poses particular problems, as each phase of a flight has different requirements. Light must be adequate for note-taking and reference to charts, for instance, but during night flights the light must never be so strong as to impair the crew's night vision. Again, cabin crew visiting the flight deck must be able to see properly and move about safely without the overall level of lighting having to be increased. Toulouse folklore has it that someone from Porsche had been very impressed with the floor-level lighting in a brothel in Bangkok, and in an inspired piece of lateral thinking applied it to Airbus.The men from Boeing naturally wouldn't know about such things. They still feel that the 757/767 and 747-400 have the edge in overall human factor design, though they recognise rather ruefully that the promotional effort Airbus has put into this area has paid dividends.

Before the development of the cathode ray tube, the instrumentation on the flight-deck of an aircraft consisted of an bewildering array of mechanical dials and gauges, each of which could normally display only one type of information. Cathode ray tube displays, which resemble small television screens, are extremely flexible and offer almost limitless possibilities for displaying information on a time-sharing basis. Airbus say that they have "taken advantage of new technology to make a completely fresh approach to the presentation of systems operation and warning information." Boeing do not dispute this, but offer the additional information that most of the technology in question was developed by them.

The technology evolved out of work done on the American supersonic challenge to Concorde in the late 1960s. When the SST programme was abandoned, Boeing continued the work in association with NASA, and the results had their first application in the 757/767. It was this Boeing-developed technology that Airbus applied to the A310. Today, the cathode ray tube displays used on the Airbus A320, the McDonnell Douglas MD-11 and the Boeing 747-400 are all roughly comparable. McDonnell Douglas and Boeing have both gone for 11-inch displays, Airbus favour a slightly smaller 10-inch.

Flight-deck display offers a good illustration of how sharp the competition is in both design and marketing. In this as in every area, the manufacturers watch each other like hawks and are very quick to adopt and adapt what the other side has done. When, for instance, Airbus followed Boeing in the first applications, they added an airspeed tape to one of the systems. The customers liked it, and Boeing were quick to offer it on the 737.

There are several areas of the market place where it is possible to observe that the design philosophies of Airbus and its American competitors are sharply distinguished. One has to do with what is known as envelope limitation. This is a system that has as its object to improve flight safety by preventing the pilot from exceeding the aircraft's designed limits—to disallow any action, accidental or intentional, that would have the effect of pushing the aircraft outside its "envelope." Such a system keeps the pilot from flying too fast or too slow, from going beyond the structural load limits of the aircraft and from exceeding its prescribed limits of pitch, roll, side-slip and angle of attack.

The Airbus claim for the fly-through-computer technology of the A320 is that it provides the pilot with full and automatic flight envelope protection. "If the pilot pulls the stick fully back, the aircraft automatically maintains lift and power, whilst retaining full lateral and directional control with no risk of stalling. The pilot can safely demand, and get, the aircraft's maximum capability without using any physical or mental dexterity, freeing him to take considered, executive decisions and actions."[8]

Boeing first started flight testing envelope limiting systems as early as 1970, but have reached different conclusions from Airbus about their application. The view taken in Seattle is that Airbus are "protecting" the pilot from actions it may be necessary for him to take; their preference is for allowing the pilot to exceed the normal envelope when he judges it to be necessary. Boeing maintain that they build planes with handling characteristics that allow them to be flown out of any upset condition without structural failure. The most important consideration relates to acceleration. Airbus include what is known as a "hard" limitation of 2.5g on the load factor a pilot can pull, even when the plane may have additional structural capability available.[9] Boeing agree that a pilot should be deterred from exceeding 2.5g, but achieve this by applying only a "soft" stop; they believe that the pilot should be able to override this limit in an emergency, and pull up to 5g if necessary.

There are signs that Boeing, traditionally cautious in such matters, may be contemplating a shift in their philosophy. Work on the abandoned 7J7 programme may have persuaded them that advances in avionics justified some change; certainly, the 777 will incorporate a three-axis "fly-by-wire" control system. They still have a gut feeling, however, that there could be cases in which envelope limitation could work against a last-ditch effort by a pilot to avoid disaster. Bob Perdue, then a Boeing vice-president on the sales side, made the point in crisp, untechnical language. The Airbus position, he said, was "just a bunch of garbage." "If I'm about to run into a mountain or another airplane or the side of a cliff, I want to pull the goddam wings off that airplane if that's what it takes, because I've bought the farm anyway."[10]

Apart from hazards like a mountain suddenly appearing out of the mist, pilots also occasionally encounter freak atmospheric conditions. An occurrence at Andrews Air Force Base on August 1, 1983, is well-documented:

At 1404, Air Force One, with the President of the USA on board, landed on a dry runway, with a windspeed of slightly less than 20 knots. At 1409:20, windspeed began to increase, reaching a peak of over 120 knots one minute and twenty-five seconds later. At 1412:20, in the eye of the microburst, windspeed was only 2 knots. One minute and ten seconds later, a second peak was reached, of 84 knots, diametrically opposed in direction to that of the first gust. At 1418 windspeed was again below 20 knots: the event had lasted about 10 minutes and substantially damaged buildings and trees on the eastern side of the base.[11]

That is a description of a phenomenon known as windshear. It is now recognised as a significant hazard during both takeoff and landing and has been the cause of more than 30 major accidents since the early 1960s, with the loss of almost 700 lives. In a report on a windshear accident to a Lockheed Tri-Star at Dallas–Fort Worth in August 1985, the American National Transportation Safety Board compared a microburst to a high-pressure air-hose pointed at the ground. Meteorologists are able to predict the type of day on which microbursts are likely, but are not yet able to pinpoint the time and place.

That being so, the standard advice traditionally offered to aircrews about windshear—to avoid it—was not hugely helpful. Beyond avoidance, Airbus and their American competitors disagree about the next line of defence. Airbus claim that they have designed into the A300 and all subsequent planes the capability to detect and avoid extremely rapid attitude and speed changes, and that their aircraft are therefore automatically protected against windshear and a number of other low-speed handling problems.

Boeing describe the Airbus claim as "overzealous."[4] They regard "protection" as a dangerous word to use, believing it could induce a sense of false security. Their bleak contention is that there are windshears that it is simply impossible to fly through, and that in most cases the automatic application of full thrust would not be sufficient. Boeing also hold that if a pilot pulls full stick back as soon as he encounters windshear, the aircraft will give up more airspeed than it should and drain off energy too early. The plane might therefore not make it through some windshear encounters that it could conceivably survive by more gradual control inputs. Their view is that until more reliable systems of detection are developed, the best line of defence is pilot training devised to increase the probability of recovery. They provide windshear detection and guidance on planes with digital flight-decks, but stop short of the confident claims made by their European competitor.

We are touching here on a cluster of issues that do more than most to raise the competitive temperature, because they all impinge on questions of safety. It is a long-standing convention in the industry that safety should not form part of a sales pitch, and it is the American contention that Airbus have broken that particular taboo. Airbus deny it. "Absolute arrant nonsense," said Bryan Slater, their general manager, sales operations. "It's something you don't do. That's not to say there isn't a little chuckle behind the hand somewhere if a competitor has an unfortunate experience, but nobody wants to see anybody having safety problems."[12]

Bob McKinlay of British Aerospace gave a more qualified answer: "Well, it's tradition that you don't sell safety in our business, because if all the aircraft are certificated, they're all equally safe. And yes, if you push on safety, you will get up people's noses. I'm not always entirely happy with the way that Airbus play the technology side of it. Ten years ago, the Airbus approach was that to beat the Americans simply on production efficiency, which is cost, would be very difficult for the Europeans, and that the Europeans would therefore have to use technology as a weapon—it would be part of their image, the *marque* of the European aircraft would be its technology. And I think that was sound. I think we've now moved into a field where we have to match them on production technology and cost, because we've got to get profit out of the business. The line we should follow is that we use technology as a way to make the aircraft more efficient and to make the production process cheaper. I don't think you can stress safety, personally."[2]

Airbus, however, subtly but unmistakably, do stress it. The safety standards to which aircraft must be designed are the responsibility of national authorities. In the United States, the code drawn up by the Federal Aviation Administration is known as the Federal Aviation Requirements Part 25 (FAR 25); in the United Kingdom the British Civil Airworthiness Requirements (BCARs) are issued by the Civil Aviation Authority; in Europe, there has been a measure of standardisation, and 11 countries have worked together to produce JARs—Joint Airworthiness Requirements. Airbus, in a publication on Flight Safety, points out that although JAR 25 is based on the American FAR 25, it is in some respects more stringent: "In fact, a European airline operating to JARs and purchasing an American aircraft is liable to be presented by the manufacturer with a bill for several hundred thousand dollars to bring the aircraft up to JAR standards."[13]

The pamphlet describes a specification produced by Airbus Industrie in 1979 for fire-resistant cabin furnishings: "The FAA have now (in 1985) issued a Notice of Proposed Rule-Making which will bring their certification requirements up to the level already achieved by Airbus Industrie." It continues with a description of how Airbus has evolved a procedure with the authorities to enable certification requirements to evolve to keep pace with technological change instead of becoming a constraint—clearly an intelligent and enlightened initiative. There follows, however, a glancing embellishment: "A problem, incidentally, with which the American automobile industry failed to cope: safety laws were not progressively amended as technology improved, and in many respects American vehicles became technologically backward, though satisfying the unmodified letter of outdated law." As delicate a piece of character assassination by proxy as one could hope to see.

There is more good stiletto work in the next two paragraphs:

In other areas there are fundamental (and legitimate) differences in design philosophy between various manufacturers. For example, all Airbus Industrie aircraft are designed to "stay in one piece" in the event of a survivable crash or in the case of a wheels-up landing: the pylons staying on the wings, and the engines staying on the pylons. The European design philosophy in this respect is fundamentally different from the American philosophy, which favours separation of the pylon (and engine) from the wing—an attitude which evolved in the early days of military jet aircraft when engines were unreliable, but which still persists in the USA, 40 years later.

Although the European philosophy has an inevitable weight penalty, we believe that the reduced probability of fuel leakage and fire justify the weight penalty . . .

Whoever wrote that clearly knew his *Martin Chuzzlewit.* Mr. Pecksniff himself could not have put it better.

There is further evidence of Airbus' taboo-breaking instincts—though of a less direct kind—in Lew Bogdan's massive and disorderly book *L'Epopée du ciel clair.*[14] Bogdan, whose original aim was to make a series of television programmes, is romantically admiring of Airbus, and there's a good deal of the purple prose that seems to afflict so many writers about aviation. For someone whose concern is with Airbus, however, Bogdan is extraordinarily well informed about the various misfortunes that had overtaken Airbus's competitors over the years—he does seem to linger rather over his descriptions of air crashes (those involving American aircraft, that is). I also had the impression that he quite enjoyed describing the period when nothing was going right for Boeing and the 747. In Bogdan's account, Boeing, to honour its contract with PanAm, had pushed Pratt & Whitney to have the engines ready in three years instead of the more usual five. The result was that the engines started blowing up on the test bench—they lost 60 out of 87, and the 747s, writes Bogdan, looked liked castrated phoenixes. I don't know whether *schadenfreude* can operate retrospectively, but I thought I could detect a whiff of it from time to time in Bogdan's 500 pages.

Whether there have been occasions when Airbus has in fact put a toe over that invisible line and breached the convention about "selling" safety will remain a matter of opinion. What is a matter of fact is that over the years the Airbus safety record has been extremely good. Then in the summer of 1988 they got a bad fright. An A320 belonging to Air France crashed at Mulhouse Habsheim near the Franco-Swiss border. Three people were killed and 133 injured. The plane was completely destroyed. Air France and British Airways immediately suspended all A320 flights until the cause of the crash was known. At Airbus Industrie headquarters in Toulouse, the alarm bells sounded very loud indeed.

The airline had taken delivery of the plane only three days previously, and it had been chartered to give a display at an airshow. Two Air France captains were at the controls. They made a low-level pass over the runway, landing gear down. "Look at that," said the airshow commentator, "how magnificent . . . how sleek." Three hundred yards beyond the runway, however, the forest began, and the plane failed to clear it. "I tried to boost the power," said the captain, "but it didn't respond."

Press speculation naturally centred on whether the accident had been caused by some fault in the "most intelligent plane in the world" or whether it was due to pilot error. Officials of the pilots' union were quick to rehearse all the arguments about safety that they had deployed when the controversy about two-man crews had been at its height in the early 1980s.

Airbus, like their American competitors, had had to tread a careful path on this issue. Although the pilots made much of the safety argument, the root cause of their hostility had been classically Luddite—they were opposed to the idea because it would mean fewer jobs. Which was, of course, one of the main attractions to the airlines—they would save on salaries and training costs, and a reduction in the space needed on the flight deck could translate into greater seating capacity and increased revenues.

The two-crew flight deck, as it is called in the trade, had long been a gleam in the eye of the manufacturers, and by the late 1960s it was common ground that they would move to it as soon as advances in design and automation made it a proposition that was both safe and efficient. It was an objective in the early design work on the A300, but the technology at the partners' command at that time did not permit it, and Airbus's first certification came more than 15 years after Boeing's for the 737 and McDonnell Douglas's for the DC-9.

That did not prevent it from figuring prominently over the years in Airbus promotional literature as one of many areas in which Europe was out in front. "The Airbus Industrie lead in flight deck design was confirmed in January 1982 when the digital A300FF became the first wide-body transport certificated for two-crew operation," *The New World* asserted glossily in 1983,[6] and a more recent publication includes the two-person cockpit in a catalogue spread over a couple of pages under the heading "Airbus technological 'firsts'."[15] "Airbus' level of experience with two-crew flights," said Boeing, in a withering return of service, "is about 0.5% of total free-world two-crew flights."[4]

Let it never be said, however, that European antennae are insensitive to the need for a change of emphasis. A few days before the publication of the findings into the causes of the Habsheim crash, a long letter was printed in *Le Monde* from Henri Martre, the président-directeur general of Aérospatiale. The tone was detached, almost scholarly. Today, he said, more than 3,000 commercial airplanes—almost half the world's fleet, belonging to 218 airlines—had two-man crews. From now on, the concept of the three-man crew was destined to go the way of the sailing ship. He owed it to the truth to say, however, that marvellous plane that it was, it was not the A320 that had pioneered the two-crew flight deck. That distinction belonged to the Americans, and specifically to Douglas, who had taken the initiative with the DC-9 more than 20 years previously. The time had come, however, Martre asserted, for European plane makers to follow suit if they wished to remain competitive . . . [16]

Nécessité n'a pas de loi, as the French say. Any port in a storm. It was as elegant a piece of historical rewriting as one could wish to see. And Airbus could have found employment for one or two redundant pilots as revisionist pamphleteers . . .

*   *   *   *   *

The view taken of Airbus by their competitors does not, understandably enough, tally in all respects with that of the airlines who are their customers. By the beginning of 1992, their number had risen to 108. The roll-call began with Aeroquetzal and ended with VASP. Air Niugini, the flag carrier of Papua New Guinea, had taken delivery of one A310 and had another on order. At the other end of the scale Northwest Airlines had signed up for a total of 130 aircraft of various types; Lufthansa, with 61 aircraft already in service, was the world's largest single Airbus operator.

Although Lufthansa is the flag-carrier of one of the Airbus consortium member countries, a proportion of its fleet is still American, because Airbus is not yet able to meet the airline's need for six different types of aircraft. Reinhardt Abraham, Lufthansa's deputy managing director, took the view that there was little to choose between the three manufacturers in terms of quality, but he made no bones about preferring to buy European if the scheduling and other requirements of the airline were met. "That is our economic responsibility," he said. In time, he expected the balance within the fleet to swing in Airbus' favour, although even with Lufthansa's policy of renewing planes after between eight and ten years, that would take some time.[17]

Abraham, a ferocious chain-smoker, can keep a beady eye on the comings and goings of that fleet from the picture windows of his office in the Lufthansa headquarters at Frankfurt airport. He joined the airline's technical division in 1956, after studies in physics, aeronautical engineering and business administration. He is an important figure in the industry, and Airbus owes him a great deal. He denied that the Lufthansa board has ever been leaned on, whatever the complexion of the government in Bonn, and said that Franz-Josef Strauss, a member of the supervisory board until his death in October 1988, had always given the management strong support in their fleet procurement plans even when they had been for the purchase of aircraft from Boeing. "I have not been aware of political pressure either on the board or outside it. In Germany the initiative lies with the executive board. The supervisory board only can approve or disapprove." This was an assertion that was felt in some quarters to need qualification. Don Carty, American Airlines vice-president, finance and planning, for example, did not think that Lufthansa's product decisions had always been reached on a basis of commercial independence: "I recall at least one instance when I was told by the Germans what aircraft they were going to select, and the next morning woke up to find they had bought a different one."[18]

Airbus has not alway enjoyed Abraham's uncritical support, for all that. He was furiously angry with them early in 1987, and there was a period of about two months when it seemed possible that the airline might pull out of its commitment to the A340 and opt instead for the MD-11. Abraham believed that everyone concerned—Toulouse, the partners, the member governments—had been far too slow in facing up to important decisions that should have been made in the course of 1986, but he reserved his strongest criticism for Airbus Industrie for trying to rush the engine manufacturer (the definition work for the programme had originally specified a superfan engine that was to be developed by IAE, an international consortium consisting of Pratt &Whitney, Rolls Royce and Japanese and other interests). "For some time the question was certainly open again," Abraham said. "Once the change to a CFM 56 engine had been decided, the margin of advantage over the MD-11 was halved. We had a standing offer from McDonnell Douglas to come back to the conditions that we had finally negotiated with them."

Abraham believed that it was the dilatoriness of the consortium during 1986 that gave McDonnell Douglas the chance to get their nose in front and launch the MD-11. "It was possible for McDonnell Douglas to organise a conservative clientele who were sceptical of whether Airbus would make it and whether the programme would be approved, and this also meant passing up the possibility of getting together and competing jointly against Boeing." Abraham, like everybody else in the industry, had clearly not forgotten the disastrous shoot-out that had taken place only a few years previously between McDonnell Douglas and Lockheed. "Everybody knew that one programme would have been better. We always said to the manufacturers 'Make a good and healthy competition at the design stage and then let the airlines decide'."

So far as sales campaigns were concerned, Abraham felt that Airbus had learned a great deal from the Americans since the late 1970s in the matter of how to make a written presentation, but that they still trailed in speed of response: "The top management in Toulouse has not enough power to make the crucial decisions. They have to go to the partners for confirmation of decisions about major changes, decisions about pricing."

He also noted progress in another important area. "Airbus after-sales service was inferior to the Americans' for a long time. We all had to work very hard to speed them up in this respect, and I have to say that they have improved their field support and their field organisation.They have also improved to some extent as far as engineering support is concerned. For many years, if you had a technical problem or a modification requirement, the documentation field was critical. The speed at which the proper documentation is available and up-dated has improved—in general they are now of world standard, which was established by the Americans. If there are still some shortcomings they are mainly connected with the fact that not everything can be done in Toulouse. They sometimes have to go back—to MBB, to BAe or to Aérospatiale—and that takes time and occasionally produces friction. Things began to get better in this respect only in the eighties."

Further north in Europe, Airbus have had a long relationship with SAS, the Scandinavian airline owned jointly by Sweden, Norway and Denmark.[19] SAS made a decision to buy a number of A300s in the late 1970s and had four of them in operation from the early 1980s. A change in management brought a change in philosophy. The A300s no longer fitted, and they were put up for sale, which caused a certain coolness between Toulouse and Stockholm. It did not make Airbus any less determined to get back into an important sector of the European and international market, however.

SAS, looking ahead to liberalisation in Europe, see a reduction in the number of airlines, and have every intention of being one of them. "We use the slogan 'One of five in ninety-five'," said Ulf Abrahamsson, the vice-president for Aircraft and Fleet Development of the SAS Group. "We think that competition will increase dramatically, and for the last couple of years we've been gearing ourselves to meet that. We think that we have to be very active now to position ourselves, so that when liberalisation hits us we are sitting very firmly on slots in the system."[20]

Abrahamsson does not think that the effects will be as dramatic as those of deregulation in the United States. "There, many airlines have disappeared, and you have a number of companies which enjoy a near monopoly situation. Prices go up, they don't give good service, it's really bad, I think. We're trying to change that with our cooperation with Texas Air and Continental. We believe very firmly that unless we become very efficient we shall have all the big American carriers flying in to Europe, and all the very big and very good Asian operators, too—JAL, Thai, Singapore. They could kill the whole system. And that is one reason we are fighting costs very heavily. We are restructuring our technical division, getting rid of some of our resources and preparing to be a buyer of services instead of doing everything ourselves."

Abrahamsson, who chairs the SAS fleet planning group, passed the corporate character of the three rival manufacturers in dispassionate review. "Boeing? Very professional, very dark suits. Everthing is extremely well organised. They're very nice guys, but they remind me a bit of IBM." (He made this sound like a slight defect of character, for which one might perhaps undergo therapy in a Swedish clinic.) "The Douglas people from California are more easy-going. Very easy people to deal with."

"Airbus? They try desperately hard all the time to get into the airline. They sometimes come on a bit strong—that's certainly the impression some of their top people have made on our top people, and it hasn't always been to their advantage. Pierson is very different from his opposite numbers in Boeing or McDonnell Douglas. He's been very bullish, I think. We've had a couple of meetings with him, and he was a little bit too firm. But they are a bit less pushy now than they were. We've rubbed off some of their corners."

The specific offence of Airbus seems to have been their tendency to try and elbow their way to the top on all occasions. "I report either directly to Jan Carlzon," Abrahamsson said, "because my group here is a staff function within the SAS group, or to him through the boss of the SAS Airline, so in some cases there are two levels above me, and in some cases just one. And then of course above Mr Carlzon you have the SAS Board, which is the final decision-making body. But we have a clear understanding in our company that our top management does not want to see the manufacturers. 'Ulf, they say to me, that's your job'."

"I have a colleague who is responsible for drawing up the contracts; he's parallel to me on the commercial side, so once we've decided on what to buy and when and how many, usually they see me and my people and him. And Airbus say, 'We want someone else, Ulf, we know you.' 'Well, I say, you'll have to live with that.' Of course occasionally, when we have the very top people from Boeing or Airbus, Mr Carlzon meets them and might have a quick lunch with them, but otherwise not."

Airbus also seem to have been slow to grasp that Stockholm lies at the junction of the Baltic and the Gulf of Bothnia and not somewhere east of Suez. "Some of their people, sensing that we were not going the Airbus way, were having contacts with people in Norway and Sweden," Abrahamsson said, "trying to put political and diplomatic pressure on us to buy European, to buy French. It seems to be part of the French way of doing things. Airbus harmed themselves by being active in that field. When we had the commuter operation we had similar activities from the French people for their ATR programme. Airbus have been very active in trying to get that kind of commitment from Scandinavian industry, more so than the others—'If SAS buys this, you will get such and such a job from us.' They tried that sort of thing a great deal, with Saab and others, but it was counter-productive."

Airbus fell into the same hole with SAS as they had done with Lufthansa over the A340 but had less luck in scrambling out. The Scandinavians had been actively considering how best to replace their DC-10s, Abrahamsson said. They had actually signed a letter of intent with McDonnell Douglas for twelve MD-11s and were one of a small group of launch customers. "Then Airbus came along in January with the A340 with the superfan engine, and we said, 'Hey, Mr. Douglas, we want to see what Airbus is offering, it looks interesting.' We fairly quickly realised, though, after about three or four weeks analysis, that they couldn't make it with that very big IAE superfan engine—it looked very good on paper, and we spent some time with aircraft and engine manufacturers, but we decided it was completely unrealistic in the timescale that they mentioned. And we were right, because a couple of months later, the engine manufacturers pulled out. It's a good engine, and will be something in the future, but not for 1992."

SAS make it plain to the manufacturers that there are certain conventions they like to see observed even in the excitement of making a sales pitch. "We make it very clear that we do not want any comparisons made with anybody else's product," Abrahamsson said firmly. "We want to know about *their* product: we can make the comparison ourselves. Sometimes, of course, in a very tight competitive situation, they forget, and in such cases we just don't listen. All three are guilty of that. But they know that we don't like it, and I'm sure they know that others don't like it either."[21]

Abrahamsson indicated discreetly that Airbus had sailed close to the wind on this point by making invidious comparisons between the four-engined A340 and the twin-engined Boeing 767 in the matter of their suitability for long-haul operations. "But they stopped immediately," he said, "because they have a twin-engined A310 which is used for long-haul operations, so it wasn't an argument." "I hope," he added, and there was a touch of mild frost in his voice, "that as an industry we will refrain from using that as an argument in the future—'come fly safely with us in our four-engined aircraft as compared with the other guy's twin-engined one'."

Two engines or four, Airbus will continue to be made welcome in SAS's new glass and metal headquarters just outside Stockholm. "I would hate to see Airbus disappear," said Ulf Abrahamsson, "and I say that from both a personal and a professional point of view. They have good products. We would hate to have less than these three manufacturers."

Airbus had to wait quite a long time to hear that view expressed on the other side of the Atlantic. The Eastern and PanAm sales had both in a sense been false dawns, and the consortium had to wait until well into the 1980s before it could add to its list of customers the names of any of the new breed of cash-rich, confident mega-carriers—companies such as American and Northwest—which had successfully ridden the postderegulation wave.

"It took Airbus a long time to get into American Airlines," said Don Carty, the Canadian who is the company's senior vice-president of finance and planning. "We bought aircraft over the years primarily from Boeing, and in recent years we've done a fairly innovative deal with McDonnell Douglas and bought some of their airplanes, but we had done very little business with Airbus, and in fact had very little interaction with them. We probably had some preconceived notions about Airbus that dated back to the very early years: 'Can a European supplier really supply and back you up?' and so on. I think we probably also had some assumed perceptions about technical leadership and technical strength. Techical evolution had come to us from Boeing and from McDonnell Douglas and we assumed that was where it would always come from."

In 1985, American had begun to consider what they needed to serve the Caribbean, which was an important part of their route network. As they began to look at what was available, it became plain to them that Airbus was a potential supplier that they needed to look at seriously. "It was also clear that Airbus was prepared to deal with us on our terms," Carty said. "Let me explain that a little bit. As a relatively successful company in the post-1980 era, American has been looking for the manufacturers to change some of their commercial practices, to be more responsive to their markets just as we'd had to be more responsive to ours. That had to do with everything from the way down payments are made on airplanes to the way they are financed and the way prices are escalated over time—there are a hundred clauses in a contract that are of significant commercial importance, never mind all the thousands of technical issues that need to be negotiated as well."

"Now it became obvious to us that we had in Airbus a supplier that was willing to talk about those things. That doesn't mean they were willing to roll over and give them all away, but what it did mean was that they were willing to listen to why this clause or that clause was a bad idea, and what they might do to frame things differently from the way we've historically framed them. Sometimes in an industry the most successful company is the slowest to make those changes, and on the commercial front, without pointing any fingers, it wasn't McDonnell Douglas and it wasn't Airbus that were the slowest to change. It was obvious to us that the Airbus people were willing to sit down and to talk on any dimension of the business. We weren't going to be haunted with hours and hours of arguing about things that were nonsensical but had just been there for a hundred years in those aircraft contracts.

"It also became clear that Airbus had an awareness of some of the financial needs of our big companies," Carty said. "At that time in particular it was our concern not to increase the financial burden on the company and the company's balance sheet. And at the same time we wanted the capacity. And I think it's fair to say that the Airbus people got into bed and they took some risks. With what's transpired in the financial markets since that time they haven't done badly out of it at all—in fact I think they've done a little better than they anticipated. But they took a risk. American is an airline that can really assure the success of any aircraft programme by itself, and Airbus recognised that it was in their interest, if they really wanted American as a customer, to take on that commercial risk."

At this point, with both Boeing and Airbus eager to sell American the 25 aircraft they had decided they needed for their Caribbean routes, the transaction took an unexpected turn. "We were very lucky in that either aircraft could have met our needs," Carty said. "So we got a good old-fashioned commercial contest going, and both manufacturers got more aggressive. In the end, both of them comfortably crossed the boundary of what we considered to be attractive propositions." So attractive, indeed, that it occurred to American that they would be foolish not to take both—the Airbus for the Caribbean, the Boeings for the North Atlantic. "We didn't want to mislead either of the manufacturers," Carty said, "so we went back to them both and we said, 'Does your offer still stand if we take both orders?' The Airbus people said, 'You bet,' and the Boeing people said, 'Well, we're going to moderate our offer a little bit,' and they agreed to give us the airplanes but only fifteen of them."

Why did Boeing respond in this way? "I'm sure a number of things entered into their deliberations," Carty said. "They had reached a long way for this order—at least in their view they had: since then I think they have learned more about how competitive their market place is becoming. But they had really stretched for it, and I think they thought they'd get a couple of things in return—they'd get the order and they'd get American to stay a loyal Boeing customer across the board. What we were now telling them was they wouldn't get both those things, and they decided that they didn't want to invest that much of their company resource if they weren't going to get all the benefit."

Boeing dispute some of the detail of this. Bob Perdue, who at the time was the vice-president in Seattle most concerned with the deal, said, "Number one, they didn't tell us—we had to ask. I kept getting these rumours, and I finally told the salesman, 'Call down there, and ask the specific question. Did they take the Airbus deal as well as ours?' Now, you know what they say in sports—'a tie is like kissing your sister.' Well, we were not interested in kissing our sister. We wanted to win, and we had made them a very attractive offer. So when we found out that all we'd gotten was a tie, we decided to back off a little bit. There was some feeling around here that we shouldn't do any."[22]

That illuminated the Boeing attitude to the deal, but to the lay mind, at least, left one apparently simple question unanswered: other things being equal, is it not a more attractive proposition to sell 25 aircraft than 15? Enlightenement came from Dick Albrecht, Boeing's senior vice-president: "The problem in your description of the transaction is the verb. You have them buying, and you have us selling. What they wanted, and what they demanded in their term-sheet when they began the competition, was basically a rent-a-plane deal: we'll take these airplanes from you, you lease them to us, we have the right to return them to you on thirty days notice at any time during the life of the airplane." It was, said Albrecht, "rather an onerous term-sheet," and Boeing resisted the terms strenuously. "It was only when we were told, 'Well, your competition's willing to do this,' that we finally acknowledged that American Airlines was an important enough customer and that we would stretch and offer them terms that we'd never offered before."[22]

It was not only the first time, Albrecht said, it was also, on that sort of transaction, the last. "We are not in the operating lease business; we are not in the finance business—at least we try not to be. But when we thought we were in a winner-take-all competition we were willing to do it for up to 25 airplanes in order to get them committed to 767-300s. When you're no longer in a winner-take-all, you say to yourself, 'Wait a minute—am I really willing to devote that many resources to get our airplane into American Airlines when we haven't succeeded in keeping the other guys out?' And we have taken enough criticism from other customers about the fact that we were willing to do that for one customer, that I think we would probably not do it today for any customer."

It was a striking illustration of the power that the new mega-carriers exercise in the market place. The word Don Carty used to describe such deals was *innovative,* and American had first pulled one off with McDonnell Douglas some years earlier. "They came to us, actually. They were in deep, serious trouble. Nobody was buying airplanes, the industry was flat on its back, it was shortly after deregulation, and they said, 'We'd like you to take some MD-80s.' We said, 'Absolutely not, we can't afford new airplanes, we're struggling here, we'd love to have some, but we can't afford it, our balance sheet can't take it.' And they said 'Well, what would induce you to take these airplanes? We'd like to keep this thing going and not end up out of commercial aviation'."

American replied coolly that they would have to give them the planes on a month-to-month basis. They would pay monthly, and if they got to the point where they didn't think they could run them properly, they would hand them back. "Well," Carty said, "they choked on that for a while, and then they came back and asked how much we would pay them a month, and I said we'd pay them what we'd save by grounding one of our older airplanes. Well, the price of fuel was higher, but it wasn't all that high at that time, so it wasn't a lot of money, and they said, 'Well, you've got to give us some upside, because it's a new airplane, and you'll save some maintenance costs, and you'll do a little better on revenue'."

In the end, Carty said, the only way he could see of bridging the gap between what McDonnell Douglas needed and what he was prepared to pay was to say, 'Look, if the airplane is better than I think it is, and generates more revenue for us, and more profit than I forecast, I'll split it with you.' "So we had a profit-sharing deal and a month-to-month lease, with a low lease rate."[23] It was a situation well described some 80 years earlier by a character in P.G. Wodehouse: "We have got them where the hair's short. Yea. Even on toast."

American's appetite for finding new ways of doing things was by no means sated by this remarkable coup. Having got the manufacturers on toast, they applied their fertile corporate mind to ways of keeping them there. "Once we'd found our feet, and had a strategy for changing the company and going forward," Carty said, "we said to McDonnell Douglas, 'Now we want another kind of innovation. We want you to imagine that every airplane coming down your line is not different. We're talking Model Ts here. How much cheaper can you make 'em than the way you make 'em today?' And they said, 'Well, in that hypothetical situation we could probably save a lot of money in production.' So we said, 'Fine, we'll buy 100 airplanes.' Which was a huge order in those days—nobody bought 100 airplanes. And of course since that time we've added another 117 on top of that, so we're now firmly committed for between 220 and 230 MD-80s, and we have every intention of committing for a minimum of 250."

American Airlines and the handful of other mega-carriers in the United States are now so powerful that they take the financing of these enormous deals in their stride. "When we started into major aircraft acquisition after deregulation," Don Carty said, "leasing was awfully important to us. Today that's no longer true. We're a very cash-flush company. In fact we have a little too much cash, we're sitting on something like $1.3 billion, and we'd like to work that down a little bit, because that's too much investment not productively utilised."[24]

"However, because of the structure of U.S. tax code, what we try to do is make optimum use of the tax attributes that come with an airplane—the depreciation, if you like. We can only use so much, though, so every time we hit that point, we look for leasing arrangements. We go to the leveraged lease market, where we can effectively pass back the tax attribute to independent investors, and we then see the benefit of that in the lease rate. These so-called leveraged leases are leases where owners of the aircraft invest a limited amount of money and then go out in the market and borrow the rest against our credit. So essentially it's our name that's being parlayed out there. But our credit is good, and our pockets are deep, so generally we'll just literally write cheques for airplanes."

One device that is becoming increasingly popular is what is known as a double-dip lease. This allows both parties to a transaction—a U.S. airline, say, and a German or French or Japanese leasing company—to take the tax benefits of depreciation under their own tax code, which creates certain economic advantages in the rates of the lease. American Airlines resorts to it extensively, and so does Northwest, another big Airbus customer. Steve Rothmeier, Northwest's chief executive, said that of the next $2 billion worth of aircraft that they would be acquiring, $1.6 billion would be financed in this way.[25]

"Airbus themselves have learned a fair bit about those kinds of financing," Carty said. "My Treasury people tell me they've gotten pretty creative. They're doing some double-dip financing where they'll find French investors to own the airplane in France, and U.S. investors to own the airplane in the States, and two or three different people are taking tax benefit out of it. And that's one of the ways they've managed to do a little better on their lease rate than they anticipated, so they've been able to achieve the guarantee they gave us. Some of the double-dip French leases are a lot easier to do round a French product than they are round a U.S. product, so because of that French bias the world financial markets today tend to be every bit as receptive to Airbus airplanes as they are to Boeing's."

Cause and effect are not always easy to trace, but there have clearly been radical changes in the way the game is played. "I don't know how much of it is due to the presence of Airbus," Boeing's Dick Albrecht said, "or how much of it is because the market and the world have changed, but we are doing things today that ten years ago people holding my position would have never dreamed of. We have done some things by way of offset and counter trade that we resisted doing for years. I guess it's now four or five years ago, but we put together a deal through a financial intermediary involving ten 747s for Saudi oil—that's the sort of thing that five years earlier would probably never have been dreamed of." Were some of his predecessors spinning gently in their graves? "Yeah," Albrecht said drily.

"And they're probably also spinning at the thought that we can't get the catalogue price for all of our airplanes."[22]

Albrecht also acknowledged that Airbus had been been very resourceful in North America. "They recognise that political pressure isn't going to help them sell any airplanes in the United States, so they don't really try to utilise it. But they have been very astute in showing awareness of political sensitivities here. They cover their bases very quickly if they're about to place an order—they make sure that the Congressman from so-and-so doesn't object. I also think they use the American government lobbying system and the PR image-building system very effectively."

Although Don Carty had been critical of what he saw as a slowness to respond on Boeing's part, he paid handsome tribute to the coherence and strength of their corporate culture. "The Boeing personality has tended to be the most predictable and stable and self-confident about their product, and while I'm sure they don't like to lose, they'd rather lose than compromise the integrity of their overall commercial strategy. Boeing scrambles less than the others do. They have been consistently managed— that doesn't mean they've always been right, but they've kept a very even keel. And they've struggled less than the other two guys to establish their product line. They've had product lines that have languished for a long, long time—the classic case was the 757. That airplane literally sat there doing nothing for five or six years, and they didn't fire-sale it. They just waited."

Although all the manufacturers had shown themselves willing to take more significant risks over the past four or five years, Carty thought that it was Airbus that had gained the most. "The pay-off for the risk they undoubtedly took is that we are now an Airbus customer. We will seriously look at any Airbus product that comes down the road, and that was a big hurdle for them to come over. So whether they sell us more airplanes in the next year or the next five years is not so important as that they've now crossed the bridge with American, and we see them as a very viable supplier."

That was a view echoed a thousand miles to the north in Minneapolis by Steven J. Rothmeier, the chairman and chief executive officer of Northwest Airlines. Rothmeier, whose family was originally German, joined Northwest in 1973. His whole career has been with the airline, and he moved into the top job at the beginning of 1985. In his spare time he interests himself in scripopholy—collecting old stock and bond certificates— and the walls of his office are hung with some rather splendid specimens from pre-war Germany.

One would have to go back to Borman of Eastern to find someone who has carried the Airbus banner in the United States with such unqualified dedication. Quite soon after becoming chief executive officer he had been faced with big decisions about fleet enlargement and replacement. The acquisition of Republic Airlines had propelled Northwest into the mega-carrier category. They flew to 130 cities on three continents and had more than 33,000 employees. The fleet numbered more than 300 aircraft, and a large number of Boeing 727s and McDonnell Douglas DC-9s were coming up for replacement.

The choice was between the Boeing 737-400, the McDonnell Douglas MD-88, which was a derivative of the MD-80 and the Airbus A320. "Basically what I was looking for was a low cost of operation, the best technology we could buy, and very strong customer appeal," said Rothmeier. "A very important criterion was the operating efficiency of the airplane, because it was our theory that if you could combine good labour contracts with the latest high technology equipment you would produce a lower cost operation over the long pull. We had the unique feature of being a late arrival in the mega-carrier group, because of the acquisition. This was good in some respects and bad in others, but the good part of it was that we had an opportunity to leap-frog the competition in technology. We also had a very strong balance sheet, so the idea was to take advantage of that to buy high-tech equipment that had lower unit costs and that, coupled with our good labour contracts, would give us the competitive edge."[25]

"The A320 clearly emerged as having the best technology," said Rothmeier. "The interesting thing was that contrary to popular belief, the price of the Airbus was actually higher than we would have paid for the 737-400 or for the MD-88. The reason we were willing to pay more per unit is that the savings on operating costs over the life of the airplane would clearly justify the higher capital cost for the advanced technology. What I was impressed with—I visited the Airbus facilities at Toulouse, and MBB in Hamburg and Deutsche Airbus in Munich—was the introduction of automation and advanced techniques of assembly. It was really a first class operation. It was like buying a Mercedes-Benz or a BMW."

The agreement was signed in October 1986. It called for Northwest to make a firm commitment on ten A320s for delivery in 1990 and 1991. Ninety more aircraft were to be available to the airline in a series of six blocks of 15 each. The total value of the contract, including spares and support, was of the order of $3.2 billion.

With Northwest, Airbus were to experience none of the difficulties in getting the ear of the top man that they had experienced with SAS. "Compared with Boeing or McDonnell Douglas, Airbus is a more Byzantine structure," Rothmeier said. "At Boeing or McDonnell Douglas you can see very clearly what the organisation chart is and who is doing what—at Airbus that's less clear. So I put much greater reliance on being able to deal directly with Pierson, and there is more of a CEO-to-CEO axis in dealing with Airbus than there is with either McDonnell Douglas or Boeing."

Another factor making for an easy relationship was Rothmeier's admiration for Franz-Josef Strauss. "I thought he was an incredible man and a marvellous leader. Interestingly, he'd been one of my heroes from the days that I was at the University of Notre Dame here in Minneapolis and at the University of Chicago for my MBA. It was when I was at Chicago in the early 70s that I really got imbued with this whole free market concept. I thought he was absolutely superb. I mean the guy was brilliant—a real quick study, a thorough understanding of the technology, a sound business man in his own right. I first met him at breakfast in his office in Munich. My family came from the Sudetanland originally, so when we sat down and were exchanging pleasantries, he said, 'Rothmeier? I know that name very well. My first sergeant in the Army was called Rothmeier. He was a tough man. Very demanding—very difficult to deal with.' So I said, 'He was not related to me, Dr. Strauss,' at which he burst out laughing, and we just hit it off very well from that point on."

When Rothmeier spoke about the Airbus style of salesmanship, it was in the language of a bridegroom in the very early days of a honeymoon. "Having been subjected to more presentations by airframe and engine manufacturers than I care to remember, the Airbus people were clearly superior. There was a structure in their presentation that really focussed on what the key issues were. They were well prepared, well organised, and their message was very clear and succint. The presentation that they made to me, as CEO, was exactly what I wanted to hear—I mean, you can't get into detail on every single panel on the airplane and how much is lithium/aluminum, that type of thing. And yet there was enough technical detail to give you confidence that everybody on that Airbus team knew the product and knew it very, very well. There was never any BS-ing, if there was a question they couldn't answer they said we don't know but we'll find out for you. They understood our company, I think they did their homework exceptionally well. It is a very, very professional organisation."

Rothmeier had raised with Airbus the past failure of European manufacturers in the matter of product support, and had spent some time whem he was in Hamburg inspecting their parts depot and quizzing them about their distribution system. It had sometimes been argued that because the main Airbus customer base was in Africa and the Middle East and other Third World countries there might be a question mark over their ability to service big-time carriers, but Rothmeier stood this objection on its head. "If that product can go into Third World countries and into areas that don't have normal product support as we know it in the U.S. and still have the highest despatch reliability in the industry, they've got to be building a pretty good product, and somehow they're supporting it, because those airplanes aren't flying round without parts in those areas of the globe. Those airplanes obviously do very well in extremely difficult operating conditions, and I would see that as an argument in favour of what they are promising in product support."

In the spring of 1987, six months after the A320 deal, Northwest signed another substantial contract with Airbus. The airline agreed to purchase up to 20 A340s and took options on ten A330s. "We felt that we probably had a unique opportunity with the A340 because of our large international route system," Rothmeier said, "and particularly our presence in the Pacific.[26] The A340 is built for range and it's built for medium-density markets, and we saw it as being a unique fit to our system. I think that probably there was a similar feeling at Lufthansa. Just starting with a clean sheet of paper, the unique size of the A340 and all the new technology that was in the airplane, it just worked out much better than the MD-11."

Rothmeier had not sought reassurances from the U.S. government about what the position of his company might be in the event of a trade war. "In all honesty I have never had a conversation with the USTR, with anyone in his office, with anyone in the White House, or anyone in the Commerce Department about the Airbus issue." He denied categorically that he had been influenced by any noncommercial considerations in the A340 sale. "There was a rumour that went around in the summer of 1987 about the offering of route authority," he said. "It was absolutely untrue. We would never even consider that type of concession. Any government trade-off of route authority in exchange for a product would be totally anathema. We would show them the door very quickly if that sort of thing came up."

There might seem to be an element of irony in the fact that Rothmeier, a product of Chicago, the citadel of free-market beliefs, an early advocate of deregulation, should embrace so uncritically the Byzantine processes of Airbus with its heavy reliance on public funds, but he evidently did not find himself in any intellectual difficulty over this.[27] "In this capitalist system we have to pay attention to the owners' interests, and we do. Whatever political issues might exist are for the government to resolve. The Europeans are not going to compete in the global economy by exporting wine and cheese and agricultural goods; they've got to be in high-tech, and those countries obviously made the decision that the high-tech area they wanted to compete in was the airplane business. So, much as there might be a desire for protection by McDonnell Douglas or Boeing, it would be unrealistic to think that you could enforce that global duopoly."

That was a harder line than the one taken by Don Carty of American Airlines, who expressed some sympathy with the view that the American manufacturers were facing unfair competition. "In the long run there is an argument that does need some resolution at government to government level. We can't have a major supplier in the industry artifically propped up. That's not letting the market work. On the other hand, you can't start in your garage and build a Boeing or a McDonnell Douglas. It might have been true when Boeing started, but it's not true any more. So that does need resolution—though we're a long way from being sorry that Airbus is in business."

Back on the other side of the Atlantic, there is one major airline that over the years has remained immune to the blandishments of Airbus, and that is British Airways. This rankles in Toulouse and causes men of an otherwise sunny disposition to mutter darkly about British duplicity and subscribe to theories of conspiracy. Nor were they particularly amused by the forthrightness of Lord King, the BA chairman, when he said some years ago, "It would be nice to know who is running Airbus, and to see some accounts."

For a time, Airbus thought they had got a foot in the door. BA had swallowed up British Caledonian and they had had ten A320s on order. That British Airways wanted to retain all British Caledonian's international and domestic landing rights went without saying. Did they want all their aircraft, however? At the beginning of 1988, only a month before the first plane was due to be delivered, a Labour member of Parliament wrote to the BA chairman asking whether the commitment to Airbus was to be honoured. A copy of the reply he received got into the press, and it did not make agreeable reading in Toulouse.

British Airways *did* intend to take the aircraft, but were concerned about a serious performance shortfall from the design specification. "Due to a combination of factors—an overweight airframe, greater drag and a less efficient performance by CFM engines—the A320 is using approximately 9% more fuel for a given journey than was expected," Lord King wrote. "This will add to our costs and in addition could reduce our revenue on long flights because we would not be able to carry a full payload. We will of course look to Airbus for compensation initially and for performance improvements as soon as these can be produced."[28]

The figure relating to fuel was, in fact, an understatement. Lord King's letter was drafted by BA's director of planning, Keith Wilkins, and he said that the true figure was in the region of 11.5 percent. "The aircraft's performance fell within the absolute minimum guarantee," Wilkins said, "but it's rare that you have to take an aircraft that's only at minimum guarantee. You tend to assess the economic performance of the aircraft at the level which you got in good faith from the manufacturer. He will protect his position by writing a guarantee which is worse than that, you do your best to get that guarantee up, of course, and in the end there will be some sort of compromise. But you still anticipate a performance of a certain level which you have agreed with the manufacturer, and you base your economic case on that—with a little bit of caution, naturally. We made quite a fuss about it."[29]

It was a fuss that could not have come at a worse time for Airbus. British Airways had already made a start on the replacement of its BAC-111 fleet, which did not meet the new noise requirements due to come into force by the mid-1990s and were generally getting a bit long in the tooth. The airline also needed extra capacity to take care of growth, and the European consortium had thought it might be in with a reasonable chance. Keith Wilkins and his team had decided initially that McDonnell Douglas,

Boeing and Airbus all had something worth looking at. "The MD-80 was a real runner to begin with," Wilkins said, "in particular because there was the prospect that we would be able to re-engine the aircraft with prop-fan engines in 1993 or so. But there was no certainty that those engines would appear even if we signed an order, and we certainly couldn't have signed an order that was conditional, so eventually, and it took several months to get there, McDonnell Douglas fell out."

That left Airbus and Boeing, and Wilkins knew that he was going to be exposed to two sharply contrasting philosophies. "The only way for Airbus actually to compete is to come out with equipment that is more advanced than any of their competitors, which can bear a higher sticker price. That then gives them a basis on which to laud the relative merits of their product. And of course the Americans would argue that there is a limit to the number of bells and whistles that any airline wishes to pay for. And you have to recall that they are hardened, they have been brought up in an environment which is entirely self-supporting. There's nobody there to help you if you buy a bell too many."

Wilkins had been in the airline business for more than 35 years, initially with BOAC. A mathematician by training, he is a mild-mannered man with rather unruly white hair who might pass at a party for an academic publisher. Although the style is different, however, his technique for unsettling pushy sales directors is clearly every bit as deadly as that of his American opposite numbers: "Well, one might get onto the manufacturer and say, 'Look, these comparisons put you in a pretty poor light, dear chap, we would need a price reduction of so-and-so and these further concessions and business arrangements to make it compete.' And you know, it's surprising when you go along armed with information like that what results you can get—flexibility emerges, because rather like a second-hand car salesman, they set off with a price in the first place to test the market."

Flexibility was something that was very important to BA in these negotiations, but flexibility of a rather different kind. They knew that they had to go on growing, but they had to take account of what such things as liberalisation in Europe and the opening of the Channel Tunnel would do to their business, and these were largely imponderable. "You cannot maintain profitability unless you are growing," Wilkins said. "But you also want as much chance as possible to change your mind when things turn out to be different, as they *inevitably* will, because you will never get it right on the growth front. So you look for insurance, and insurance means being able to change your mind." Negotiations began in earnest on the 4th of July. "We thought it was a good way to mark Independence Day," said Wilkins.

Boeing and Airbus were both in a certain difficulty. "Boeing's production was largely sold out until 1993," Wilkins said, "but there were some slots available. When I knew that, the very first thing I did was to put all my effort into persuading Boeing to keep a lien on those slots for us, and to do that, I had to indicate the possible size of the business that we were really thinking about, which wasn't just making provision for 111 replacement. In the case of Airbus, there was no production availability at all until 1994, so that did curtail our interest. But then they came back into the picture very strongly with their offer of the A320s ordered by Pan American."[30]

The Boeing campaign was led by Graeme Howard, their director of European Sales. In theory, the BA requirement for flexibility suited them very well, but it was not all plain sailing. "Our 737 family started looking extremely attractive, but there was one major road block, and that was that it did not have category 3B landing capability, which is the lowest weather minimum that an airplane can operate under. We came back and reworked it, and we came up with a timetable to incorporate that on the airplane, but they wanted to start rolling over the BAC-111 fleet as early as 1990, so we had a big timing problem, because Airbus would have been able to deliver those PanAm airplanes as early as the spring of 1989, which put us almost 18 months out of synch."[22]

Howard, like Ulf Abrahamsson of SAS, remarked on the Airbus tendency to try to get the ear of the most senior man in an airline, though he thought they had recently come to appreciate that this was not always the best tactic. "If Airbus gave us an advantage in the past, it was by always trying to enter an airline at the top, because that's the guy that's going to make the decision, and they would wine him and dine him and all this kind of stuff. But there are a lot of airlines in which the top guy is just a political appointee—figurehead is too strong a word, but you know what I mean. In Boeing, our goal always is to work it from every possible direction. We'd talk to the janitor if we thought it would do us any good."

The campaign lasted until October. "I was camped in the Sheraton Skyline there for the last ten days, right across from our office at Heathrow," Howard recalled, "and we were burning the midnight oil trying to get this thing all together. Airbus was on site at that time, too, of course, and BA was spending three hours in the morning with Airbus and three hours in the afternoon with us and then going back and comparing notes."

"Airbus cut the sticker price very vigorously indeed and pursued us on a commercial deal which was as aggressive as anything I have ever seen," Wilkins said. Boeing won in the end, but not before they had committed themselves to opening a major spares store within an hour's drive of both Heathrow and Gatwick, and not before the airline's final decision was deferred for a fortnight to consider a last-minute throw by Airbus that had the sales team from Seattle extremely worried.[31] The memorandum of understanding was for twenty-four 737s, six 767-300s and one 757, together with eighteen options. The deal was worth $1.8 billion.

Asked why they had lost, one Airbus executive said sourly, "Because our name wasn't Boeing," making himself sound unintelligent when he was merely disappointed. Boeing won because the 737 comes in three versions.

The Series 300 has 124 seats. The Series 400 has 141 seats. The Series 500 has 106 seats. BA does not have to specify how many it wants of each until relatively late in the acquisition process. If there is an upsurge in air travel, they can go for more 400s. If growth tails off, then the 500 will be the answer. Flexibility. Commonality. The elimination of risk.

British Airways thus remained the only national flag-carrier among the four countries in the consortium not to have bought any Airbuses. "BA once again turns its back on the European manufacturers," wrote the French aviation magazine *Air & Cosmos* with a resigned editorial shrug. Among British politicians, there was criticism from both left and right. Michael Colvin, the chairman of the Conservative Parliamentary Aviation Committee, said, "British Airways cannot cajole us into 'flying the flag' if that flag is the Stars and Stripes,"[32] and Roger Stott, a Labour Opposition spokesman on trade and industry, said that the BA decision was "damaging and unpatriotic."[33]

There was also union criticism. The Manufacturing, Science and Finance Union happened to be holding its annual engineering conference when the announcement was made, and its national officer for aerospace, Chris Dark, said, "This is a kick in the teeth for the UK and European aerospace industry and is another example of a newly privatised company being totally unpatriotic, bordering on treachery."[32] The reaction of the business community was more pragmatic. Michael Grylls, a Conservative MP who was also chairman of the Small Businesses Bureau, saw nothing to complain about: it was a commercial decision taken by a company in the private sector. "I hope that as many British suppliers as possible will seize the opportunity of winning contracts with Boeing for the very large order."[32]

Airbus Industrie itself found it hard to master its disappointment. In a reproving letter to the *Financial Times* in London, Robert Alizart, their director of corporate communications, wrote that the paper's account of the deal would have gained in objectivity if it had paid more attention to "the benefits on offer from the world's second largest producer of civil aircraft." If British Airways or any other airline were simply to stick to one manufacturer that "it knows well," it would all but exclude effective competition. It would also result in much higher prices being paid for new equipment. "Is this policy of progressing backwards towards the future in the long-term interest of the airline or of its shareholders?" asked Monsieur Alizart.[34]

It is no great consolation to Airbus, but Keith Wilkins is convinced that their presence in the market place has toned up the performance of both McDonnell Douglas and Boeing. "What Boeing have traditionally done is get the balance just right between the price of the aircraft and the job it's designed to do. It's a sort of cooking version of the aircraft. Airbus had to take a different tack. They couldn't have got into the market if they'd taken that same line. They couldn't underprice Boeing—they are far too efficient. They had to do something more sophisticated. When they did that, they came back and they trumpeted that as being *the* advantage of going their way.

"Boeing eventually had to react to that. They simply couldn't leave their cooking versions alone, and they had to introduce some of the innovations—those that seemed to be the most cost-effective or safety-effective—that Airbus had. So Boeing were dragged along, and have been forced to increase the sophistication of their products. So that has been to the advantage of the carrier to a degree. In terms of pricing, the mere fact that there is a company offering a competing product must inevitably improve the buyer's position. Nothing more clever than that."

Wilkins did not think that he had seen the last of Airbus. "I should think they'll be back again when the dust settles, to deal perhaps with the long-haul operation.The dust might settle next year, and I would expect them to be back with a vigorous offer for A340s.

"But it has to be said that we have effectively closed off the likelihood of business at the smaller end of the market. One of the consequences of the Airbus high technology philosophy is that given the fundamental inherent cost, the only way you can continue to compete with that product is to make it bigger—you must spread those costs over a larger envelope; you can't compress it. So they would never be in a position to move down scale in their product offering, and therefore they will always be disadvantaged against a company like Douglas."

NOTES

1. *The Airbus Builders.* AI/CS 201/85 May 1985
2. Interview in Bristol, July 28, 1988.
3. *Flight International,* February 14, 1987.
4. *Boeing Leadership in Commercial Airplane Technology,* Seattle, 1987.
5. *A330/340: Advanced technology at work,* Airbus Industrie, Blagnac, 1988.
6. *The New World. Designed by pilots, for pilots: The A310 and A300-600 flight deck.* Airbus Industrie, Flight Division, Promotion Materials Group, May 1983.
7. David M. North, *Aviation Week & Space Technology* (November 30, 1987).
8. Extract from AI publication—subheading Windshear, nos. F-05-01 and F-05-02, undated.
9. g is the symbol for the acceleration due to gravity—9.8 m.[32 ft.] per second at sea level.
10. Interview in Seattle, February 1988.
11. Quoted in *Wind Shear* (New York: Airbus Industrie of North America, Inc., undated).
12. Interview in Toulouse, June 1988.
13. *Flight Safety.* AI publication no. F-03-01, undated.
14. Bogdan, *op. cit.*
15. *Presentation. Airbus Industrie,* January 1988.

16. " . . . on doit à la vérité de dire que c'est n'est pas lui qui a apporté le pilotage à deux: ce sont les Américains, et en l'espèce DOUGLAS avec son DC-9, qui en ont pris l'initiative il y a plus de vingt ans. Il était temps que nous en tirions les conséquences si nous voulions rester dans la compétition." *Le Monde,* July 22, 1988.

17. Interview in Frankfurt, December 1988.

18. Interview in Dallas, January 1989.

19. Scandinavian Airlines is, in fact, a consortium, made up of the old national airlines— ABA in Sweden, DDL in Denmark and DNL in Norway. The shareholding is split equally in each country between the government and private interests. The board, nine strong, has three members elected by these private interests, three representing the governments and three representing the staff. It is, in effect, run like a private company.

20. Interview in Stockholm, December 1988.

21. A report in the *Seattle Post-Intelligencer* for October 16, 1990 made it plain that this aspect of the competitive game can be played with varying degrees of subtlety. Boeing hit on a novel way of showing off the extra five inches it had managed to add to the diameter of its newest model, the 777. After a potential customer has toured the mock-up of the planes's interior, he is led to a second mock-up directly underneath. It is, in fact, three mock-ups in one, with a slice of the 777 interior telescoping into the narrower McDonnell Douglas MD-11 and then into an even tighter section of an Airbus A330. Stephen Wolf, the United Airlines chairman, is extremely tall. When he inspected the mock-up in the spring of 1990, he was offered a seat in the A330 section—and bumped his head on the ceiling when he stood up. This second mock-up is informally known at Boeing as "the dirty pool room."

22. Interview in Seattle, January 1989.

23. American had not, in fact, been the first port in which McDonnell Douglas had sought shelter from the storm. They had gone first to Northwest, and it was their chief executive, Steve Rothmeier, who developed thew concept of what was to become known as the walkaway lease, although in the event he decided against the deal.

24. Two months after this conversation American went on a spending spree. On March 22, 1989 they announced orders with Fokker and Boeing amounting to some $4 billion.

25. Interview in Minneapolis, January 1989.

26. Northwest had been flying Pacific routes since 1947, and in 1987 flew more passengers on them than any other U.S. airline.

27. He had written a paper about the economics of deregulation when he was studying at Chicago, and in the 1970s, when he was a director in the economic planning area at Northwest, he had had a hand in drafting the testimony which their then chief executive officer gave in favour of deregulation before a Senate subcommittee.

28. *The Sunday Telegraph,* January 31, 1988.

29. Interview in London, November 1988.

30. PanAm were in trouble. They could no longer afford the planes they had ordered from Airbus a couple of years earlier, and were hoping they could off-load them and make a handsome profit—as launch customers they had got them at a concessionary price. What would have suited Airbus best would be to find a new buyer in the United States. U.S. tax-base financing was in place, and to break that up and dispose of the aircraft outside the United States would be both complicated and costly. They had approached both TWA and United Airlines, but to no effect.

31. Stuart Iddles, the Airbus Commercial Director, was philosophical about this particular concession, and did not think it had clinched the deal: "It's all money. You either take it off the price of the aeroplane or you give it away in spares, but it's all money at the end of the day. It's very difficult to manage, that sort of thing. As a matter of policy, we do not any longer do consignment and spares jobs, because they're a nightmare to

administer." (Interview in Toulouse, February 1989.)

   32. *The Daily Telegraph,* October 22, 1988.
   33. House of Commons *Hansard,* October 26, 1988.
   34. *Financial Times,* October 22, 1988.

10

Words and Opportunities

"Ambassadors have no battleships at their disposal, or heavy infantry, or fortresses; their weapons are words and opportunities. In important transactions opportunities are fleeting; once they are missed they can never be recovered."

—Demosthenes, *De Falsa Legatione*, 343 B.C.

Although there was not much public sign of official U.S. concern about Airbus until the middle 1980s, the administration had in fact been exerting itself to contain the development of the European consortium for some time before that through diplomatic channels. Sometime in the first half of 1982, for example, the office of the Trade Representative had picked up on the Foreign Service net that feelers had been put out about broadening the participation in the Airbus A320 programme. There had been soundings in a number of countries, including Yugoslavia, Australia and the Netherlands, but the strongest push had been made in Italy and in Canada. In the case of latter, the approach had been made through the agency of the French government. The Province of Quebec had been approached for support, and there had been a vigorous attempt to secure both Canadian industrial participation (attention centred on de Havilland of Canada, which was then government-owned) and financial backing from the federal government. On June 23 Richard J. Smith, the U.S. chargé d'affaires in Ottawa, transmitted a letter from Ambassador William E. Brock, the United States trade representative, to the Canadian minister of industry, trade and commerce, Herb Gray.

The letter began in a low key by noting that international industrial participation in commercial aircraft was a growing trend, and that a number of U.S. companies benefited from Canadian involvement. "However," it continued,

a potential Canadian participation in the A-320 programme appears to differ from the traditional U.S. industrial cooperation in the following important respects:

1. It appears to involve a government-to-government negotiation and commitment. It is our understanding that consideration may be given to factors which are unrelated to the commercial merit of the venture being evaluated.

2. Significant government undertakings and investment would be required on both sides.

3. There are indications that the French sponsors of Canadian industrial participation in the Airbus A320 program would expect purchases of that aircraft or other Airbus Industry [sic] products by Air Canada to be one of the considerations in such an arrangement. Any implied or actual commitment on the part of Canada to purchase Airbus products or to encourage their purchase, as an adjunct to industrial participation would be a major concern to the United States Government . . .

The letter further expressed concern that government participation in the project might be on subsidised terms, which would place U.S. manufacturers on an unequal footing, and drew attention to the provisions of the Subsidies Code. "We ask," it concluded, "that you review this matter and would urge that any government monies advanced for industrial participation be on a commercially competitive basis and that there not be any government influence on aircraft selection by Air Canada if an industrial arrangement is made . . . " A letter couched in similar terms was sent to Italy. Neither country, in fact, became associated with the programme.

The year 1982 had also seen the beginning of a dialogue on trade matters between the U.S. administration and the industry, and prominent on the agenda was the 1979 Agreement on Trade in Civil Aircraft. The American industry had realised all too quickly that its authors must have been very familiar with the *Confessions* of St. Augustine—"Give me chastity and continency—but not yet!" The preamble was full of OK phrases such as "the ever-greater liberalisation of world trade" and "fair and equal competitive opportunities," but the text as a whole had been most expertly weaselled. Restrictions or distortions of trade, for example, were not simply to be done away with, but "reduced or eliminated to the fullest possible extent." Again, a sentence about the adverse effects on trade in civil aircraft of governmental support in development, production and marketing ended up by recognizing rather lamely that "such government support, of itself, would not be deemed a distortion of trade."

American dissatisfaction with the agreement had come to centre on Article 4, which dealt with government-directed procurement and inducements, and Article 6, which was concerned with government support, export credits and marketing. Article 4 stipulated that purchasers of civil aircraft should be free to select suppliers on the basis of commercial and technological factors and enjoined signatories not to require airlines to buy aircraft from any particular source. (The phrase *unreasonable pressure* was used at one point—the question of what constituted reasonable pressure was presumably left to the ingenuity of individual governments.) This was also the article under which signatories agree that aircraft should be purchased only on a basis of competitive price, quality and delivery, and that no inducements of any kind should be attached either to sale or purchase.

Under Article 6 the signatories agreed that the pricing of civil aircraft should be based on a reasonable expectation of the recoupment of all costs. The text here was unambiguous and specified the inclusion of nonrecurring programme costs, identifiable and prorated costs of military research and development, average production costs and financial costs. The article also noted that the GATT Agreement on Subsidies and Countervailing Measures should be held to apply to trade in civil aircraft, and the signatories affirmed in that context that they would "seek to avoid adverse effects on trade." What followed, however, turned this part of the agreement into a lawyers' paradise: "They also shall take into account the special factors which apply in the aircraft sector, in particular the widespread governmental support in this area, their international economic interests, and the desire of producers of all Signatories to participate in the expansion of the world civil aircraft market."

The view of one old hand with a long memory at GATT headquarters in Geneva was that the American negotiators had quite simply been outwitted: "The Community negotiated it, but behind the Community were the British, who know a thing or two about how to negotiate, and who whittled the language away until a lot of it meant nothing. I think it was a very good idea on the part of U.S. industry, but it was poorly negotiated and what they got was a lot of hot air."

The British negotiator was Roger Maynard, then an official in the Department of Trade and Industry, later British Airways vice-president for commercial affairs in North America, and during the negotiation he formed a close alliance with his French opposite number, Michel Lagorce. Lagorce said that initially there was a lot of discussion in France about whether such an agreement would be to their advantage.[1] "We were beginning to sell aircraft. Our main interest was in the removal of tariffs. There was a uniform tariff schedule, and all aerospace products were paying something of the order of 6 percent. On the Airbus Eastern deal, Eastern had said to Airbus, 'Look, we would be delighted to buy your planes, but we don't want to pay any duty, so you'll have to pay that for us'—which meant 4–5 percent on the price of an aircraft which was selling for $35 million or so. So we were certainly interested in the elimination of tariffs. What the Americans wanted was a code of practice that would regulate subsidies and government intervention. There were several high level meetings here in France, and there was considerable reluctance, because they were afraid that we should be obliged to accept lots of constraints that would put us at a disadvantage. But Roger Maynard and I were confident that we could negotiate a code in terms that would not tie our hands at all."

The *entente cordiale* certainly appears to have operated to some effect during the period of the negotiations. "There was a great rush to get it finished," Maynard said, "but rush by GATT standards is not quick. It was at least 18 months. I was going to Geneva at least once a month for what seemed ages."[2] Asked whether he was surprised that the Americans had acquiesced in the final wording, Lagorce laughed, and said, "At the time I was not. I was too young. Nine years later, my feeling is that if I had been in their shoes I would not have signed."

Maynard is unsure about whether the American side realised at the time that it had not got what it wanted. "It was their idea, of course, to have an agreement. They came traipsing round Europe to persuade us this was a good thing, and I think that by the time we had reached a conclusion, it was very difficult for the Americans to walk away from it. It would be easy to say we outnegotiated them, but I wouldn't want to claim that. I think they misled themselves. I think they assumed they had got more out of it than they really had, and in order to sell it to Congress and everyone else, they had to bolster it, they had to believe their own rhetoric, if you like. I think the agreement was just as we had expected it to be, and as they should have expected it to be."

Maynard did not have an altogether easy time with his own political masters. "I have to say I had considerable difficulties getting British politicians to sign off on it—they were very 'iffy' about it. They saw the benefits of the free trade, but they were concerned that it could be used to restrict their freedom of manoeuvre to support what they regarded as a strategic industry. But in the end they went along with it. I think we did actually get a good deal for Europe out of it. I think the Americans were just rather naive about the value of the language."

There was provision in the agreement for review and for the settlement of disputes. A Committee on Trade in Civil Aircraft was established, which was to consist of representatives of all the signatories and to meet not less than once a year. The text concluded in conventional manner—"Done at Geneva this twelfth day of April nineteen hundred and seventy-nine in a single copy, in the English and French languages, each text being authentic . . ."

It did not take the United States side long to conclude that it read very much better in the French version. "I remember I was appointed the first Chairman of the Committee," Roger Maynard said, "and the Americans brought their first 'case' to the first meeting and quickly discovered that the language didn't mean what they hoped it meant. The Europeans said, 'Well, this is what the wording says, what is it you are trying to get us to do? It's not consistent.' I think think they found out very early on about article 4, in particular, which is the one about inducements. There was quickly a disagreement over that. They obviously thought it meant a lot more than the Europeans did. The key phrase was 'unreasonable pressure'—it's a beautiful word: what does it mean? We always recognised that if you disallow 'unreasonable pressure' then it's obviously quite legitimate to have reasonable pressure, whereas the Americans had assumed it really meant that you never put any pressure on at all. But they signed it, and basically they've been trying to renegotiate that agreement ever since. That's in essence what this trade dispute is all about—it's an attempt to renegotiate something they discovered late in the day they didn't like."

The dialogue begun between the administration and the major companies was resumed the following year, and in January 1983 the chief executive officers of five of the biggest aerospace companies—Boeing, General Electric, Lockheed, McDonnell Douglas and United Technologies—had a meeting in Washington with the secretary of commerce, Malcolm Baldrige, and Ambassador Brock.

The industry spoke very much with one voice. They urged the need for a more coherent export policy that would foster trade, keep U.S. markets open and create new jobs in aerospace for workers laid off from other industries that were shrinking. Unilateral measures, which were seldom effective and invited retaliation, should be avoided, and there should be no resort to protectionism: the selective use of political leverage, however, should not be excluded. They did not feel that the financing available from the Export-Import Bank was adequate, and they suggested changes in the policies of the bank and its removal from the federal budget. They also emphasised the need to strengthen and enforce international trade agreements, and for good measure they threw in appeals for a revision of the antitrust laws governing joint research, more favourable tax treatment and an increase in R&D funding to NASA and other appropriate agencies.

Summing up for the industry, T. A. Wilson, Boeing's chairman and chief executive officer, suggested that representatives of all those attending the meeting should be formed into a task force to implement their specific proposals and that there should be a cabinet-level working group, perhaps chaired by the trade representative, which would be asked to come up within six months with a draft of a trade policy along the lines suggested.

The government side responded in more-general terms than the industry could have wished, but were not unsupportive. Ambassador Brock said that he was looking into the terms of the charter of the Export-Import Bank, and undertook to remind the British and German governments of their obligations; the French, he added, were less approachable on such matters. The idea of a task force was accepted in principle; to the proposal for a group at cabinet level they didn't say yes and they didn't say no. The administration representatives appealed specifically to the industry for their support in resisting the protectionist trend that they anticipated in Congress in the course of the year.

Later in the year, Ambassador Brock had the benefit of the views of the Aerospace Industries Association of America, which had been reviewing the operation of the agreement in its first two and a half years. The president of the association, Karl G. Harr, Jr., wrote that the agreement had proved to be an appropriate vehicle in many areas, although he noted that like GATT itself, it had what he described as "problems involving satisfactory and timely discipline." He called for the provisions about procurement to be strengthened and for an enlargement of the scope of the article about export credits. Signatories should agree to eliminate all subsidies in official government direct-loan financing and accept that the Illustrative List of Export Subsidies contained in the GATT Subsidy Code Annex were applicable to the agreement.[3] In his reply, the trade representative indicated his readiness to pursue the points made by the association, although he felt that in particular cases it would be more effective to deal directly with the governments concerned—"as we did last year in countering foreign government pressures being applied in Italy with regard to Alitalia's fleet requirements."[4]

Ambassador Brock was also kept posted with details of the industry's suspicions about dirty tricks in the market place. In 1984, for instance, Boeing formed the view that a sales campaign in Turkey, where the 767 was pitted against the A310, had not exactly been conducted according to Queensberry rules. It was certainly the case that Franz-Josef Strauss had been in Turkey at the time, and he did not behave like a conventional tourist. He turned up a few days before the airline was scheduled to make its decision. He met the prime minister, the foreign minister, the minister of defence and the minister of transport.

France, as it happened, was not in Turkey's good books at the time. It had been slow to recognise the newly installed régime, and had caused further offence by permitting the unveiling of a monument commemorating the alleged Armenian genocide of 1914. *Kein Problem!* said Dr. Strauss. Airbus, as was well known, was a German aeroplane.They could buy with confidence. He congratulated his hosts on the large numbers of Turkish workers who had found employment in Germany . . . He passed in review his country's extensive economic and military aid to Turkey . . . What better way could there be of greasing the slips for entry to the European Community than a demonstration of Turkey's belief in the superiority of European industrial products?

The U.S. trade representative was prevailed upon to remonstrate with the Federal German minister of economics, Martin Bangemann. It was a little naïve to expect him to tangle with the uncrowned king of Bavaria— they should have known in Washington that Bonn's writ did not run in those parts. Herr Bangemann, clearly a student of British naval history, placed his telescope to his blind eye. "The Federal Government has at no time been in contact with the Turkish airline," he replied virtuously. "On government level it is the Federal Government's policy to reject any linkages of private business transactions with political considerations." Quite so. The man who once said that only the whole truth is wholly true was only a philosopher, after all.

In general, however, Airbus competed with a thousand other issues at intergovernment level, and interest was sporadic. Politicians—European ones, at least—do not for the most part have a long span of attention, and one has the impression that in the middle 1980s ministers entered the fray with no more than moderate enthusiasm and only when prodded by their officials.

In the United States things are rather different, and July 1, 1985, saw a change of cast in Washington, with the swearing in as trade representative of Ambassador Clayton Yeutter, a man with a lot of government experience during the Nixon and Ford administrations and a former president of the Chicago Mercantile Exchange, the world's second-largest futures market. The ambassador held both a Ph.D. in agricultural economics and a law degree.The press announcement of his appointment said that he was still remembered for having worked on both these graduate level programmes simultaneously, while at the same time managing a 2,500 acre farm.

The industry naturally exerted itself to bend the ear of the new ambassador. In a speech to the Aero Club of Washington in late November, Dean Thornton, the president of the Boeing Commercial Airplane Company called for "some jawboning from the highest levels" to aid U.S. manufacturers. He said that the process of negotiation through such mechanisms as GATT was "too cumbersome and slow." Thornton stressed that his company was not asking for subsidy, but conceded that the Airbus sales strategy was exerting tremendous pressure. "We have tried to remain competitive, but we have elected not to give away the farm in order to sell the current crop," he said. "Product performance is served up but lost in a plate full of price concessions, financing deals, government linkage and political machinations. Maybe we should be flattered to be a 'targeted industry' . . . "[5]

There was another broadside from Boeing a few weeks later at the rollout of their new 767-300 in Seattle, this time from Tom Bacher, their director of International Business and Government Affairs. The company, Bacher said, had been patient for more than ten years, "but now it is getting pretty damned mad."[6] He went on to question whether it made economic sense for Europe to have an aircraft industry—"You build good train systems and things like that in Europe, and we do not." It was a phrase that was to have wide currency and bring a hornet's nest around his ears. Many thousands of miles away in Aberdeen, Scotland, an indignant reader of *Flight International* took up his pen and wrote at length to the editor. "Perhaps," he concluded with heavy irony, "we should capitulate to the Americans and not have an aircraft or helicopter industry. Let us stick to the things we are good at, such as finding new ways of putting ourselves down and encouraging the talented to go overseas."[7]

In December 1985, Ambassador Yeutter had received a long letter, too. His was from the British secretary of state for Trade and Industry, Leon Brittan—also a lawyer, though lacking Yeutter's agricultural expertise. The minister understood that the *Annual Report on National Trade Estimates*, recently published by the trade representative's office, alleged that the governments of Airbus partner countries had intervened politically to promote sales in a way that was inconsistent with the Agreement on Trade in Civil Aircraft. He also understood, he wrote, that it expressed doubts about whether government launch aid for the A320 was permissible under the agreement . . . "I wanted to write to you personally to say that I cannot go along with this as a fair representation of the facts."

Yeutter had a small surprise in store, because this "personal" letter was also copied to the commerce secretary, the treasury secretary and Secretary of State Shultz, but he would only discover that when he got to page three. The first two pages were taken up with a smooth defence of Airbus, a bland exegesis of Article 6 of the agreement and a glancing observation or two about the different forms taken by governmental support in different countries . . . Brittan ended by confirming that Her Majesty's Government, together with the governments of the other Airbus partner countries, would welcome further informal talks with the U.S. as soon as possible at the level of senior officials. The European governments had obviously concerted their views; Mr Yeutter had similar letters from Bonn and Paris, the latter rather more terse in tone.

The consultations were arranged for the following March in Geneva and the trade representative asked Bruce Wilson, his assistant for industry and services, to lead the U.S. delegation. There is a curious sentence at the end of a letter Ambassador Yeutter wrote at this time to the West German minister of economics, Martin Bangemann, which could indicate that he thought they were not going to be easy—"Martin, it is important that we work together to ensure that our colleagues succeed in these talks so that we do not have to become personally involved in the details." Whatever his reasoning, it was not an involvement he would escape very much longer.

The meeting took place at the West German Mission in Geneva (West Germany was the current chairman of the intergovernmental Airbus Committee) and lasted for two days. Dieter Wolf, *Ministerialdirigent* at the Federal Economics Ministry, led for the Europeans, and Bruce Wilson's team included representatives from the Departments of State, Commerce, Justice and Labor as well as the U.S. Embassy in Paris and the U.S. Mission to the GATT in Geneva. There was an observer from the European Commission present, but he did not speak. Outside the meetings, the U.S. team had the benefit of industry advice from representatives of the AIA, McDonnell Douglas and Boeing. Alan Boyd, Airbus Industrie's North

American chairman, was also in Geneva.

There were four sessions, and the discussion ranged over five broad issues—the competitive environment, financial support, political influences and inducements, procurement by national airlines and supplier selection. The tone of the exchanges was generally friendly, although the temperature rose several degrees when the discussion turned to subsidies and the American side produced its estimate of $7 billion as the amount of aid Airbus had received from the member governments—a figure one-third to one-quarter higher than the total amount of assistance disclosed in the national budgets of the member nations.

The Germans gave no figures, maintaining—correctly—that so far as they were concerned, they were available in published budget documents. The British admitted only to the £250 million provided as launch aid for the A320. The French, whose style on such occasions normally makes Stonewall Jackson's performance at Bull Run seem wimpish, came up with a figure of 8.7 billion francs for the period from 1969 to the end of 1986, and claimed to have recouped 25 percent of the sums provided. The Europeans occasionally varied their tactics by carrying the argument briskly into the American camp, asserting that their support for Airbus, though direct, was really different only in form from assistance provided to their American competitors—R&D for defence, defence procurement, military "flow-through" to civil aircraft development and research funded by NASA.

On the question of inducements, there appeared to be more of a meeting of minds. There was little recrimination and hardly any reference to specific cases, though the Europeans slipped in a passing reference to what they saw as U.S. government intervention in Thailand, Japan and Kenya. There seemed to be agreement that intervention was to be deplored. Ideas like illustrative lists of what was permitted and what was not were explored, and there was some interest in the idea of a "hot-line" between governments to air complaints.

At the end of two days, the joint press statement proposed by the Europeans seemed to the Americans to do little more than reiterate the objectives of the Aircraft Code and paper over differences, and each side accordingly went public with its own version of the state of play. A further meeting was agreed for June, and the heads of the German and British delegations, more concerned than the French about the effect of possible American retaliation, accepted invitations to visit the United States and hear the industry's case from the horse's mouth.

In the middle of April, Clayton Yeutter picked up his pen once more and wrote identical letters to his European ministerial colleagues. (In the United Kingdom, Leon Brittan had now been succeeded by Paul Channon.) He characterised the consultations as "lengthy, frank and honest." He understood that there seemed to be some prospect of progress on inducements, but that the two sides were still far apart on subsidies. He hoped they would urge their delegations to be "flexible and forthcoming" at the next meeting, and suggested that any understandings reached then should be formally recorded, perhaps by an exchange of letters between governments.

He raised a second matter. It was common knowledge by now that the Airbus partner governments were considering the question of launch aid for the new A330 and 340 programmes, and the trade representative registered his government's concern. He did not beat about the bush. "Our own preliminary economic analyses do not persuade us that there is a solid economic basis for providing government aid to launch these aircraft programs. The market potential appears too small to allow for recoupment of such government aid, including interest charges, in a manner consistent with Article 6.2 of the GATT Aircraft Agreement . . . "

The most thoughtful reply he received was from Martin Bangemann, who said that although it was the federal government's policy to reduce the level of public support to German industry, the financial position of the aerospace industry posed special problems. He recalled that for "political reasons" the industry had been allowed to resume activity only in the mid-1950s. For a number of years after that, most aerospace defence items had either been purchased in the United States or manufactured under licence. For these and other reasons the industry was still undercapitalized and still needed time before being able to finance civil aircraft programmes from its own resources.

From Michel Noir, the French trade minister, there came an elegantly dusty answer. He parried the subsidy point by referring to the funds for research and development that he claimed the American industry received from NASA and the Defense Department. On the question of the A330 and 340 he invited the Americans, in the nicest possible way, to mind their own business—it was, he said, a matter for internal decision, on which France and her partners would employ their own judgement.[8] This unaccommodating tone was echoed in a position paper prepared for the benefit of the European delegations attending the June meeting. It was plain that there was little genuine interest in any amendment to the terms of the agreement, and that the officials who were spending the sticky days of the Washington summer drafting forms of words could as well have gone boating on the Potomac.

All the Americans were able to squeeze out of this second round of informal discussions was an "agreed minute" (the European side used the French term "procès verbal"). This document was not made public, and its force and status were obscure. The delegations of the Airbus governments had no authority to negotiate on issues of trade policy, which is the prerogative of the European Community, and the minute did not therefore constitute a legally binding interpretation of the Aircraft Code.

There was some satisfaction on the American side that for the first time the definition of inducements had been broadened to include more than landing rights and that a process had been agreed for resolving complaints. To that limited extent the area of disagreement had been narrowed. On the major issue of government support, however, the two sides remained as far apart as ever, and a page and a half of the agreed minute was taken up with describing the width of the gulf between them. The Airbus side did not concede that governmental support was in itself a distortion of trade. In their view, a government was obliged to provide information on support for their civil aircraft industry only when there was evidence of such distortion, and they insisted that they knew of none. The U.S. delegation took the view that the provisions of Article 6 of the agreement amounted to an obligation to provide support to civil aircraft programmes only on a commercial basis, and elaborated on what information they believed to be necessary to ensure the effective operation of the agreement.

There had, of course, been an undeclared American objective, which was to try and keep the Europeans off balance in the matter of the A330/340 launch. One tactic for achieving this was to create uncertainty about what the United States's next step might be. Talking to the press at the conclusion of the talks, Bruce Wilson emphasised that the United States was fully reserving its rights under existing international trade agreements and outlined the various courses of action open to them—the discussions with the Airbus governments could be formally raised to the political level; consultations with the EEC could be initiated under GATT; a GATT case could be initiated to force an interpretation; amendments could be sought to the code; or the U.S. government could embark on unilateral actions. There was no great confidence in the American industry that this goal would be achieved. There was also some anxiety that the administration might, as one Boeing executive put it, be lulled back to sleep by procedural concessions that were essentially without meaning. The option that would best suit their book was the escalation of the talks to the political level so as to maintain pressure on the central issue of government support.

In Paris a few weeks later there was evidence that on the European side nothing very much had changed. The French transport minister, Jacques Douffiagues, was the guest of honour at a dinner-debate, and one of the journalists present bowled him a very gentle ball—"After Boeing's attempt to brainwash the French press in Seattle two months ago about the European governments' subsidies of the Airbus programmes, what are your conclusions following the recent discussions in Geneva?" "The communiqué released after the meetings reports in moderate terms the frank discussions and the positions of the two parties," the minister replied. "However, the debate will not move towards an eventual understanding as long as we do not get the answer to the question still unanswered about the exact financial contribution of US government business to Boeing's total profits."

During the summer, the Department of Commerce picked over the scanty data that had come out of the Geneva meetings and revised their estimates of the amount of launch aid advanced to Airbus since 1969. Their new figure was $4.6–4.7 billion—$7 billion with the addition of simple interest, $9 billion if compounded. The industry kept up its pressure on the administration, urging the escalation of the consultations to the political level and increased activity in the GATT Aircraft Committee for the amendment of the Aircraft Code. A month before the October meeting of the Committee, the president of the Aerospace Industries Association of America sent to Ambassador Yeutter a detailed note on the strategy they would like to see adopted by the administration, but little was achieved, and by the end of the year the association had raised their sights and were addressing their concerns to the secretary of state, George Schultz.

The Supervisory Board of Airbus had authorised the "completion of the definition" of the joint A330/340 programme at the end of January 1986, and when Chancellor Kohl came to Paris at the beginning of March for one of his regular twice-yearly meetings with the French president they had lent their support to the project. The Americans knew very well that a firm decision to launch the A330/340 would mark a watershed in their relations with the European consortium. Airbus salesmen had quite a good line in gallows-humour—"Buy a Jumbo and get a 737 free," they used to say when they felt the need to keep their spirits up, and their masters in Toulouse had made no secret of their belief that the key to commercial success in the long term lay in finding a way to compete with Boeing's "cash cow," the 747. To extend their range in this way would allow them for the first time to emulate the Boeing strategy of offering a complete family of aircraft, allowing airlines to achieve substantial savings through commonality.

The United States also knew that the although the campaign to secure government financial backing was being vigorously pursued, the channelling of large sums of public money into such ventures was being increasingly questioned. In the United Kingdom, the government and British Aerospace were facing each other down over how much of the taxpayers' money should be committed this time round. The company had initially said it would only take part in the project if the government picked up the tab for the whole of the design and development cost of the wings, but the Department of Trade and Industry was sceptical about the commercial prospects for the programme, and it seemed unlikely that the government would come up with more than half that amount.

In Germany, too, there were signs that the government was stirring itself to shift some of the burden of financing the consortium away from the public sector. The government was exploring ways of involving a number of large industrial concerns. Bosch and BMW had been mentioned, and so had Siemens and Daimler-Benz. Franz-Josef Strauss was not disposed to make things easy for the government. In a letter to Martin Bangemann, extensively leaked to the German press in December 1986, he painted a garish doomsday scenario. Not only would it be impossible to make up any reduction in the government's commitment to the programme from the private sector: Deutsche Airbus in fact urgently needed further subsidies if it were to stave off bankruptcy.

It even seemed possible that things might be changing a little in France. The finance minister in the new centre-right government, Edouard Balladur, proposed to finance some of his tax cuts by a reduction in subsidies to the public sector, and Jacques Chirac had appointed as his minister of industry Alain Madelin. Madelin had been trained as an engineer and a lawyer, and was one of the architects of the programme of privatisation and deregulation on which the French centre and right had come to power. This 40-year old son of a Communist worker spoke a language that had not been much heard in the Paris ministries: "Producers come to the government for the money capitalists and consumers have decided to deny them because of poor performance"; "It is not French producers who are no longer competitive: it is the French state." One of his early decisions had been to refuse to cover the record deficit of the nationalised Renault company until a plan had been prepared for getting it out of the red in two years.[9]

The United States administration decided it was time to step up the pressure. There had been a good deal of lobbying both from the AIA and from individual companies, urging that the discussions with the Airbus governments be elevated to cabinet or sub-cabinet level, and on December 5 the Economic Policy Council adopted a plan of action. Ambassador Yeutter was instructed to arrange for a delegation to visit Europe for talks at ministerial level early in the New Year.

These took place in early February 1987, and the U.S. team consisted of Bruce Smart, the under secretary of commerce for international trade, and Michael B. Smith, Clayton Yeutter's deputy, the most hawkish of the senior administration officials involved in the Airbus issue and the man who had signed the Civil Aircraft Agreement for the United States in Geneva eight years previously. According to Bruce Wilson, who was next in line at the USTR's office after Smith, their instructions from the cabinet were clear: "They went to deliver a political message—that the U.S. government was not going to stand idly by and accept the unfettered subsidisation of Airbus, particularly when that unfettered subsidisation was leading to a displacement of U.S. exports by the no.1 manufacturing export industry in the U.S."[2] They went first to London, where a meeting had been arranged with Geoffrey Pattie, the junior minister at the Department of Trade and Industry, and they met with a reception that was distinctly unfriendly.

Sally Bath of the Commerce Department was in the U.S. party. She said that she was appalled by the behaviour of the British minister, and thought that some of his own officials were, too. "I was very, very angry," she said. "I mean, I'm a brief-case carrier, I'm there to open doors, but I was absolutely livid. And when I looked at some of the people I knew on the other side of the table, there were eyebrows going up and a couple of small *mea culpas* coming across the table at me like this" (Bath's fingertips came together just above the level of her desk). "And when I saw this little tent come up like this above the table, I thought 'You're reading it the same way I am, and you know I'm mad!'"

Pattie's offence seems to have been that he decided attack was the best form of defence. That a country with 80 percent of the world airline aircraft market should complain about European competition he characterised as "bizarre." The United Kingdom, he said, took exception to being lectured on its financial support for its aircraft industry by a U.S. government which awarded large contracts to its own aircraft manufacturers. There might, he suggested, be a link between the pricing of Boeing's 767 aircraft and what he called the "monopolistic" pricing of the 747. The world's airlines ask for competition, he said. "It is astonishing that the U.S. should cry foul in the light of U.S. protectionism." Pattie, schooled in the rough-house of Westminster, clearly enjoyed himself. "Imagine words like that being used across the table at 10 o'clock on a Monday morning to people who had jet lag," Sally Bath said. "It was not a wonderful meeting."

Having said it once in private, Pattie said most of it again later at a press conference. Journalists like nothing better than an outspoken politician, and wrote it all up with zest. They are also essentially a lazy breed, however, and they went on writing more or less the same story when the scene shifted to Paris and Bonn later in the week, although in fact the tone of those meetings was notably less sharp.

Sally Bath conceded that some people had seen the trip as an attempt by the United States to "draw a line in the sand." As things turned out, the American delegation felt it had not had much of an opportunity to make its case. "You've got to realise that a trip like that is planned over a period of several months," Bath said. "In between the plan for the trip and the time of the trip, things got a little interesting in Europe on a marketing perspective, and you had two organisations out each trying to cut the ground out from underneath the other—McDonnell Douglas with the MD-11 and Airbus with the A340."

"The U.S. company was constrained in how much of a price concession it could give by the instructions of its board of directors, which basically said "we're not going to lose money on this aircraft," because even on your launch you can cut so far but no further. The Airbus marketing team didn't seem to be under any such constraints, and as a result, when we got ready to go to Europe, Bruce Smart and Mike Smith were both quite upset about what they were hearing about these absurd price concessions that were coming out on the A340. It was very hard for us to understand how a four-engined aircraft of all-new technologies could be sold even on a launch price concessionary basis at $65 million each. It didn't make sense. If the aircraft had all these bells and whistles on it that were going to create wonderful operating economies for the airlines, the airlines should have been willing to pay for it, even in a launch situation. That was something that unfortunately got in the way of some of the statements of principle."

Airbus had, in fact, had a considerable boost only a few weeks before the talks when it had been announced that Lufthansa had provisionally agreed to buy 15 A340s, with an option on 15 more. Reinhardt Abraham, Lufthansa's vice-chairman, rejected any suggestion that their decision had been influenced by political considerations, but it was not thought likely that Franz-Josef Strauss, wearing one of his many hats as a member of the airline's supervisory board, had opposed the idea.[10] No financial details were disclosed, but one analyst specialising in West German equities for Merrill Lynch in New York said, "I'm sure they got pristinely beautiful financial arrangements." He underlined the significance for Airbus of a big deal with an important airline as an incentive to other buyers, but added, "Airbus has always shown a willingness to go ahead with programs whether they make any sense or not."

Smith and Smart flew home, bloody but unbowed, and their report was discussed at a meeting of the Economic Policy Committee of the Cabinet on February 13, 1987. The following day, in Toulouse, Airbus rolled out the A320: a highly theatrical occasion, complete with laser beams, clouds of dry ice and angel voices—presumably on tape. The French prime minister was there, and so were the heads of the 16 airlines that had ordered the plane. There were a great many speeches. The Prince of Wales said that collaboration on technology was a good thing. Franz-Josef Strauss, allowing himself to be a shade more controversial, had a little sly fun with the Smith/Smart mission, which he described as "acoustical interference" from the United States. "We will not allow political agitation to distract us from the successful path we have chosen," he said.

When nobody could think of anything more to say, the Princess of Wales swung a very large bottle of very good champagne. The Airbus ministers of the four countries were there, too, of course, and took advantage of the occasion to put their heads together, rather as if they were at a royal funeral. Afterwards they put out a communiqué, which said, yet again, that they "noted with satisfaction that the A330/340 met the requirements of the air transport market." Jean Pierson and his Airbus Industrie colleagues had naturally hoped that they would say what their satisfaction amounted to in hard cash, but on that they were silent.

In Washington, the pace quickened. At the February 13 meeting of the Economic Policy Committee, the administration had come pretty close to lighting the touch paper. "Some pretty tough options were considered by the cabinet," Steve Falken of the Department of Commerce said, "but at the last minute McDonnell Douglas had a change of heart—they decided that when they had a lot of customers and potential customers in Europe the government's efforts would simply contribute to the building of a fortress Europe mentality and that action would be counterproductive to their sales efforts. I think their expression was "Keep your powder dry'."[2]

Not everyone in the administration was best pleased at the company's indecisiveness. There was some feeling that McDonnell Douglas had marched them up to the top of the hill and marched them down again. "It will be a long time before McDonnell Douglas will get anything from the government," one official was quoted as saying. "The U.S. government is not a marketing tool."[11] The upshot was that the Economic Policy Committee called for a special meeting of the GATT Aircraft Committee to interpret two articles of the Aircraft Code—Article 4 (inducements and pressure on airlines) and Article 6 (subsidies and pricing). The Department of Commerce was also instructed to commission a study of the economics of the Airbus operation and to keep a beady eye on any attempts by Airbus to woo MD-11 launch customers away to the A340. If there was evidence of trade practices deemed to be unfair, the issue would go back to the cabinet for action. The aim should be to settle things by July.

The Department of Commerce placed its commission with Gellman Research Associates Inc., a company run by a prominent transportation economist that had its head office in Jenkintown, Pennsylvania. The brief was "to examine the subsidy questions and undertake an economic analysis of the support and pricing of existing and proposed Airbus aircraft programs," and by the middle of May the department had received a bulky technical proposal for how the work should proceed, complete with the sort of diagrams so dear to the hearts of consultants that demonstrate things like conceptual methodology. The company had assembled a large study team, dripping with doctorates and bristling with expertise, and proposed to enlist additional consultancy support in both the United Kingdom and the Netherlands. A good deal of the brushwood had obviously already been cleared. Gellman did not propose to hang about. A final report was promised within 60 days of the award of the contract.

The interested parties had meanwhile all shuttled back to Geneva for two days of meetings that were due to begin on March 19, but the start had been delayed by wrangling over procedure. The Europeans, sensing a new determination in the American delegation, went on the offensive and said in effect that they would not negotiate on interpretation with a pistol to their heads. After much manoeuvring, the U.S. side agreed to withdraw its formal "request" for the meeting, but on the condition that the Europeans agreed to a schedule of meetings leading to a conclusion of the discussions in July. In the brief two-hour session that this left time for, the U.S. delegation elaborated on its proposed interpretation, and the EEC delegation riposted with a legal critique in which they they claimed that the Americans were in effect trying to renegotiate the code.

At the end of April, Ambassador Smith deputised for Clayton Yeutter at a panel discussion organised by the Aerospace Industries Association, and told his audience what they wanted to hear. The aerospace industry, he said, embodied the height of high-tech. It was crucial to the economy and to exports. The time had come to get a "meaningful handle" on the deficiencies of the existing international disciplines in aircraft. He hoped they could come firmly to grips with the issue over the ensuing three or four months, but that really depended on the Europeans. At one point he said, "I will try to be diplomatic, recognising that there are members of the Fourth Estate here," but the newspaper reporting of the February visit plainly still rankled. "It was reported in the press that we retreated from Europe after our discussions on the Airbus. I can't speak for Bruce Smart, but coming from Marblehead the word retreat is not in my vocabulary."

Preparations for the next round were quickly underway. Boeing, alive to officialdom's predilection for the dispatch of business and a quiet life, decided that it would do no harm to mark the Department of Commerce's card and got off a letter to Bruce Smart. "We have stressed on several occasions that our major problem with Airbus stems from its extensive and unlimited subsidization. These subsidies lead to launch of new programmes without viability, incorporation of technologies that cannot pay for themselves, building of whitetails which are offered at fire-sale prices and widespread underpricing to gain market share." Boeing saw the resolution of this issue as basic, and urged that the government negotiators should not settle for a partial agreement that dealt only with secondary matters like the offer of inducements in sales campaigns. An agreement on subsidies and on the requirement for complete and continuous disclosure should be the first order of business.

Meetings were held monthly. There was one on May 26 and 27, and an internal report on it, prepared by the staff of the European Commission, throws interesting light both on the European stance and on the relationship between the member governments and the EEC. The commission had clearly now realised that the Americans were not just playing around and had won approval from the member states for the view that it was no longer sufficient simply to refute the United States interpretation—"The Community should offer some (admittedly preliminary) views on how it understood certain of these provisions and, in particular Article 4, without, of course, making any concessions of substance at this stage, *in order to avoid providing any pretext for the US to abandon this consultation process"*(author's italics).

The staff work of the Airbus governments seems to have been a shade chaotic. They had produced two informal working papers on their interpretation of articles 4 and 6, but made them available only during the meeting, which meant that they were of little use to the commission team. The member states were present, but sat silent throughout, though at the end of the proceedings they thanked the commission spokesman for the way he had conducted the consultations. This seemed to please the EEC team inordinately—"One of the most remarkable results of this meeting certainly is the confidence the Commission was able to gain from the Member States. It has established itself as the generally recognised spokesman of the Community in this matter, which can only be regarded as a positive basis for future proceedings."

There had never really been much doubt that the member governments would come up with the necessary launch aid for the A330/340 programme. From the middle of May onwards, beginning with the United Kingdom, they each made known the terms that they were prepared to offer. Airbus Industrie decided not to wait for the Paris Air Show and announced the formal launch of the programme on June 5. They said that ten airlines had announced commitments or expressed interest, a total of 130 aircraft. The United Kingdom would contribute £450 million, the Federal Republic DM 2,996 million and France FF 6,000 million. The Spanish contribution was not immediately disclosed. Certification of the A340 was planned for May 1992 and of the A330 for the following spring.

The official American response came in the form of a statement from Clayton Yeutter a week later, and in the light of all that had gone on earlier in the year, it sounded curiously muted. The U.S. government, it said, was unpersuaded that the launch programme could be justified by a reasonable expectation of recoupment of the investments with interest. The study of the Airbus subsidy question which the Economic Policy Council had ordered several months previously would soon be ready, and the administration would be using it to determine whether the recent decision was consistent with the GATT Aircraft Agreement. The aim of reaching an understanding by July on ways of clarifying and strengthening the agreement might now be more difficult.

Before those crucial July sessions, the issues had an exhaustive airing in Washington. The House of Representatives Committee on Energy and Commerce has a subcommittee on Commerce, Consumer Protection and Competitiveness. Its chairman was James J. Florio, an intense and serious-minded Italian-American Democrat from New Jersey, and at 9:33 A.M. on June 23 he called his members to order and directed their attention to the morning's business—the competitiveness of the US commercial aircraft industry.[12]

A starry list of witnesses had been summoned to appear. Bruce Smart was there for Commerce and Ambassador Smith for the USTR. McDonnell Douglas's corporate vice-president for Aerospace, James E. Worsham, was on parade, and so was Orvil M. Roetman, Boeing's vice-president for International Business and Government Affairs, and the industry team was completed by Don Fuqua, the new president of the AIA. The odd man out in this high-powered team was Alan S. Boyd, who had been secretary of transportation in the Johnson administration and was now the chairman of Airbus's North American Board. Before he left Room 2123 of the Rayburn House Office Building at the end of the morning he would have reason to remember some words of Dean Acheson, who when he was secretary of state in the 1950s said that appearing before a congressional committee was like "entering an abattoir."

They had all come with prepared statements and they were all subjected to questioning. It was plain from the chairman's opening remarks that he saw no particular merit in coming to the matter in hand with an open mind: "Our trade partners should understand that the Congress cannot and will not ignore the failure of negotiations to produce an acceptable agreement. The aerospace industry is too important to this nation's trade, economic and defense interests to allow this situation to continue."[13]

Bruce Smart spoke first. He had just returned from the Paris Air Show, and it had been plain to him that the United States lead in aerospace technology was being strongly challenged by a number of countries. He gave a forceful account of the administration's concern. He said that the Airbus governments had made it clear that they believed it was their right to have a commercial aircraft industry, whether it was profitable or not, and seemed to be determined to do so "in an expanding fashion." He predicted that Airbus would continue to be a loss leader, serving principally as a technological showcase and as an employment generator for its sponsor governments.

"Airbus supports are the major industrial trade issue that we now have with Europe. When the President created his Trade Strike Force in 1985, we in that strike force placed Airbus very high on our list of concerns." He quoted a Salomon Brothers report on pre-tax operating margins in the commercial divisions of the major U.S. companies. In the previous three years, the Boeing figure had never been higher than 4.7 percent on sales and had been as low as 0.3 percent. McDonnell Douglas had fared even worse, ranging from a high of 3.6 percent to a loss of 2.7 percent. "There is no way that private companies can compete for long against determined efforts by governments who ignore market forces and spend taxpayer money to achieve non-economic goals." He drew a comparison with the EEC's agricultural practices, where the community had asserted a right to 20 percent of the world market for wheat and used whatever subsidies had been necessary to get it—"we cannot have the aerospace industry and the civil aircraft industry become another grain fiasco."

Ambassador Smith, who followed him, concentrated on trade policy issues. The fundamental question, he said, was "the degree to which governments can, will or should intervene in the promotion or production of a product." The Aircraft Agreement had been a sincere and ambitious effort to lay out a common set of disciplines, but it had proved unsatisfactory. He reverted to his February mission to Europe with Bruce Smart—"In a nutshell, the meetings were disastrous." Since then the partner governments had agreed to find another $3.3 billion for the launching of the A330 and 340. If these were, as the member governments maintained, not subsidies but investments that would produce a reasonable rate of return, why were the private markets not flocking to invest? Airbus had the second largest backlog of orders in the industry. If these airplanes were such a success, why was government support still needed? Was it still an infant industry?

Then it was Alan Boyd's turn. He gave the committee a thumbnail history of the consortium. He conceded that Airbus had not yet achieved profitability, but said it had every reasonable expectation of doing so by 1995. Until 1974, Airbus Industrie had no product and zero market participation. "It has been an enormous struggle to obtain a sufficient share of the market to permit it to become a viable entity." The consortium had proposed the development of a family of five related aircraft types as early as 1973. It was only with the recent launch of the A330 and A340 that this was in place. They aimed to obtain approximately 30 percent of the market over the next 20 years.

When it came to questions, the committee, or rather the chairman and one other member of it, gave Boyd a hard time, largely because they found it difficult to grasp the complexities of the GIE structure and to appreciate that he was the chairman only of a whollyowned marketing subsidiary. Boyd, who is a large, calm man, remained totally unflustered. "I don't have the vaguest idea," he would say, or "I'm not trying to play games with you, Mr. Chairman. I just don't have any concept." After this had gone on for some time, the record shows the Chairman becoming more than a little exasperated.

> *Mr. Florio:* Let me go to basics. Maybe we should have done this earlier on.
> *Mr. Boyd:* OK.
> *Mr. Florio:* What exactly do you do?

Shortly afterwards, Congressman Howard C. Nielson of Utah, who had drifted in late, caught the eye of the chair. "I was involved in another hearing. I apologize. I didn't hear your testimony, but I do have some questions." The answers which these elicited from Boyd quickly made the congressman hot under the collar, however. "You haven't been candid once, not once," he told him. "You say, 'No, I don't know. I don't have access to the books. I couldn't hazard a guess.' I haven't heard a direct answer either to mine or the Chairman's question." "Sir," replied Boyd, "if you would like me to give you my personal opinion on things about which I do not have knowledge, I'll be delighted to do it. I have opinions on almost everything."

He then opened his shoulders and offered the committee a considerable range of opinion, and with some forthrightness:

My personal opinion is that the A300 program will never make a profit. Now I expect some derivative will show up to be profitable in the future. I question whether the A310 program will ever show a profit. I think it's entirely appropriate for those two types of aircraft to be sold at whatever price they were sold at, in order for Airbus to obtain market participation. That's a standard practice. It's done by Procter & Gamble; it's done by everybody. If you're not in a market and you want to get in a market, you sell at whatever price you have to to get in the market—agree or disagree, that's the fact.

Later, Nielson wanted to know how Airbus picked its vendors. "On the basis of the most advanced technology, quality and price," said Boyd succinctly. Nielson then observed that the U.S. share of Airbus vendor sales was declining. Was that because they were no longer competitive? The main reason, Boyd said, was that there was no 100 percent U.S. engine for the A320—both were being manufactured by international joint ventures. But there had been a political factor, too:

There is no question that the Europeans made some effort to draw back from U.S. vendors as a result of two unilateral actions taken by President Reagan, one which prohibited the export of Airbus aircraft—that was the effect of it; it wasn't direct—to Libya where Airbus had had an order for 10 aircraft, and one of which did not affect Airbus at all was an order impacting sales of European equipment to some Russian gas or oil pipelines, which, according to the press at the time, was taken without any consultation with the European governments, and I can tell you, sir, that it made the Europeans very angry and raised some severe questions as to whether or not they could afford to rely on U.S. suppliers in the future.

Alan Boyd had been around in Washington a long time, and looked back on his morning in the lion's den with equanimity. "I knew that it was a 'beat on Airbus' day," he said, "and there was nothing to do but go up there and be the target. I didn't have to, but I just thought it would be better to do so. I had no illusions—I've testified before that committee for about 15 years. I think people in Toulouse were quite angry about it. I take it the French Chamber of Deputies doesn't do things in that way, but to me it was all in a day's work. You have to be a realist."[2] "He had a very tough time," Steve Falken of the Department of Commerce said. "I don't know who advised him to go there. They changed their attorneys after that."[2]

Alan Boyd was followed by Jim Worsham of McDonnell Douglas, a man not given to elaborate preliminaries. "To give birth to a new small commercial airplane these days, it costs about $3 billion U.S. dollars. For a larger long-range airplane, it is $5 billion in excess of that. You must go at this very carefully, because you bet your company and if you are wrong, you lose your company." He offered the committee one or two facts and figures about Airbus, saying that at current prices, funding by the

European governments amounted to some $12 billion. "The governments are truly risk absorbing partners." There was an interruption from the chair:

> *Mr. Florio:* Mr. Worsham, how do you know these things? Mr. Boyd doesn't know them. Where do you get your information from?
> *Mr. Worsham:* We survive in this business by understanding the business and trying to understand our competitors. A lot of this is public knowledge. My survival depends upon knowledge of the competition.

Worsham went on to itemise his company's main concerns. "We with our MD-11 which we launched in December, are head to head competitors with Airbus' A340. We have been building commercial airplanes since 1920 and think we understand how much they cost. We have had a team of our people carefully studying the design of the A340. To the best of our knowledge, the A340 is priced $14 million under its cost. That assumes they sell 500 A340s plus 500 A330s and we do not believe the market will sustain such sales."

Worsham said that such pricing was impossible to explain in commercial terms. Although the two planes were comparable in size, basic costing factors favoured the MD-11. The total launching cost for the MD-11 had been less than $1 billion. The launch aid commitment made by the Airbus partner governments amounted to $3.4 billion. No U.S. private company could compete indefinitely with the national treasuries of the most powerful European governments. The damage might manifest itself slowly, but could be fatal in the long term. And the damage translated directly into lost jobs. A 15 percent loss of market share for the U.S. industry meant the disappearance of 90,000 jobs.

When the time came for the Boeing spokesman, Orvil M. Roetman, to address the committee, the preceding speakers had used most of his best lines. He questioned Alan Boyd's contention that Airbus had found a market niche that the American manufacturers had overlooked, pointing out that in the first five years only 57 A300s had been delivered, and that even after ten years, combined deliveries of the A300 and the smaller A310 had reached only 240 units. Boeing, he said, was not challenging the decision of the sponsoring governments to go ahead with the additional programme. Now that the Airbus family was complete, however, they believed the consortium should operate on the basis of commercial terms and conditions.

He shared the chairman's scepticism about the outcome of the GATT discussions. If they were to succeed, however, Boeing believed there would have to be agreement on a number of specific points, and first and foremost on the elimination of future launch assistance. They attached importance to the pricing of aircraft to recoup all costs, and there must also be agreement to establish financial disclosure and end government and political inducements in sales campaigns. "If such agreements are not reached in July," Roetman said, "it is hard to predict how the issues will be dealt with." He believed that fair competition would improve Europe's capabilities in the industry, and quoted approvingly from something *The Economist* had written on the subject two years previously: "Competitiveness is not a virtue that governments can buy or ordain. It is a virtue learned by exposure to an unprotected market."[14]

The chairman clearly thought that both the industry and the administration had been pussyfooting around the issue. "Why do we have to remain optimistic? I mean, we've got the last 6 or 7 years of optimism that hasn't resulted in a whole heck of a lot, not only in this area but in other trade areas." He wanted to know what the industry saw as what he called "the timeframe for alternative action," and Mr. Worsham and Mr. Roetman agreed that it was the late summer of 1987.

Mr Florio also wanted to know about the negotations that had been going on between McDonnell Douglas and Airbus. Worsham jibbed at the word *negotiation,* but confirmed that there had been discussions with some of the Airbus governments and some of the Airbus partners on what he described as "the possibility of win-win cooperation." They would, he said, probably be confined to small and narrow-bodied airplanes.

The McDonnell Douglas and Boeing spokesmen agreed that since the Eastern sale, both their companies had felt obliged to lease aircraft to airlines, although it was not something they liked to do. Nor did they build "whitetails"—airplanes without a home, as Worsham described them. "The price of carrying that kind of inventory would just put us out of business," Roetman said. He also said that if an export license had been available, the business in the Libyan campaign mentioned earlier by Alan Boyd would have gone to Boeing and not to Airbus. "I don't believe they really suffered there. They took a risk of implementing aircraft for a customer knowing full well we had been turned down for export licenses in the United States, so that was a business decision of theirs to proceed anyway."

The last witness was Don Fuqua, the president of the Aerospace Industries of America and a former member of the House of Representatives. He concentrated on the importance of the industry to the economy of the United States, the complex relationship between trade policy and support for research and development and the increasing internationalisation of aircraft manufacture. He rejected the claim that defence contracts constituted a subsidy for commercial aircraft manufacturers. While some sharing of technology did occur, there were fundamental differences in mission and design criteria. For military aircraft, the emphasis was on high performance. For commercial aircraft it was on reliability and economy. Increasingly, technology was being transferred from commercial to military programmes rather than the other way round.

It had been a long morning. Fuqua was asked to speculate on the strength of the market but refused to be drawn on whether there was room for more than two players. Asked what he would recommend if the GATT talks got nowhere, he took refuge in sporting metaphor: "Then I think we have to huddle. We are about at fourth down then. We either have to decide whether we are going to punt or try to make the first down."

Lunch time loomed. "I commend you for coming here," said the irrepressible Congressman Nielson of Utah. "I'm glad to see there is life after Congress." The committee stood adjourned at 12:58.

Political interest in the issues raised by Airbus was also mounting in France. A month after the Florio hearings, a delegation from the French Senate spent ten days in the United States meeting representatives of the administration and the industry; and their report provides useful evidence of how the issue looked to European eyes in that summer of 1987.[15]

They sketched in the background to Airbus's penetration of the North American market, dwelling with particular satisfaction on the success of the A320. Steve Rothmeier, the boss of Northwest Airlines told them that he could have bought cheaper, but had opted for the A320 on grounds of quality and economy. They were not disposed to take too seriously American concern about the commercial impact of Airbus, and reinforced their point of view with a mischievous little statistic provided by an enterprising attaché: the average annual value of Airbus imports over a period of six years worked out at $830 million, which was a little more than half of what the United States had spent in 1986 on importing toys from Taiwan.

The delegation met both Bruce Smart and Mike Smith. The former told them that McDonnell Douglas had seriously considered pulling out of the civil market, but the latter, in what they described as "a very muscular performance," had said that the administration would never let the company die. The delegation was left in no doubt about how offensive the support made available to Airbus was to the American free market philosophy, and the account they gave in their report of the United States position was both comprehensive and dispassionate.

Unsurprisingly, that was by way of prelude to an elaborate deployment of the case for Airbus. They rehearsed the familiar litany of arguments about public support to the American industry through NASA and the Department of Defense. They said that in the matter of inducements, the record of the United States was far from lily-white, and made a number of specific allegations: that in Thailand in 1985, for example, the U.S. ambassador had threatened a 6 percent increase in duty on Thai textiles if Airbus were preferred; that in South Korea in 1987, the government's choice had been improperly influenced by considerations concerning the U.S. deficit with that country.

On the question of economic return, they were frank—it could not be denied, they said, that the profitability of some programmes would be "only mediocre." In spite of improvements, for instance, the A300-600R would continue to suffer a penalty in fuel consumption because of the outmoded design of the wing.[16]

When they turned to the question of capital injections by the state into the partner company, however, all they had to offer was a rock-like reaffirmation of the classical French position, and a curt indication that the matter was not even debatable.[17] The French system, they insisted, was radically different. The French industry was in the public domain. The role of the state was therefore that of shareholder and financier. The state, indeed, in their view, had not always performed its duty as shareholder in a satisfactory manner—its attitude had been "unnecessarily chilly" ("exagérément frileuse"), and they endorsed the 1985 annual report of the *Cour des Comptes* which had said that Aérospatiale was undercapitalised.[18]

The senators went home convinced that there was a major risk of confrontation. The tone in which the message had been conveyed to them had ranged, they said, from the firmly polite to the brutal.[19] The consequences were incalculable and could well be catastrophic. A complaint to GATT seemed to them less likely than a resort to American legal procedures; these would be quicker and have a more direct effect on imports of Airbus. They offered a lucid analysis of the scope of U.S. trade legislation, describing the antidumping and countervailing duty procedures as "extremely inquisitorial." They also pointed out that all current contracts between Airbus and their American customers contained a clause providing that any duties levied would be met by Airbus—there was no corresponding clause in the contracts in force between Boeing and such European airlines as Air France, Lufthansa and British Airways.

The senators identified an enormous gap—which they characterised as 'tragic'—between the informed state of public and political opinion on the Airbus issue in the United States and the ignorance they discerned in France among public and parliamentarians alike. French tradition dictated either that the issue, because of its international importance, should be dealt with at the highest level, or that it should be regarded as technical and confidential. In the United States, by contrast, it was regarded as a public issue and treated accordingly. European publications on the subject compared very unfavourably with the documentation put out by the Americans. Boeing material, in particular, seemed to them to be of high quality. A recent Airbus equivalent seemed to them to be less aggressive, designed to instruct rather than persuade.[20]

They noted that the protectionist tendencies of Congress, already pronounced because of the U.S. trade deficit, had been sharpened by the results of the previous autumn's elections, and observed that the Trade Bill that was then under discussion would reinforce the U.S. arsenal of trade legislation. The possibilities for a European response were three in number—action under Article 86 of the Treaty of Rome aimed at establishing that in the matter of 747 sales Boeing was guilty of abusing its dominant position; action under community regulations aimed at Boeing's pricing practices with the 757; possible action under U.S. antitrust legislation. It could not, of course, be excluded that the dispute would spill over into other areas.

The senators turned their minds finally to the possibilities for conciliation. When they had asked Boeing whether they saw a place for three manufacturers in the market place, "Rusty" Roetman had replied "Maybe two and a half?", and this had been their cue to consider the prospects for international cooperation. On the one hand, it seemed to them that American collaboration with, say, the Italians or the Japanese could lead to the closing of certain markets to Airbus. The possibility of some sort of arrangement between Airbus and McDonnell Douglas, however, was an altogether different matter. They had devoted quite a lot of the five hours they spent talking to Jim Worsham exploring that, and their conclusion was that collaboration in some shape or form offered the best hope in the long term for taking the heat out of the issue.

The senators flew from Long Beach to San Francisco and wound down for a day with a visit to a national park and a California winery before boarding a UTA flight for Paris on July 26. The latest round between the European Community and the United States had finished two days previously and had achieved next to nothing. The European side had proposed a further meeting in September, but Bruce Wilson, who led the American delegation, said that he must first seek guidance from his "political principals" in Washington. Wilson expressed his disappointment. There had been no convergence of views over Article 6. "The Community has one interpretation," he said, "and we have quite another."

During the talks, the American delegation had warned the Europeans that a failure to make progress might well trigger action by Boeing or McDonnell Douglas. Lawyers representing the U.S. manufacturers stood poised to submit complaints to the International Trade Commission in Washington. The European side had apparently not found this an especially blood-curdling piece of information. The statement they put out described the talks as "constructive." One of the few things that was agreed was that a list of prohibited government inducements should be drawn up, though the Community stipulated that it would have to be "illustrative and non-exhaustive" rather than comprehensive.

August came, and produced some exchanges of the sort Washington Irving must have had in mind when he wrote about "dog-day whim-whams." The AIA had published a slim brochure with a title almost as long as the text: *Does the United States Support Its Commercial Transport Manufacturers Like Europe Supports Airbus? That's the European View*

. . . But There is a Difference. It was, in fact, one of those that had been singled out admiringly by the French Senate delegation the month before, but when it was drawn to Jean Pierson's attention in Toulouse he got on his high horse and dashed off letters to a number of AIA member companies—Sundstrand, Garrett, Rockwell—with whom Airbus had business dealings.

The brochure, wrote Monsieur Pierson, contained contradictions, omissions and innuendos. "As a supplier to Airbus Industrie, your association with such a document impacts unfavourably, although hopefully only temporarily, on the working relations, mutual trust and cooperative spirit which have always subsisted between our two companies. I am confident that you will take all necessary steps to restore mutual confidence in our relationship . . . "

Don Fuqua, AIA's president, sent an accommodating reply. No offence intended. The aim had been simply to clear up misunderstandings and create a healthy trading environment. "PS. I have enclosed a copy of our brochure entitled *Continued International Cooperation in Aerospace* in case you have not seen it."

Two months after Airbus announced the launch of the A330/340 programme, Boeing made public its decision to postpone development of the 7J7. Boeing didn't say as much, but the two statements were not unconnected. The launch of the 7J7 had been projected for 1987 so that it would be ready for delivery in 1992. The design of the twin-aisle plane had incorporated new-generation electronic components and lightweight structural materials as well as a fuel-efficient propfan engine to be made by General Electric. A cross-section of the fuselage had been on display at the Paris Air Show in June and an intensive sales campaign had been launched, but there had been no orders. Steven Udvar-Hazy, the president of the International Lease Finance Corporation of Beverly Hills, had been present at one of the presentations. "Everybody was saying ooh and aah about the technology," he said, "but nobody was ready to sign up."[21]

The most obvious explanation was that airlines were currently more interested in economy than in new technology. Low fuel prices had removed some of the incentive to replace ageing fleets, and competition between the Boeing 737-400, the McDonnell Douglas MD-80 and the Airbus A320 had brought the price of all three planes down to attractive levels. Boeing have a very good eye for clouds no bigger than a man's hand, and they had been clear for some considerable time that Airbus pricing practices represented a serious threat to the 7J7 programme.

An analysis made by the company as early as April 1986 accepted that potential 7J7 technical gains were extremely vulnerable to relatively modest financial infusions by Airbus. The aircraft had been given a tentative catalogue price slightly below that of the A320, but it was recognised that the economic viability of the programme with such a pricing structure would depend upon dramatic cost reductions compared with the 757 and 767 and moderate concession levels. Both of these requirements were described as "fragile."[22]

Boeing's market intelligence told them that the A320 was currently selling at $5–6 million below the sticker price, providing direct operating cost parity with the 7J7 at its proposed catalogue price. Assuming a moderate 7J7 concession level of 6–8 percent (about $2 million), Airbus would need to discount the A320 by only a further $2 million to retain that parity. It seemed to Boeing a foregone conclusion that they would do that. If they were then to respond, earning levels would be eroded. If they were to make further concessions in the $2.5–4 million bracket, profitability would fly out of the window.

With the market split 70/30 in Boeing's favour, the incremental cost of playing the discounting game would be much less to Airbus than to Boeing. Boeing would be absorbing the loss in 70 percent of the market, Airbus in only 30 percent. Boeing calculated that the total cost to Airbus of maintaining direct operating cost parity would be of the order of $600 million. For another $1 billion, they could escalate concession levels still further and 'put Boeing away' entirely.

It was calculations like these that lay behind the vigour with which the American manufacturers had prodded the administration throughout 1986 and 1987. The Boeing paper quoted above ends with the words, "This may involve some changes in prevalent Boeing attitudes concerning data disclosure and endorsement of aggressive U.S. trade counteractions." It is also the case, of course, that Boeing's decision to delay investment in the 7J7 freed substantial sums that would otherwise have been spent on research and development. Analysts speculated that the figure might be as high as $500 million, a sum that would come in very useful in striking back at Airbus in the market place.

It was not only the upper house of the French Parliament that was interesting itself in the question of Airbus in the summer of 1987. Between the 3rd and 7th of August Gilbert Gantier, a member of the National Assembly and a vice -president of the Commission des Finances was also in the United States. Although his visit was shorter than that of the Senate delegation, the report of this package-tour Tocqueville was an altogether more incisive and more political document than that produced by his colleagues.[23]

He began with a bold comparison. The economic might of Japan was not explained by its natural resources or a particularly favourable climate. Nor did it rest on a privileged geographical position. It flowed from the hard work of its inhabitants—their energy and the use to which they put their intelligence. That, asserted Monsieur Gantier, was how the French must behave if they wished to escape the decline with which they were threatened. Airbus offered a model of how this might be done, although on two conditions. The first was that the danger posed by the conflict with the United States must be removed. The second was that certain adjustments were required in the way the enterprise was organised.

Monsieur Gantier then embarked on a brisk analysis of the Airbus issue and an examination of American attitudes. His conclusions, and the tone of voice in which he presented them, differed markedly from those of many of his compatriots. He identified the mood in the United States as one of exasperation. Although he believed there was an element of hypocrisy in American criticisms, he was persuaded that the Europeans were faced with a real problem. He described the existence of Deutsche Airbus as a "provocation" to the Americans, arguing that the volume of financial resources committed to Airbus by the Federal Government made them vulnerable to American attack and that this in turn exposed a European flank.

His political assessment of the issues was acute. He was aware that the U.S. position was far from monolithic and that there were hawks and doves in the industry no less than in Washington. He also observed that European commercial loyalties were fairly widely distributed, noting that Italy, for instance, was both a good customer and a subcontractor of McDonnell Douglas.

He had clearly been a forceful ambassador for Europe, presenting the case for its aircraft industry with some robustness and giving his American hosts quite a hard time—there could be no question, he said, of Europe's capitulating before the selfish interests of the American manufacturers. In his conclusions, however, he came down firmly on the side of those who argued the need for change in the consortium. The present situation, he wrote, was untenable. The American market must not be lost at any price. Where else he asked, could one pick up orders for a hundred aircraft at a time?

Monsieur Gantier conceded that there was a period when the needs of the "infant" industry gave it a legitimate call on public funds. That period could certainly be held to have extended to the signing of the GATT Aircraft Agreement, arguably even to the launching of the A320 in 1986. Beyond that, the case for what he described as "relatively orthodox" methods of financing seemed to him unanswerable. This would imply that future programmes would be expected to be profitable—something, he added, "which is, after all, in tune with the liberal philosophy of the present government."[24] (No prizes for guessing which segment of the political spectrum Monsieur Gantier occupied in the Chamber of the National Assembly.)

He had little time for the idea of collaboration with McDonnell Douglas—often presented, he said dismissively, as "la solution miracle" to the conflict with the United States. He advised caution. The failure of such a scheme could make matters worse, giving the Americans the impression that all the talk had merely been a delaying tactic. The course he recommended was an infinitely safer one—"S'engager, pour l'avenir, dans une voie plus commerciale, et moins étatique". He was convinced of the need both to change the methods by which production was financed and to modify the juridical structure of the consortium, and he believed it was a matter of some urgency.

A few weeks after the publication of his report, the French deputy's views about Deutsche Airbus found a powerful echo in the federal republic itself. The German government receives a report once a year from a body called the Independent Council of Economic Advisers. The council, which is five strong, is influential and well regarded. Its reports are debated in Parliament, and the government is required to respond to the advice offered. Their report for 1987–88 appeared at the end of November, a meaty document of almost 400 pages, and it reflected growing unease at what was seen as an increasingly open-ended commitment.[25]

The Council noted that although there had for some years been calls for a reduction in subsidies, federal spending under this head in 1987 had amounted to DM 67 billion, an increase of 3 percent over the previous year. The lion's share—DM 10 billion—had gone to mining, which represented DM 52,000 for each job in the industry, but subsidies for shipbuilding, agriculture and the aircraft industry had also been increased. Aid to the aircraft industry, indeed, most of which was earmarked for Airbus, had grown by some 50 percent compared with the previous year.

They described the subsidies made available to Airbus as massive—for the A330/340 programme alone, a total of DM 11 billion. They conceded that there had been substantial benefits—Airbus had been established in the market, new technologies had been developed, the results of R&D benefited other companies and products and the brain drain had been slowed down. But they observed that the enterprise could also be viewed in another light. It was not certain that it would ever be an economic success. It had not yet achieved profitability. There was no prospect of the A300, the A310 or the A320 breaking even in the foreseeable future, and calculations of the profitability of the 330/340 were purely speculative.

They noted that a request that had been made for exchange rate guarantees to protect Airbus from fluctuations in the value of the dollar and pointed out that this would lead to incalculable risks for future budgets. It would also discriminate against other companies, which had to pay high insurance premiums to protect themselves against fluctuations in the exchange rate. In the council's view, long-term reliance on subsidy militated against the achievement of cost efficiency. They questioned how efficiently Deutsche Airbus was managed, pointing out that their R&D costs were higher than those of their opposite numbers in the United Kingdom.

They considered the international repercussions. Subsidies for market access and for sales both caused problems, and they registered that there was disagreement over the extent to which the sort of subsidies paid to Airbus conformed to international agreements. They dismissed the European claim that U.S. manufacturers got indirect subsidies in the form of military contracts, pointing out that that is precisely how European planemakers managed to make ends meet.

Their conclusion was that payments aimed at easing market access, and repayable over a limited period, were economically justified. Subsidy, however, once embarked on, quickly came to resemble the primrose way to the everlasting bonfire. They did not think it would be practical politics to expect the federal government to withdraw from Airbus—that might well kill the project, and would be damaging to European cooperation. The most it was realistic to hope was that the government should find some way of gradually easing itself out of the programme and encouraging German industry to play a larger part. They had no suggestions to make about how the hard-nosed men who wrought the German economic miracle might be persuaded to raise that particular chalice to their lips.

There were two more opportunities before the end of 1987 for the two sides to find words to bridge their differences. At the end of October, the trade ministers of the four member countries and Ambassador Yeutter sat down together in London, and seemed to edge a little closer together. The talks went on three hours longer than scheduled. When they were over, Mr. Yeutter flicked through the deck of carefully graded responses that are used on such occasions, and selected the one which said "cautiously optimistic."

Officials were instructed to examine the issues further in preparation for yet another ministerial meeting some weeks later between the United States and the European Commission. This time Secretary of State George Shulz headed the U.S. delegation and Willy De Clerq, the commissioner for External Affairs, led for the Commission. If it had been one step forward in London in October, it was two steps backwards in Brussels in December. "Airbus, pomme de discorde," said a French headline. "Fundamental differences remain." The long-suffering officials got out their diaries and noted glumly that they must get down to it again early in the New Year.

The prize for the best quote of the year went to Monsieur Michel Noir, the French trade minister, for his cheerful remark to a journalist: "International trade politics is not a ladies' tea party. It is a rugby international, and you can easily come away with a broken nose."

NOTES

1. Interview in Paris, November 1988.
2. Interview in Washinton, October 1988.

3. Letter Harr—Brock, October 4, 1983.

4. Letter Brock—Harr, October 18, 1983.

5. *Aviation Daily,* December 2, 1985.

6. *The Seattle Times,* January 16, 1986.

7. *Flight International,* February 15, 1986.

8. "Bien entendu, il s'agit là d'un processus de décision strictement interne, dont l'appréciation relève de notre seul jugement, et de celui de nos partenaires européens."

9. See an article by François Guillaumat in *The Wall Street Journal,* August 27, 1986.

10. Interview in *Interavia Air Letter,* February 3, 1987.

11. *Inside U.S. Trade,* February 27, 1987.

12. In November 1989 he was elected governor of New Jersey.

13. *Competitiveness of U.S. Commercial Aircraft Industry.* Hearing before the Subcommittee on Commerce, Consumer Protection, and Competitiveness of the Committee on Energy and Commerce, House of Representatives, June 23, 1987 (Washington: U.S. Government Printing Office, Serial No. 100-59, 1988).

14. *The Economist,* November 2, 1985.

15. Sénat, prèmiere session extraordinaire de 1987–1988, document no. 222, January 22, 1988.

16. "L'A300-600R constitue le dernier développement de l'A300 d'origine, mais souffrira, malgré les améliorations substantielles incorporées de façon permanente, de la conception ancienne de sa voilure, et par conséquent d'une pénalité, en termes de consommation en carburant."

17. "Il convient d'être parfaitement clair sur ce point: les apports en capital de la part de l'actionnaire, l'Etat, ne peuvent en aucun cas être critiqués."

18. Cour des Comptes, *Rapport au Président de la République,* 1985.

19. "Souvent de façon ferme mais courtoise, parfois de façon assez brutale, la partie américaine a clairement fait savoir qu'il y avait un risque majeur d'affrontement, de crise, entre les deux parties."

20. "Une plaquette d'information de qualité, mais a vocation pédagogique, et sans présenter le caractère résolument offensif des plaquettes américaines."

21. *The Wall Street Journal,* August 24, 1987.

22. Boeing internal document, *7J7 Program Vulnerability to Airbus Subsidies and Pricing Practices,* dated April 18, 1986.

23. Assemblée Nationale, première session ordinaire de 1987–88, document no. 960, November 4, 1987.

24. "Ce qui correspond après tout à la philosophie libérale qui anime le gouvernment."

25. *Jahresgutachten 1987/88 des Sachverständigenrates zur Begutachtung der gesamtwirtschaftlichen Entwicklung.* Deutscher Bundestag, 11. Wahlperiode, Drucksache 11/1317, November 24, 1987.

11

The Faro Table
of Governments

"War is the province of chance. In no other sphere of human activity must such a margin be left for this intruder. It increases the uncertainty of every circumstance and deranges the course of events."

—Karl von Clausewitz, *Vom Kriege (On War)*, 1833.

"Jaw-jaw is better than war war," said Winston Churchill. It is a dictum to which the executive branch has been readier to subscribe than has Capitol Hill, but if the United States decides at a given moment that talking is not producing results on the international trade front and should give way to action, it has a formidable armoury of statutory instruments at its disposal.

If, for instance, it is found that imports are being sold at less than their fair value and that this is resulting in material injury, duties may be imposed equal to the margin of dumping. Again, if the Department of Commerce establishes that imports are being subsidised, countervailing duties may be levied equal to the amount of those subsidies. More broadly still, if it is determined that U.S. rights under a trade agreement are being violated or that U.S. commerce is being "burdened or restricted" by foreign acts deemed to be unreasonable or discriminatory, the president is empowered to take "all appropriate and feasible action." This offers scope for a wide range of retaliation, from the imposition of tariffs or other import restrictions to the withdrawal or suspension of trade agreement benefits.

There is a considerable degree of ignorance in Europe about where power lies in the United States both for the formulation of foreign economic policy and for the regulation of foreign trade. Article I, Section 8 of the U.S. Constitution, for instance, is specific, in listing certain express powers of the Congress, that it falls to the legislature "to lay and collect taxes, duties, imposts and excises . . . to regulate commerce with foreign nations, and among the several states . . . ," and the Congress has always been very jealous of its prerogatives in the regulation of such international transactions.

Within the House of Representatives, jurisdiction over trade matters rests with the Committee on Ways and Means, and it has always kept a beady eye on such matters as tariffs and unfair trade practices as well as taking very seriously its responsibility for the authorisation and oversight of the departments and agencies that carry out federal policy. In the early 1930s, however, Congress came to recognise that it simply wasn't practical politics to retain full control over trade matters within the legislative branch, and 1934 saw the first significant delegation of authority in this field from Congress to the President. The Reciprocal Trade Agreement Act of that year vested in the White House authority to negotiate international agreements for the reduction of tariffs.

Since then, the degree of authority delegated to the president has varied, providing a barometer both of congressional concern about trade matters and of the state of relations between the legislature and the executive. When the delegated authority to negotiate trade agreements expired during the presidency of Lyndon Johnson, for example, there was a period of seven years during which it was not renewed. In the Trade Act of 1974, presidential authority was extended to cover nontariff as well as tariff negotiations, but the *quid pro quo* was that both before and during negotiations the president should be under certain obligations to notify and consult the Congress so that domestic interests might be protected.

Not everybody admires the sort of trade remedy regime with which the United States has equipped itself. One senior British diplomat in Washington, with long experience of trade issues on both sides of the Atlantic, saw the 1974 Trade Act as having had a destabilising effect because it had effectively removed the discretion that the administration had previously enjoyed in the imposition of countervailing duties. The recognition of the right of private action had introduced a number of what he described as "mechanistic triggers." Before 1974, the various U. S. administering agencies had, as he put it, "stuffed countervailing petitions into the drawer." Since then, if private petitioners could establish injury, countervailing duties were imposed more or less automatically, and the government's power to exercise discretion in the national interest had been removed.

In his opinion, this was one of the consequences of a long drawn out battle between Capitol Hill and the White House in which the Congress had been trying to claw back some of its former authority. On this view, the sort of trade remedy regime that emerged in the United States in the 1970s was open to criticism on the ground that it set out to do things in a mechanical way. "Don't mistake me, I'm not trying to say that subsidies are harmless and don't have repercussions and don't need controlling," he said. "I just don't think they can be controlled in this mechanical way, because what it means in effect is that one sectional interest or another can lob in its petition and hold the whole show up to ransom, as it were. To put it another way, governments can no longer aggregate interests very well, and that's something they have to be able to do if they are to cooperate with each other properly."

The imposition of antidumping duties is governed by a section of the Tariff Act of 1930, although there has been legislation offering protection against dumping in the United States since the time of the First World War. Congress first passed an Antidumping Act in September 1916, and this provided a civil cause of action for private damages in the federal courts. Some of the requirements under this statute, however—the need, in particular, to demonstrate evidence of intent—proved difficult to meet, and the measure gave way five years later to a new act that was to remain on the statute book till 1979.

During the negotiations to set up an International Trade Organisation after the Second World War the United States proposed a draft article on dumping based on the 1921 Act, and this became the basis for Article VI of the General Agreement on Tariffs and Trade. Although dumping was not an issue during the Kennedy Round, a widespread feeling had emerged that antidumping actions constituted a potential source of abuse, and as a result the GATT AntiDumping Code of 1967 was established. During the Tokyo Round, in the 1970s, this was amended to bring it into line with the newly negotiated Agreement on Subsidies and Countervailing Measures. Congress approved this in 1979, and in the same year responsibility for administering the antidumping law was transferred from the Treasury to the Department of Commerce. The legislation has been most recently modified in the Trade Act of 1988.

For an antidumping duty to be imposed, two conditions must be met. The first is that the Department of Commerce has to determine that the merchandise in question is being sold at less than its fair value. The second relates to the question of injury caused by such imports. What has to be established (by the International Trade Commission) is that a U.S. industry is either materially injured (or threatened by such injury) or that the establishment of an industry in the United States has been materially retarded. If both conditions are met, an order is issued imposing duties equal to what is known as the dumping margin—the difference between the foreign market value and the U.S. price.

"Lawyers and painters can soon change white to black," says an old Danish proverb, and there is clearly a lot of lawyers' language here, with much scope for the profession to lick its chops over definitions and interpretations. Foreign market value is assessed in one of three ways: by home market sales, by third-country sales or by what is called constructed value; the test is to be applied in that order. Constructed value is calculated by a formula that is set out in the statute—the sum of the costs of production plus a minimum of 10 percent for general expenses and at least 8 percent for profit.

What is "material injury?" "Harm which is not inconsequential, immaterial or unimportant," say the act. Establishing whether such harm has been caused involves the International Trade Commission in an elaborate analysis of the volume of imports and the effect of those imports on U.S. producers of similar products. This cannot be done without examining such things as productivity, market share, return on investments, profits and utilization of productive capacity.

An investigation into a suspected case of dumping may be initiated by the Department of Commerce, but interested parties may file a petition, too—a manufacturer or producer, a trade association, a recognised union and even a group of workers within the affected industry. If a small business wants to have a go, it can call on the Department of Commerce for technical assistance.

The Department gets 20 days to decide whether there are grounds for an investigation. The ITC is allowed 45 days to decide whether there is a "reasonable indication" of material injury, and in this case the burden of proof rests on the petitioner. If by the end of a period of 160 days the department thinks there is a case, it must order the "suspension of liquidation" of all entries of the goods in question and obtain a cash deposit or bond for any other merchandise coming in to the value of the suspected margin of dumping. This preliminary finding also triggers what is known as a final injury investigation by the ITC.

The department is now into the home stretch. It has another 75 days to publish its findings (135 if the importer has a good lawyer). All it then has to do is sit back and wait for the ITC to come up with its final determination. It can then leave the rest to the Customs Service—unless, that is, it feels inclined to have a last little bit of sport in the shape of a suspension of the investigation.

This can happen if those responsible for most of the imports under investigation are prepared to do a deal. They must agree to one of three things: to stop exporting the goods within six months; to raise their prices to close the dumping gap; to raise their prices so that the injurious effect on the U.S. industry is removed. This does not happen very often. In fact between January 1980 and January 1987 it happened six times. In that same period 365 petitions were received, of which 14 were dismissed and 103 subsequently withdrawn. The number of final antidumping orders made was 74.

The history of U.S. legislation aimed at offsetting any unfair advantage resulting from foreign subsidy is rather longer than that relating to dumping. The first countervailing duty law was passed in 1897, and it too remained on the statute book largely unaltered until 1979, when it was modified in accordance with the agreement reached during the Tokyo Round.

The law of 1897 said that duties might be levied on imported merchandise that had benefited from a "bounty or grant." In 1922

Congress broadened the provision so that it also applied to subsidies on manufacture or production. Originally there was no injury test, but that was one of the fundamental changes that was made in 1979 with the application of the GATT Subsidies Code to U.S. law. Responsibility for the administration of the statute passed in 1979 from the Treasury to Commerce, and the 1984 Trade and Tariff Act extended the scope of the countervailing duty law to include "upstream subsidies"—subsidies made available for components that are then used in the manufacture of a finished article subsequently exported to the United States.

As in the case of the antidumping legislation, the main players are the Department of Commerce and the International Trade Commission. The department's role is to determine that a subsidy, direct or indirect, is being provided and to establish its net amount; the ITC has to establish the fact of material injury. A countervailing duty (CVD) will be payable whether the goods are imported direct or from a third country, and whether or not they are in the same condition as when they were exported.

There are, once again, rich pickings for lawyers. The legislation does not contain an explicit definition of what is meant by subsidy, although it indicates that it shall mean the same as "bounty or grant," and provides an illustrative list of examples. Direct cash benefits, credits against taxes and loans with artificially low interest rates are all held to be included.

So far as material injury is concerned, the standard is the same as under the antidumping law, and the procedure for investigation is also very similar. As it happens, exactly the same number of final CVD orders was made between 1980 and 1987 as was the case with antidumping orders, although appreciably fewer petitions (293) were received. Eight of these were dismissed and 84 withdrawn.

It is clear that both the antidumping and the countervailing duty legislation could inflict substantial damage on Airbus, and it is known that the major manufacturers have cases sitting ready in the offices of their Washington attorneys. There is, however, a third shot in the U.S. locker, and it is one widely regarded as giving them the trade war equivalent of nuclear capability. It differs considerably in both scope and procedure from the measures already described and is usually known simply as 301. This is shorthand for Chapter 1 of Title III of the Trade Act of 1974, though that statute has been amended and strengthened in subsequent legislation, most recently in the Trade Act of 1988, with which Congress and the White House played shuttlecock for a few months in the last year of the Reagan presidency.

What was mainly different about 301 when it was enacted was that it placed the authority to enforce U.S. trade rights and to respond to unfair foreign practices directly in the hands of the president.There had been similar provisions in the Trade Expansion Act of 1962, but the 1974 legislation stiffened these in a number of ways, including the introduction of specific time limits on the various steps involved in investigating petitions and taking action on them. The United States saw the 1974 Act as providing a domestic counterpart to the GATT dispute settlement procedures. These included provision for consultations to seek a solution without resort to dispute procedures and the right to a panel of impartial experts from countries not involved to review the dispute.

The scope of the powers granted to the president under 301 was broad, and not confined to countries that were members of GATT or other trade agreements, and the authority conferred on him was equally wide ranging. He was required not only to enforce U.S. rights under any trade agreement. He was also obliged, much more generally, to respond to anything that "is unjustifiable, unreasonable, or discriminatory and burdens or restricts U.S. commerce." The legislation was not simply permissive. If a case was made out, the President *had* to act, and was obliged, in the sonorous words of the statute, "to take all appropriate and feasible action within his power to enforce such rights or to obtain the elimination of the act, policy or practice."

There were also certain discretionary powers. The president was entitled, for instance, to suspend the benefits of any trade agreement concessions with the country in question or impose duties or other restrictions. Most importantly of all, the act conferred on him the right to take action against goods in any sector, regardless of whether they were involved in the particular practice that had given rise to the dispute. Officials in Washington are understandably reticent when asked hypothetical questions about how things might develop if 301 were invoked against Airbus, but the manufacturers, some of whom speak like characters in an advertisement for Marlboro cigarettes, are less inhibited. When I discussed trade actions in Long Beach with R.C.P. Jackson, McDonnell Douglas's vice-president for special assignments, he sketched me a scenario with some relish.

"In a standard war," he said, "I put duty on, you put duty on, but 301 doesn't work that way. You pick the nation which has a favourable trade balance with you, and you pick the product which is most important to him. A 301 action is quite unlike a duty action—it is not product-specific. It could be agricultural things, it could be almost anything—that's what's so dangerous about it to the the people on the other end. Let's use Germany as an example—it's a nice neutral country." (This with a grin.) "What you'd find would be that the trade action would be on Mercedes, not on airplanes. The whole purpose of a 301 is to be able to do this worldwide and to do it in whatever battlefield you choose, not necessarily the one where you're aggrieved."[1]

These are weighty matters, but Jackson evidently did not feel that they were so serious that jokes were precluded, and he produced a memorably economical definition of the difference between the various trade remedy laws we had been discussing. "CVD and dumping? That's a kangaroo court.

For 301, you don't have any court—you just have an executioner!"

Execution, however, is not summary. Any interested party may file a petition, and the U.S. trade representative is empowered to initiate an investigation on his own authority provided he has consulted the appropriate private-sector advisory committees. Another section of the act, however, requires that in parallel with the domestic investigation there must be an attempt to resolve the matter through consultations with the country concerned. The trade representative is required to set that process in motion on the day he decides to initiate a case. If that doesn't produce results, and if the issues are covered by a trade agreement, he must press the button that starts up the appropriate dispute settlement routines.

An important element in the effectiveness of 301 is that there are time limits—opportunities for spinning the game out are strictly limited. It cannot go on longer than a year, and in certain cases the USTR is obliged to make recommendations to the president within seven months. The trade representative must also keep a weather eye on Capitol Hill. An account of progress must go to the Congress every six months, but in certain circumstances an additional report may be called for setting out the reasons why a particular dispute has not been settled, describing the state of play and giving an account of what USTR proposes to do about it.

Heavy artillery is not for every day, and not just because of the price of ammunition, but the United States policy of sparing but aggressive use of 301 has paid off, against trading partners both big and small. In July 1986, for instance, Korea agreed to offer significantly greater protection to intellectual property, including trademarks, patents and copyrights, settling a 301 case that had been initiated by the U.S. administration. Later the same year, Taiwan agreed to open its beer, wine and cigarette markets to U.S. exports after the president had instructed Ambassador Yeutter to propose retaliatory action.

In July 1986, Japan agreed to open its market to American semiconductor sales and said it would take steps to discourage Japanese companies from dumping computer chips in the United States and third-country markets. This settled a 301 case that had been initiated by the American industry and two antidumping cases that had been initiated by the administration. The following April, President Reagan imposed sanctions of $300 million because Japan had not fully implemented the agreement. Within two months, dumping in third markets by Japanese companies had been reduced, and the sanctions were partly lifted. Also in 1986, the European Community agreed to give American citrus producers increased access to the European market, ending a 16-year dispute over the Community's special treatment for Mediterranean citrus imports. This agreement came nine months after President Reagan had retaliated under 301 against the European citrus preferences by raising pasta duties.

301 has given rise to substantially fewer cases over the years than either

the CVD or antidumping laws. In a 12-year period beginning in January 1975, for instance, only 7 cases resulted in retaliatory action. 5 petitions were rejected, 11 were withdrawn and the number of cases terminated by a resolution of the dispute amounted to 27. The figures demonstrate clearly that the legislation has a strong deterrent effect. They also prompt the question put to Sherlock Holmes in *Abbey Grange:*

"Is there any other point to which you would wish to draw my attention?"
"To the curious incident of the dog in the night-time."
"The dog did nothing in the night-time."
"That was the curious incident," remarked Sherlock Holmes.

The curious incident for some in the confrontation with Airbus is that although the United States has at its disposal the panoply of weapons described earlier in this chapter, it has never got beyond fingering the safety catch on any of them.

Alan Boyd, the former U.S. secretary of transportation who is now the Airbus president in North America, offered a succint explanation: "It's not a situation where you can drop the atomic bomb on Hiroshima and it's all over and nobody on your side gets hurt."[2] Jonathan Menes, an old hand in the Department of Commerce, elaborated on the same point: "In almost all cases, a solution to a trade problem involves an element of shooting yourself in the foot. You retaliate against the other person, but that retaliation usually takes the form of making it hard for them to sell their products in your market. Now that can be entirely legitimate or legal, but it imposes a cost on you as well as them. And in purely economic terms, there will always be those who will argue that the pain you are inflicting on yourself exceeds the benefits you are going to get out of it. Negotiating with an ally isn't easy. You have a lot of relationships with them in a lot of different areas, and you can very quickly get beyond the gristle and into the bone."[2]

The GATT headquarters in Geneva is another reservoir of ripe reflection on all matters relating to Airbus. "I think the U.S. administration is caught in a draught," one seasoned observer told me. "This is an area in which it is very hard to count your own sheep, because the whole aerospace industry is now in effect so multinational. Everybody is married with everybody else on different projects—it's practically incestuous. It's much easier to identify your own agriculture, because farmers are on your own territory, they're in Iowa or wherever and you know where they are, but that's no longer so with aircraft."

Reviewing his three year involvement with the issue in the fall of 1988, Bruce Wilson, one of the USTR negotiators, was inclined to think that the fortunes of the companies at any given time were always a major factor on the tactics and timing of the government. "If the companies are prospering commercially, then there's less pressure on the government, particularly as the companies themselves—Boeing more so than McDonnell Douglas—are vulnerable in Europe." He also thought it might be difficult, with bulging order books and the assembly lines working flat out, to demonstrate material injury.[2]

The alliance between the administration and the industry on the Airbus issue has not always been an easy one. "Alliance implies a community of interest." Sally Bath, office director for Aerospace Policy and Analysis at the Department of Commerce, told me. "I think you'll find that the government looks at most issues of this type from a broader perspective than just simply what is good for the industry. In any case, the aerospace industry itself does not have a commonality of view. So the government has to look at the issue in the context of our overall trade policy and our overall governmental objectives. Obviously we are servants of the people, but the people include the airlines and the travelling public as well as the manufacturers."[2]

For anyone trying to get a feel for the way the administration sees the Airbus issue, the number of government departments or agencies in Washington that have a finger in the foreign trade pie is daunting. Trade policy, however, is a major strand in both economic and foreign policy. A decision, say, to raise quotas or impose tariffs can clearly have far-reaching implications for the domestic economy, and there is an obvious need for machinery to coordinate diverse activity and reconcile conflicting interests.

Although Congress insists on the periodic nature of the authority it delegates to the president and emphasises that it is limited in scope and time, the authority that it has granted to federal agencies to administer such things as the trade remedy laws is permanent, although subject to congressional oversight—not least in the small matter of appropriations.

Until the late 1950s the State Department was in the driving seat, and the Trade Agreements Committee, on which eight agencies originally had representation, was chaired by the secretary of state. In the early 1960s, however, the need was felt to establish a better balance between competing domestic and international interests, and the Trade Expansion Act of 1962 empowered the president to establish the Office of the Special Representative for Trade Negotiations. The special trade representative was given the rank of ambassador extraordinary and plenipotentiary. These were the years of the Kennedy Round, so he was also given two deputies. One was based in Washington, the other in Geneva, and they shared responsibility for the conduct of trade negotiations until the conclusion of that particular GATT round in 1967.

The 1974 Trade Act further increased the importance of the office, establishing it within the Executive Office of the president and enlarging the responsibilities of the representative, who was now raised to cabinet rank and made directly responsible to the president and Congress. In 1980 he was redesignated United States trade representative, and it was specified that he was the President's principal adviser and chief spokesman on trade, including advice on the impact of international trade on other U.S. government policies.

The number of agencies represented on the Trade Policy Committee has now risen to 14—the departments of Agriculture, Commerce, Justice, Defense, Energy, Interior, Labor, State, Transportation and Treasury, the Office of Management and Budget, the Council of Economic Advisors, the National Security Council and the International Development Cooperation Agency. The donkey-work is done at office director level by a group called the Staff Committee, and it can draw on the efforts of more than 30 subcommittees and task forces. Between them and the Trade Policy Committee there is a Review Group, which is staffed at assistant secretary level. Issues on which they fail to agree go upstairs to the committee proper for submission to the Cabinet.

If all these good people were laid end to end they would stretch quite some way up Pennsylvania Avenue, and it is not surprising that complex trade issues make their way through the bureaucratic machine at a fairly stately pace. Ex-President Reagan gets the credit for tidying this stretch of the waterfront up a bit by his creation in 1985 of the Economic Policy Council and the Domestic Policy Council, because these two bodies took the place of an Interagency Group on International Economic Policy and seven other cabinet councils.

The president himself chairs the Economic Policy Council, or in his absence the secretary of the treasury. Apart from him and the USTR, the other members are the secretaries of State, Agriculture, Commerce and Labor, the director of the Office of Management and Budget and the chairman of the Council of Economic Advisors. Various National Security people drop in as appropriate, and the vice-president and White House chief of staff serve ex-officio.

An obvious question, with so many players on the field, is whether they don't sometimes get in each other's way and find it difficult to see the ball. Most of the older hands in Washington say no. Some of them do own to an occasional sense of frustration and a rather more than occasional sense of *déjà vu*, but after a decade and more of brooding over the Airbus issue that is scarcely surprising.

Sally Bath has sat through more interagency meetings than she cares to remember, and finds it easy to take a long view. "It makes developing a consensus more difficult, but I'm not sure that's all bad. I think that the process we have probably ensures that the result will be one we can live with through many administrations." If you listen to her very carefully, Bath might also just be suggesting, with enormous delicacy, that there could sometimes be more than one view about the performance of USTR in the driving seat. "They are the ones who lead our delegations. I'm not sure how much they steer the boat." (When not preparing for, attending, or recovering from interagency meetings or trips to Geneva, Miss Bath likes to sail.) "I think on occasion the boat is steered in accordance with a pre-plan, with the helmsman following instructions."

Bath sees the Department of Commerce as having responsibility for the broad industrial health of the nation. "In this particular office we analyse the aerospace industry, we are aware of its international competitive posture, we look at the trade problems as one part of their business, but not the totality of their business. We also look at their domestic customers, which obviously in this country includes the Department of Defense and NASA, and we consider what is required of government policy to ensure that aerospace remains a technologically advanced industry that is the right size and shape for the future."

There are at least as many views on the issue as there are agencies, but there is no hard and fast division into hawks and doves. Arnold Levine, the director of the Office of International Transportation and Trade, told me that the positions of the agencies on Airbus was not as polarised as he had seen it on many other issues. "This has not, for example, been an issue that has been pushed to cabinet level for a decision on whether to take trade action. There has been enough unanimity at sub-cabinet level, the inter-agency level, and only very occasionally does it rise up to the cabinet. They've generally said, "Yes, keep up the good fight," and it comes back down again."[2]

Levine's own agency, the Department of Transportation, tends to find itself at the dovish end of the spectrum. "We speak for the users of the aircraft," he said. "We represent the point of view of the U.S. airlines whose interest is obviously in having as competitive a market in aircraft and engines as possible. So when we come to the table we take that point of view—that more competitors are better than fewer competitors." I asked him whether this meant there was a sense in which the Department of Transportation was pro-Airbus. "We realise that even if Airbus never sells another plane in the U.S., its presence as a supplier has a significant competitive effect, so that from that point of view, yes, I suppose you might say we *are* pro-Airbus."

Levine and those who think like him see themselves as free-traders. "Our view has been that there is a great deal of value to having three suppliers in this market, and that we should not take any hasty action to precipitate a confrontation that might result in the exclusion of that third supplier from the U.S. market or in retaliation against U.S. airframe manufacturers abroad. We have consistently run back to the numbers on this, looking at what Boeing and McDonnell Douglas are doing, how many planes they're selling, what their finances look like. If we thought either company was being seriously injured by the presence of Airbus in the market or unfair practices being pursued by Airbus, then my office would strongly urge a migration towards the hawk side on this. But in the absence of convincing evidence, we have tended towards the free-trader side".

The other end of the spectrum is occupied, not very surprisingly, by the Department of Labor. Its primary concern with such issues lies in their impact on employment. There is a statutory requirement in the United States for labour advice on trade negotiations, and as the main channel for that it falls to Labor to feed into the interagency discussions the concerns and resentments of the unions. Richard B. Schulman, of the Department's Office of International Economic Affairs, was involved in the original Aircraft Code negotiations in the 1970s and therefore has a longer memory than most for the twists and turns of the Airbus saga. "The labor unions are very sensitive on the issue," said Schulman. "They are told by free market administrations that you have to let the chips fall where they may and that if you're not competitive in the international economy you must take your lumps. They've done that, and as a result they've lost substantial employment. Here is a high-tech sector where we lead the world. Aerospace is our major industrial export. To have that natural comparative advantage jeopardised by artificial government props is simply intolerable. They have memories of the cyclical nature of the business. There are good times and bad. They remember the massive lay-offs, and they're very concerned about the long-run effects."[2]

Organised labour in the United States has less muscle than does its European counterpart, and aerospace workers do not all belong to one union. The Machinists' Union has most of Boeing organised, the United Auto Workers represents most McDonnell Douglas employees, and the Electrical Workers' Union tends to be strongest among subcontractors and smaller firms. None of them takes it as axiomatic that what is good for McDonnell Douglas or Boeing is good for them. An offset deal by Boeing in Spain, for instance, might not be greeted with unalloyed enthusiasm by the employees of American subcontractors who saw themselves being cut out of the business. The unions would also look very closely at the sort of joint venture that has been under discussion between McDonnell Douglas and Airbus. Work moving from Europe to the States would be fine, traffic in the other direction less so. The conviction that Airbus is essentially an ambitious European jobs programme is deeply rooted. "The unions don't want to hear that Europe is trying to export its unemployment over here just because they have more rigid social policies and can't lay people off if there's a downturn," said Schulman.

The State Department, like foreign ministries the world over, is frequently cast as pig in the middle, mistrusted in equal measure for its tiresome tendency to think that there can sometimes be two sides to a question and for a certain disposition to think better of foreigners and their motives than the average run of the citizenry does. Robert Deutsch, as Officer in Charge of European Regional Economic Affairs in Washington, brought to the job the perspective gained during an assignment to the U.S. Embassy in Paris. "Our basic function is to try and help manage the different trade issues between us and the European Community in a manner that preserves U.S. interests but reduces frictions. Our basic mandate is to try and keep the inevitable conflicts from spilling into the broader areas of the relationship. And I guess that we may be seen somewhat as a motor for trying to convince the U.S. government to compromise, to be somewhat more reasonable, and to understand better the motives of the Europeans in promoting the Airbus consortium and the European commercial aerospace industry."

When the material for this book was being gathered, the Justice Department turned out to be the proving exception to the general Washington rule of openness, and it was therefore necessary to form a view of their position at second hand. A former government official who had observed them at interagency meetings told me that in his experience they tended to take a very soft line, in his view for reasons of ideology. "Basically their approach is that competition is a good thing, and never mind where the money's coming from. The AntiTrust Division is the one that's involved. There are obviously antitrust implications in industries as concentrated as this, and there is in the Justice Department, and particularly in the AntiTrust Division, a pronounced aversion to current U.S. policy in the area of enforcement of unfair trade laws. They tend to view the enforcement of these statutes and the issuance of antidumping and countervailing duty orders as anticompetitive, anti–free trade devices. And there are those of us who take pretty strong exception to that view of life."

The same informant, who himself saw things from a fairly hawkish perspective, also confessed to some surprise at the position taken by the Treasury. "Treasury, oddly, was a bit soft on everything until it came to the idea, which surfaced late in the negotiations, that the European manufacturers were going to be given exchange rate guarantees, and at that point even Treasury got upset. For about a year and a half before that, though, Treasury was hardly visible in this process. They rarely showed up at the meetings, and when they did—at delegation meetings, that is—they rarely talked."

The Treasury naturally takes a less unflattering view of itself. "We see ourselves as an economic agency whose function is to try and improve the efficiency of the operation of the U.S. economy," William E. Barreda, deputy assistant secretary for trade and investment told me. "I guess we were a little slow to learn that international trade cannot now be divorced from the American economy as a whole. Our view can sometimes be distinct from that of Commerce, who might be closer to what industry is thinking, and from USTR, who have to be quite responsive to Congress." People in the Treasury, he said, tended to be reasonably free traders, their views often close to those of the Council of Economic Advisers, but maybe not quite as theoretical—an assertion he then cast doubt on by adding, rather text-bookishly, "Airbus is interesting to us intellectually because it's an example of oligopolistic competition internationally, which is a little different from the classical model."[2]

Divergences of view can of course stem from individual temperament as well as from differences of professional concern, but there are shades of opinion not only between agencies but also between different offices in the same department. Within the Department of Commerce, for instance, the Office of European Community Affairs considers Airbus as a classic example of industrial targeting. For them the core issue is that the European goverments have chosen, for both political and economic reasons, to pour resources into a high-tech industry. They regard their Aerospace colleagues in the International Trade Administration (Sally Bath's neck of the woods) as inclined to be pragmatic, which I take to be a Washington euphemism for overaccomodating. They argue that unless the United States takes a hard line, the Europeans will assume that the principle has been conceded and will feel free to pursue the same strategy in another industrial sector such as semiconductors.

That is a position that could be strengthened by the provisions of a measure finally passed into law in August 1988—Public Law 100-4118 of the 100th Congress. "An Act to enhance the competitiveness of American industry, and for other purposes," says the title page, adding helpfully, "Short Title—This Act may be cited as the 'Omnibus Trade and Competitiveness Act of 1988'." Omnibus is the word. It is a vast catch-all of a measure that sprawls over 230 unnumbered pages and appears to have something for everybody. Section 2209 expresses the sense of the Congress on Japan and the Arab boycott of Israel; Section 1745 records temporary changes in the tariff treatment of fluazifop-p-butyl; Section 6201 concerns the development of literacy corps programs; Section 7002 lists amendments to the Buy American Act of 1988. It is also the technical instrument that bestows on the president the authority to pursue negotiations in the Uruguay Round.

It is a great marvel that it is as short as it is. The bill went through the Senate and the House of Representatives in different versions, each the best part of a thousand pages long. The task of reconciling the two documents fell to 199 members of Congress drawn from 23 committees. The first time it went to the White House, President Reagan vetoed it. He was unhappy mainly about the mandatory requirement for businesses to give advance notice of closings or layoffs, but there were other sticking points, too, ranging from the proposal for a Council on Competitiveness (it would "open even more venues for special pleaders," the President said) to the expansion of ethanol imports which could harm U.S. grain producers.

In the form in which it finally reached the statute book, there are a number of provisions that have a bearing on the Airbus issue. Since 1985 the Office of the United States Trade Representative had been producing a plump document entitled *National Trade Estimate Report on Foreign Trade Barriers*—a requirement under the Trade and Tariff Act of 1984.

There had clearly been some feeling in Congress that this had never got to be more than an exercise in tailwagging by the USTR's office, and that it needed to be more sharply focussed. Under the new legislation it will no longer be sufficient simply to pass the catalogue of trade barriers in ponderous review. The Trade Representative is now called upon to determine which foreign practises are particularly burdensome and to indicate priorities for action, and the terms of section 301 under which such action would be taken have been strengthened.

A number of other passages in the act will have been scrutinised with particular attention in Brussels and Toulouse. Section 1327 provides that in certain instances leases shall be regarded as equivalent to sales and defines the considerations that apply—whether, for instance, the product subject to the lease is integrated into the operations of the lessee, and whether the lease transaction would permit avoidance of antidumping or countervailing duties. Another section with a clear application to Airbus is 1315— "Treatment of International Consortia." The provision here is that if members of a consortium receive subsidies from their respective home countries, "the administering authority shall cumulate all such subsidies, as well as subsidies provided directly to the international consortium, in determining any countervailing duty upon such merchandise."

"War is the faro table of governments." The words from which this chapter takes its title are Tom Paine's in *The Rights of Man.* The Americans clearly know very well that a trade war is just as chancy a business as the shooting variety, but it would be foolish of the European side to think that the United States's apparent preference for the negotiating table over the green cloth of the casino is a law of nature. "We don't expect to negotiate eternally," said Sally Bath. "We do expect to finish things within a certain time frame—even in this industry where marketing campaigns can go on for five-ten years. So we don't want to beat an issue to death, we don't want to make a career out of it, and we do want to finish these things when we get into them."

If it's going to be faro, Europe should perhaps reflect on the rules of the game. The chances between dealer and punter are, of course, equal—except that if the cards are alike, the banker wins half the stake.

NOTES

1. Interview in Long Beach, October 1988.
2. Interview in Washington, October 1988.

12

Four Wise Men

"It requires wisdom to understand wisdom; the music is nothing if the audience is deaf."

—Walter Lippmann, *A Preface to Morals,* 1929.

By late 1987 it was plain that negotiations between Europe and the United States were getting nowhere. A degree of political concern became apparent in the member countries of the consortium, and there was a growing acceptance that unless there were changes in the system, there was a European flank that would remain vulnerable. A small group was set up, and each of the four countries supplied a member. They were charged, in the slightly wobbly grammar of the ministers' letters of appointment, "to consider the organisation of Airbus and to advise if the current structure and organisation is the most appropriate." They became known, inevitably, as 'The Four Wise Men'.

For their nominee, the French found it natural to go to the heart of their aeronautical establishment. At the time of his appointment. Jacques Benichou was the president of GIFAS (Groupement des Industries Aéronautiques et Spatiales), the body that corresponds to the Aerospace Industries Association in the United States. A product of the Ecole Polytechnique and of the Ecole Nationale Supérieure de l'Aéronautique, he had worked as an engineer in the public service before stepping across into the higher reaches of the industry. He had run Messier Hispano Bugatti in the 1970s, and since 1982 had been at the head of SNECMA, the engine manufacturers. If there was anyone in the industry Benichou did not know, it could be taken that it was an acquaintance not worth cultivating.

The German Wise Man was Peter Pfeiffer. Born in Munich in 1922, he had graduated as a lawyer and then entered the Bayerische Vereinsbank, serving as a director there from 1962 until his retirement 25 years later, and sitting on a number of supervisory boards—including those of MBB and Deutsche Airbus. A member, that is to say, of the formidable Bavarian *mafia* that was so solidly ensconced in the councils of the aerospace industry in the Federal Republic.

Spain volunteered the services of Emilio González García, deputy general manager of the Banco Español de Credito, although an aeronautical engineer by training. In the early 1970s, when he was on the board of Iberia, he had been a member of the government commission that had negotiated Spain's entry to the consortium. He was also a former chairman of CASA, and from 1975 to 1978 had served on the Airbus Supervisory Board.

The only member of the group with no experience of the aircraft industry was the British nominee. Sir Jeffrey Sterling (later Lord Sterling of Plaistow), a self-made millionaire, was chairman of P&O—the Peninsular and Oriental Steam Navigation Company. Trained as a classical violinist, Sterling had worked for some years as a stockbroker and then gone into property. He had come to the attention of Margaret. Thatcher in the early 1980s. He was also a friend of Lord Young, then secretary of state for Trade and Industry, and had acted as an adviser to his department on the government's programmes for privatisation and for the reform of broadcasting.

Between them, the Four Wise Men clearly knew where quite a lot of the bodies were buried in Toulouse and the various other centres of Airbus activity, and they went quickly to work with their picks and shovels. Between January and April 1988 they had meetings with Franz-Josef Strauss, the top management of the four partner companies and senior staff of Airbus Industrie in Toulouse. Their report[1] filled a mere 17 pages of typescript, but in spite of its even tone it was as devastating as it was brief.[2]

They began by paying tribute to what Airbus Industrie had achieved and to the universities and research establishments that stood behind that achievement. They had picked up Airbus Industrie's bad habit of lumping together firm orders for aircraft and options—1,100 at the time of their report, they noted, of which 400 had already been delivered. They also recorded that the consortium had secured between 15 and 20 percent of the world market and that they now numbered among their customers five out of the ten largest American airlines.

Airbus was not yet, however, a commercial success, and the Wise Men needed no help from the Circumlocution Office in Dicken's *Little Dorrit* in their account of why this should be. The GIE structure was "ill-adapted for consolidating the remarkable technical success achieved so far into an economic success." They recognised that it could not be swept away overnight, but they were clear that there were urgent changes that could not wait:

It is imperative to establish as soon as possible a system in which decisions, the power to take them, and the background knowledge appropriate to the decisions vest clearly in particular manager or groups of "managers" inside a tightly defined reporting system. It is clear to us that, unless such management changes take place immediately, problems for Airbus can only increase, leading in particular to serious production delays, severe extra costs and worst of all, the loss of goodwill of major airlines. After such a promising start, it would be a tragedy were Airbus to founder upon problems of management and administration.

The Wise Men conceded the Airbus contention that it was still at too early a stage in most of its programmes to have reached a break-even point, that they had had to compete for market share and that their problems had been exacerbated by the fall in value of the U.S. dollar. They insisted, however, that these were inherent difficulties for the aerospace industry generally, and they identified certain other problems that they attributed to "a certain lack of adaptability and organisational efficiency" in the Airbus organisation itself.

These were three in number. The first they described as a lack of correlation between the marketing of aircraft and the financial aspects of the programmes. This they attributed to the fact that sales and support were essentially an Airbus Industrie responsibility, whereas the four industrial partners negotiated their prices among themselves and with Airbus Industrie but kept their costs to themselves. Secondly, they noted the absence of an overall balancesheet at Airbus Industrie level, which meant that both AI and the governments lacked what they termed "objective decision-making criteria." Thirdly, they remarked on the proliferation of committees within the Airbus structure and the general unwieldiness of the organisation, observing that the rule that required decisions to be backed by partners holding 81 percent of the shares was, in effect, a unanimity requirement.

The Wise Men made no claims for originality in their analysis, remarking that all earlier studies and reports had reached similar conclusions: "What is required is an Airbus Industrie structure which would be more responsible for all parts of the programmes, more concerned with profit and loss, and less dependent in its day-to-day operation on each industrial partner. The partners, on the other hand, need to control more closely Airbus Industrie's decisions, since they bear all the risks."

The question of structure was paramount. The Wise Men acknowledged that their preferred solution, the setting up of an "Airbus PLC" (i.e., public limited company), would take a long time and would pose thorny problems of valuation and capitalisation, not least because of the mix of private and state-owned companies. Given the present level of Airbus activity, it would also be difficult to envisage an immediate positive cash flow, and that implied that for some years it would be necessary to make injections of capital.

To pave the way for a transition to PLC status, it would be necessary to devise an improved management structure to enable the consortium to compete successfully (i.e., profitably) in the market place. The Wise Men believed, however, that such a decision would quickly bring them up against what they described as "a fundamental reality of the aeronautical industry"—that no major civil manufacturer could expect to be profitable without the contribution they received from defence and space research, and the military orders that resulted in better returns and dampened the civil aircraft order cycles. The latter they characterised as "welcome," the former as "indispensable."

A PLC structure did not seem realistic before 1992, but they had given some thought to what form it might take, and even sketched out in an annex what is known in Brussels English as an organigramme. Airbus Industrie would become a sort of holding company. It would continue to look after sales and support and programme coordination; it would also take on most research and development and become responsible for the manufacture of the main elements and for the final assembly line.

Under such an arrangement, the partners would have to assign to the new company their design facilities, some of the laboratories used for general research and development trials and the main sites at present devoted to Airbus manufacture—MBB's Finkenwerder plant in Hamburg, Aérospatiale's St. Martin facility in Toulouse and the British Aerospace factories at Chester and Filton. The four partners would continue to exercise control as main shareholders, but the Wise Men, although recognising that they were talking about an industry characterised by high risks and low margins allowed themselves a modest fantasy— at the right side of the organigramme, attached by a thin umbilical line to Airbus Industrie Holding, is a box marked "Other financial investors."

The land of Cockaigne is likely to require visas, however, and the Wise Men had a number of suggestions about how the consortium should complete its application form. "We believe it will be very important for the efficiency of the system that the relationships between AI and the partners are simplified and streamlined."

They paused first over the Supervisory Board, noting that it was some 20 strong, that it met roughly twice a year and that its main function was to ratify decisions made elsewhere. Their conclusion was that it ought to play a far more dominant role in decisions about programmes, cooperation agreements and strategic control not just in Toulouse but in the partner companies—that it should, in fact, become the main instrument of policy of the consortium as a whole. It should be reduced drastically in size, and consist of only five members—the president of Airbus Industrie and the presidents or chief executive officers of the four partner companies. If the occasion demanded, it ought to meet on an *ad-hoc* basis and despatch urgent business, and to make that easier, alternates should be appointed and given authority to speak for their companies.

They recommended that the Supervisory Board should be the main interface with governments, and they trod delicately round the question of what the French called the presidency and the British the chairmanship. (Franz-Josef Strauss was still alive when the report came out, and appeared to some to have been there since time began. "I don't know who appointed *him*," British Aerospace's Sir Raymond Lygo said. "God, I suspect—I mean, I can't think of anyone else capable of appointing Strauss."³) "It is important for Airbus," the report said, "to have as its President a familiar and respected international figure. We acknowledge, though," (a tell-tale signal, this, that what follows is in code rather than plain English) "that under the system of management recommended in this paper, the President of Airbus may find himself—as will all the partner Presidents—having to devote much more of his time than hitherto to Airbus business."

The Wise Men then turned their attention to the senior executives. Their first recommendation was entirely conventional and followed from what they had said earlier about a move towards PLC status. There should be a managing director, and he should be the administrateur gérant of Airbus Industrie GIE. He should also chair an Executive Board which would be directly responsible to the Supervisory Board, and his would be the responsibility for the day-to-day operation of the entire Airbus system.

Then there was the small matter of finance. The Wise Men had observed that the central accounting of the Airbus system was restricted to the management accounts of Airbus Industrie in Toulouse, and that these covered only the sales and service functions. The Airbus books of partners were not open either to their fellow partners or to Airbus Industrie. For the managing director to be able to carry out the role envisaged for him, it seemed to them that it would be necessary to establish a central accounting system comparable to that existing in the head office of a PLC:

We consider that our recommendations concerning the remit of the finance director and his place on the Executive Board are at the heart of our proposals. Indeed, if Airbus Industrie does not take steps to constitute itself in the organisational manner we propose and to introduce full transparency of costs and profits together with producing comparisons between AI and its partners, we doubt whether Airbus can ever reach long-term profitability.

The powers with which this new financial director was to be invested were sweeping. He was to head an accounting function separate from any other central administrative functions of the Airbus programmes. The Airbus accounts of all the partners and of Airbus Industrie itself were to be fully open to him. He was to have full control and authority over all cash-flows within Airbus Industrie. This stopped short of giving him authority to issue instructions to any of AI's operational directors, but was to mean that all plans and programmes would require clearance from him. He was to have the mandatory right to require full details of their programme costs from the partners and to see invoiced prices and profits and losses arising from work contracted to them by Airbus Industrie. In other words, he was to see to it that there was full openness of accounting throughout the Airbus system.

Most significant of all was the place he was to have in the pecking order, which the Wise Men described in one short, flat sentence—"He should report to the Supervisory Board, the Managing Director and the Executive Board." As will be seen, they were the fourteen most highly charged words in the report.

The Executive Board was to be a sort of Board of Directors, which would be the main instrument of control over agreed programmes with agreed prices. A membership of seven was proposed—a senior manager from each of the partners and three representatives of Airbus Industrie—the managing director, the finance director and a commercial director, who would be responsible for marketing, sales and after-sales activities. The partners were urged to appoint as their representative the most senior man within their companies with day-to-day responsibilities for Airbus activities and to regard them as plenipotentiaries. This board would replace the existing, but rather looser, executive committee. Its remit would be broader, and would include responsibility for pricing policy. The managing director and financial director would both report to it.

The Wise Men were not content to leave these bodies to write their own rules of procedure, however. They stipulated first of all that the Supervisory Board should meet at least four times a year, and that on the recommendation of the Executive Board it should concern itself with all matters relating to the launching of new programmes and the subsequent decisions about work-sharing. While doffing their cap to the merits of consensus, they recommended that a vote should be taken where necessary and even detailed a procedure. Major decisions about new programmes (or the cancellation of existing ones) should be made on the basis of partnership shares and require a 75 percent vote in favour; other major decisions should be on the basis of a simple majority of partnership shares; all other matters should be determined by a simple majority between the presidents.

The most important recommendation about the Executive Board was that the partners should accept that its decisions were binding. It would hold monthly meetings, and in the absence of a consensus should generally reach decisions by a simple majority vote. An exception to this was made in the case of certain decisions with financial consequences for the companies, and here at least two partners, controlling at least 51 percent of the shares, must be in favour. As its first task, the Executive Board was enjoined to produce a rule book for itself and get it approved by the Supervisory Board.

The Wise Men also had things to say about the mix of nationalities within Airbus. They had formed the impression that the system of temporary transfer from the partners to Airbus resulted in a lack of commitment, prime loyalties remaining with the parent companies. They wanted to see the introduction of contracts of employment directly with Airbus.They believed that this would lead to the evolution of a career structure, and that this would be good for morale and foster a stronger spirit of cooperation.

Nothing , it seemed, was to be sacred:

At present some roles within Airbus are reserved for particular nationalities: the President is "traditionally" German, the Executive Head is French, the Head of Accounting of Toulouse is British etc. We recommend that all such reserving of jobs for nationalities should cease, both at the Executive Board level and within the administrative and technical functions. "The best man for the job" should be the only selection criterion . . .

Perhaps one of the Wise Men had been reading the correspondence of Admiral Sir John Fisher, the father of the Dreadnought, at the turn of the century: "Favouritism was the secret of our efficiency in the old days . . . *'Buggins's turn'* has been our ruin and will be disastrous hereafter!"

There were a number of further recommendations on specific financial and management issues. It had been brought home to the Wise Men that a partner's only prospect of profit from Airbus work lay in the performance of contract work on advantageous terms. This meant that the partners exerted themselves to ensure that their share of work as contractors was at least equal to their partnership share in the consortium—any losses incurred as partners could then, at least in theory, be made good by profits earned as subcontractors. There had been occasions when this had led to the contract's not being placed with the best supplier, and that was clearly not at all in the interest of the Airbus system as a whole. The report recommended that in future, profits and losses should be apportioned in accordance with the partners' invoiced work-shares and not in proportion to their partnership shares.

The Wise Men had also detected a nonsense in the way that funding for modifications was provided. All development work took place at the partners' factories, and the funding for it came only from the partners or their governments. The inflexibility that this gave rise to had led to a good deal of frustration, and the report recommended that the Supervisory Board should make a certain sum of money available (a figure of 5 percent of total development funding was suggested) so that modifications could be developed to solve design problems as they arose and on the initiative of the Executive Committee.

Subcontracting was another area in which there seemed to be scope for greater flexibility. The Wise Men did not challenge the proposition that there should be no competition for mainstream contacts. They did not think that should apply at the margin, however, and they urged the introduction of a system that, while guaranteeing each company subcontract work up to an agreed proportion of its partnership share (perhaps 80 percent), would leave the rest to be awarded by the Airbus Industrie Executive Board on a competitive basis. Such work would be offered in the first instance in the country that held the lead on the part of the aircraft in question, but if Airbus Industrie judged tenders from the home country to be uncompetitive, it should be allowed to open the bidding to firms in the other three countries or eventually beyond. The Wise Men saw this as a reform that would greatly enhance the efficiency of the consortium.

A greater role for competitive market forces was also seen in the equipment area, where the Wise Men saw logic in the extension of direct tendering. They conceded that there might be some difficulties, but pointed out that Airbus already benefited from this in its purchase of engines, a cutthroat market where nonrecurring costs were borne directly by the engine manufacturers.

In conclusion, the Wise Men addressed two recommendations to the governments that had appointed them. The first related to the territoriality of equipment supply, where they were not convinced that the partners always awarded contracts on a strictly commercial basis. When, for instance, a contracting partner dealt with a subcontractor from another of the participating countries, the partner was not required to help that subcontractor with nonrecurring costs; what happened was that any costs not borne by the equipment supplier himself fell to the partner in that country. The result was that there was no incentive to the negotiating partner to push for the most cost-effective contract. The change suggested by the Wise Men was that a subcontractor's nonrecurring costs should in future fall upon the partner awarding the contract. They felt that this would be particularly appropriate where equipment development costs were no longer mainly a charge on government, a shift in policy that had already taken place in the United Kingdom.

Their second suggestion related to export credit. The existence of four separate export credit agencies in the member countries seemed to the Wise Men to result in inefficiency and delay and to put Airbus at a disadvantage in competing with the Americans. They recommended the creation of a European import-export bank to provide full credit facilities comparable with those available from the Export-Import in the United States. They also saw the founding of such an agency as a further step towards a united Europe.

There was a short coda to the report that combined a brief pat on the back for Airbus with a sober glance into the crystal ball. "Having already won a significant place in the market (15–30 percent) and having as a result less need than formerly to achieve sales at the same rate as before, it should be possible to achieve a break-even point over the next five years, particularly for the A320." They emphasised, however, that they only saw that happening if the new management structure they proposed was rapidly put in place. This was a prerequisite for increased competitiveness, substantial reductions in programme costs and increased efficiency. They looked to the new team for one other thing, too—"the encouragement of a reappearance of a true spirit of cooperation in the Airbus programme as a whole."

The ministers of the four partner countries met in Madrid on April 12, 1988. They welcomed the report and instructed the industrial partners to present detailed plans for implementing its proposals by their next meeting, which was due to take place in Hanover on May 5. Kenneth Clarke, the British Trade and Industry minister, said that he and his colleagues wanted to make final decisions on the new management structure before the year was out so that it could be in place by the beginning of 1989.

There was not a great deal of political interest, and the press found meagre pickings in the story. *The Economist* observed that tougher controls were long overdue and that Airbus had been handled like the delicate child of indulgent parents.[4] There was speculation that Franz-Josef Strauss was under pressure to step down as chairman on the grounds that his style was no longer appropriate. An article in the *Frankfurter Allgemeine Zeitung* on the eve of the Hanover Air Show certainly did not mince its words. Under the heading *Das fliegende Subventionsgrab*(The Flying Subsidy Grave) it took Airbus comprehensively apart, noting Strauss's inability to meet criticisms of the consortium other than by attacks on Boeing, and comparing his performance to that of a mercantile prince.[5] In Britain, Lord Bruce-Gardyne, a treasury minister in the first Thatcher administration, wrote waspishly that for Herr Strauss, Airbus was essentially "a scheme to carry on the good work of the Common Agricultural Policy by other means, sustaining his faithful voters in Bavaria in the style of life to which they are accustomed."[6]

When the ministers met in Hanover, however, it was announced that Dr. Strauss was staying put, at least for the time being. The announcement was made by Erich Riedl, the state secretary in the Bonn Economics Ministry and a protégé of the Herr Doktor's, who also expressed the satisfaction of his colleagues that the industrial shareholders had endorsed the Wise Men's proposals. The French transport minister, Jacques Douffiagues, described the reforms as "indispensable," but said that they were not sufficient to give Airbus "a full industrial dimension." Kenneth Clarke's script made statesmanlike but vague references to the coming to maturity of Airbus and the need for a unified European market from 1992.[7]

It was a curious experience in the months after the report appeared to go the rounds of the companies and of Airbus Industrie and try to establish what they actually thought of it. The immediate response of almost everybody was to say that it was all very sensible—"Much of what was in the Report was very close to what we said to them," said Robert McKinlay of British Aerospace. "The title of the presentation I gave them was 'Airbus Industrie—the need for change'," Adam Brown said in Toulouse. "I spent about three hours with them on all the things we felt needed tackling if the system were to become more efficient. I would say their report has addressed every single one of the problems, and I say '*Chapeau!*'"

In general, people in Toulouse tended to think that the proposals would mainly affect the companies, and people in the companies seemed to think that they were mainly aimed at . . . Toulouse. It did not, however, take a great deal of probing to discover that the partners liked some of the recommendations much more than others. Their response was very much that of enterprises everywhere to the prescriptions of company doctors— they tended, that is to say, to pick and choose, and to push anything they did not fancy to the side of the plate.

There was some feeling that the job had been rushed. That was certainly the view of Henri Martre, at that time the boss of Aérospatiale, who had spent only one morning with the Wise Men. "For example, they set the majority for a vote at 75 percent, a suggestion made primarily at the instance of the British Wise Man, Sir Jeffrey Sterling. That seemed OK to my German colleague and me, but Sir Raymond Lygo of BAe pointed out that this would not be permissible under British law. And it would, of course, have meant that if the French and the Germans had been in agreement, they could have imposed a decision on their British partner." Martre had also felt that the philosophies of the individual Wise Men had been very different and that they had not totally understood each other. Not a bad report, for all that, he said. It made some interesting suggestions. French is a marvellous language for damning with faint praise.[8]

Martre was in no doubt about the most important recommendation. "An enterprise in which decisions are not taken is an enterprise which is dead. The central weakness of the Airbus consortium is that the decision-making process is more painful than in any other industrial organisation. And that is scarcely surprising, because effective financial responsibility rests not with the consortium but with the partners—they are the people who have the money and run the risk. So the most important reform which is now proposed is that the Executive Board should be able to make decisions about financial matters on a majority vote. That is the fundamental reform—we have established an effective decision-making process. Previously, when the rule of unanimity applied, there were often occasions when decisions were not taken and had to be deferred to the next meeting."

For the finance director proposal he had no time at all—"If you will forgive me for saying so, it is ridiculous. The idea that the financial director should have authority over everybody in a company makes no sense—I have never come a cross a company where the financial director had authority over everybody else. That would make him managing director, not financial director." (This had occurred to somebody else, too. The question had been raised in an interview with Jean Pierson at the 1988 Farnborough Air Show—might it for him be a resignation issue? There was a longish pause. The gaze was inscrutable. It was not clear whether he was considering how best to reply or waiting for the appalling noise the Soviet MIGs were making over-head to die down. It was also a very warm day, and the Airbus chalet lays on a very good lunch. The answer, when it came, was delivered absolutely dead-pan. "That," he said, "is a very interesting question."⁹)

The Airbus PLC notion did not have much appeal to Aérospatiale's senior management, either—"Très franchement, je ne la trouve pas bonne," Martre said. "Consider what the situation would be. We create this Airbus PLC with factories in Toulouse and in Hamburg, and on the world scale it would be quite small. It would offer no sort of challenge to Boeing. Boeing would have between 60 and 70 percent of the market, this little enterprise 15 percent. Apart from its commercial activities, Boeing undertakes a range of activities for the Pentagon, and from the point of view of financial capacity these activities bulk very large. In the U.S. the profit margin is of the order of 10 percent for military orders—on the civil side, it is much more modest. What's more, Boeing's domestic market is much greater than its overseas market. For a little company called Airbus PLC the domestic market isn't even a captive market—sales in Europe constitute a relatively minor part of her sales. So if you compare the two, the conclusion must be that Airbus would disappear at the end of four or five years. It does not make sense to think of separating the commercial side from the military side in an aerospace company."

Martre was equally dismissive of the concept of full transparency. "It's a completely artificial idea. I buy aluminium to make my aeroplanes, but I've no idea of what sort of profit you make on aluminium. Transparency in the matter of costs simply does not exist. We would also have to have common accounting conventions. That would take an enormous amount of work. Would it apply to subcontractors? To the suppliers of engines? I don't see the object of the exercise. Is it to transfer money to those who are making a loss? Or to require those who are making losses to get themselves organised so that they don't? What would we gain? Frankly, as a private citizen, when I go out to buy things, I'm not remotely interested in transparency. If I buy a hi-fi, I have no interest in what profit the man in the shop is going to make. All I want to know is what the price is. Then I might try and beat him down a bit. Whether the retailer is making a profit or a loss when he sells me the equipment interests me not at all—in fact if he told me afterwards that he'd lost his shirt on the deal, I'd be delighted. C'est pas normale! C'est pas le bon réflexe! Le bon réflexe, c'est négotier."

On the question of contracts of employment with the consortium, he was more than a little sceptical. "That's something that individuals must negotiate. 'Airbus—how long will it last? What if I don't like it after three years? Will my old job still be there?' I think most of those who come will want to keep their contracts with their own companies. I think we've got to be very careful. To start changing things for reasons of principle because the Wise Men have suggested it—none of that counts. What counts is people. And you'd have to pay people four times as much as elsewhere to compensate them for the insecurity".

There was as much plain speaking about the Wise Men at British Aerospace's head office next to Charing Cross Station in London as there had been in the 16th *arrondissement* in Paris. Admiral Sir Raymond Lygo, a former vice-chief of the Naval Staff who joined BAe at about the time that Britain rejoined the consortium, has all the bluntness of speech traditionally associated with those who have spent a life on the ocean waves. Some of his indiscretions are no doubt calculated and some of them are not. He was a popular chief executive because everybody in the company knew exactly where they were with him, even if public relations officers who sat in on his interviews sometimes looked slightly unwell. "I thought it was a good report. I also thought it was a somewhat unnecessary report, in the sense that a well-run business should have come to those conclusions itself and not have had to produce Four Wise Men. I would not be very happy if somebody had to come and tell me how to run BAe."[10]

For Sir Raymond's money, the report did not go far enough. "The concepts they came up with are very straightforward and obvious. My wish, expressed to the Wise Men, was that they should tackle the fundamental question by saying we intend to privatise Airbus Industrie and we intend to turn it into a PLC. I don't know of any other discipline which is capable of exerting the necessary constraints and motivations on a company."

"Now I'm the first to admit that the consequence of that would have had to be the restructuring of the management of AI in a way in which somebody was in charge of it. Secondly, the company would have to be capitalised in a proper and satisfactory manner. It is a tradition in British politics that when you privatise something you write off all the debt—you can't privatise something which has got a massive debt round it's neck. That's understood by everybody. And if the European governments were to be faced with the fact that they had a once and for all chance of writing off the debt of Airbus Industrie—putting it on its feet, capitalising it properly, and saying, 'Now, run it as a business'—then I believe that would have been the most clinically clean way of solving the problem, and I do not believe myself that the problem *will* be solved until that simple fact is faced."

Sir Raymond's colleague Robert McKinlay, who had been BAe's executive director, Airbus, since Britain rejoined the consortium in 1979, felt that the difficulties of establishing a PLC should not be underestimated, and did not believe that the Wise Men's suggestion that it might take the form of a holding company would really meet the case. "If you set it up as a shell PLC, then the airlines will see it for exactly what it is, and all the liabilities and all the guarantees and all the warranties would have to go back through the shell to the parent companies."

"So you have to set up something which is solid in the eyes of the customer. The customer is buying an article which he needs to know is going to last for 20–30 years, so the PLC has to overcome the problems of finding which construction it should be technically, French, German or British or European, and it has to be capitalised in such a way that it is seen as being a really solid and respectable body. My own view is that it cannot be just a holding company. It has to have physical resources. That is the only way that the airlines would believe that we're going to be around in the next 20 years—if we have physical resources to protect."[11]

For Sir Raymond Lygo and his BAe colleagues the proposal to set up a PLC clearly marked a major point of difference with their French colleagues. "There was an argument advanced by Henri Martre," said Sir Raymond, "—and I understand it perfectly well—which was that this was not possible, because in the whole history of aviation, no civil aircraft have been produced except with the support of a military capability in the country concerned. To which I said, "What you're saying is that you cannot produce civil aircraft without a subsidy." Now I don't believe that can be true, because if it is, what are we trying to do? If you say it must be hidden behind the skirts of some military requirement, then I understand it, but I can't go along with it."

This had not, however, been the main thrust of Henri Martre's argument. The main problem for him in Aérospatiale's membership of Airbus was the enormous investment that was called for, and it was the search for a solution to that which led him towards the idea of complete amalgamation. "That would produce an aerospace company on a European scale—one could perhaps look to add Aeritalia— a company not quite on the scale of Boeing, but it would rank fourth or fifth in the pecking order."

Martre has a very firm grasp on political reality, however. "Would Mrs. Thatcher, for instance, accept the degree of industrial amputation which that would imply?" (He was speaking before the Iron Lady's departure.) "Because whether you like it or not, aerospace companies are inextricably caught up in politics, and that applies whether they are in the public or private sector. And there is no such thing as a transnational or multinational aerospace company. So the minute I talk about amalgamation, I encounter a political obstacle, and in my view the concept of Europe is not sufficiently advanced for such a solution to be admissible. But from the industrial and commercial point of view, that's what ought to be done."[8]

Sir Raymond was less hostile to the finance director proposal than was his French counterpart. "In any well-run PLC, there is always a dotted line from the finance director to the chairman or the nonexecutive directors, so that if at any time he thinks that the managing director or the chief executive has got his hand in the pot or is not doing something properly, he can automatically go to the Chairman and say, 'Look, I think you have to know that the Chief Executive has gone balmy.' That is a perfectly adequate check and balance."

He was every bit as indifferent as Henri Martre to the happiness of subcontractors, but quite happy about the right of the financial director to know full details of programme costs. "Mind you, if you were in an open tender situation—and I was in favour of that, I wanted everything competed for—then you wouldn't need that, because it wouldn't matter. I don't care what my subcontractors costs are. I'm only interested in their price, and if I can compare that price with a and b and c and d, I know I'm getting a good deal. In the case of Airbus, the work share is allocated, and that means that you don't have any idea of how much profit the individual partner is making."

"Now we all know—or we think we know—what our profits are going to be from the work we take from Airbus. What we don't know is what our share of the overall profit or loss is going to be at the end of the year. And you reach the ridiculous situation where the partners put in their prices to Airbus Industrie, they add the prices up, and that exceeds the total at which you can sell the aeroplane. You then have to say, 'Right, the aeroplane can be sold at 100 units. At the moment, the prices you have put in come to 110. We have therefore got to abate the price of the aircraft that you've put together by 10 points'—and that means that you are into a loss immediately. Now what you didn't know—nobody knew except the individual partner—was how that loss stacked up against the profit he was making out of his section price."[10]

Bob McKinlay emphasised that he saw positive commercial benefit in opening up the books to the new financial director: "We believe that the core of the exercise is that Airbus Industrie has to be more competitive. In looking at the books of BAe or Aérospatiale we don't want the guy to be looking at it just to find out what the horse died of, we really want to be able to look at all the situations and say, 'Well, that's not competitive enough in the market; what are we going to do about it?'"

Lygo saw no great problem about establishing an overall balance sheet for the consortium, but very much doubted whether it would withstand the assaults of human nature. "Let me tell you that when this question of the exposure of our costs was being discussed, I was the only president who said, 'Fine, our books are open. Not all our books—I can't let you look at what it's costing us to build Tornadoes or Harriers or anything like that, but the books relating to AI will be open to you.' The next thing however, is that the French say, 'This is ridiculous. What is the point of this?' And when I said it was so we could know what the costs are, they said, 'But that's ridiculous, because everybody will have two sets of books.' And I thought, 'Christ, you're innocent, Lygo!'"

Sir Raymond shared the view of the Wise Men that Europe was not competitive with the U.S. in the matter of export finance. "We won't say who is the most difficult horse in the team," he said, "but let me give you an example. There was a sale to Turkish Airlines some time ago, and they were looking for credit. The French credit agency came up and said yes, we'll give cover. The German lot said yes, too. Britain's ECGD said no— no cover for Turkey. So Pierson gets on the phone to me and says, 'We're going to lose the Turkish sale because the British government won't play,' and I say, 'Oh, I'm sorry about that, I'll get on to them.' 'That's right,' they said, 'there's no cover for Turkey.' Pierson said, 'But this is crazy,' so the thing was escalated. Then the DTI comes back to me and says, 'Why don't you pick up the recourse in BAe?' I said, *'Me?* My partners don't pick up recourse, I'm not picking up recourse. The sale will be lost.' Twenty-four hours pass. 'Well, would you pick up 50 percent of the cover in BAe?' 'No, I will pick up nothing. All same Queen Victoria me, all white men together.' So then the phones start buzzing, and Kohl gets onto the PM and Mitterand gets onto the PM—and we get cover for Turkey. Now that's no way to run a railroad."

On the question of cutting costs, Sir Raymond was bullish so far as his own company was concerned, sceptical about the system as a whole. "If you had a rational organisation you should be able to get the costs down by at least 25 percent, I would say. But that's Cloud-cuckoo-land, I'm afraid. So far as BAe is concerned, we are setting out to achieve productivity targets that were never heard of before. With the A330/340, the target is up there on the board in Bristol. On the 737, it takes Boeing 26–27 days to manufacture a wing. We are planning to do it in 20. Now that is getting it right. At the moment we're sitting at something like 40, because we're right at the beginning of a learning curve, but we are driving it down, and the lads are absolutely determined that they're going to beat Boeing, and they will.[12] Now, if all the partners did the same, it would have a dramatic effect, but you'd then have to sort out this bloody nonsense of sending things from A to B to C to D to E to F to G."

Bob McKinlay was slightly more cautious on the question of costs, but thought it should be possible to make savings "ranging from the substantial to the dramatic." "Airbus at the moment is a $2.5 billion a year programme. In six or seven years it will be the best part of $15 billion a year. You really ought to be targeting for saving a minimum of 10 percent and perhaps as much as 20 percent. You're talking about very substantial amounts of money."

It was considerably more difficult to form an impression of what the German industrial partner thought of the Wise Men's proposals. This was partly because at the time the report was published they had one major domestic preoccupation that dwarfed all others—the talks between the government and the industry about a possible takeover of MBB by Daimler-Benz were already at an advanced stage. It also had something to do with temperament. The Germans tend to be a good deal more reticent than their French and British colleagues, and there has never been much inclination to wash linen in public. On a visit to the German Airbus partner, anyone interested in areas where there is less than complete agreement must listen very carefully to what senior managers say in conversation—and reflect even more carefully on what they leave unsaid.

Hartmut Mehdorn, MBB's cheerful and bustling vice-president, did not share the Wise Men's view that the GIE structure had outlived its usefulness, but on most other points felt that they were on the right track. "I personally accept what they have said.There's a hell of a lot of overheads that we shouldn't have in the future, though it was not wrong to have them in the past, because that was our learning process. Also, we have now done each deal once, so we don't need to invent each time a new sales contract. Let's use one of the hundred different sales contracts which we already have, we don't need to invent the next five hundred."

Mehdorn was born in Warsaw in 1942 and studied mechanical engineering in Berlin. His experience of Airbus is long and varied. At the age of 32 he was programme manager for the A300, with direct responsibility to Corporate Management, and in the early 1980s he spent three and a half years in Toulouse as head of the Production and Industrial Planning Division.

There was more than a hint of impatience with what he evidently saw as a misplaced tendency to perfectionism in the system. He felt there were occasions—and this applied both to design engineers and to salesmen—when Airbus allowed the best to become the enemy of the good. "Airbus people always want to be first. If they are not world champions, they don't even start. Sometimes it's enough to be second." It was also fairly clear that he though the sales side of Airbus had been allowed too much freedom to paddle its own canoe.

Not everyone in MBB favoured the idea of the Daimler-Benz takeover, but Mehdorn was very clear that there was only one way to go. He saw a restructuring of the aircraft industry in Germany as essential to its stability and to its competitiveness—and he was looking not only at established competitors across the Atlantic but at the possibility of new challenges that he saw emerging in Asia. "The future lies with still larger groupings. In the field of high technology you don't just have to be intelligent, you've got to be able to afford to use your intelligence. If you buy a good piano, get a proper pianist—it's no use playing with two fingers."[13]

Governmental reactions to the report were in general favourable. "We thought pretty well of it on the whole, and would be happy for it to be implemented more or less as it stands," said Dieter Wolf, *ministerial-dirigent* at the Economics Ministry in Bonn and the most senior German official concerned with the Airbus issue. He had one minor reservation: "We were not entirely happy with what they had to say on the question of territoriality. Our legal situation doesn't allow our partner to spend taxpayers' money on activities conducted outside our territory. If taxpayers' money is spent it must not create jobs outside our territory. But that would change in 1992, of course."[14]

It was Wolf's impression that feelings ran a little higher elsewhere. "It has emerged that those running the business in Toulouse do not welcome the idea of too much structural change. There are also the divergent interests of the industrial partners and the governments. It's plain that the time is not yet ripe for them to accept willingly the proposals about making appointments on merit regardless of nationality. The French are insisting on keeping Pierson in place, and also wish to have the new finance directorship. The German view is that that would be too much. The British are also claiming the finance directorship, and the Germans would accept that." Wolf did not believe, however, that the proposed new structure would do anything to rectify the central weakness of Airbus, which he saw as the divorce between the production and the sales sides. "The ideal structure? A European statute. Until that becomes possible, some degree of criss-cross shareholding might be helpful."

Wolf's opposite number in Paris is Michel Lagorce, of the Direction Générale de l'Aviation Civile, yet another member of the formidably equipped aeronautical establishment turned out by the French *grandes écoles*. Lagorce (hobbies: gardening and reading) passed in turn through the Lycée Louis-le-Grand in Paris, the Institut de Sciences Politiques, the Ecole Polytechnique and the Ecole nationale supérieure d'aéronautique before adding for good measure a master's degree from the California Institute of Technology at Pasadena. He views the Airbus issue in a very long perspective, having served as Air Attaché in the embassy in Washington from 1969 to 1974 and been the French negotiator in the talks that led to the GATT Agreement on Civil Aircraft at the end of the decade.

Lagorce saw the report as a means of shaking off the last vestiges of the old Concorde-style "committee management"—a matter on which he speaks with some authority, as he was the commercial director of the Concorde programme from 1974 to 1979. "As one of the Wise Men said, if Airbus Industrie wants to compete against Boeing or McDonnell Douglas, it should have the same kind of management and commercial structure as they do."[15]

Lagorce believed that the appointment of the financial director was of crucial importance, but would be agreeably surprised if it produced speedy results. "There are obstacles, and those obstacles are the four industrial partners of Airbus. They do not want transparency—they do not want to lose power, to lose leadership and to give it to Airbus Industrie. That certainly applies to the French partner, and it certainly applies to the British. So far as the German partner is concerned it is hard to tell—with the reorganisation that is in train, we don't really know who the German partner is at the moment".

The British government official with day-to-day responsibility for Airbus matters was Paul Lawrance of the Department of Trade and Industry. In his early days with the department, in the late 1970s, he found himself briefly involved with Concorde. His views on the Wise Men's report were of particular interest, because he acted as the group's secretary. Perhaps because of the emphasis placed in the report on the idea of PLC status for Airbus, there was an assumption that it was mainly the work of Sir Jeffrey Sterling, but in fact the French member Jacques Benichou took the chair, and Lawrance said that by the end he was a "drafting chairman."

"It's a damning report," Lawrance said. "It really is astonishing that nearly 20 years on into a project ministers have to say 'Wouldn't it be a good idea if you knew how much your products costs?' That, I think, was what concerned the Wise Men most—the way the organisation appeared to exist to make aircraft and not make money. Everyone was perfectly happy going along churning out their parts so long as at the end of the year what they managed to book the organisation for as subcontractors more or less balanced out with what they'd had to stump up as Airbus Toulouse losses."[16]

Lawrance felt that Airbus Industrie in Toulouse had in general impressed the Wise Men more than the partners had done. "It does what it's set up to do. It sells large numbers of aircraft within the price parameters it's set. Nobody knows if those are sensible parameters, because no one knows the real costs of building the aircraft. But what it's put there to do, it does." When asked to identify the main obstacle to speedy implementation, Lawrance, like Michel Lagorce, put his finger on the extreme reluctance of the French partner to open up its books. "Aérospatiale is a company featherbedded beyond the wildest dreams of a British nationalised company - effectively refunded every two years."

Lawrance threw interesting light on some rather bald words that were quoted earlier from the last page of the report—a sentence about the need to encourage "a reappearance of a true spirit of cooperation in Airbus programmes as a whole." "This is a theme that emerged in virtually every meeting the Wise Men had—that in the early, buccaneering days of Airbus people, sat down and got things done. They wanted to create this product and get it in the air, and who did what and how much money each company made didn't really matter. They were engineers with a new toy to play with. Now without exactly having been overrun by accountants—would that it had been—the whole thing has somehow changed, and the only question that seems to get asked is, "How do we screw more money out of the Airbus system?" British Aerospace have told us that until two years ago they made regular small profits out of their participation."

A certain vicarious nostalgia for those early days might account for at least some of the unhappiness that Jean Pierson obviously felt about certain of the Wise Men's recommendations. It was not something he was prepared to discuss except with his familiars. In December 1988, shortly before the ministers were due to meet in Toulouse to push things forward, a senior Airbus official described the atmosphere inside the organisation as "charged." "These ministerial meetings have made everyone jumpy," he said. Requests for appointments with Pierson beyond that date did not meet with an accommodating response. "What if I've walked out by then?" he said aggressively to one colleague who pressed him.

One thing that might have prompted him to walk out is that the new paraphernalia of boards and committees, although presented as leaner and more coherent than the structure they replaced, still represented a degree of bureaucratisation that was profoundly uncongenial to the essentially freewheeling instincts that can still be detected among some members of the top management in Toulouse. More specifically, however, there was the uncertainty that had come to surround his own function. "He doesn't understand the setup", Sir Raymond Lygo said. "He believes that the *administrateur-gérant* must be responsible directly for marketing. And what we, the presidents, are saying is 'No, you must devolve the marketing task to the commercial director, and you must be a bigger man than that and run the company.' But he doesn't understand that, because what he is is a very nice, slightly overweight Gallic salesman."[10]

There was a pill with a still more bitter taste, however, and that was the proposal to appoint a finance director. The Wise Men were not the first to suggest it. Some years previously, when Robert Whitfield had been seconded from British Aerospace as vice-president, finance, his parent company had pressed hard for him to have a very similar reporting structure, something, as Whitfield diplomatically put it, "which wasn't really fully accepted by the management down here," and which he himself quickly recognised as politically unrealistic. [17]

By the end of 1988, however, the political climate in Toulouse had changed considerably, and it was plain from conversations with Pierson's senior colleagues that he must have considered resignation very seriously. "Given that his mandate runs out in 13–14 months time, I think he's taken the decision that it would be unconstructive to resign on the basis of those concerns today," Robert Whitfield said early in 1989. "The current wording, and the fact that he is to report to the Supervisory Board, makes it clear that the finance director is to control not just the partners but also the managing director, and I think by his nature it is more difficult for Jean Pierson than most to accept somebody in that role. In the past he has resented the role of the finance committee,[18] which in many cases consists of people who are much junior to him and have much less experience of the industry, and to be frank if he was uncomfortable about such people seeking to look over his shoulder and say he's doing the right thing or the wrong thing, then inevitably, the finance director will confront that dilemma very early on."[19]

Temperament is very unevenly distributed around the Airbus Industrie building in Toulouse, and some of Monsieur Pierson's senior colleagues have clearly not lost any sleep over the Wise Men and their report. "I never read it, actually. It wasn't circulated within the organisation," said Stuart Iddles, the matter-of-fact Mancunian who is the senior vice-president, commercial. Iddles's curriculum vitæ reads very differently from those of the smooth technocrats who are so much in evidence in the French industry. His career began at the age of fourteen with the British Aircraft Corporation at Filton, and he worked during his student apprenticeship for a degree in aeronautical engineering from the University of Bath. In 1969 he became a sales engineer with Hawker Siddeley, and for the next 15 years he sold planes in Canada, North and West Africa and Mexico.

"Clearly the one thing that has to be welcomed is anything which is going to tell us in Airbus Industrie what it costs to build an Airbus," Iddles said. "It seems nonsense to be here fighting to justify striving for profits if we don't actually know what half of the equation is. I think the fundamental achievement is to get an executive board which works on the principle of majority voting for decisions, which I think is going to be very good for getting higher production rates voted, or specific deals approved. Because we don't do any deals that aren't approved by the board, despite what you sometimes read in the press from the chairmen of the partner companies— the board approves every single deal we do."[19]

Iddles, who was obviously one of the colleagues Pierson was most likely to come into conflict with under the new dispensation, also approved of the recommendations about future structure. "It's not because I'm from British Aerospace, but I do support the idea of trying to create an Airbus PLC, because only when we have an Airbus PLC will we be the true masters of the business, and we need to be, I believe. The senior management of Airbus Industrie actually needs to be in control of the production process and the design process in order to get the most effective result. It's very difficult to hold the management here accountable when it doesn't have the responsibility."

"There is a commonly held view in the world that nobody can make money building civil aeroplanes if you start from scratch on day one and say, 'I'm just going to build civil aeroplanes.' Well, everybody's had a big leg up through the military business one way or another over time; I think that's undeniable. Whether I would take the view that it cannot work, I'm not sure, because there are many things that you can do to help make a go of it. I think you would run into problems—an Airbus PLC would certainly run into problems raising the necessary funding for a future programme—but it could probably make a go of turning what we've done into a profitable enterprise."

The formal start to that process was slower than the ministers had hoped, although this was partly due to their own inability to get themselves together in one room on the same day. They were to have met in Farnborough at the time of the 1988 Air Show, but there had been ministerial changes in the host country. Kenneth Clarke, who as number 2 at the British Department of Trade and Industry had previously looked after Airbus, had moved on. The secretary of state himself, Lord Young, had taken the issue onto his own plate, which was already piled high. In theory, this was good news for those who wanted to see things pushed forward. Lord Young, after all, a rich lawyer and property man who had come late to politics, was the minister of whom Mrs. Thatcher had once said, "What I like about David is that he doesn't come to me with problems, he brings me solutions." What it meant in practice was that his bulging official diary was the despair of his officials, and the note of urgency that there had been earlier in the year was muted.

Then, on October 3, Franz-Josef Strauss died. He, too, was a man whose diary had always been full. He collapsed while out with a hunting party and died from heart and circulatory failure. He was 73. "He was not," wrote the Berlin paper *Der Tagesspiegel,* "the kind of man to sit out his old age in a rocking chair." He was mourned like a king. His coffin was draped with the white and blue flag of Bavaria. Flanked by Alpine musketeers, it was borne through the streets on a horse-drawn carriage to the beat of drums. There was music by Bruckner and Beethoven. The state president said of him that he had sometimes been more liberal than many of his progressive opponents, which he might or might not have taken as a compliment. What would certainly have pleased him was that he succeeded, in death as in life, in injecting controversy into the proceedings— prominent among the congregation at the midday mass in Munich Cathedral was President P. W. Botha of South Africa.

Strauss left as big a hole in Airbus as he did in German politics, and the task of filling it fell to the ministers when they next met in London in mid-November. No doubt they pondered the advice of the Wise Men: "The President is 'traditionally' German . . . We recommend that all such reserving of jobs for nationalities should cease . . .'The best man for the job' should be the only criterion . . ." It did not, however, cause enormous surprise when the best man turned out to be . . .a former German politician.

At 57, Hans Friderichs had had something of a chequered career. A member of the Free Democrats, the small German Liberal Party, he had from 1972 to 1977 been federal minister of economics in the second Brandt/ Scheel cabinet, and had also, from 1974, been the leader of his party. He left politics in 1977 to become chairman of the Management Board of the Dresdner Bank. Two years later he was also appointed chairman of the Supervisory Board of AEG Telefunken, which was in difficulties, and embarked on a successful reorganisation of the group.

In March 1985, however, Friderichs was named as defendant in legal proceedings over funding for the Free Democrats, and he gave up the chairmanship of the bank. In February 1987 he was fined for tax evasion, but cleared on a charge of accepting bribes. A month after joining Airbus, he also became chairman of the supervisory board of Co op, one of West Germany's largest food retailers, and was plunged into negotiations with the group's 140 or so creditor banks to find ways of rescheduling Co op's debts in an attempt to fend off bankruptcy and restore it to stability.[20]

Having found their man, the ministers felt that he ought to be allowed a little time to get his feet under the desk. At a meeting in Toulouse in the middle of December, they stopped the clock and asked him to come up with his proposals for how the Wise Men's recommendations should be carried out by the end of January 1989.

Inside Airbus Industrie, first impressions were favourable. He certainly gave the job more time than his predecessor had done and in a more orderly and methodical way. Robert Whitfield felt that even in his first few weeks he had been showing signs of being able to get the company presidents to reach agreement on major issues more often and more quickly. "If the supervisory board, meeting monthly, is seen to be more dynamic, and if he can develop the pursuit of the consortium interest rather than the individual interests of the companies, that will give an important lead to the executive board. Indeed, if the executive board doesn't then make decisions itself and just passes the buck to the supervisory board, it could degenerate into a post office and risk losing its function. The crucial question that remains is whether we can make the majority voting rule apply when we need it to. If a partner decides to dig in its heels and claim that its vital interests are affected, then we shall be back to square one."[19]

Questions of organisational structure apart, there were straws in the wind towards the end of 1988 to indicate that Toulouse had hoisted aboard some of the Wise Men's advice about other areas. It emerged at the time of Farnborough, for instance, that Airbus Industrie had significantly revised its policy for the selection of equipment suppliers, and that so far as the A330/340 programme was concerned, there was to be a new emphasis on lower costs and improved product support. Heribert Flosdorff, Airbus Industrie's executive vice-president and general manager, said that the partners would now have full responsibility for selecting the equipment supplier. Airbus Industrie would retain the right of veto, but only for reasons of commonality, product support or technical risk. The only exceptions to this would be for the engine and nacelle.[21]

Flosdorff also said that the consortium was abandoning its previous efforts to increase the percentage of European equipment on its aircraft. He claimed that the decision to seek a high European equipment content for the A320 had been a response to the U.S. blocking of A300/A310 sales to Libya because there was such a high percentage of American equipment on board. "Now we're back to a more competitive policy for which we no longer are implying certain preferences with a European angle," Flosdorff said.

There was evidence, too, that the partners were seeking out non-European firms to assume some production responsibility for the basic airframe of the A330/340. In certain cases this was being done to meet the offset requirements imposed by some countries, but Flosdorff said that the partners were all looking for "dollar zone" companies, so that they could counter the impact on their balance sheets of the weak U.S. dollar. British Aerospace, for instance, had signed a contract with Textron Aerostructures of Tennessee, which made the U.S. company a risk-sharing partner in the development and production of the wing for the A330/340. The work was valued at some $700 million for the first 600 shipsets. Textron would produce a 20-metre section of the wing leading edge and a 30-metre portion of the wing's upper skin assembly.

How comprehensively and wholeheartedly were the senior managements of the industrial partners and of Airbus Industrie itself prepared to embrace the Wise Men's proposals? What degree of political will existed among the member governments to crack the whip if the need arose? Finally, how long would it all take—or, a rather more deadly question, how much time was there available?

The essential volatility of governments and politicians makes any answer to the last two questions wildly speculative. Within the Airbus system in Europe there is undoubtedly a core of gifted and impressive men prepared to exert themselves prodigiously to make the enterprise succeed on commercial terms—the Scot Bob McKinlay of British Aerospace is one such, the Englishman Stuart Iddles of Airbus Industrie itself another; nor, until he stepped down in mid-1992, was it entirely eccentric to include in such a catalogue Aérospatiale's clear-sighted Henri Martre, even though his Gallic vision of how things should be driven was markedly different.

None of them would take offence at being called pragmatic. Nor, on the other side of the Atlantic, would Alan Boyd, the much-respected Democrat who was secretary of transportation in Lyndon Johnson's administration and whom Airbus shrewdly recruited to head their North American operation in the early 1980s. "The current relationship has been in effect since the early 1970s," he said, "and it certainly isn't going to be easy for the partners to start looking at substantial change. What's the old Chinese proverb—'It's better to light one candle than to walk in the darkness'? I think this is one candle. I think it's a start."[22]

The new order took effect in Toulouse on April 1, 1989, and the changes were described in a communiqué put out in the name of the Supervisory Board.[23] As expected, the status of Airbus Industrie as a GIE was left unchanged. Jean Pierson remained at the helm, and Heribert Flosdorff's designation was changed to chief operating officer (directeur général opérationnel). The tussle for the finance director's job had been won by the British and went to Robert Smith, who had held the same position at Royal Ordnance since it had been acquired by British Aerospace two years previously.

"I see great similiarities between the two jobs," he said. "The essence of the challenge is to take an organisation accustomed to a sheltered public-sector existence and instil in it a commercially accountable, profit-driven culture."[24] Smith acknowledged that the dual role of the partners posed problems, and said that he wanted to move towards arrangements that would require them to compete harder for Airbus work. A decision by the supervisory board the previous week had made that ambition seem less unattainable that it might have done in the past. In tendering for the proposed "stretched" version of the A320, the partners would have to submit competing bids for the whole project.

The name Smith was not the best guarantee of a cordial reception in Toulouse. The remarks made by the other Smith—Roland, British Aerospace's chairman—about Airbus being "loose-limbed and unaccountable" had not been forgotten. Bob Smith was asked by his interviewer how he would feel if the elder Smith continued to snipe, and his reply demonstrated at least that he was quick on his feet. "I'd hate him to be making those sorts of statements in a year or two's time," he said. "Then I would know we had totally failed."

NOTES

1. *A Report on the Airbus System,* April 1988.

2. Even so the report, according to Paul Lawrance, the British civil servant who was the group's secretary, was twice as long as the Wise Men wanted it to be at their first meeting.

3. Interview in London, October 1988.

4. *The Economist,* April 16, 1988.

5. *Frankfurter Allgemeine Zeitung,* May 4, 1988.

6. "A bumpy ride with the Airbus," *The Spectator,* May 14, 1988.

7. *Financial Times,* May 6, 1988.

8. Interview in Paris, October 1988: "Très franchement, les Wise Men n'ont pas eu suffisamment de temps pour se pencher sur cette affaire. Et puis, ils étaient de philosophies très différentes, et je crois qu'ils ont eu quelques difficultés à se comprendre totalement. Très franchement, je trouve que le rapport n'est pas mauvais, si vous voulez— il est même bon, et fait des suggestions intéressantes."

9. Interview in Farnborough, September 1988.

10. Interview in London, October 1988. Sir Raymond retired in 1990 and was succeeded by Richard Evans, previously chairman of the group's defence companies.

11. Interview in Bristol, July 1988.

12. In their annual report for 1988, published in March 1989, BAe claimed to have got the figure for the A320 wing down from 67 days to 23.

13. Interview in Hamburg, July 1988.

14. Interview in Bonn, November 1988.

15. Interview in Paris, October 1988.

16. Interview in London, August 1988.

17. Interview in Toulouse, June 1988.

18. Whitfield chaired this body, and the companies were represented on it.

19. Interview in Toulouse, February 1989.

20. In October 1990, Having resigned from Co op over a policy difference, he became

chairman of the supervisory board of Adidas, the German sports equipment company.

21. *Aviation Week & Space Technology,* September 5, 1988.
22. Interview in Washington, October 1988.
23. *Air & Cosmos,* March 25, 1989.
24. Interview, *Financial Times,* March 21, 1989.

13

Vox Populi

"History is a drama without a dénouement; every decision glides over into a
resumption of the plot."

—Pieter Geyl, *Encounters in History,* 1963.

The title of this chapter is misleading. The popular voice has never been
much heard on the Airbus issue on either side of the Atlantic. During 1988,
however, it was necessary to consult the people in both France and the
United States about who they wanted to be their president, and this meant
that the Airbus issue, along with a good many others, found itself moved
onto the back burner.

In France, there had been two uneasy years of *cohabitation*—a Socialist
president and a right-wing prime minister. The defeat of François
Mitterand by Jacques Chirac would not in itself have had much effect on
the fortunes of Airbus. Chirac's views about liberalisation and privatisation
coexisted quite happily within his political philosophy with strong support
for the French aircraft industry in general and Airbus in particular. He had
gone out of his way at the rollout of the A320 to make strongly supportive
noises and to warn the United States that any trade action would meet with
retaliation.

In the United States, a change of administration could well have led to a
more aggressive stance on trade issues. "When the chief executive fails to
assume the role of advocate and lightning rod on trade matters, as was the
case throughout the Reagan years, the protectionist pressures are almost
impossible for Congress to withstand."[1] Congress, with its Democratic
majority, had certainly responded to those pressures, most notably in the
framing of the Omnibus Trade Bill.

At the turn of the year, Airbus Industrie looked back on 1987 with
considerable satisfaction. They had rolled out the A320. By adding options
to firm orders, they were able say that they had passed the magic 1,000

mark.[2] Most important of all, they had secured the necessary funding to launch the A330/340 programme. "A classic year of achievement," said an immodest heading in one of their publicity handouts. "The Airbus family is completed as sales continue to increase."[3]

During January, Jean Pierson spoke at press conferences in both Paris and London, and on both occasions he was in attacking mood.[4] He flourished what he said was a computer listing of the 60,000 or so contracts of all kinds that the U.S. government or its agencies had placed with American aerospace companies since the signing of the Aircraft Agreement in 1979. He also said that the previous September, Airbus Industrie had made available to American officials their market studies and cash-flow analyses for the A330/340 programme. Evidence produced by auditors from an American capital venture company had played a part in convincing them of the soundness and profit potential of the programme—"If Airbus Industrie was not a GIE, they would recommend American investors to put money into it with expectation of a good return."

He said that the consortium had challenged the U.S. authorities to file claims if they believed they had evidence of trade violations, and he made an outspoken attack on his American competitors: "It is Boeing's paranoia concerning Airbus Industrie that leads to the U.S. company's exaggerated efforts to prevent us from widening our customer base," he asserted. "Boeing has money to try to block us from adding new customers because it has cash that had been earmarked for the 7J7 program, and because it makes a profit of about $30 million per 747 due to its monopoly on this end of the market."

Airbus had embarked on a major cost-cutting exercise. "We are launching a programme to cut costs by 30 percent over three years," he said. The exercise was partly aimed at reducing the consortium's vulnerability to currency fluctuation, which Pierson acknowledged was having a marked effect on sales revenue. He once again floated the idea of selling in a "basket" of currencies, using a mix of of dollars, marks, francs and pounds, in which each currency would account for perhaps a quarter of the total contract value.

He confirmed that British Airways would be taking delivery of the ten A320s they had inherited when they took over British Caledonian, though he admitted that Airbus Industrie would be paying compensation to the airline because the planes were not initially going to meet the performance predictions made for them. He described the sum involved as "insubstantial"'—little more, he said airily, than it would cost to repaint the aircraft in the British Airways livery.

He also confirmed reports that Airbus was having discussions with a number of East European airlines, and he did not think that the question of technology transfer would be an insurmountable problem; he pointed out that their American competitors were active in the same market. Talks were also being held with Lockheed. These centred on the possibility of Lockheed's involvement as a risk-sharing partner and the setting up of a production line at Lockheed's Georgia facility for an aircraft "with less than 200 seats." That was relatively straightforward, because, said Monsieur Pierson, "we have no conflict on the product line." What the journalists would have been much more interested to hear about was how the discussions about possible forms of collaboration with McDonnell Douglas were getting on.

Something that was not generally appreciated was that the two companies had been talking on and off for years, and had in fact done some business with each other as far back as the early 1970s. "Our first association with Airbus goes back to about 1970–71, when they were organising their resources to do the A300", said Bob Jackson, who as McDonnell Douglas's vice-president, special assignments, had been closely involved in the relationship. "Roger Beteille, who was their chief engineer at the time, came over here to talk to us about supplying the power eggs (i.e., the engine housing) off the DC-10 as a way to cut down the resources which would be required for the airplane and get a complete power package that had already been demonstrated to be satisfactory rather than starting over again and designing. We made a business deal, and we supplied those power eggs for about the first 300 airplanes. Then somewhere along the line there were pressures placed on the people who actually built the power eggs to construct a facility in France or face the loss of the business. So they put a facility into Toulouse to do the final assembly of the power eggs over there, and we got out of the middle of the game."[5]

McDonnell Douglas saw further possibilities, however, Jackson recalled. "After we finished the negotiations on the power eggs I said, 'Well, Roger, you're starting from scratch; I know this is a struggle, the industry in Europe has got a lot of experience and built a lot of commercial airplanes over the years, but from the business standpoint let me make you a suggestion—why don't you take the fuselage off the DC-10?' And I got about three hours of eloquent French engineering logic as to why a fuselage had to be 9 inches smaller in diameter and why that was the optimum diameter. And I suddenly realised that my way of approaching things as a businessman, even though I'm an aeronautical engineer, was entirely different from the Airbus way of approaching an airplane. In simple words they are technology drunkards. They don't pay, they don't know what the cost is, they don't care. I've just never been round people like that. I was raised in an environment which was highly cost-competitive, highly business-oriented, and I find them difficult to understand."

Where then, lay the appeal in a revival of dialogue with these technology drunkards from Toulouse a decade and more later? When he appeared before the Florio Committee, Jim Worsham had made a robust assertion of McDonnell Douglas's determination to stay in the commercial aircraft business: "We plan on standing and fighting," he said. (He also quoted the cable that the Associated Press once received from Europe saying 'The report of my death was an exaggeration,' but the stenographers seem not to have known their Mark Twain, and in the official transcript 'death' came out as 'debt.')

McDonnell Douglas were under no illusion that the fight would be easy, however. Airbus had already relegated them to third position in terms of market share, and if the government negotiations came to nothing, they would be in an infinitely more exposed position than Boeing. Bob Jackson was very frank about the strategic considerations that were uppermost in their minds. "My Chairman, Johnny Mac, looked at this whole thing and said 'Let's face it, we and Airbus are two small people, and Boeing is very big. They have a larger customer base than we have, and in the long run, in fifteen or twenty years, it would be wise if the McDonnell Douglas Company and Airbus could build a rational product line. It would serve a lot of purposes—we would not have to fund the whole product line, as Boeing would, and on the other side, the European governments could hope that the thing would be done on an economically rational basis, and they could stop putting money into Airbus with little hope of ever getting it back'."

The Airbus interest had been fuelled by rather different concerns. "It's been driven very largely by what's happened to the dollar against European currencies," Adam Brown said. "One of the consequences of the historical U.S. domination of our industry is that prices in the market are in dollars, and no airline is ever seriously going to be persuaded to accept pricing on any other basis. So our partners in Europe are facing some big risks, and one obvious way to reduce the risk is simply to increase the dollar content of the aircraft and that's what our British partner in particular is doing. The other thing is that just as long as the dollar remains where it is the basic pricing is good, and we've had some price proposals which are just incredibly attractive."[6]

Brown said that he also also saw subsidiary marketing benefits in increasing the U.S. content of Airbus. "Putting on a 'Made in the USA' label may help to overcome some reluctance of U.S. airlines to buy. It's more difficult for anyone seriously to suggest that Airbus is taking jobs out of America if at the same time Americans on American soil are actually building our airplanes."

The talks with McDonnell Douglas were in their nature different from those that had taken place with other companies such as Lockheed. "In the case of other manufacturers, many of whom are looking at a downturn in military procurement, they have got huge production facilities and factories really running out of work, and they are eager to bid, purely as subcontractors, for bits of work. Douglas is in the market with a product line which competes with us, and the talks there are of a much more global and strategic nature and much more complicated."

Airbus was at one with McDonnell Douglas in relishing the prospect of doing an injury to Boeing—"the original 800 lb gorilla," as Alan Boyd, the Airbus North American chairman, obligingly described the competitor from Seattle. "From a classic point of view," Adam Brown said, "it has to make sense, in any industry where there's an absolutely dominant number 1 player, for number 2 and number 3 to get together and see—within the constraints of U.S. antitrust laws—whether they can't somehow combine forces and develop a stronger competitive thrust against number 1."

Brown confessed that American antitrust concerns were a considerable inhibition. "You see, obviously the sort of thing we have to sit down and explore is a rationalisation of our two production lines. Now the moment you use a phrase like that, it's almost in the book for what is illegal. I don't know whether you know, but a contravention of Section 1 of the Sherman Act isn't just a civil offence, it's a criminal one—the idea of Long Beach County Jail is not too bad, but a federal penitentiary is a different kettle of fish altogether."

Over the years, the talks between the two sides had ranged very widely—"Man, God and the Universe," in Adam Brown's phrase. "Our concept was that it was not practical to envisage anything other than a global cooperation, so we proposed a cooperation that spanned a whole raft of airplanes. You see, at the moment if you look at our product line we are about to have a kind of continuum of products—we will shortly have a set of five airplanes, nicely spaced, satisfying particular discrete categories of airline demand. What you've got to consider is whether there isn't a need for something down at the bottom at 125 seats, and something up at the top of 600-plus."

"We've had a whole process of preparing for summits," Brown said—"I'm like a sherpa, carrying oxygen bottles and things. We've had a set of four separate specialist working teams, each with Airbus people, but in many cases people brought in from the partners, too. I'll give you an example of the problems. We have designed an absolutely spectacular airplane. It's called the AM 300. It takes an MD-11 fuselage with another 35 feet in length. It takes an A330 wing. Put the two together and you end up with a three-engined airplane that can absolutely wipe the floor with the 747. It's a much more efficient airplane, it carries more people, it flies the same sort of distances, burns 30 percent less fuel, it carries more cargo, it's just a terrific airplane. What could be simpler, combining forces, using the best of each company?"

"Simple question—how are we going to sell this airplane? Because you have to bear in mind that we have an A340, and they have an MD-11, which are in competition with each other, and that each of them is also going to be in competition with this new plane, because to some extent it is going to draw business from its parents. So it needs to be sold in combination with MD-11s to airlines which have already bought MD-11s, and it needs to be sold in combination with A340s to airlines which have already bought A340s. And it's a terribly simple question—my small son would ask it—how are you going to sell it? And we have already devoted many man-weeks with many powerful brains sitting round various tables trying to find an answer. We haven't yet found one."

Initiatives from the European side have not come exclusively from Toulouse. A few years ago, when things seemed bogged down, Sir Ray Lygo of British Aerospace decided that a free-lance intervention was called for: "I woke up at 4 o'clock one morning and said, 'Christ, this is madness,' and I got onto an aeroplane and went over to talk to McDonnell Douglas, and I said 'Look, this is stupid,' but I couldn't get them to listen to me. Then Airbus Industrie discovered what I'd been doing and told me, publicly—I mean, there was a great scene with Strauss in the chair—'You have been going behind the backs of your partners.' 'No I haven't,' I said. 'I've been doing something which is commercially sensible. That's what I'm paid to do.' Well, a resolution was passed, and in future the only contact with them was to be through AI, so I thought well, that's the end of that."[7]

It wasn't quite the end, in fact, and talks on the AM 300 continued for some considerable time. "It's technically feasible," Bob Jackson said, "and by cooperating it could be done for a rational amount of money—$1 billion, $1.5 billion, that kind of thing, whereas to do a brand new 747 from scratch is probably $8–9 billion." Although there was joint technical work and joint market analysis, however, McDonnell Douglas were not able to persuade Airbus to do any costing work. "This is how we learned the difference between their system and ours," Jackson said. "We start making cost estimates when we have a piece of paper with a sketch on it, and we just keep working our way up, because it always has to be sound technically and it always has to be sound financially. They do the design first, then they worry about the workshare and get that settled, and *then* they worry about what the damn cost structure is, which to me is incredible, just absolutely incredible." Jackson gave a disbelieving laugh. "At first I thought they were pulling my leg," he said.

Jackson believed that the main stumbling block for Airbus so far as the AM 300 was concerned was quite simply that the aircraft was going to look like an MD-11. "Flosdorff finally said, 'You know, you people are talking about this thing as if it were a technical problem—it's not a technical problem, it's an image problem. It doesn't look like an Airbus.'" Reflecting on the issue some months later, Adam Brown maintained that it had not been a sticking point. "It was an element that had to be taken into account in trying to achieve an overall balance. It sort of pulled the scales down on one side, but that could have been overcome."

McDonnell Douglas's reservations related more to the question of collaboration on a broader front, because it seemed to them that their share of what was proposed would not amount to more than about 35 percent. Airbus, who must have had somebody trained by the Jesuits in their team, advanced the ingenious argument that this would make them the biggest single partner in the consortium. "That was a very large bone to chew upon," Jackson said. The men from Long Beach and St. Louis are quick chewers, however. "The result was that fifteen minutes after they had made that offer, our Chairman told them 'We're breaking off negotiations on a broad product line. If that is your idea of equality, we can't negotiate'."

McDonnell Douglas seem to have been genuinely regretful. Both sides needed a big airplane. Airbus lacked the production capacity, and it was difficult to expand capacity in Europe, particularly for a short-pulse programme. They also needed an assembly facility to stretch the A320. "We'll build one in the U.S., build some of the parts and build the airplane for you," McDonnell Douglas told them. "It's nothing to do with market sharing—it's strictly a business arrangement about how vehicles are produced, not how they're sold."

Adam Brown, however, continues to believe that it was precisely on the inability of the two sides to agree about the practicalities of selling that the talked foundered. "We just couldn't see how two organisations who were competing against each other in one sector of the commercial aircraft market could collaborate in another sector. We just couldn't see how we could be hammering on trying to kill Douglas with our A320 against the MD-80, and they could be trying to kill us with the MD-80 against the A320 and how at the same time the two of us could somehow be out there in some love and brotherhood relationship jointly selling the new airplane. They were convinced that the difficulties could be overcome, that one could simply establish an organisation and depute people."

Sir Raymond Lygo took the view that not all the McDonnell Douglas objections were openly declared. He believed that they finally jibbed at the idea of a stretched MD-11 fuselage and an A330 wing because of the impact they realised it would have on the rest of their range. "I mean, you can do it, but it's a high technology wing. Now that means a high technology cockpit, that means a fly-by-wire system, that means the whole MD-11 has got to change, and that means that every other aeroplane made by McDonnell Douglas is now not compatible. End of story. What I said to John [McDonnell] and James [Worsham] at the end of the day was, 'This reminds me of a Greek tragedy.' They looked at me, and since I knew they hadn't seen a Greek tragedy in St Louis, I said "To help you, I can tell you that if ever you watch a Greek tragedy, you can't believe what's going on in front of your eyes, but one thing of which you can be absolutely certain before the curtain comes down is that everybody on the stage is dead.' And that finally got home."

Formally, the talks were suspended, though informally the lines were kept open in case anyone came up with new thoughts on how to square the circle. The ministers of the Airbus governments were not best pleased, because they had made it plain that they would welcome some form of collaboration. "At one point the ministers took it upon themselves to issue what they called a mandate," Adam Brown said. "I have what's called a negotiating mandate issued by the four ministers. It strongly encouraged Airbus to come to an agreement, although nobody has explained the mechanism by which Airbus is constrained to take notice of this. At the same time it stated very clearly that this was not to be taken to imply that there was going to be any money available. That's a fence that I guess is going to have to be jumped at some point, but we haven't yet rounded into that straight."

Adam Brown's slightly waspish tone was understandable. The so-called mandate had emerged from a meeting in Paris in early March, chaired by the French transport minister, Jacques Douffiagues. The communiqué put out at the end of the meeting said that Airbus had been given a mandate to continue "with necessary diligence" its negotiations with McDonnell Douglas, aimed at reaching an agreement for balanced cooperation that would benefit both sides. Given that the two sides had been at it for several years, there was no particular reason to think that they could pull a rabbit out of the hat by June. Nor was it clear what the ministers could do about it if they didn't.

What of course was mainly in the ministers' minds was the need to position themselves for the next encounter with the Americans which was due to be held in Konstanz later in the month. Neither side seems to have entertained hopes of more than a modest degree of progress. Willy de Clerq, the EEC commissioner for external affairs, questioned in the European Parliament in the week before the meeting, said that agreement on the outstanding issues would require "further rounds of very difficult negotiations." The talks, he said, should provide the negotiators with "final guidance." The Wise Men were still at work on their report, and the French presidential election was only two months away. There was some inclination in the United States to think that the Europeans would yet again be disposed to play for time, and there was also a recognition that their own presidential election, with is much more extended timescale, might already be making its anaesthetic influence felt on decisionmakers in Washington.

The two sides met for five hours on March 18. Both said afterwards that matters had moved forward, although as on previous occasions, it was the noises emerging from the European camp that suggested the greater degree of progress. Willy de Clerq announced that there was agreement that future government aid to Airbus would be granted only for research and development and not for production, although there would be a clause allowing governments to step in with assistance if companies ran into financial difficulties that had not been foreseen. There had also been agreement to observe the GATT rules on inducements and on the setting up of consultative machinery.

They were close to agreeing in principle that there should be similar rules for direct and indirect subsidies and on the terms for the disclosure of subsidies and the appraisal of the commercial viability of programmes. Three central issues remained unresolved—the precise terms on which government support would be permitted; a definition of what constituted acceptable commercial practices; and the arrangements for "transparency" that would allow third parties to assess the actual level of subsidy.

Clayton Yeutter, however, made it clear that substantial differences of interpretation remained. He said the ban on future production support was an important step, but disputed the EC assumption that it would not apply to the A330/340 programme. The decision to treat direct and indirect subsidies alike posed a problem of quantifying such subsidies that remained to be addressed. He also rejected the EC claim that the agreement would permit financial assistance to offset the fall in the value of the dollar. Frederick Barbarossa is reputed to have signed the peace of Konstanz in the town in 1193. This had clearly not been a rerun of that occasion. Yeutter said there was no point in setting another deadline, but that if there was to be an agreement, it would need to happen "relatively soon." The two delegations seem to have agreed informally to aim at June or July and went their separate ways.

Back in Washington a couple of weeks later, Ambassador Yeutter felt it necessary to go on the record with a lengthy statement redefining the U.S. position. The trigger was the Airbus study examined in Chapter 8, which had been tossed into the discussions at Konstanz and had clearly got under Yeutter's skin. "The Airbus Industrie study is being widely publicised and given credence in some quarters despite its poor scholarship and false conclusions," the statement said. The talks had dragged on for too long. "The central issue under discussion is subsidies for the development of commercial projects, not the amount of money American taxpayers spend in defense of the free world." The United States remained willing to discuss the issue of indirect supports, but on the basis of "a reciprocal exchange of government-validated information," so that the issue could be disposed of rapidly. This would allow ministers to focus on the more difficult issue of disciplining direct government support for civil aircraft development. "We will not hold such discussions on the basis of a 'study' that has no credibility."[8]

On the European side, much of the negotiating at the senior-official level had been conducted by Mogens Peter Carl, head of division in the Commission's Directorate General for External Affairs; a quiet, sophisticated Dane, trained as an economist. Carl had detected some initial uncertainty and unevenness in the American performance at the negotiating table and attributed this in the main to McDonnell Douglas's having blown hot and cold. To begin with, the company had pressed very hard for the U.S. government to file a complaint, but then late in the day they had backed off very considerably, much to the irritation of the administration. Carl did not wish to intrude on private grief, but speculated politely on what might have caused this about-face—perhaps there had been a belated realisation that a trade conflict over civil aircraft could spill over into the military field and affect their European sales.

After some 15 months of largely tactical sparring, it seemed to him that the central American concern was to obtain binding disciplines on future programmes—a commitment from the European governments that they would only grant support that was conditional on there being a real rate of return and a more or less fixed schedule of reimbursement. The European side was alive to the fact that there was no close identity of interest between the two major American manufacturers, McDonnell Douglas's most obvious concern being with the A330/340, Boeing's more with future programmes.

Carl felt he was reasonably clear about what the Americans would accept on future programmes, much less so on the type of discipline they sought for the A330/340. The Europeans, he said, were prepared to offer a so-called effects mechanism—"we would, for example, be willing to envisage a commitment not to provide further support that would permit Airbus to undercut prices any further—a kind of standstill, if you wish." The Americans had not, however, been prepared to discuss the proposal, apparently because of antitrust considerations.

On questions of financial accounting, Carl's own view was that a reasonable degree of transparency would be of enormous value both in lowering the temperature and advancing the debate, but he did not need to be told that such an accommodating view made him pig in the middle. He went rather wearily through the catalogue of "reasons why not" advanced by the European side: that it would be shooting oneself in the foot; that it wasn't necessary because the facts were already in the public domain; that the partners enjoyed a sovereign right not to provide such information if they did not so choose. "Of course," he added evenly, "the last argument ignores the fact that we have a commitment in the GATT to provide other contracting parties with information about our subsidies."[9]

Although he conceded some exaggeration in the statements made in Europe about the amount of indirect support available to the industry in the United States, Carl argued that transparency must cut both ways. "It's going to be extraordinarily difficult to obtain mirror-image transparency for indirect support in the United States. We do want to resolve this conflict peacefully, but there are limits to what we would accept in terms of commitment regarding transparency on direct support in the absence of something meaningful on the other side." Carl distanced himself with some delicacy from the emphasis that Airbus Industrie had been putting on the extent of indirect support available to the American manufacturers—"You asked me to concentrate on the essential point, and the essential point is direct support."

Asked which parts of the European case he found it most difficult to find good arguments for, Carl needed only as much time to think about his answer as it took to say, "I must be very diplomatic about this one," although what he then said extended the definition of the word considerably. "What I don't like to have to say is that we have to subsidise because of our inefficient industrial structures. That's very unpleasant. But it's true. We are compensating for inefficiency. Mind you," he added, engagingly, "while that is an embarrassing argument to have to use, it does suggest another line of thought, which is that if we are only compensating for industrial inefficiency, our subsidies can't really be contributing to trade distortion."

Questioned about the atmosphere in which the negotiations had been conducted, Carl said, "The tone has been amicable and straightforward. No histrionics, no threats—or at least if there are threats, they are usually very carefully worded." He felt that his American opposite number, representing only one government, enjoyed a slight advantage and was better placed to take initiatives. The mix of backgrounds and attitudes on the European side sometimes made for more cumbersome procedures.

What if there was no accommodation and the dispute turned into the trade equivalent of a shooting war? That, he said, would depend on how it broke out. "Let me give you two extremes. It could take the form of a U.S. company filing a suit under section 301. That would be at the low end of the scale. At the high end of the scale would be a successful antidumping or countervailing duty complaint by the United States. That would mean a total conflagration. I'm virtually certain that within 24 hours we would have a counter-suit filed by European companies or governments. And that would lead us into a tit-for-tat situation which would be virtually uncontrollable."

Was it accurate to talk about a certain hardening in the European position? On a visit to Airbus Industrie headquarters a few weeks previously a note of confidence had been detectable—mild aggression even—that contrasted with the rather defensive noises that had been emerging from Toulouse not so very long before. "Well," Carl said mildly, "it is not Airbus in Toulouse which negotiates. They are under the impression that their study of indirect support in America provides them with an extraordinary amount of protection against United States activity in this area . . . " Pause. "I don't want to comment on that."

He went on to say that he sensed much less of a push than there used to be from the American side, something he put down to the fact that Airbus and McDonnell Douglas were talking. If those talks got nowhere, or if there were major new infusions of cash into Deutsche Airbus or British Aerospace, that would be a new situation, and the temperature could rise sharply. Things had certainly hardened in late 1987/early 1988. "What we were hit with then was a set of completely unrealistic and almost offensive American proposals which would have put us out of business completely."[10] What had changed outside the ambit of the negotiations was that the member governments had urged Airbus to pursue their discussions with McDonnell Douglas. That could be construed as signalling concessions to the Americans on the industrial side rather than at the level of an international agreement.

If the American negotiators have problems in reconciling the divergent ambitions of their own rival manufacturers, they do at least all speak the same language. The EC negotiators are in effect driving a coach and four, and the horses are not all that closely matched. Carl was philosophical—"It is our daily work. Normally we do it with twelve member states, not just four. It's what we're paid for."

Many of the difficulties stemmmed from the differences between the industrial partners. "You have companies in Britain and France which are reasonably profitable, at least some of the time. In Germany, you have an industrial situation which is uncomfortable—very high costs and a level of government intervention which is much greater than in France. There is also an apparent need—I read this in the newspapers—for the German government to provide very substantial further infusions of cash into MBB both to cover accumulated losses for old programmes and perhaps to meet further losses on the A330/340. It's a big mess."

The philosophical complexion of the partner governments was a consideration, too. "The general attitude of the present United Kingdom government towards free competition and the like has come through very clearly in the positions taken up by our British colleagues—they've shown themselves much more understanding of the American line on disciplines for public support." Ideology had been tempered by pragmatic considerations, however—"the British government seems at least as keen as any other European government to maintain a certain sovereign choice."

It was surprising to hear from Carl that he found the French more relaxed than anybody else—"perhaps because their industry happens to be rather efficient"—although that did not prevent them from adopting what he called "rather strong positions" on the terms of a possible agreement.

The German position he described as "complex and paradoxical." In spite of the federal government's strong traditional attachment to a free-market philosophy, the Germans had been more reluctant than any of their partners to contemplate the types of discipline for which the Americans had been arguing. "The German aircraft industry has obviously been supported with vast sums of money by its own government. They know that if they were to accept such disciplines and implement them, that would render the situation in Germany virtually untenable."

It was the position in Germany that was to preoccupy the Americans more and more as the year wore on. The two sides came together in Washington for two days in early June, but in the words of Boeing's Ray Waldmann, "things kind of fell apart." "It was quite clear by that time that there had been a lot of retrenchment on both sides", Waldmann said, "certainly on the European side away from the ministerial declaration of London. So the conclusion was we might as well forget about this approach; we were just arguing back and forth across the table without any progress, and Mike Smith decided it was time to go back to the Cabinet, report all of this and ask for further instructions."

A new phrase found its way into the diplomatic vocabulary at this time with talk of the declaration by the United States of a "hostile truce"; Brussels would be asked to come up with fresh proposals and would be threatened with trade sanctions if it failed to do so. This was seen as a face-saving device that would defer the need for immediate action but leave open the possibility of returning to the charge at a later date.

The Economic Policy Council of the Cabinet met at the end of July and decided as a first step to request another meeting. Ambassador Yeutter was directed to inform the Europeans that if substantial new subsidies were provided his instruction were to return to the Council with "appropriate recommendations." The Cabinet reserved all options available to the United States under the law, including Section 301.

A curious state of affairs had arisen concerning the Gellman Report which the Commerce Department had been instructed to commission the previous year. The study had been completed, but nothing had been published, although the industry was not alone in urging that it should be. "We've had Congress screaming at us," said Steve Falken at the Office of the USTR. "It confirms a lot of concerns that we have had in a very detailed way. If that study got out, it would raise the heat, and perhaps for that reason it hasn't been released. Once the report got out, the absence of a quick negotiated solution would force a 301 case."[11]

The administration therefore found itself in the bizarre position of having fashioned a weapon that was too powerful to be used. They had expected Gellman and his colleagues to provide them with a case of mortar bombs, but it seemed that they had taken delivery of an atomic device. The Cabinet accordingly took refuge in the formula that it would "continue to review" the report (a number of agencies, including the State Department, the Office for the Management of the Budget and the Council of Economic Advisers, had not yet, in fact, had the opportunity to do so), and release it "if the circumstances warranted it."

High-level contacts continued after the cabinet meeting. Ambassador Smith had bowed out by this time to seek an opening for his aggressive talents in the private sector, and his place had been taken by Alan Holmer, who had previously been the USTR's chief counsel. Holmer made a trip to Europe. His talks in London and Paris were fairly inconsequential, but in Bonn he was briefed on the proposed Daimler-Benz takeover of MBB and did not at all like the sound of what he heard.

It had been known since 1986 that Deutsche Airbus and its parent company had their backs to the wall. The letter leaked to the German press in December of that year (see page 173) had urged the need for further subsidies to avoid bankruptcy, and when MBB's accounts for the year were published the following July, they disclosed that capital transfers to Deutsche Airbus had resulted in a deficit of DM 103.7 million, and forecast an only slightly smaller loss of DM 95 million for 1987.[12]

The West German government had first put out feelers to Daimler-Benz about the possibility of greater involvement in the aerospace industry in May of 1987. It was well known that BMW and Bosch had turned the idea down, and that Siemens, which already owned a 10 percent share in the company, had said that it did not wish to increase it. Daimler-Benz had taken the first serious step down the road to diversification two years earlier. It already held 50 percent of the equity of Motoren und Turbinen Union (MTU), which manufactured large engines and propulsion units for tanks and ships and aircraft, and in February 1985 it snapped up the remaining 50 percent from the truck manufacturer MAN. Four weeks later, Daimler moved again. The Dornier family, which had large holdings in the aviation and space travel company of the same name, wanted to get out of the business. There was a good deal of interest, notably from Mannesmann, the large mechanical engineering and electronics concern based in Düsseldorf, but with the help of the then prime minister of Baden-Württemburg, Lothar Späth, Daimler-Benz carried the day. Before the end of the year they seized a third opportunity. The electrical engineering concern AEG had been going through bad times. Daimler saw its chance and acquired a majority shareholding.

By 1987, then, Daimler-Benz was already a powerful presence in the aerospace sector, and it remained the board's strategy to diversify still further away from vehicles and into other high-tech industries. There was therefore nothing particularly surprising in the government's suggestion that it should acquire a majority holding in MBB, though it was initially proposed that the four aerospace companies should accommodated within a new holding company rather than merged.

Daimler-Benz is based in Stuttgart, and the board trod round the suggestion with appropriate Swabian caution. The profits being made by MTU and Dornier were not big enough to absorb the losses that MBB was making on Airbus. By the late summer of 1987, the company was already making conditions. If the takeover went ahead, they would want the activities of MBB's Hamburg and Bremen facilities to be merged and the facility at Speyer to be closed down. They would also want funding for the Dornier Do 328 regional aircraft project—a request that had previously been turned down—and it would be a condition of any Daimler-Benz investment that the Franco-German helicopter and Eurofighter programmes should be kept going.[13]

The result of any such arrangement would clearly be that Daimler-Benz would acquire a position of near monopoly in the German aerospace industry. In the space and weapons sector, this would deprive the government, as a customer, of the element of competition that it had always insisted was of such importance. A Ministry of Defence study showed that of 146 R&D, development and manufacturing projects currently being managed by the ministry, 78 would be in the hands of the new group.

This would obviously be unpopular with the political left in Germany, and almost certainly with the Federal Cartel Office, which had been unhappy about the acquisition of AEG two years earlier. The small Free Democratic party, with its enthusiasm for market forces and its belief that medium-sized was beautiful, might also be restive. The current head of the party, however, was Martin Bangemann, the federal economics minister, and he, in his eagerness to be rid of the burden of Airbus subsidy, might be expected to swallow his principles, carry his small band of followers with him and, if necessary, exercise his right to overrule the Cartel Office.

By the end of 1987, Daimler-Benz was known to be insisting on a new condition, which was that the German states should divest themselves of their holdings in MBB (between them, the *Länder* of Hamburg, Bremen and Bavaria held 52 percent of the company's stock; shares were also held by the Dresdner Bank, Robert Bosch, who were Daimler-Benz suppliers, and the Blohm family, who had big interests in aircraft and shipbuilding in Hamburg). It was thought unlikely that the states would be prepared to do this in one single transaction, but that they might be willing, in an initial stage, to reduce their stake.

Two developments in November made it easier for Daimler to countenance the idea of the takeover. The first was the Bonn government's decision that it would play a larger part in the European space programme than it had originally seemed inclined to. The second was the decision to proceed, jointly with the French, with the development of the PAH-2 antitank helicopter. Both meant a healthy slice of new business for MBB. Edzard Reuter, the 60-year old Daimler-Benz chairman, was no pushover, however. He was the son of Ernst Reuter, the former mayor of Berlin, and although he carried an SPD card, he had never been active in the party. He was on record, indeed, as saying that a business cannot be managed from a social democratic or from a Christian democratic point of view—only well or badly.

By early 1988 he was making it very clear that he had no intention simply of doing the government a favour. "We have one big problem in those talks," he told a group of American journalists. "We are by no means keen and we are by no means ready to get ourselves mixed up in the Airbus business."[14] On current form, he said, Germany's involvement in Airbus could not be economically viable before the end of the century. Daimler-Benz had other problems that bore on the matter. The three major aerospace and technology companies it had acquired since 1984 had still not been fully integrated. One possibility might be to break the Airbus interests out of the MBB group; the company's non-Airbus operations would make a very satisfactory fit.

This idea did not appeal to Hanns Arnt Vogels, the MBB chairman, who saw little to be gained from separating civil and military research and development. The various MBB divisions were closely interlinked and would become more so. Airbus, for instance, benefited from the experience gained in work for space missions—from electronic controls and the use of new materials.[15] He also saw a firm link between Airbus and the European Fighter Aircraft: "From the point of view of assuring our production capacities, also in technology transfers between the two programmes, these two projects are a condition for Western Europe's technological competitiveness in coming decades." There at least Vogels got what he wanted, because it was announced during the 1988 Hanover Air Show in early May that the federal government had given the go-ahead to the EFA project.

At the Daimler annual general meeting at the beginning of July, Reuter repeated his view that the German aerospace industry must be reshaped to meet international competition, and said that the company had left no doubt of its willingness to take part in such a process so long as the politicians created the right conditions. "Those conditions are now mostly in place," he said. The company was not prepared to enter into what he called "an unpredictable adventure," but a political readiness was emerging to remove the financial risks of the Airbus programme from MBB. Translated into deutschmarks, this meant that the government was now prepared to take over the existing Airbus debt, thought to be of the order of DM 4 billion, and offer guarantees to cover exchange-rate losses on sales.[16]

The Social Democratic opposition was strongly critical. Wolfgang Roth, their spokesman on economic affairs, said that coming from a government committed to deregulation, the proposal was grotesque. The result would be a state within a state. It would lead to the creation, for the first time in the Federal Republic, of a military and industrial complex.[17] The mayor of Hamburg, Henning Voscherau, used the same expression, and Reuter hit back hard. The concept of a military and industrial complex, he said, was to be found in the writings of Lenin and the vocabulary of terrorists. It was not something which Mercedes-Benz had any intention of building.[18]

There was quite a lot of opposition in the press, too. A writer in the *Deutsches Allgemeines Sonntagsblatt* waxed biblical and painted a lurid picture of the emergence of a latter-day Moloch. In lighter vein, *Handelsblatt* published a cartoon showing three battered taxpayers lying in hospital beds. They were all giving blood. The tubes ran from their arms into a fuel hose—which disappeared in turn into the maw of an Airbus. "Life support system," said the caption.

Not for the first time, however, the paper that really stripped off the gloves was *Der Spiegel*. Its cover for the edition of August 1 carried a picture of a warplane bristling with rocketry. "The armaments giant Mercedes-Benz", said the title. "Waffenschmiede der Nation"—"Armourer to the Nation." Inside, one of the illustrations to the article was a photo of Hitler taking the salute—in an open Mercedes, naturally. Underneath was reproduced a greetings telegram which the führer had sent in April 1939 to the Mercedes generaldirektor. A Messerschmitt Me 109 fighter plane had just set a new speed record of 755 kilometres an hour. It was powered by a Daimler-Benz 601 engine. "I send you my heartiest good wishes. Adolf Hitler."

Hostility to the idea was laced with uncertainty about the outcome. *Die Zeit* reported that Johann Schäffler, the former Airbus Industrie number 2 who now ran Dornier, had bet a journalist six bottles of champagne that the issue would not be resolved in 1988. By the autumn, however, there was broad agreement between the government and the company on the outlines of a deal. The matter was also becoming pressing, as any additional public expenditure on Airbus would need to be taken into account in the government's budgetary planning for 1989.

A cabinet meeting on November 2 empowered Martin Bangemann and his colleague Gerhard Stoltenberg, the finance minister, to conclude negotiations. The government was prepared to make an additional DM 4.3 billion available for the period up to the year 2000. Daimler-Benz would take a 30 percent stake in MBB, valued at DM 800 million, and West Germany's 37.9 percent share in the Airbus consortium would pass to a new holding company owned 80 percent by MBB and 20 percent by the federal government. Daimler had insisted on a direct government stake to limit the company's exposure in the event of any such unfavourable developments as protectionist moves by the United States, but the company would undertake to buy that stake back by 1999. There would be an exchange-rate guarantee covering any movement in the dollar down to DM 1.60. The government would assume 75 percent of the risk until 1998, and in the two following years the risk would be equally spread.[19]

At this point the going got rough. The Social Democrats and the Greens had been vehemently critical from the start, but late in the day a new source of opposition emerged from a less expected quarter. Martin Bangemann had been succeeded as chairman of the Free Democrats by Count Otto Lamsdorff. "Der Graf," as he was known, the great nephew of a former foreign minister in Tsarist Russia, had trained as a lawyer and had a background in banking and insurance. He had lost a leg on the eastern front during the Second World War and in 1984 he had lost his job as economics minister after charges that there had been irregularities in the way contributions had been made to party funds.The count had been the FDP's treasurer, and it was alleged that he had been a party to the Flick industrial group and others channelling money through charities to avoid taxes. (One of his co-defendants was Hans Friderichs.) After a trial that lasted 18 months he was found not guilty of corruption but fined for tax evasion. He had continued to defend free market policies long after they had ceased to be particularly fashionable in Bonn and was a stern critic of the government's lack of drive in deregulating the economy.

Lamsdorff now raised last-minute objections to the Daimler-MBB deal, and succeeded in having the decision put off for five days. He complained that his party had learned of the details only from news reports (Bonn is a small and leaky capital), and expressed "deep reservations." In the view of the FDP, the plan would not lead to the desired reduction in Airbus subsidies. Nor were they persuaded that MBB could only find happiness in the arms of Daimler-Benz: "A bride as richly attired as this isn't just interesting to one bridegroom," said the count.[20] This late intervention was seen by some as a manoeuvre by Lamsdorff to assert his authority in his own party—his victory in the contest for the chairmanship had been a narrow one—but it gained the support of some Christian Democrats, and the postponement brought the government uncomfortably close to the date (November 9) by which final allocations for the 1989 budget had to be made.

In the event, Lamsdorff backed off. The Cabinet agreed to some modifications of the text, and the FDP parliamentary group gave it qualified approval. Lamsdorff acknowledged that if the leading role in developing Airbus was to pass from the state to private industry, there was no real alternative. "We cannot simply jump off a moving train," he said.[21] His performance, which seemed to his opponents to combine opportunism with inconsistency, was not much admired, and the SPD opposition accused him of capitulation. This seemed a little hard on Der Graf, because the concessions he had won were not without substance: the assurance that any profits arising from the military business would be applied to the Airbus programme, for instance, and the stipulation that the funding should be subject to a "qualified block," which meant that no money would be released without the approval of the Budgetary Committee of the Federal Parliament.

Rumbling was not confined to the political parties. West Germany has the most stringent antitrust laws in Europe (though they do not match those of the United States) and Herr Wolfgang Kartte, the president of the Federal Cartel Office, had more than once indicated that he had misgivings about what was proposed. Kartte, who had run the Cartel office for twelve years and occupied a spacious office in Berlin with a cuckoo clock on the wall, would now have up to four months to consider whether the agreement would give the new group dominance in certain market sectors. Dr. Bangemann had hinted that it might be necessary for some activities in areas like electronics to be sold off to conform with the law.

In London, there was a slightly jaundiced reaction from a spokesman for

British Aerospace, partners with MBB in Airbus but competitors on other fronts: "If our partners get more assistance than we do for Airbus, they have more money to spend on other things." The Bonn correspondent of the *Financial Times* was both severe and patronising: "The affair highlights the ponderous provincialism which still surrounds debate on economic matters in Western Europe's largest economy . . . West German industry and banking remains endemically opposed to large-scale risk-taking."[22] The Frankfurt Stock Exchange, however, took a cheerful view. Daimler-Benz shares went up DM 16 to DM 760.50, and Deutsche Bank shares registered a more modest rise of DM 5.50 to DM 525.50.[23]

The position inside Daimler-Benz was far from monolithic. The chairman of the group works council, Herr Herbert Lucy, said that association with the defence industry would adversely affect the core motor business and that union members on the Daimler board would oppose it. Even on the management side, there were those who wondered whether they might not be inviting American reprisals. There were, after all, the 55 mph speed limit notwithstanding, a great many Daimler-Benz products cruising up and down the freeways and interstate highways of the United States.

The American response, issued late on November 7, was sharp and immediate.[24] It came in the form of a statement from Clayton Yeutter, and he described the plan as a very disturbing development. It was, he said, particularly unacceptable coming as it did during ongoing discussions about key provisions of the GATT Aircraft Code. What he didn't say, but what a number of people in Washington thought, was that the Germans had played a dirty trick with the timing of their announcement and that it was calculated to catch Uncle Sam standing on one leg the day before the presidential election.

Ambassador Yeutter claimed in his statement that the German decision knocked away a major underpinning of the negotiations, namely a bilateral standstill. Again, he didn't say so, but there was some feeling in the United States that the Europeans were once more trying to bounce them, just as they had over the launch of the A330/340, and it did nothing to increase American confidence that the other side was negotiating in good faith.

The United States trade representative was particularly troubled by the provision for exchange rate guarantees, and he struck a note of rhetorical exasperation: "It is an essential tenet of private enterprise that business firms absorb the risks associated with commercial ventures, including exchange rate risks. Thousands of firms throughout the world hedge their own exchange rate risk. Why should aircraft manufacturers be any different? And why should Airbus be singled out for special treatment?"

Yeutter pointed out that earlier in the decade the strong dollar had resulted in a loss of U.S. price competitiveness, but that they had not responded by "inventing new ways to subsidise exports." For West

Germany, a country enjoying an extraordinarily large trade surplus, to do so was "incongruous and indefensible." They were resorting to "privatisation based on massive subsidisation." The statement ended with a clear warning that the United States was fingering the safety catch: "We will carefully review the final action taken in Bonn and examine the consistency of such support with the Federal Republic of Germany's international obligations."

The arrangements still had to be approved by Daimler-Benz, and it was generally held to be the most controversial decision in the 101-year history of the company. The Supervisory Board met in Stuttgart on November 10 under the chairmanship of Alfred Herrhausen, who was also the head of Deutsche Bank, and they remained in session for nine and a half hours— more than twice the length of a normal meeting. The board was made up of ten representatives of the shareholders and ten representing the workforce. The latter, led by Herbert Lucy, were solidly opposed to the merger, and a statement made by Edzard Reuter to the press immediately afterwards showed why. Reuter insisted that the parent company should have full management control of MBB, and his refusal to give guarantees about preserving jobs in the company's 16 plants made it clear that there were plans to slim the 38,500-strong workforce. The board agreed that it would meet again and make a final decision before Christmas.[25]

In a long interview with the *Financial Times* a few weeks later, Herr Reuter was candid about the degree of scepticism that persisted about the deal within both the supervisory and the management boards. "The task of bringing about a new structure is going to be a difficult job," he said. "I estimate the process will take about five years."[26] He told his interviewer that he had his eye above all on bringing more private-sector corporate influence to bear in Airbus and on the reduction of the decision-making importance of governments. To this end, he wished to explore the idea of a network of cross-shareholdings between the member companies. (Aérospatiale already had a 10 percent share in MBB, and Daimler itself had a stake of just under 5 percent in Matra, the French electronic and defence company.)

Reuter, whose family had been forced to flee to Turkey in the 1930s, was understandably unhappy about some of the opposition to the deal, and in particular the portrayal of it in some quarters as a revival of fascism. He also rejected the idea that he had played a skilful game of poker and taken the government for a ride. "The word is not appropriate because this entails an element of bluff. I set down from the start the conditions for us to participate in this project. That was never negotiable. I am still not sure today if all these conditions can really be fulfilled." He was adamant that Daimler-Benz would only go ahead with the takeover if they had an entirely free hand to carry out the necessary degree of restructuring at MBB. One important appointment had already been made, however. Jürgen Schrempp, currently sales director for commercial vehicles and a man with no aerospace experience, had been made chairman of Daimler's new Deutsche Aerospace division, which would own the stake in MBB. Herr Schrempp was 44. "He can accept his task as a long-term one," Herr Reuter said.

In mid-November, with the U.S. election out of the way, Clayton Yeutter made a quick trip to Europe. Dieter Wolf, who was present when he lunched with Martin Bangemann in Bonn, said that he seemed relaxed. They got onto Airbus only in the last fifteen minutes, and Yeutter confined himself to reiterating the American dislike of the exchange-rate guarantee proposals.[27]

Thorough as always, he had asked his old stomping ground, the Chicago Mercantile Exchange, to brief him on the pros and cons of foreign exchange hedging. Hedging, they told him, appeared to be a prudent business decision by the manufacturing partners. They then blinded him with science over six pages, exploring the cost, the impact on profitability and competitiveness and the range of instruments available. Their conclusion was unremarkable: "These derivative currency markets . . . will continue to develop optimal combinations of swaps, forwards, and options such that risk managers will be able to customize the alterations to their FX risk profiles."[28]

The German side maintained that what they were proposing was not a unique arrangement. So far as hedging was concerned, the market would not offer cover for the sort of periods necessary in the case of Airbus; the most they could hope to get was 18 months, and Airbus needed 20 years. They had calculated that hedging would cost about DM 6 billion, a sum equal to the total hedging activities of German exporting industry as a whole.

Airbus was in any case not the only ripple on the mill-pond of U.S.-European trade relations. There was the forthcoming mid-term assessment in Montreal of the GATT Uruguay Round to consider and, more immediately, the differences that had arisen about hormones in beef. Yeutter took his hosts into his confidence and told them that it was his swansong as USTR, though he did not tell them—if indeed at that stage he knew—that he would be staying on in the Bush Cabinet as secretary of agriculture. Either way, Clayton Yeutter, the very model of a modern trade commissioner ("The Good Lord has blessed me generously with talents"), was beginning to turn his mind to other things.

His successor was Mrs Carla Hills, a 54-year-old former secretary of the Department of Housing and Urban Development. She had also been assistant attorney-general in the Ford administration, and she had little experience of trade issues—"a tough, no-nonsense attorney," President Bush said of her when he announced her appointment, though he probably did not mean to be unflattering. She comes from California, and rounded off her Stanford and Yale Law School education with a brief stay at St.

Hilda's College, Oxford. Her first Washington job was in 1974, when Elliot Richardson was attorney- general, and she ran the civil division of the Justice Department, which meant that she dealt among other things with the Nixon tapes.

Her performance before the Senate Finance Committee at the end of January 1989 won her swift and unanimous confirmation of her appointment. The chairman of the committee was Senator Lloyd Bentsen, Governor Dukakis's running mate on the Democratic presidential ticket, and he had some stern and fatherly words for her about the need for a close working relationship on trade issues between the administration and Congress. The Reagan administration, he said, had gone its own way on trade, and had, as he put it, got "stiffed" in negotiations.

The Republican senator who introduced her said she had "the guts of a lion," and Mrs. Hills quickly decided that some fairly vigorous language would be in order. She would, she said, "use a crowbar" to prise open markets for U.S. goods. While retaliation could not be the goal of U.S. policy, the credible threat of retaliation provided essential leverage. "Thus, actual retaliation will be used, albeit reluctantly, to preserve the credibility of the threat." She described the Airbus issue as a top priority. She repeated that the administration was "very troubled" about the level of subsidy, particularly in West Germany, and said that there were some "very strong unilateral tools" available. "We will seriously consider them if our bilateral negotiations do not succeed."

The Daimler-Benz board had, in fact, reached final agreement on the terms of the MBB takeover only a few days previously. Edzard Reuter announced that Daimler would take control of MBB in two stages. First, it would participate, at a cost of just under DM 1 billion, in a rights issue, which would give it a 30 percent stake. Secondly, Daimler would spend a further DM 700 million on buying out most of the existing private-sector shareholders. Allianz, Europe's largest insurance company, had agreed to sell its 4.63 percent holding, and the eventual departure of Dresdner Bank and the Bayerische Vereinsbank would leave only Siemens and Aérospatiale with substantial corporate interests. The combined holding of Bavaria, Hamburg and Bremen, which was just over 52 percent, would come down to 36 percent. Herr Reuter hoped to have his majority by the end of 1989 or early 1990 at the latest. The marriage of elephants, as the German press called it, had been agreed, if not yet consummated.

Early in March, the proposal went through yet another statutory hoop when the European Commission gave its approval. "The proposal will strengthen the overall competitiveness of the sector," the Commission statement said, "and thus will contribute in a concrete way to the common European interest." The Federal Cartel Office took longer to pronounce, and there were sections of the German press that urged it to dig in its heels. "If this is the market economy," wrote Klaus-Peter Schmid in the Hamburg weekly *Die Zeit*, "then the textbooks should be rewritten." He reminded

Helmut Haussmann, Martin Bangemann's successor as economics minister, of his declared intention to adhere "embarrassingly closely" to monopolies procedures. "This self-assured Liberal must show that everything that is good for Daimler is not necessarily also good for the German economy."[29]

Two weeks later, in a document that ran to 136 pages, the Federal Cartel Office made it easier for the minister to follow that advice by ruling against the planned merger. Herr Wolfgang Kartte, the office president, had formed the view that it would lead to overconcentration of industrial might in the arms sector. He was believed to have been influenced by the criteria observed three years earlier by the Monopolies and Mergers Commission in the United Kingdom when they had rejected a proposed takeover of Plessey by the British General Electric Company; in the MMC's judgement, this would have given the resulting conglomerate a position of unacceptable dominance in the British defence market.[30]

The Cartel Office view was that the proposed Daimler-MBB merger would create or strengthen "market dominating positions" in the arms, aerospace and truck industries. Competition for contracts in the early stages of weapon development was vital, because the prime contractor decided what proportion of the work would go to other companies. Daimler-Benz and MBB had argued that the existence of international competition voided the cartel objections, but the Cartel Office believed that it would not be possible for foreign companies to match the market presence of the merged conglomerate, because weapon procurement was still largely nationally oriented. Although some 70 percent of West Germany's defence contracts involved international cooperation, no foreign company had a chance to compete for the German portion of a project. That situation was unlikely to change, even with a single European market.

The Cartel Office was also concerned at the political power that the merger could put in the hands of the enlarged company. With 60,000 of the country's 68,000 defence industry employees working for one concern, politicians could find themselves confronted with the argument that a particular contract was vital in order to maintain employment.

Herr Reuter took a relaxed view of this setback, and said that the group would go ahead with the development of its aerospace activities even if it was not allowed to buy into MBB. He pointed out, however, that this would require greater cooperation with foreign partners, especially in the United States, adding silkily that for West Germany, this would entail a loss both of suppliers and of skilled employment.

The political parties were once again quickly shouting the odds. Herr Max Striebl, the prime minister of Bavaria, which was a 24 percent shareholder in MBB, announced that he would not accept any splitting off of MBB's defence business as a condition for the merger to go ahead. Opposition parties, notably the Social Democrats and the Greens, remained hostile to the deal, articulating growing criticism of the Federal Republic's military links within NATO. Nor did the government coalition speak with one voice. Rumblings continued within Herr Haussmann's own party, the Free Democrats, and he was obliged to rebuke Herr Erich Riedl, his state secretary with responsibility for aerospace, for suggesting that a ministerial waiver of the Cartel Office veto was a foregone conclusion. He promised the Bundestag a resolution early in September; it was, he said, the most difficult decision of his career.

At the beginning of May, Daimler-Benz lodged a formal response to the Federal Cartel Office's rejection of its bid. In a 50-page letter to Haussmann, the company argued that the merger would be in the interest both of Germany and Europe. It would improve European aerospace competitiveness. It would promote Deutsche Aerospace to a position in Europe second only to that of British Aerospace. It would also, by the year 2000, save the Federal Republic the sum of DM 3 billion in subsidy payments by shifting German participation in Airbus onto a private-sector basis.

Meanwhile, in the United States, May 1 1989, saw the publication of the National Trade Estimates Report, a 214-page deadpan inventory of foreign trade barriers that the United States saw as inimical to American enterprise. It was the fourth annual report of its kind, but the previous year's trade legislation gave it enhanced significance as a point of reference for the U.S. trade representative in the event of her deciding to activate Super 301. Japan was still very much the villain of the piece—the US trade deficit for the previous year was listed as $55.4 billion—but the European Community (U.S. 1988 trade deficit $12.8 billion) was in third place, close on the heels of Taiwan, and the report recorded that Airbus subsidies remained "a primary area of contention," along with the beef hormone ban and the strong "buy national" policies of certain EC utilities and agencies. There had also, the report stated, been continuing allegations of unfair trade activities, "such as intervention in third-country sales through political and economic inducement to promote Airbus sales."

The report occasioned a good deal of unfavourable comment on U.S. trade policy in the European press. In London, the *Financial Times* saw it as a sign that a truculent Congress was determined not to let President Bush slip into what it perceived as the malign neglect of trade of his predecessor. Super-301, the paper said, was "a fundamentally flawed provision and incompatible with the smooth working of the mutilateral trading system on which all countries, including the U.S., ultimately depend." It set the United States firmly on a path of seeking bilateral solutions to its trade problems. This could lead quickly into the realm of managed trade, and all too easily undermine efforts to strengthen the multilateral system through the Uruguay Round. The only real guarantee of economic security, the paper concluded, was a more balanced fiscal policy.[31]

There had been no immediate response to the report from the European Community (the offices in Brussels were closed for the May Day holiday), but two days later it retaliated with a 41-page document detailing U.S. practices that impeded EC exports. "The difference between theirs and ours," said a Community official, "is that theirs triggers an automatic procedure outlined in the Trade Act." In the Community, he added virtuously, there was no legal link between the report and any subsequent action.

The following week, United States and EC officials came together again for two days of talks in Geneva. The American side argued that by subsidising Daimler's purchase of a majority holding in MBB the Bonn government would be in violation of the General Agreement on Tariffs and Trade; specifically, they were critical of the exchange-rate guarantee that was included in the proposals. The EC refused consultation under the subsidies heading, arguing that the special aircraft code took precedence over the more general subsidies agreement; the two sides eventually agreed to let the legal issue ride while they discussed the substance of the American complaint against the Daimler-MBB deal.

The EC contention was that there was no case to answer because there was no distortion of trade. Airbus, with a 1988 market share of only 17.2 percent, could not be held to constitute a serious threat to its American competitors at a time of sharply expanding demand. European officials pointed out that in 1979, when there had been three American manufacturers, the U.S. share in sales of large aircraft had been 75.3 percent. Now, despite the disappearance from the scene of Lockheed and the expansion of the Airbus range, that figure had risen to 79.3 percent. McDonnell Douglas had taken on 22,400 new workers in the previous three years and had reported a 23 percent growth in turnover. They claimed that Boeing's market share had risen from 51.6 percent to 62.5 percent during 1988, that its profits had increased by 28 percent and that over the previous four years it had taken on 66,400 workers. They repeated the allegation that Boeing was using profits of at least $30 million per aircaft from its 747 sales to cut the price of models competing with the Airbus range. It was, said Dieter Wolf, throwing the economic text book at them, "a classic case of monopolising strategy"—cross-subsidising from one product to another to keep prices down despite strong demand.

The European side, and the Germans in particular, were indignant at the U.S. challenge to the Daimler-MBB deal because they felt it went back on an undertaking given at the ministerial meeting in London the previous October not to hinder efforts to privatise the Airbus consortium. The EC was also dismissive of the renewed American suggestion that Airbus and MBB could cover themselves against fluctuations in the dollar by normal commercial hedging on capital markets. This was precluded by the long lead times typical of aircraft projects—hedging is normally practised for periods of up to three months. It would also be ruled out on grounds of sheer volume. The Germans calculated that the amount required to cover their Airbus participation would be equivalent to the total forward exchange dealing in the German economy.

President Bush made his long-awaited decision about which countries to cite under the Super 301 provision at the end of May 1989. The European Community was not included; at the beginning of September, the West German government gave the green light to the Daimler takeover of MBB. Haussmann announced a series of conditions that showed some sensitivity to the concerns that had been expressed—the opposition parties had kept up a barrage of criticism during the summer, and the previous month, the chairman of the Advisory Monopolies Commission (Monopolkommission) had resigned over the issue. Daimler and MBB would both be required to divest themselves of their profitable marine defence technology activities (turnover DM 900 million) within two years and MBB would have to give up the manufacture of small pilotless aircraft and sell its 12.5 percent share in Krauss-Maffei, the maker of West Germany's Leopard tanks. Further stipulations were that Daimler and MBB should sell four military procurement planning and service companies, and that no Daimler representatives should sit on the boards of other German arms companies. Finally, Daimler would have to assume full responsibility for MBB's Airbus activities by the end of 1996—three years earlier than previously envisaged.

Carla Hills was in Europe a few days later, and the tenor of her speeches reflected renewed American concern about the EC's progress towards market integration. "Of late," she said in Paris, "some provisions and directives give us pause." In a speech to a joint session of the American Chamber of Commerce in London and the Royal Institute of International Affairs she indicated that the Airbus dispute was still high on her agenda. "Of all subsidies," she said, "that which would destroy the price mechanism is the most egregious."[32] She met Nicholas Ridley, the British Trade and Industry Secretary. One of his junior ministers, Lord Trefgarne, said afterwards that the United Kingdom would be pressing its Airbus partners to play a constructive part in the next round of talks due to begin in October. "The buoyancy of the market has created an opportunity for resolving the issue," he said.

The publicity given to the Daimler-MBB merger served to distract attention from a serious disagreement over Airbus production arrangements that had arisen between France and Germany. The Germans had long wished to acquire a larger work share but had encountered strong French resistance to their proposal that final assembly of the A320 should be transferred from Toulouse to Hamburg. At one of their regular meetings earlier in the year President Mitterand and Chancellor Kohl had agreed to commission a report that would analyse the economic implications of the proposal.

The Germans put forward as their representative Herr Jürgen Krackow, who had been a senior steel executive. The French offered the services of

Monsieur Jacques Benichou, who had been their nominee on the group of Four Wise Men two years previously. Entirely predictably, they failed to reach agreement on any joint recommendations, each effectively restating the position of his own government. Herr Krackow estimated the annual savings of a move to Hamburg at $80 million (£50.9 million); Monsieur Benichou arrived at a much more conservative $9 million. He also questioned the MBB assertion that a move to Hamburg could reduce the final assembly cycle of the A320 from 65 working days to 42. (Boeing took 43 days to assemble the 737 and 63 days for the 757.)

The idea that the production arrangements for Airbus was something that could be decided bilaterally between the French and the Germans did not go down well with their Spanish and British partners. There was concern in London, in particular, that such talks could further politicise the Airbus programme and hinder attempts to make it commercially viable. The Spanish and British governments accordingly decided to recall to the colours their two Wise Men, Emilio González García and Sir Geoffrey Sterling, and they put their names to a study that was clearly intended as a shot across the bows of Bonn and Paris.

The study deplored government interference in Airbus and reiterated the view that the consortium must be allowed to run its programmes as commercial ventures. They acknowledged that moving the assembly line to Hamburg might produce some savings but feared that it might also disrupt production and damage the aircraft's credibility with airline customers. More broadly, they questioned whether the recent reorganisation of the Airbus management structure went far enough. They reiterated their belief that the consortium should become a PLC, and advocated the appointment of a "totally objective" deputy chairman and a strengthening of the powers of the recently appointed finance director.

Before 1989 was out, however, that particular horse had already bolted. Robert Smith, appointed finance director only the previous April, had quickly become disenchanted. One of his tasks had been to get the partners to change their reporting procedures and provide more information about their costs, but he had run into a stone wall. He also felt that he had not been sufficiently involved in the decision to seek finance for the research and development programme for the A-321 from the commercial banks.[33]

Smith's resignation came only weeks after the sudden departure of Adam Brown, the Airbus vice-president concerned with strategy. Although Brown had been at Toulouse for many years, he had remained on the payroll of British Aerospace. He was notable for his lack of inhibition, and like many of his Airbus colleagues was not infrequently critical of his parent company's attitude to the consortium. During the summer, in an interview with the Industrial Editor of *The Guardian,* he had spoken even less guardedly than usual not only about British Aerospace, but also about its chairman. "Roland Smith has never been to Toulouse. Next time you see him, ask which hotel he stayed in," he said tartly.[34]

It was believed in Toulouse that Roland Smith and his colleagues in London were putting it about that there was nothing to stop a lucrative stock-market flotation of Airbus as early as 1993; Jean Pierson and his associates took the view that 1998–99 would be a more realistic date. Airbus officials were also irritated by hints dropped by Professor Smith that a closer relationship between BAe and Daimler-Benz, possibly involving a degree of cross-shareholding, could have an important influence on the development of the consortium's affairs.

Boeing finally decided in December 1989 that the time was right to announce that it was going ahead with a new model. The plane would be larger than the 767-300 but smaller than the Jumbo, and the company was setting up the New Airplane Division, headed by Phil Condit, to develop it. Boeing made its plans known in a characteristically guarded and low-key fashion. "We don't launch airplanes," said Dean Thornton, the president of Boeing's commercial operations. "Our customers do when they sign firm orders."[35]

There was a powerful illustration of how important Boeing was to the economy of the United States when the U.S. trade figures for November 1989 were published. The company had been hit by its first strike in 12 years when its machinists (the 57,000 members of its 109,000-strong labour force who were members of the International Association of Machinists and Aerospace Workers) refused a new contract that would have increased their pay by $13,800 over three years. In the first nine months of 1989, Boeing, as America's largest exporter of manufactured goods, had helped to hold down the U.S. trade deficit with more than $8 billion of net exports. The 48-day strike reduced aircraft exports by $900 million from the already depressed October level, and the trade deficit widened to $10.5 billion, its highest level of the year.

Early in 1990, an industrial dispute affecting British Aerospace underlined the vulnerability of Airbus Industrie's federal structure. The British partner in the consortium had become the focus of a campaign by unions to secure a 35-hour working week for some 1.5 million engineering workers, giving them similar conditions to their European counterparts. BAe, an important target because of its size, bore the brunt of a rolling campaign of strike action, with about 7,000 workers on strike at three of its plants, mainly concerned with the production of wings. By the second week in January, the dispute had cost Airbus an estimated $100 million in layoffs around Europe. Production had slowed from 12 aircraft a month to two, and final assembly in Toulouse was within days of grinding to a complete halt.

British voices had always been loudest in calling for a more market-oriented approach to the management of the consortium, often to the irritation of their continental partners. Those partners were now not slow to express their irritation at what they saw as a demonstration of British managerial ineptitude. Jean Pierson, in particular, had a number of old scores to settle. "The art of good management," he said acidly, "is also the art of handling labour relations."

There was talk of invoking article 7 of the Airbus regulations that would make BAe liable to pay about 40 percent of the cost incurred by Airbus as a consequence of the strike. It was particularly galling that it came just as Boeing was getting back into its stride. Pierson made it clear that a production shut-down would seriously affect the consortium's credibility—87 airlines and leasing companies had planes on order. He was not disposed to let the British down lightly, and adroitly turned one of their favourite arguments against them. "If we were a public limited company," he said pointedly, "I suspect we would have asked ourselves if we should keep all wing production at one plant. If you have a turbulent plant in a multinational group, you usually consider shutting it down."[36]

By the middle of February the strike was in its 16th week, and BAe's partners were getting distinctly restive. At the Singapore Air Show Jacques Plenier, the head of Aérospatiale's aircraft division, described the strike as "an act of sabotage by BAe management and the UK unions." Henri Martre, Aérospatiale's chairman, said that before it arose, Aérospatiale had been expecting to report its first profit on its Airbus operations. He confirmed that he would be pressing for compensation. BAe continued to insist that Article 7 did not apply because the strike constituted a case of *force majeure.*[37]

By the time the stoppage came to an end in early March, it was estimated to have cost the consortium some $300 million. The BAe management conceded a reduction in the working week from 39 hours to 37, and the workforce nodded in the direction of increased productivity by giving up their time-hallowed tea-break. On the day they voted to return to work, the Airbus Supervisory Board, meeting in Hamburg, gave its approval to the setting up of a German assembly line for the A321. The French unions huffed and puffed, but the blow to Aérospatiale and to Gallic pride was softened by a decision that so far as the A330/340 programmes were concerned, aircraft customization—the fitting-out of the passenger cabins to airline specifications—should be transferred from Hamburg to Toulouse. The board also announced that this measure of rationalisation would apply to all future programmes.

In the middle of February, the attention of Jean Pierson and his colleagues had been diverted from the BAe strike in the most unwelcome manner possible. An Indian Airlines A320, in service for less than two months, crashed on landing at Bangalore, killing 89 of the 153 people on board. It was the first major crash involving an Airbus. The entire fleet of fourteen A320s operated by the airline was grounded. Indian Airlines also announced that they would not for the time being take delivery of the additional A320s they had on order.

In France, the accident reopened the debate on the reliability of the aircraft, although the authorities rejected a call from the pilots' union for it to be grounded pending inquiries into the crash. Pierre Gille, the president of SNPL (Syndicat national des pilotes de lignes), pointed out that with only 80 A320s in service around the world, this was the second crash in two years, an accident rate unprecedented in civil aviation. He was critical of the tendency of DGAC, the French Directorate General of Civil Aviation, always to blame pilot error. In his view (he was himself a Boeing 737 pilot with no experience of the A320) the electronic command system meant that the pilot could not be totally in control of the aircraft; he also believed that it was a mistake that the controls operated by the pilot and the co-pilot were not coupled as they were in aircraft of more-traditional design. Airbus, in its pursuit of innovation, had pushed ahead too rapidly. His members were no longer sure whether the plane's qualities outweighed its defects. Few Air France pilots had been happy to fly the A320 for more than a year.[38]

Relations between France and India were quickly soured. The Indian government refused a French request that a transcript of the black box recording should be made available to Airbus Industrie, saying that was a matter for the court of inquiry. In parallel to the inquiry, the minister of Civil Aviation, Mr. Arif Mohammed Khan, set up a committee under an air marshal to consider whether Indian Airlines and Indian airports had the infrastructure necessary to handle the aircraft.

The French and Indian press were full of rumour, speculation and innuendo. A writer in *Le Monde* recalled that when an Indian Airlines Boeing 737 had crashed at Ahmedabad in 1988 with the loss of 131 lives, media interest had been slight; in the aftermath of the Airbus crash, by contrast, India seemed to be in a state of mass hysteria. He conceded that there were, for all that, questions to be answered. One was whether Airbus provided adequate pilot training. Another was whether it was sensible to sell such sophisticated aircraft to countries culturally and economically ill-equipped to operate them safely.[39]

Airbus Industrie was understandably sensitive to the prospect of adverse publicity. On February 20, Jean Pierson wrote to the International Civil Aviation Organisation to protest at the behaviour of the Indian government. He claimed that in refusing the national authorities that had certified the aircraft access to the inquiry, India, a member of the organisation, was in breach of its rules.

Corruption is endemic in the public life in India. When V. P. Singh campaigned against Rajiv Gandhi in the 1989 elections, it had been on a ticket of cleansing the Augean stables of government. It therefore caused little surprise when the Indian Central Bureau of Investigation got in on the act, and at the end of March they filed preliminary criminal charges. It was alleged that in 1985, when Rajiv was prime minister, Airbus Industrie and the aero engine consortium, International Aero Engines, had paid bribes to eight former Indian officials to cancel a letter of intent to buy 757s from Boeing and agree instead to a $1.47 billion contract with Airbus for the purchase of 38 A320s. It was the third investigation ordered by the Singh government into the transactions of its predecessor. The CBI was also looking into the purchase of artillery guns from the Swedish Bofors company and into the acquisition of submarines from the West German concern Howaldt Deutsche Werke. In each case there were suggestions of corruption in high places.

In the Airbus case, large sums were alleged to have been deposited in Indian and foreign banks for the benefit of the Indian officials. They were said to have altered both the air-traffic projections on which the Boeing deal was negotiated and the nature of Indian Airlines fleet requirement. The news magazine *India Today* reminded its readers that Rajiv Gandhi, an Indian Airlines pilot before entering politics, had spent a "well-publicised" half-hour in an A320 cockpit at the 1985 Paris Air Show.The implication was obvious. One of the accused was S. S. Sidhu, India's former civil aviation secretary; he was now, by a piquant twist, working in Montreal as secretary-general of the ICAO—the United Nations body to which Jean Pierson had addressed his complaint only a few weeks previously. The CBI charge sheet claimed that Airbus had been awarded the contract without a proper evaluation of the aircraft, and that after the A320 crash near Paris in June 1988, the serious doubts expressed about the airworthiness of the aircraft had been dis-regarded. The crash cost Indian Airlines dear. By the end of July, the pro-longed grounding of the Airbus fleet had already cost them £22.3 million, and the airline looked like being in the red for some years.

Differences between the United States and Europe flared up briefly again in the summer of 1990. The two sides had given themselves until the end of July to reach agreement, but a week before the deadline the Bush administration decided to force the pace by announcing that it had decided to make a formal complaint to GATT. At issue was the undertaking given by the Bonn government in 1988 to shield Daimler-Benz from exchange-rate fluctuations with a subsidy of up to $2.63 billion if the dollar fell below DM 1.60. The American move took the European side by surprise. They did not regard the talks as having broken down; only ten days previously they had offered a firm commitment to ban all production subsidies on large aircraft with more than a 100-seat capacity and had also offered to cut development subsidies to 50 percent of the investment from the the existing figure of 75 percent. The Americans did not think this went far enough, and were looking for a limit of 35 or 30 percent, but after further exchanges they decided on a tactical softening of their line and agreed for the time being not to proceed with their formal complaint.

The heat was quickly turned up again, however. In early September the U.S. Department of Commerce decided that the time had come to release the Gellman Report, long talked about in hushed tones in the corridors of Washington as Uncle Sam's weapon of last resort.[40] The report traced the familiar details of the inroads made by Airbus into the market share of the American manufacturers. The U.S. share of commercial aircraft unit orders had declined from 87 percent in 1980 to 64 percent in 1989. Over the same period, the Airbus share of large commercial aircraft unit orders had grown from 7 percent to 27 percent. The report set the amount of direct government support to Airbus programmes at $13.5 billion, a figure that would rise to $25.9 billion if interest were computed at normal commercial rates. Of that total West Germany had contributed 59 percent, France 25 percent and the United Kingdom 16 percent. Three-quarters of the total development cost of all Airbus programmes had been met by the member governments. Of the $5.4 billion dollars disbursed to that date in development costs, $500 million had been repaid.

Gellman saw none of the Airbus programmes as commercially viable, i.e., earning a positive rate of return taking into account the cost of capital. They saw no prospect of a positive cash flow for the consortium before 1996. They estimated that by the year 2008, Airbus would have a cumulative negative nominal cash flow of $30 billion at 1990 prices.

The report concluded with a resounding statement of the obvious—if Airbus Industrie continued to sell below cost, U.S. firms would see their profits reduced below what they otherwise would have been. "Despite this sector's current strength," said J. Michael Farren, the U.S. under secretary of commerce for international trade, "subsidies to Airbus Industrie member companies provide an unfair advantage over U.S. manufacturers and could injure the industry's future competitiveness." As a trumpet player, Mr. Farren was clearly not in the same class as Joshua. The walls of Jericho showed no sign of tumbling down.

In October 1990, in the presence of 10,000 guests, President Mitterand opened the new facility that Aérospatiale had built on a 130-acre site at Toulouse to build the A330 and A340—the largest aeronautical complex in Europe. The event did not go entirely as planned. French farmers, furious at what they saw as their government's failure to defend them against cheap meat imports, seized the opportunity to publicise their concerns. Several hundred of them burned tyres and straw outside the Toulouse-Blagnac airport and spread liquid manure on the roadway. The police fired tear gas into the crowd to force them back from the perimeter fence, and a 21-year old farmer had his hand blown off as he picked up one of the canisters.

The new plant had been conceived three years earlier, at the start of an unprecedented buying cycle. It represented an investment of some FF 7 billion, 1 billion of which had been spent on an enormous, partly-robotised assembly hall reminiscent of the Boeing plant at Everett. (The French, like the Americans, favoured sporting comparisons, but chose different games—each door was described as the size of five tennis courts. For good measure, they threw in the information that the hall was the same height as the Statue of Liberty.) Less than a week later, it was Boeing's turn to seize the headlines with an announcement that it had taken the largest order for new aircraft in aviation history—United Airlines had signed a $22 billion contract. They had agreed to buy 30 747s, with options on 30 more. Much more importantly, from Boeing's point of view, the deal also included 34 firm orders and the same number of options for the 777. With United aboard as launch customer, the Boeing board gave the programme the formal go-ahead before the month was out.[41]

At the beginning of 1991, for the first time since the consortium was set up, Airbus announced an operating profit. Jean Pierson declined to disclose precise figures, but claimed they were substantial. (When European aerospace ministers met in Dresden in March a figure of $105 million was given.) A month later he said gloomily that he expected the order intake to be less than half the volume for the previous year. His pessimism was widely shared. In the wake of Iraq's invasion of Kuwait, assumptions about the future of the aerospace industry were being drastically reappraised. Until then, the changes in the Soviet Union and eastern Europe had pointed to a reduction in defence spending and a corresponding boost to the commercial sector, but the Gulf crisis suddenly made it seem that the "peace dividend" might be an altogether slimmer affair than had been anticipated. By the early months of 1991, growing recessionary pressures, higher oil prices and the fear of flying induced by hostilities in the Gulf and the possibility of terrorism had combined to catch airlines in a vicious double bind of rising costs and collapsing revenues.[42]

There were also signs that Deutsche Airbus's success in the matter of the A321 assembly line had by no means exhausted its ambitions. The German group was now showing interest in developing a regional jet, possibly in cooperation with Aérospatiale and Alenia, the Italian aerospace group (earlier talks with British Aerospace had broken down); British Aerospace, for its part, was contemplating an enlarged version of the BA-146. Pierson maintained that Airbus should be allowed to develop a 130-seat version of the A320, and that attempts by the individual companies to go it alone or forge new partnerships could undermine the cohesion and credibility of the consortium. (Airbus rules stipulated that partners should not separately develop new aircraft that would compete directly with consortium products.) He argued that a smaller version of the A320 could be developed for $400 million. The German proposal could swallow up to $4 billion, and even to stretch BAe's 146 might cost as much as $1 billion.

When the German, French and Italian companies signed an agreement early in March, United Kingdom officials urged them to reconsider and look again at the Airbus proposal. Britain was particularly anxious about the prospect of the German government's agreeing to a development subsidy for the new project. She told the European Commission that she was concerned not only about distortions in the European aerospace industry but also about a possible exacerbation of the EC dispute with the United States. Government aid to such a new project (Deutsche Airbus was said to be asking Bonn to meet half the German share of the development costs) would constitute a wilful misallocation of resources—precisely one of the things that the planned European single market was intended to discourage.

That the pursuit of national advantage in all this was so thinly disguised did not augur well for the future of Airbus as an exercise in European collaboration. The British interest was to prevent the emergence of a continental regional aircraft consortium from which British Aerospace was excluded; the United Kingdom, so often criticised for its detachment, suddenly seemed to be speaking in accents more European than the Europeans. The German interest was to secure the leading role in a large international project. Weary of the part it had been obliged to play in the postwar world, and despite the mounting budgetary cost of reunification, the new Germany wished to break out of its subcontracting chrysalis and assert itself as a fully formed civil aerospace manufacturer. It was a desire reinforced by the decline in defence sales, which accounted for roughly half of DASA's revenues; with the reduction in East-West tension, the company's intake of new orders had shrunk by 43 percent in the previous year.

The British and the Germans had seemed to be the two partners most determined to force the consortium into a proper commercial mould. With Daimler-Benz and British Aerospace pulling in different directions, it appeared doubtful whether that impetus towards rationalisation could be maintained. "The old-world urge to subsidise, to protect jobs and to create national champions remains depressingly intact," wrote *The Economist*.[43]

The dispute with the United States returned to the front burner at the beginning of March 1991. The subsidies committee of GATT agreed to establish a dispute-settlement panel to examine a U.S. complaint that the German exchange-rate insurance scheme for Deutsche Airbus violated the GATT Subsidies Agreement. A European Community plea that the matter could be dealt with under the GATT Civil Aircraft code was rejected. Washington claimed that Bonn had already paid out more than DM 390 million under the scheme, and that this represented an export subsidy of $2.5 million on each aircraft delivered.

The Commission's response was to propose that the Civil Aircraft Agreement should be renegotiated because its references to subsidies and competitive practices were not sufficiently precise. The Europeans conceded that production subsidies should be prohibited but argued that support for the development of new programmes should be permitted on certain conditions: these were that it should be limited to an agreed percentage of the development costs and that governments had a reasonable expectation of re-coupment within a given period. They also harked back to their contention that the American manufacturers derived indirect benefit from military programmes and argued for the inclusion of a clause that would prevent this.

Jean Pierson, speaking at the Cranfield School of Management in England at the end of April, was aggressive and uncompromising. The European Commission, he said, would use "every legal weapon" at its disposal to defend Airbus. He maintained that the European side had been prepared to be accommodating, agreeing for example that direct government support for research and development should be limited to 45 percent. He suggested that the Americans had intensified their attacks with an eye to the approaching first flight of the A340, scheduled for October. He also reiterated the European charges about indirect government support to Boeing and McDonnell Douglas; the figures he quoted in support of them were not new, however, and appeared to be drawn from the 1988 Airbus publication analysed in Chapter 8.

It emerged during the early summer of 1991 that the United States had it in mind to broaden its attack and was once again contemplating unilateral action against Airbus, which might include special duties and quotas on Airbus sales in the United States. The thrust of recent U.S. negotiating efforts had been towards limiting government launch aid for new programmes to 25 percent of their overall development and production costs, although in the face of the strong EC preference for 45 percent they had been prepared to agree to a 3-year transitional period. The compromise had not found favour with the American manufacturers; Ray Waldmann, Boeing's director of government affairs, described it as "an open invitation for European governments to throw money at Airbus during the transitional period." As things turned out, the proposal was rejected by the European side.

In Paris for the 1991 Air Show, Herr Johann Schäffler, the deputy chairman of Deutsche Aerospace, attributed the latest hardening of the American line to anxieties about a new Airbus challenge to Boeing at the top end of the market. Stuart Iddles, the Airbus senior vice-president for commercial affairs, confirmed at a *Financial Times* Aerospace conference that the consortium planned to start talks in September with a number of airlines currently operating large fleets of 747s. The aim would be to explore their requirements for airliners seating more than 600 passengers. The intention was not to compete with the current Jumbo, but to develop a new aircraft for the 747 replacement market early in the next century. In what was plainly an attempt to disarm critics, Mr. Iddles said that Airbus should be able to finance the project from its own resources. A $4–$5 billion development programme would require some 5 percent of turnover. That, he said, should be "not insuperable." He added that if Airbus went ahead with a 130-seat version of the A320—the A319—that too would be financed through the commercial markets.[44]

Shortly after the end of the air show, Airbus Industrie entered the international bond market for the first time with a five-year Eurolira issue of L 150 billion. This first issue, intended to help the financing of the A321, was reported to have been reasonably well received by continental investors, despite some weakness in the Eurolira market. The bond carried a coupon of 12.25 percent and was swapped into floating rate dollars, allowing Airbus to borrow more cheaply than if it it had tapped the Eurodollar market direct.[45]

It was notable during the summer of 1991 that Boeing was becoming more vocal than it had previously been. (In the earlier stages of the dispute it was McDonnell Douglas that had seemed more disposed to put its head above the parapet, although it did so with no great consistency.) "We kept a low profile while the U.S. and EC governments were trying to resolve the issue," said Frank Shrontz, the Boeing chairman. "We did not want to be considered in the industry as a crybaby." Frustration with Washington's lack of success in negotiating a compromise was clearly having an effect. "Enough is enough in our view," Shrontz said. In September 1991, the U.S. renewed its attempts to bring pressure to bear through the machinery of GATT with a new complaint to the Subsidies Committee. The European Commission, while accepting conciliation, again stressed that what it saw as its rights under the Civil Aircraft Code should also be respected. It proposed that the United States should resumes bilateral negotiations on the dispute, and that these should proceed in parallel with multilateral negotiations for the improvement of disciplines in the Civil Aircraft Agreement.

Airbus morale had been boosted during the summer of 1991 by a number of important orders. It had been announced at the Paris Air Show in June that Kuwait was to re-equip its fleet with an order that spanned almost the entire Airbus product line. A month later, there was jubilation in Toulouse when Federal Express, of Memphis, the world's largest express transportation company, placed a firm order for 25 A300-600 freighters with an option on a further 50.

There was a change of mood in August when the consortium was once again pipped at the post by Boeing in a fiercely fought contest to supply British Airways. Airbus had been offering the A340, but BA plumped for the Boeing 777. The British flag-carrier had long been Jean Pierson's King Charles's head. He chose October 4, the day on which the A340 was unveiled in Toulouse, to make a not particularly festive announcement. The consortium, he said, wanted Brussels to investigate whether Boeing had a case to answer on grounds of unfair competition—an official complaint had been lodged with Sir Leon Brittan, the relevant commissioner, and he would also be asked to look at the commercial practices of British Airways. As the champagne corks popped, there was an unmistakable whiff of sour grapes.

In the event Airbus did not press the issue, but in early December 1991 the European Commission reentered the fray with what was essentially an attempt to counter the Gellman findings. It published a report commissioned from the Washington law firm of Arnold & Porter which asserted that over a period of 15 years the U.S. commercial aircraft industry had benefitted from "massive and systematic" government support to the tune of $41 billion. The report claimed that these subsidies had been channelled to U.S. companies via R&D grants from NASA and the defense department and that Boeing and McDonnell Douglas had received substantial "crossover benefits" because of the overlap between commercial and military aeronautics technology. Boeing acknowledged that it had received military contracts worth $39.9 billion in the previous ten years, but claimed that the value of military contracts gained in the same period by the three main Airbus partners amounted to $85 billion.[46]

At the beginning of January 1992 nerves were set jangling in Toulouse when an Air Inter A320 coming in to land at Strasbourg crashed into a mountain with the loss of 87 lives. After a preliminary examination of the flight recorders, the French air-safety authority said that it could find no reason to justify grounding other A320s, but although pilot error had been blamed in the two previous A320 crashes, the accident prompted renewed worries over the role of new technology in the cockpit and how pilots were adjusting to it. Herr Hans-Ulrich Ohl, of the German Federal Office for Air Safety, expressed the view that pilots were "understretched" by having too much technological assistance. He said that this led to boredom, which meant that mistakes were not spotted in time.[47]

Some weeks after the Strasbourg crash, an Air Inter pilot reported a malfunction on an aircraft flying from Lyons to Bordeaux, and this led both Air Inter and Air France to impose an indefinite ban on landing A320s using the VOR-DME navigational system. Airbus Industrie acknowledged that they were conducting tests to establish why one particular instrument was behaving erratically, and it emerged that Lufthansa had quietly imposed a similar ban late in 1991 after difficulties with the same system, which works by picking up signals from a network of radio beacons on the ground. Airbus did not neglect to point out that the two manufacturers who supplied the VOR-DME equipment, Collins Government Avionics and Bendix, were both American.[48] The preliminary report of the independent investigation into the Strasbourg crash did not identify the cause of the accident. It did, however, express concern that cockpit displays might lead to confusion between an instruction by the pilot to the aircraft to descend at a set angle and one to descend to a set height; its recommendation that the layout of the descent controls should be reviewed was immediately accepted by the French government and Airbus Industrie received an instruction to that effect from the minister of transport. [49]

The accident at Strasbourg did little to harm Airbus's commercial credibility—in March 1992 they won an order worth $675 million for nine A310s from Delta, the third-largest U.S carrier. Boeing, who had been offering the 767-300, (and who had just announced a 27 percent increase in fourth-quarter earnings) cried foul, alleging that there had been a "walk-away" clause in the agreement and that Airbus had provided "creative lease financing." The European consortium denied the charges, insisting that Delta had made an outright purchase; it also spoke about "predatory pricing" on Boeing's part in winning a recent order from Emirates, the Dubai-based airline and harked back to the deal with British Airways the previous summer, which it ascribed to Boeing's "special relationship" with the British flag-carrier.

Both sides knew that further negotiations were imminent between the United States government and the European Commission. It was also public knowledge that the United States had set a deadline of March 31, and had once again been making threatening noises—if agreement was not reached it would seriously contemplate either unilateral action against Airbus, or the lodging of a formal complaint with the subsidies committee of GATT. As the American presidential elections loomed, it was time once more to recall the grand old Duke of York to the colours.

NOTES

1. Editorial, *Foreign Affairs,* Winter 1988/89.

2. News editors don't have such good memories as they used to. When firm sales *did* pass the 1,000 mark in February 1989, Airbus got a second bite at the cherry—and the benefit of a few more column-inches.

3. *Airbus update,* No.3, January 1988.

4. *Ibid.,* No. 4, February 1988; *Interavia Air Letter,* No. 11,419, January 21, 1988; *Aviation Week & Space Technology,* January 25, 1988.

5. Interview in Long Beach, October 1988.

6. Interview in Toulouse, June 1988.

7. Interview in London, October 1988.

8. Press release, Office of the United States Trade Representative, Washington, D.C., April 6. 1988.

9. Interview in Brussels, June 1988.

10. With hindsight, Ray Waldmann, the former U.S. assistant secretary of commerce who had moved to Boeing as director of government affairs, was inclined to agree: "I think one of our problems with that text was that it was too specific, too detailed, too legalistic in tone—it tried to tie up a lot of loose ends in a contract style of agreement which I think was offensive to the Europeans, and therefore it was rejected out of hand as a basis for discussion" (interview in Seattle, February 1989).

11. Interview in Washington, October 1988.

12. *Süddeutsche Zeitung,* July 22, 1987.

13. *Interavia Air Letter,* No. 11,307, August 11, 1987.

14. *The Wall Street Journal,* February 24, 1988.

15. *Hannoversche Allgemeine,* May 7, 1988.

16. *Financial Times,* July 2, 1988; *The Wall Street Journal,* July 4, 1988.

17. *Die Welt,* July 13, 1988.

18. Interview in *Stern,* July 28, 1988.

19. *Handelsblatt,* November 2, 1988.

20. "Eine derart vergoldete Braut ist nicht nur für einen einzigen Bräutigam interessant." *Der Spiegel,* November 7, 1988.

21. "Aus einem fahrenden Zug können wir nicht einfach abspringen." *Frankfurter Allgemeine Zeitung,* November 8, 1988.

22. *Financial Times,* November 11, 1988.

23. *Frankfurter Allgemeine Zeitung,* November 9, 1988.

24. Press release, Office of the United States Trade Representative, Washington, D.C., November 7, 1988.

25. *Frankfurter Allgemeine Zeitung,* November 11, 1988.

26. *Financial Times,* December 1, 1988.

27. Interview in Bonn, November 1988.

28. *Airbus Industrie Foreign Exchange Hedging Study.* Prepared by the Currency Products Marketing Group of the Chicago Mercantile Exchange. Undated.

29. *Die Zeit,* April 7, 1989.

30. *Financial Times,* April 21, 1989.

31. *Ibid.,* May 2, 1989.

32. *The Wall Street Journal,* September 15, 1989.

33. It took Airbus the best part of a year to find a replacement. In November 1990 they announced the appointment of Mr. Ian Massey, a British Aerospace executive, and said that he would have full access to information about the production costs of each of the four partners.

34. *The Guardian,* July 21, 1989. Brown was soon back in Toulouse, as director of planning— and on the strength of Airbus Industrie.

35. *The Wall Street Journal,* December 11, 1989.

36. *Financial Times,* January 10, 1990.

37. *Ibid.,* February 13, 1990.

38. *Le Figaro,* February 20, 1990.

39. Alain Faujas, "Airbus dans les turbulences," *Le Monde,* February 22, 1990.

40. *An Economic and Financial Review of Airbus Industrie,* Gellman Research Associates, Inc., Jenkintown, PA., September 4, 1990.

41. A second order followed in December when All Nippon Airways placed 15 firm orders and took options on further ten. At the same time they ordered five A340s and placed options on five more. Airbus had complained of U.S. political interference earlier in the year when it lost out against McDonnell Douglas in a bid for business with Japan Airlines.

42. Figures published by the International Air Transport Association in March 1991 estimated that airlines had lost more than $2 billion during the first two months of the year. *Financial Times,* March 27, 1991.

43. *The Economist,* April 27, 1991.

44. *Financial Times,* June 12, 1991.

45. *Ibid.,* June 21, 1991.

46. *Ibid.,* December 4, 1991.

47. *Ibid.,* January 25, 1992.

48. *Ibid.,* February 10, 1992.

49. *Ibid.,* February 25, 1992.

14

Compromise and Barter

"All government,—indeed, every human benefit and enjoyment, every virtue and every prudent act,—is founded on compromise and barter."

—Edmund Burke, *On Conciliation with the American Colonies*, 1775.

If you were moving round the Washington cocktail circuit in the last year of the Reagan presidency, a book you absolutely needed to have glanced at the reviews of was *The Rise and Fall of the Great Powers*. It was written by Paul Kennedy, an Englishman who taught history at Yale, and for a few months in the summer of 1988 it became a tract for the times in the way that Servan-Schreiber's *American Challenge* had been 20 years earlier.[1]

It was a blockbuster of a book that surveyed the world scene from 1500 to the present day. Some of its propositions were less remarkable than others—one hardly needed, for instance, to wade through 678 pages to agree that in the long run the rise and fall of states normally reflects their relative position in the world economy. What excited most interest, however, was what Kennedy was understood to be saying about America's place in the sun in the late twentieth century and the policy prescription he seemed to be offering. He wrote at one point about "imperial overstretch"—the situation a great power finds itself in when the sum total of its global interests and obligations exceeds its power to defend them all simultaneously. Some of his readers who had skipped a few pages took this to mean that unless Americans got a grip of themselves, the United States was destined before the end of the century to join the Moguls, the Hapsburgs and the British Empire on the discard heap of history.

The role and influence of the United States was a preoccupation well beyond the Georgetown cocktail belt. In the same summer of 1988, two former secretaries of state, Cyrus Vance and Henry Kissinger, looked ahead to the post-Reagan era and passed the nation's prospects in sober review. "By the end of this century a number of the pillars on which the global order was rebuilt after World War II will have changed significantly. For the United States . . . our relative share of the world economy will be less than half of what it was forty years ago."[2]

There was, they noted, a growing list of constraints on America's actions. Her ability to shape the world unilaterally was increasingly limited, and they were not thinking solely of traditional diplomatic and political concerns. "When we served as secretaries of state, only a relatively small portion of our time was spent on international economic issues. Our successors do not have this luxury . . . U.S. political leadership in the world cannot be sustained if confidence in the American economy continues to be undermined by substantial trade and budget deficits."

There were those who took a chirpier view. "The American press and public have been sold a bill of goods," asserted Milton Friedmann in *The Wall Street Journal:* "They have become convinced that the so-called twin deficits—the federal budget deficit and the foreign trade deficit—are time bombs that will sooner or later undermine prosperity and prospects for growth. Nothing could be further from the truth."[3] Friedmann regarded the twin deficits as politically convenient scarecrows put up by liberal Democrats. For him, the real threats to growth and prosperity continued to be wasteful government expenditure, excessive regulation of the individual and of businesses—and the recent trend to protectionism.

It was a trend that had become unmistakable, as Vance and Kissinger had recognised obliquely in their manifesto: "Great emotion is now attached to discussions of international trade and financial questions in our political debates—especially how we can restore our competitive position. Moreover, our citizens worry that the American standard of living is directly affected by economic decisions taken in foreign capitals that are less politically and militarily powerful than our own."[2]

It had looked for a time during the early months of the 1988 presidential campaign as if trade issues were going to bulk large. Congressman Richard Gephardt used them to make a strong populist pitch for the Democratic nomination, and late in the day, when the Dukakis campaign was running out of steam, the Governor of Massachussets reverted to some of the same themes. (Neither of them had the confidence to carry their populism as far as William Jennings Bryan did when he ran for Congress in the 1890s. "I don't know anything about free silver," he said. "The people of Nebraska are for free silver and I am for free silver. I will look up the arguments later.")

As it happened, the electorate preferred the message they were invited to read on the lips of George Bush. Even so, Ronald Reagan had lost his year-long game of shuttlecock with the Congress, and the Omnibus Trade and Competitiveness Act of 1988 had finally passed into law. The authors of the legislation believed that the burden placed on the United States by its own deeply ingrained free-enterprise philosophy was too heavy. It had been bad enough in Carter's time, but the advent of Reaganomics had made things worse. Its declared objectives of strengthening U.S. trade laws and improving the management of U.S. trade strategy clearly meant that the Bush administration would be obliged to handle such issues with a closer regard to what Congress saw as the national interest than its predecessor. The vice-president of the U.S. Chamber of Commerce put it more plainly: "The view of the Congress that some of our major trading partners do not play fair, that they cheat and take us for patsies, is gut level."

Those trading partners viewed the Act with a mixture of suspicion and apprehension. The Japanese Trade and Industry minister said that it was racist. The French government said that the protectionist complexion of the measure made it doubt the commitment of the United States to bringing the Uruguay Round to a successful conclusion. Some of the things that Europeans said about the Trade Act were couched in exactly the same language that Americans were beginning to use when they contemplated the approach of the single European market in 1992. *The Economist* caught the mood of the confrontation with a witty cover that transposed it to medieval times, and it sustained the metaphor in its main article:

From within their newly armoured siege-towers, the Americans watch Europe's masterbuilders at work. Surely they are building a fortress? No, say the Europeans, by 1992 we will have created a great market whose wide avenues will be open to fair-minded traders from every land. The watchers are not convinced. They note that Europe's masons hold their plans close to their chests. They watch brick after protectionist brick—an anti-dumping suit and a reciprocity clause here, a local-content rule there—being added to Europe's agricultural earthworks. Soon the taunts fly as never before, with both sides prophesying war.[4]

Given that the main pan-European structure already in place—the Common Agricultural Policy—relied heavily on trade distortion to support European farm incomes, *The Economist* thought American suspicions were understandable: "The risk is that project 1992 could end up creating a common industrial policy as ugly as its country cousin."

Willy de Clerq, then the Community's commissioner for external relations, had maintained in a speech in London in the summer of 1988 that there was no question of the emergence of a "Fortress Europe": the intention, he said, was to use the Community's growing influence "to ensure that the liberalisation process which we are pursuing in the Community is accompanied by increasing liberalisation of world markets."[5]

There was more than one view about that in Europe, however. David Henderson, head of the Economics and Statistics Department at the Organisation for Economic Cooperation and Development, offered a personal view in a paper he gave to a Plenary Meeting of the Group of Thirty in Frankfurt that September.[6] He noted that the creation of the original Community of the Six had given a strong impetus towards a more liberal world system of trade, and conceded that 1992 could well have a similar effect in improving the climate for reducing the extent of protectionism. Against this, he pointed out that the trade regime of the Community over the past 20 years had moved in a nonliberal direction. The main instance of this was the Common Agricultural Policy, but he also cited specific subsidies, both to exports and to "problem" sectors.

In his judgement the EEC was now more protectionist than it had been in the early 1970s; more seriously, the main forms that protection took had become more discretionary and less transparent. "The Community," Henderson concluded, "has contributed to weakening not only the GATT but also the fundamental idea that international trade policies should be governed by a framework of accepted rules." He saw little prospect of a change of direction: "There is at present little visible evidence of a renaissance of free trade ideas in the Community." He maintained, however, that the debate about "Fortress Europe" was largely beside the point. "It is not the spectre of Fortress Europe that gives ground for concern, but the reality of some long-established characteristic features of the Community's present trade regime."

In Henderson's view, this trend has been mirrored by a similar departure from liberal trade policies on the part of the United States, and there was now not a great deal to choose between the two trading entities. The 1988 Free Trade Agreement with Canada had moved towards special preferential arrangements; support for domestic agriculture had been increased; and the new Trade Act considerably widened the scope for retaliatory procedures. The prospects, then, for a return to multilateral trade liberalisation were dim.

In another essay that he wrote at about the same time, Henderson came at the same issues from a different direction.[7] He pointed to a seeming paradox, which was that the economic policies of many developed countries had for some years been marked by a striking dualism. It was something that had also been remarked on by a number of those involved in the Airbus issue in the United States—that since the late 1970s, there had been a domestic trend in the direction of more freedom and less control, with more reliance on prices and markets and less on regulation. This move towards economic liberalism (Henderson employed the phrase in its European sense) was by no means confined to the America of Ronald Reagan or the Britain of Margaret Thatcher. It also happened in France between 1982 and 1986 and, most dramatically, in New Zealand after the election of a Labour government in 1984.

The reason Henderson described this trend towards economic liberalism as "uneasy" was that it had not extended to all areas of policy. It had not, specifically, extended to trade, and it was Henderson's view that on balance the trade regimes of the OECD countries were less liberal at the end of the 1980s than they had been at the end of the 1970s. He ascribed this to the fact that those who fashion economic policy are not particularly receptive to classically liberal ideas of where economic advantage lies. His tone was one of tolerant regret—"though academically respectable and even orthodox, these views are not widely held." Instead, economic interest was perceived in terms that were "staunchly nationalist and mercantilist," the policies that resulted testifying to what he described, with a slight wrinkling of the nose, as "the power of do-it-yourself economics."

Henderson argued that although the progressive establishment of a genuinely open multilateral trading system would be of general benefit, that benefit would extend beyond material prosperity and would make a contribution to international stability and security:

Because of its centralised and discretionary character, administrative protectionism gives rise to an unending series of complex arguments and disputes in which governments are directly involved. In addition to the waste that these constant litigations represent—since the time and energies of highly skilled people are committed to activities which are unproductive or even damaging—they are a constant source of friction between states.

Quite a few veterans of the Airbus dispute on both sides of the Atlantic would give a sigh of recognition at that insight.

Henderson also pointed out that the prospects for stability and security depended to some extent on the readiness of states, especially the most powerful ones, to accept and lend support to internationally recognised norms of conduct, and that in the sphere of international trade such norms exist, and can usefully be given legal form. It would not be for a senior official of the OECD to say so, but one of the unfortunate facts of international life that is highlighted by the dispute over Airbus is the ineffectiveness of the GATT—"The General Disagreement" as *The Economist* unkindly called it in a review of the state of play at the halfway mark of the Uruguay Round.

The General Agreement on Tariffs and Trade had been signed at the Palais des Nations in Geneva in October 1947. All that the 23 nations represented had been asked to do was draft a charter for a body to be called the International Trade Organisation, which would take its place beside the International Monetary Fund and what was later to become the World Bank. In November of the same year, 56 countries assembled in Cuba to consider the text, and four months and 602 amendments later, all but three of them put their signature to it. The process of ratification was acrimonious, however, particularly in the United States. The Americans had wanted the ITO to have the authority to enforce a "code of laws," but some of the other signatories jibbed at the idea of such a code's being policed by an international regulatory body. Two years later Washington announced that the Charter would not be resubmitted for ratification by the Congress, and the GATT found itself promoted from midwife to fostermother.

During the next two decades, the winds of trade expansion and liberalisation blew steadily. Since the middle 1970s, however, it has been a different story, with escalating farm subsidies and continual trade disputes, and there were many who applied to GATT the description that Israel's Abba Eban had pinned to the United Nations 20 years earlier—"the runaway policeman." When the organisation celebrated its 40th anniversary in 1987, Arthur Dunkel, the former Swiss civil servant who was its third director-general, did not beat about the bush. "The GATT rules exist to help governments cope with change. If governments are unable to do so, and seek to block the process of change by protectionist means, then trade growth will slow down and with it the rise in living standards. That is exactly what has happened as some governments have sought relief through new forms of import restriction or attempted to give their traders a competitive edge through subsidies."[8]

Although the United States remains formally committed to free trade, the reality is that for some years now it has effectively been operating a policy of managed trade, and there are few who believe that will now change. Raymond Waldmann, who was an assistant secretary of commerce for international economic policy in the Reagan administration before moving to Seattle as Boeing's director of government affairs, wrote a book on the subject in 1986 and rehearsed the steps that would be necessary to reverse the trend:

To achieve truly free trade would require dismantling the European Common Market and the East bloc's COMECON; ending the special and differential treatment promoting development in poor countries; removing governments from the airlines, communications, trading, insurance, and shipping businesses; eliminating OPEC; outlawing financial and tax incentives for new investment; and most importantly, throwing open protected sectors in all countries to the harsh forces of international competition. Only then would the preconditions be in place for buyers and sellers to make decisions without government interference.[9]

Waldmann's view was that the United States must collaborate with the inevitable. Its aim should be to enlarge the area within which free trade principles operate by a judicious use of the principle of reciprocity and by negotiating new free trade areas with those countries prepared to do so. It should also work for the strengthening of the GATT. Beyond that, he advocated a United States initiative for some new free trade area arrangement that would seek to minimise and eventually eliminate government intervention—in effect a sort of "super-GATT." The inducement for other countries to join would be the prospect of access to what is still the largest and most lucrative market in the world.

A variant on Waldmann's theme found forcible expression at a meeting of the World Economic Forum in the Swiss ski resort of Davos in January of 1989. "GATT is dead," announced Lester Thurow, dean of the Sloan School of Management at the Massachusetts Institute of Technology, adding (rather redundantly, some thought) "Let's drop the Uruguay Round."[10] Thurow viewed the development of large trading blocs with equanimity. The emergence of free regional economies should be seen as a step towards a world economy, he said.

The Round was certainly looking sickly. It had been launched in the small seaside resort of Punta del Este in 1986. By the time the trade ministers from the 96 signatory nations met in Montreal in December 1988 to review progress at the halfway stage, there were deep disagreements between the EEC and the United States over agricultural reform. Incensed by the behaviour of the Community and the United States, a group of Latin American states, led by Argentina, brandished the diplomatic equivalent of an Exocet missile—unless the farm issue was settled, they would block progress in the 11 areas (out of 15) where outline agreement existed.

One set of proposals that the ministers had before them would have strengthened the authority of the GATT as an institution—a new system for monitoring the trade policies of member countries (the United States had volunteered to be first on the ducking stool), proposals for greater ministerial involvement and a tightening of the procedures for the settlement of disputes, which by common consent were cumbersome and ineffectual.

"No deal is better than a bad deal," the deputy U.S. trade representative said bleakly. Everything was put on ice until the following April and the GATT director-general was charged with finding artful language that would save the Round from the fate of Humpty Dumpty and the GATT itself from the undertakers. Four months later, it seemed that Dunkel's attempts at administering the kiss-of-life had succeeded—just. But the second half of the road begun at Punta del Este proved every bit as long and stony as the first. As this book was going to press, in the late spring of 1992, the trade talks in Geneva remained snagged, mainly on the issue of agriculture, and the landscape was littered with expired deadlines and phoney ultimatums.

The specific disagreement at Montreal had been about the lowering of agricultural trade barriers and the phasing out of subsidies. Within weeks, Europe and the United States were again at odds over agriculture when the Community announced that it intended to ban imports of hormone-treated meat for human consumption. The effect of this would be to exclude American exports worth some $100 million a year, and Washington immediately announced that it would retaliate by blocking boned ham, canned tomatoes, instant coffee and fruit juice from Europe.

European unease on hormones dated from 1980, when a number of Italian mothers became convinced that certain infant foods containing a growth-promoting substance called DES was causing their offspring to grow breasts. Green parties, notably in West Germany, climbed aboard the issue, and in 1985 the Commission imposed a ban, although the scientific evidence pointed the other way. Suspicions that the ban had more to do with the European beef mountain than any health hazard were not confined to the United States.

When he pronounced GATT dead in his speech at Davos, Professor Thurow also said that 1989 was going to be a year of "incredibly sharp trade disputes." Before the end of the month American telecommunications exports had joined the lengthening list of areas where friction might be expected (this flowed from a provision in the new Trade Act), and in one of his last acts as USTR Clayton Yeutter had served notice on the European Commission that the United States wished to open negotiations on market opening measures.[11] Economic liberals, preparing in 1989 to mark the hundredth anniversary of the death of the radical John Bright, were clearly not going to have a happy year.

Two years later, as presidential hopefuls for 1992 began to declare their candidacies, it was clear that even though the U.S. trade deficit had fallen substantially, some Democrats would once more turn to economic nationalism as a way of distinguishing themselves from Republicans and appealing to "Reagan Democrats." The cry was once more "Get tough on trade." Tom Harkin, the Democratic senator from Iowa, was one of the first to throw his hat into the ring, and a staple line in his stump speeches was that $160 billion was spent on subsidising Western Europe and would be better spent at home.

Richard Gephardt, though not himself a candidate this time round, was also back in the fray. In September 1991, the House majority leader announced that he and Sandy Levin, the Democrat from Michigan, would introduce new legislation to replace the Super-301 provision of the 1988 Trade Law which had lapsed earlier in the year. During the campaign for the New Hampshire primary in February 1992 Patrick Buchanan, the right-wing Republican challenger to President Bush, took a strong "America first" line on trade and called for retaliation against Airbus Industrie by the U.S administration. He said that if he were elected he would tell the governments that backed the consortium that "we are going to protect Boeing because they built the planes that kept you free." He would do so by the intoduction of countervailing duties that would raise the price of Airbus aircraft in the U.S market.

* * * * *

The conflict engendered by the success of Airbus has generally been seen in economic terms. Neither side has seen much profit in making such a connection openly, but it is instructive to place it in the context of some of the foreign policy and defence preoccupations of the parties to the dispute.

Forty-five years after the end of the Second World War, and in spite of the enormous economic progress Europe had made in that time, the United States was still making a disproportionately large contribution to western security. It was a burden that she had borne generously and without complaint, although she had never denied that her policies were fuelled by a healthy element of enlightened self-interest. One of the benefits to her European allies was that they had had rather more money available than would otherwise have been the case to pursue such policies as stimulating industrial output—which included the provision of capital to their aircraft industries and the reduction of the risk at which such industries operate. It was not a law of nature that American tolerance of such a state of affairs should be unlimited.

There was a second defence-related consideration. It is one that has seemed less urgent since events in Russia and eastern Europe went into the fast-forward mode, but the conflict in the Gulf in early 1991 showed that it would be foolish to discount it. Although it is possible to make too much of the closeness between the civil and the military side in aircraft manufacture, there is one important respect in which the military capacity of the United States is heavily dependent on a healthy commercial industry. The handful of big, household-name manufacturers such as Boeing and McDonnell Douglas are only the tip of the iceberg. Beneath them there is a huge and intricate network. It covers several major industrial sectors, and includes engine manufacturers, producers of components and suppliers of materials.

The parts and equipment that go into a single Boeing 747, for instance, are supplied by more than 50,000 companies representing every state in the Union, and that is where the hidden power of American industry lies. Because of the "start, stop, sputter" character of many defence programmes, however, the military side does far less to sustain this essential supplier base than do the more consistent civil manufacturers. At one remove, therefore, the military preparedness of the nation is closely bound up with the health of the commercial aircraft industry. If things got really rough on the international trade front, that is a consideration that the U.S. Government would be bound to have in mind.

Such concerns found a focus during the 1988 U.S. presidential campaign in the theme of burden sharing, defined in a *Newsweek* article as a code-word meaning "America is being let down by its wimpy allies."[12] Presidential hopefuls as dissimilar as Jesse Jackson and Robert Dole both found room for it in their campaign pitch, and it had to do with much more than painless ways of attacking the federal budget deficit. "Burden sharing and trade should be talked about in the same paragraph," said one of Dole's advisers. "Both reflect Americans' feeling that they're being screwed, and both focus on the same 'enemy': our allies."[12]

Senator Dole's long political nose had told him that a growing number of Americans felt that too much was being spent on the common defence, that there were too many GIs stationed abroad and that America's allies used the money they saved on defence to subsidise trade, thus making a contribution to the U.S. trade deficit. The figures for defence spending could be marshalled to support such arguments. The U.S. military budget amounted to almost 7 percent of gross national product—Britain spent less than 5 percent and West Germany just 3 percent. This meant that the average taxpayer in America had to shell out $1,209 a year on defence compared with a West German figure of $561.[13]

American defence experts such as Senator John McCain of Arizona, a Republican member of the Senate Armed Services Committee, acknowledged that there were other ways of doing the sums—that Europe provided 90 percent of the ground forces, for instance, and 75 percent of the air power—but insisted that their contribution had not grown in a way that matched the expansion of their economies.[14] Manfred Wörner, the NATO secretary- general and a former Bonn Defence Minister, appeared to concede the point: "The Americans are obviously entitled to ask whether a stronger Europe shouldn't bear greater burdens and responsibilities."[15]

American irritation was compounded by a feeling that some Europeans tended to take the NATO defence umbrella for granted. In the summer of 1988, for example, Rupert Scholz, the academic lawyer from Berlin who had succeeded Wörner as defence minister only a few months previously, contributed a long article to *Die Welt* about European security and how assymetric disarmament was the key to reaching a balance in conventional forces.[16] The views and positions of the Warsaw Pact, Mr. Gorbachev and the Federal Republic were all rehearsed at length. "Political *détente* basically starts at the level of each individual, of each European and his right to self-determination. Support for freedom, self-determination and independence, therefore, represents the guiding motto for a policy of *détente* in Europe. If true progress is made in this field many of the problems of European security would take care of themselves." Quite so. The only curious thing about the article was that at no point in it was there a mention of the United States.[17]

West Germany had ceased to be the prize pupil in Uncle Sam's Atlantic academy long before the onset of the Gorbachev "charm offensive." (He probably didn't notice it, but in his day even Leonid Brezhnev had been greeted on a state visit to Bonn by an anti-Reagan demonstration.) The leading strings had become progressively looser since Willy Brandt embarked on his *ostpolitik* in 1970. For some years before reunification, hardly a week went by without an opinion poll in West Germany disclosing that four people out of five would favour a nuclear-free Europe, that half the population would prefer to be neutral and that large numbers of West Germans entertained warmer feelings towards the Soviet Union than they did to the United States. Some Americans remembered their Heine: "Denk ich an Deutschland in der Nacht, bin ich um meinem Schlaf gebracht!"[18]

The former West German Republic played host to the most dense concentration of military forces in Western Europe, and its air space was used by seven different NATO air forces. In August 1988 67 people died when an Italian aerobatics display at the U.S. Air Force base at Ramstein went disastrously wrong. When an American A-10 Thunderbird crashed near Düsseldorf four months later killing four people and destroying 20 houses, it was the 21st NATO aircraft to crash on West German soil in the course of the year.

Small wonder that the old debate about the occupation rights of the allied armies flared up. "In contrast to its alliance partners," said a leading article in the conservative *Frankfurter Allgemeine Zeitung,* "the Federal Republic is not fully sovereign."[19] One of the speakers at a memorial service for the victims of Ramstein was the prime minister of Rhineland-Palatinate, Herr Bernhard Vogel. In the past his Christian Democrat party had criticised opponents of the airshow as anti-American, but now he felt it could never be held again in that form. "Ramstein," he said, "is an example of the burdens that the people of this country have to bear."

One of the burdens the U.S. administration felt it had to bear as the 1980s moved to a close was the sight of its European allies falling over each other to bankroll Mr. Gorbachev as he tried to do something about the shambles that was the Soviet economy. In 1988, the Soviets had sought loans on the international capital markets for the first time since repudiating the obligations of their tsarist predecessors. A British consortium led by the Midland Bank assembled a credit package worth $2.6 billion, Crédit Lyonnais came forward with $2 billion and from West Germany came the offer of loans at interest rates below those paid on German treasury securities. Americans scratched their heads and reflected that these were the hard-headed men who had not yet thought it worth investing in Airbus. For Mr. Gorbachev, who was thought at that stage to be running a budget deficit about four times as large as that of the United States, it was very cheerful news. Apart from anything else, it meant that he would not have to cut his military budget—and that was believed to be about 14 percent of the USSR's gross national product, or rather more than twice that of the United States.

None of this ever made the United States seriously consider throwing up its hands and heading for home, although Europeans occasionally made extravagant projections about the transatlantic relationship that suggested that this was inevitable. As recently as 1989, for instance, one writer was speculating in entertainingly Gallic fashion about what he called the "bucolic pacifism" of the Star Wars concept.[20] It arose, he averred, from the wish to be protected today by a nuclear shield just as the United States had been protected, at the time of the Monroe Doctrine, by the breadth of the oceans: it was an expression, in the thermonuclear age, of old-style isolationism.

That was so much salon talk, and sounded almost as absurd before the collapse of communism as it did after it. The Americans may well press for different arrangements with their allies, but Europe would be deceiving itself if it believed that either the administration or industry in the United States have been remotely affected by the "declinist" theories made fashionable by Professor Kennedy and others—least of all after the cataclysmic changes in the former Soviet empire.

Those changes, however, will inevitably have the effect of making arguments between the United States and Europe over economic issues bulk larger than they used to. Such differences were overshadowed in the past by the military imperatives of the Atlantic alliance Now that the Soviet threat has disappeared, that "security glue" is no longer as strong as it was, and American thoughts turn naturally to some of their pressing domestic preoccupations. That was what lay behind the speech that the U.S. vice-president, Dan Quayle, made at the annual Munich security conference in February 1992. The failure of the GATT talks would fuel protectionism in the United States, he said, and encourage those who wanted to pull all U.S. troops out of NATO. His remarks, which came in a departure from his prepared text, elicited a sharp response from European Community agriculture ministers who happened to be meeting in Brussels; the United Kingdom minister, John Selwyn Gummer, spoke about megaphone diplomacy, adding waspishly that Mr Quayle had no doubt not been properly briefed. The vice-president backtracked a little, denying that he had intended to make any specific linkage between the success of the Uruguay Round and U.S. troop levels in Europe There had been a number of other senior American politicians and defence experts at Munich, however; several of them had spelled out the connection very directly and none subsequently found it necessary to unsay a word.

At the time of writing, it is too early to judge whether the upheavals in the former Soviet Union could have an indirect effect on U.S.-European trade relations. If they do, it will flow from the enhanced importance of Germany, and the impact which that in turn will have on her relations with her European partners—especially France—and with the United States. In general, anything that tends to expand the market tends to take the edge off competitive hostility, and in that context both sides will be keeping a close watch on developments in Russia and the other former Soviet republics— Aeroflot is, after all, the world's largest airline. It has an estimated fleet size of more than 1,200 aircraft and in 1990 carried some 12 percent of world air traffic. It was significant that in 1991, for the first time, the USSR was included in Boeing's annual market survey.

"U.S. national power rests on the strength of our domestic economy," said President Reagan in his 1988 National Security Strategy statement. "It is in our national security interest to maintain a dynamic research and development capability which enables us to be in the forefront of technological advance."[21] The thrust to reassert U.S. leadership and the marked resurgence in aeronautical research in the United States had not, in fact, gone unremarked in Europe, and early in 1987 the European

Commission and the nine leading aeronautical companies had agreed to share the cost of what became known as the Euromart Study Report.[22] It confirmed that there was substantial cause for concern: "The competitiveness of the industry is threatened by the intensification of technological competition resulting from the powerful drive underway in the United States . . . which expresses a positive national determination to try to sustain its historical preeminence into the next century." Apprehension was also expressed about the emergence of newcomer industries in a number of developing countries—there had, for instance, been some penetration of military trainer aircraft from Latin America.

The report acknowledged that for some future projects, particularly supersonic and hypersonic transports, there would be a need to seek partnerships outside Europe "to cope with the enormous technical and financial challenges." There was an insistence, however, that the required technological capability must be acquired within Europe: the industry, it said, "cannot buy or otherwise obtain this upgraded technological skill from its US competitors *without giving up the independence it wishes to maintain.* "(author's italics)

This seemed to betray some confusion of thought. When it has suited them, the Europeans have emphasised the virtues not of independence but of *inter*dependence, stressing the global nature of the industry and claiming that Airbus was one of the pioneers of internationalisation— "360,000 man-hours of American labor go into each A300/310", said an Airbus Industrie booklet given wide currency in the United States in 1987.

The Americans initially approached the idea more warily, but they too now accept it as a fact of life—"the marketplace has changed and there is no going back," said a 1988 AIA publication.[23] The Americans have also tended to be much franker than the Europeans about their reasons:

The growth of aerospace manufacturing capability in Europe and in a number of more recently industrialised countries like Brazil, Israel and Indonesia has created overcapacity . . . Foreign government support of their aerospace industries has increased the number of market competitors and the strength of the competition, causing US market share to decrease. As a result, US firms have been impelled to strengthen their international market position through a variety of means including licensing, direct investment abroad and joint ventures.

In the last decade and a half, joint ventures have often made more sense for American firms than either direct investment or licensing.[24] The McDonnell Douglas MD-11 is one such project, involving JAMCO of Japan, McDonnell Douglas of Canada, CASA of Spain and Aeritalia. The 777 is another. Boeing announced in May 1991 that Mitsubishi Heavy Industries Ltd., Kawasaki Heavy Industries Ltd. and Fuji Heavy Industries Ltd. would all participate as programme partners in the design, manufacture and testing of portions of the airframe structure and would share in market risk.

There is also the highly successful—and significant—joint venture between General Electric of the USA and SNECMA of France which produces the CFM56 engine. "One thousand one hundred and twenty-three thank-yous!" said an advertisement in the French trade press in the spring of 1989.[25] It had been placed by Boeing. It patted SNECMA (and itself) on the back for the success of "the best-selling jet in the history of aviation" (all the new 737s were powered by the CFM56). It also paid tribute all its other French suppliers, and it slipped in a useful little statistic—the substantial French content in Boeing planes meant that the French Treasury was better off to the tune of more than $1 million a day. The implication was plain. The aircraft industries of Europe and the United States are already so intertwined that if the dispute over Airbus were to escalate, it would have some of the attributes of a civil war.

Which in turn suggested that one way of cooling things might be to persevere with the search for possible areas of collaboration. Given the constant acceleration in performance trends and the astronomical level of funding required for research and development, there is plenty of scope. There was only 25 years between the Douglas DC-3 and the Boeing 707. There was less than 20 years between the start of jet service and the advent of Concorde. It seems certain therefore that there will be dramatic advances in subsonic flight by the turn of the century and highly likely that an advanced supersonic transport will emerge not so very much later. Beyond that it seems probable that sustained application of space technology to commercial aircraft design will bring travel times down even more sensationally. The technology is not yet in place, but with sufficient effort in the areas of laminar flow, high-temperature composite structures and variable-cycle engines, the longest routes could be shrunk to as little as three or four hours.

It is not, perhaps, immediately clear who would want to buy a ticket for such a journey, but a supersonic aircraft flying at Mach 3.2 could make the round trip from London to Sydney and back all in one day, with stops at Anchorage and Tokyo on the way out and Honolulu, Los Angeles and New York on the homeward leg. Such a prospect is now well this side of fantasy—indeed some ideas have already been floated about how airline operators might combine to handle such a hair-raising itinerary. A plane on such a route would pass through many sovereign territories. Airlines might form a consortium and develop arrangements comparable with those that banks now make for leasing aircraft. A carrier would pay only for that part of the flight in which the plane traversed that airline's traditional routes. These are not the fevered imaginings of some demented futurologist. They are ideas advanced by John Swihart, formerly Boeing's chief engineer of production for the American supersonic transport program and subsequently their corporate vice-president for international affairs.[26]

McDonnell Douglas and Airbus may have failed to get together on the AM 300, but the last word has not yet been heard on transatlantic collaboration. And as hypersonic flight is an area for which the Japanese have earmarked several hundred million dollars of research effort, a spot of European-American togetherness might have something to be said for it. In a little-noticed development in the summer of 1991, Boeing and Deutsche Aerospace signed an agreement-in-principle to coordinate efforts related to the study and development of a High Speed Civil Transport.[27]

The scramble to form international alliances as a means of spreading investment costs and penetrating export markets was intensified in late 1991. Shares in McDonnell Douglas rose sharply when the company confirmed that it was in negotiations to sell up to 40 percent of its commercial aircraft business. The prospective buyer turned out to be Taiwan Aerospace, a newly-formed venture between the Taiwan government and local industry which had been capitalised at $250 million; a $2 billion sale would give MDD about half the funds it needed to develop the MD-12. "McDonnell Douglas has the good sense to prefer losing an argument to losing its shirt," *The Economist* commented drily, pointing out that a transpacific version of the Airbus consortium might well bring the American company the sort of government subsidy to which it had taken such exception over the years—when the recipient was its European competitor.[28]

Boeing's collaborative agreements with Japanese companies related to aircraft in the 100-400 seat market, but it was an emerging strand of Airbus strategy to persuade the Japanese that when it came to developing a new Jumbo they might prefer to consider the attractions of a European partnership. Mitsubishi and Kawasaki both confirmed in November 1991 that they had been approached by Airbus, and Adam Brown, speaking the following February at a conference organised by the *Financial Times* on the eve of the Singapore Air Show, played skilfully on Japanese sensitivity to the received idea that Boeing were reluctant to share their know-how on core technologies: "I raise the question," he said, "as to how much longer Boeing can hope with such an approach to satisfy the legitimate aspirations of the dynamic developing nations in the Asia-Pacific region."[29] Airbus's interest in forging new partnerships was not restricted to Asia. Henri Martre of Aérospatiale was also in Singapore. He said a few days later that the cost of developing a new 600-seat aircraft would require wider cooperation than under current Airbus arrangements and disclosed that his company had approached the Russian manufacturers Tupolev and Ilyushin to see whether they too might have an interest in collaboration.[30]

* * * * *

As the Airbus dispute entered its second decade, the three manufacturers were still all selling prodigious quantities of aircraft, their order books bulging far into the 1990s. In one seven-day period in the spring of 1989, Airbus announced firm orders from five different companies for 41 aircraft with options on 39 more—business valued at more than $7 billion. A month later GPA, the Irish leasing group, placed massive orders with all three major manufacturers—123 firm orders valued at $6.5 billion and a further $10.3 billion worth of business in options and orders subject to confirmation. Between 1988 and 1989 Boeing, traditionally conservative in such matters, revised its estimate of demand over the next 15 years to more than 8,400 jetliners—an increase of 1,500. Was it possible that the traditional feast and famine rhythm of the industry had gone haywire? Had the pendulum in some mysterious way got stuck?

Adam Brown of Airbus thought not. "I'm one of the very few people here at the moment arguing that we have to expect a downturn. I'm not sure of the timing, and if anyone tells me that he can predict these cycles, then I'm sceptical, because if he could, he wouldn't be talking to me, he'd be bobbing about on his yacht in Tahiti or somewhere. But I fear that sometime in the early nineties there will be a downturn. I hope it won't be a massive one, but I think it will be significant."[31]

Those who believed that the pendulum had seized up argued that a number of things had occurred that, taken together, represented a structural change in the market. "They point out the effect of deregulation of the airline industry in the U.S.," said Brown, "the effect of moves towards the liberalisation of the industry in Europe, and of similar trends in Canada, Australasia and Japan. They point to the awakening of China, to the progressive imposition of noise rules, to the increasing concern about ageing airplanes—all these are one-off factors that have occurred more or less together, and which are certain to drive demand. So this isn't just going to be a cyclical blip, this mean the whole market is going to take a jump."

Brown conceded the force of all that, but his memory was retentive. "I lived through the last of these downturns, where we were driving to increase the rate on the A300/A310 to seven airplanes a month. We had a thing called the operations room where the whole wall was given over to a great graphical display of all the business we were going to lose if we didn't drive production, drive production, drive production. I was as guilty as anyone—every visitor who came here we would take into the operations room and say, 'If we don't drive production up to seven a month, look at all the business we're going to lose'."

"Well, the market *did* turn down, and we ended up with twenty-four whitetails. Now you can argue that wasn't all bad—I don't think we would have got a PanAm deal if we hadn't had them available. But that sort of thing does leave scars. I still say to everybody, 'Don't forget the downside.' And my expectation is that there will be a significant downturn."

During 1990, it began to look as if Brown's judgement was correct.

Even before Iraq invaded Kuwait in August of that year, the U.S. economy had entered a period of stagnation, and recessionary pressures were apparent worldwide. As a result of a cold winter and shortages, oil prices had risen to about $19 a barrel in the first quarter. After the Iraqi invasion, the UN embargo and the fear of war increased prices to over $40. The substantial increase in fuel bills took a heavy toll of airline profits. Orders for commercial jets, which had surged to a record figure of $96 billion in 1989, eased back to $81.3 billion in 1990. In their 1991 market outlook document, Boeing's forecast of average annual growth up to the year 2005 was 5.2 percent—between 1982 and 1990 the growth figure had been 7.2 percent.[32]

Airbus announced at the beginning of 1992 that orders in the previous year had fallen to around 100 (in 1990 the figure had been 404). Some weeks later the director-general of the International Air Transport Association, Gunter Eser, told a conference in Singapore that airlines had cancelled 138 orders for new aircraft in 1991, the highest figure since the 1982 recession. At the same conference the executive vice-president of the French Banque Indosuez, Emmanuel Vasseur, said that the growing problems faced by aircraft manufacturers were largely of their own making—by encouraging airlines to acquire more new aircraft than strictly necessary in the late 1980s, they had created considerable overcapacity in the market.[33]

In the intervals of frowning over their econometric models in Seattle and Toulouse, there were matters for both sides to ponder. In some respects— and the reasons were both cultural and temperamental—the two sides still confronted each other across a gulf of incomprehension. At its widest point it was Marianne and Uncle Sam who glared at each other the most angrily. There were Americans who genuinely could not understand why people who are so good at producing camembert and perfume should want to try their hand at jet aircraft as well. They forgot that European education was not what it was. Nowadays the number of people familiar with Ricardo's theory of comparative advantage is small; those who understand it are an even more select band; those who believe it has an application to their affairs could ride comfortably together in one taxi-cab.

It seemed strange, on the other hand, that in the heart of the Old World the nation that gave birth to La Fayette and Tocqueville and Beaumont should have so little feel for the profound sense of indignation that their attitude to the Airbus issue engendered in many Americans. That should not have required too much of an intellectual or imaginative effort from the most intelligent nation in Europe.

Perhaps they were still hampered in that by their recent history. There have been two occasions in this century when France owed her liberty to American intervention, and there has always been a level of consciousness at which this was less a cause for gratitude than a source of humiliation.

Count Carlo Sforza, who was Italy's foreign minister at the time, was once asked to define the difference between the French and the Italians after the Second World War. "Simple," he replied. "The Italians must forget a defeat. The French must invent a victory. Our task is infinitely easier . . . "[34] Almost half a century later, it was as if Airbus were one of the war zones in which the assurance of that victory was still being sought.

The American and European sides both made tactical mistakes. "Speak softly and carry a big stick," said Theodore Roosevelt in a celebrated speech at the Minnesota State Fair in 1901, but 80 and some years later, Smith and Smart seem to have been provoked into getting that back to front and doing an injury to American credibility. The best work on the U.S. side of the table in the late Reagan years was done one step down the pecking order by impressive and level-headed officials of high competence such as Bruce Wilson of the Trade Representative's office. The trade representative himself is clearly not in the strongest of positions as an administration begins to run out of steam. In his last year or so in the job, before moving on to become President Bush's secretary for agriculture, Clayton Yeutter developed a tendency to finger-wagging and gave the Europeans the impression that they were being lectured. Negotiators are not helped by a reputation for big talk and small cigars.

Until the later 1980s, the Airbus touch was least sure in the fields of public relations and publicity—a general weakness for the glossy and the rhetorical, a poetic tendency to blur the distinction between options and orders, a more than occasional inclination to go over the top. The fifth Marquess of Salisbury, a Tory grandee in the Britain of the 1950s and 1960s, once inflicted serious damage on a prominent member of his own party by describing him as "too clever by half." It is a phrase well suited to some of Airbus's promotional material of a few years ago, although since Jean Pierson brought in Robert Alizart as vice-president for communications in 1986 the tone of voice in which the consortium addresses the world has matured and now seems less extravagant.[35] "It doesn't mean style is out, but flamboyance is not really the language of Airbus anymore," said Alizart. "In the old days, when we were christening an aircraft, it was Château Pétrus, and who cared if the bottle cost 1,500–2,000 francs? Well, now I do care. If Château Pétrus is absolutely called for, it will be served, but sometimes a lesser vintage will do."[36]

It was also an error of judgement on the part of Airbus to lash out at Boeing in 1988 in the manner described in Chapter 8. "Bad case, abuse opponent's attorney," is poor advice under any legal jurisdiction. Airbus showed considerable flair in reading their customers, but were less good at reading their competitors. It is easier, of course, to be laid back if you are as big as Boeing, but that is not a law of nature. Toulouse should forget the Avis Company's "We try harder" motto and remember their Talleyrand: *Surtout, Messieurs, point de zèle.*

* * * * *

As conflict over trade has been endemic in the international system at least since the late Middle Ages, it is not surprising that it has spawned a considerable literature. In recent years, some of it has become demandingly technical and abstruse. The unwary reader can quickly find himself fast in the coils of hegemonic stability theory or wrestling with multilateral assymetry. Here be dragons. Out in the narrow no-man's land that separates economics and political science some writers have built theoretical models for trade games, and these structures have splendidly evocative names—"Prisoners' Dilemma," "Chicken," "Stag Hunt," "Hawk–Dove," "Bully," "Called Bluff," "Deadlock," "Battle of the Sexes."[37]

They are rather like the games that can be played on computers, but as tools for predicting the outcome or duration of particular conflicts their usefulness is limited. In 1988 Paul Lawrance of the British Department of Trade and Industry ventured a guess that the Airbus dispute could well rumble on for a further 20 years. Even if it did, it would still have some way to go before it forced its way into the record books—the conflict between England and the Hanseatic League over the control of trade in the Baltic went on for the best part of 400 years, after all.

There is an arresting (and completely untechnical) passage in a volume of memoirs published in the United States in the late 1970s:

They often behave like two heavily armed blind men feeling their way around a room, each believing himself in mortal peril from the other, whom he assumes to have perfect vision. Each side should know that frequently uncertainty, compromise and incoherence are the essence of policy making. Yet each tends to ascribe to the other side a consistency, foresight and coherence that its own experience belies. Of course, over time, even two blind armed men in a room can do enormous damage to each other, not to speak of the room.

Henry Kissinger again, child of the old world, servant of the new.[38] He was writing, in fact, about the superpowers, but his words caught something of the way those two worlds had sometimes seemed to regard each other in the confrontation over Airbus.

When the research for this book was at an early stage Paul Lawrance of the British department of trade and industry said, "The Americans give the impression of not knowing what they want, but of not being prepared to rest till they've got it." It was a good line, but there were many Americans, even in the late 1980s, and particularly in the industry, of whom that was emphatically not so. The simplest prescription—analysis, comment, remedy all in one—came with a kindly rasp from Boeing's Dean Thornton: "Time for the kid to get off the tit and stand on its own legs", he said.[39]

Mr. Thornton comes from Idaho. For those unfamiliar with the stockyard idiom of that state, his colleague Dick Albrecht expanded a little on what the American manufacturers would settle for. "If the Airbus governments were now to say, 'OK, fellows, we have given you the money to get started in business and now you've had twenty years to build up a customer base, to learn how to provide customer support, to develop a whole family of airplanes. You're big boys now, and you're out on your own. Whether you sink or swim depends on your ability to compete in the commercial marketplace'."

"If they were to do that," Albrecht continued, "I would say, 'Fine—we will forget that they were subsidised in the past, we will forget that every one of their products was designed and developed with government money. The next airplane, or the next major derivative, they should make enough money off their existing airplanes to fund its development, just as we do in Boeing.' Now if we could get a commitment on that in which we had some confidence—though I'm not sure how you ever get that out of governments—I would happily take it off the political agenda."[40]

On April 1, 1992, shortly before this book went to press, officials from the European Commission and the Office of the U.S. Trade Representative concluded a series of meetings in Washington and Brussels. They reached tentative agreement on a number of issues and went off to seek the approval of their respective governments. How fully did that accord meet Richard Albrecht's conditions for removing the issue from the political agenda?

In any future programmes, direct subsidies would be limited to some 30 percent of total development costs, and conditions would be imposed on the timing of repayments. So far as indirect subsidies were concerned, a limit of five percent of a manufacturer's civil aircraft turnover was believed to have been agreed. On the issue of transparency, the two sides said that they would meet twice a year for consultations; new rules were also drawn up to prevent governments putting pressure on third governments to buy aircraft. The parties agreed not to initiate any new unilateral trade action against each other; either might ask for the suspension of part of the agreement if a manufacturer's business were badly affected by "external" economic or political factors.

The agreement plainly marked a relaxation of the lightly armed truce which the two sides had observed for some years. Would it, however, as Hugo Paemen, the chief European negotiator, claimed, create "peace in the valley?" Airbus were clearly relieved at the removal of the threat of U.S. trade action and the possibility of a ruling by an arbitration panel under GATT. Aérospatiale, whose level of subsidy for the A330 and A340 was believed to be of the order of 40 percent, felt they could live with the agreement. A short statement from Boeing's Lawrence Clarkson described it as "a significant step forward" and said it represented "reasonable progress towards levelling the playing field." Sir Barry Duxbury, the director of the Society of British Aerospace Manufacturers was even more cautious: "The Europe versus U.S. issue will remain pretty active for the balance of this year and in the years ahead in spite of the agreement," he said.[41]

The note of reserve was understandable. Ratification was not a foregone conclusion, and was likely to prove easier in Europe than in the United States, where a formidable number of government agencies had to be consulted. Early indications were that the defense department was not happy with the clauses relating to indirect support and there were also political rumblings— Jack Danforth, the Republican senator from Missouri and a member of the International Trade subcommittee took the view that the U.S. negotiators had given away too much: "It would be difficult to envision a worse outcome," he said.[42]

On balance, the Europeans certainly seemed to have yielded less than the Americans, who had hoped to drive the launch aid figure to much below 30 percent; European officials also claimed that the agreement marked the first implicit admission by the United States that its civil aircraft industry benefited from defence and space research subsidies. It is difficult to believe that the agreement will put an end to disputes in this specific area and on the closely related issue of transparency; the European side, in particular, has argued in the past that beyond a certain point transparency became another word for the disclosure of commercially sensitive information. The belief that one can legislate effectively in the matter of government inducements also seems a shade utopian.

Beyond ratification, further imponderables loom. The agreement is, after all, bilateral, and unless it can be quickly converted into a multilateral one, subscribed to by countries like Japan and Taiwan who are ambitious to develop their aircraft industries, it is likely to remain a dead letter. Nor can there can be adjudication on any disputes that may arise without some appropriate independent mechanism, and this points to the need for a new commercial aircraft code which can be enshrined in the General Agreement on Tariffs and Trade.

It was difficult, in the spring of 1992, to find any impartial observer prepared to express more than modified enthusiasm for the settlement. "Far from being a victory for free trade," wrote *The Economist*, 'the deal struck in Brussels is really a bilateral agreement to subsidise."[43] The past munificence of governments is now so much water under the bridge. The good faith of the parties to the agreement will only be fully tested when the manufacturers start costing their plans for ultra-high capacity aircraft— in other words when Airbus and McDonnell Douglas, very probably in collaboration with Asian partners, challenge the ascendancy Boeing has enjoyed with their 747—and when Boeing, as it assuredly will, responds to that challenge.

Adam Brown, Airbus's director of planning, said in Singapore in February 1992 that a survey by the consortium indicated interest in an aircraft with twice the capacity and 50 percent more seats than the 747. Airbus had set itself the target of 15 percent better direct operating costs per seat than the 747, and they say that this would be achieved through advances in airframe and engine technology.[44] Nobody is yet saying very much about the likely development cost of an aircraft on this scale, but it could be of the order of $15 billion. It remains to be seen whether the financial centres of Europe (and of the Asia-Pacific region) would look at such figures. If they were not prepared to, governments might once again hear siren voices that sang beguilingly of the national interest, of the importance of technological leadership and of the painlessness of offering guarantees . . . [45]

Perhaps the most balanced and perceptive insight into how the 1992 agreement left the aerospace industry appeared in a leading article in the *Financial Times*, which asserted world-wearily that self-interest remained the most effective discipline, but concluded that economic forces had irrevocably altered the terms of the argument:

Though nationalism may still colour the politics of commercial aerospace, its economics are increasingly driven by the growing international interdependence between producers and customers. The continuing globalisation of the industry is the best guarantee of fair trade in the future.[46]

The cast all remain on stage—it's clear to them that *Dogfight* will run and run. Behind them, however, the scenery has changed, and it looks as if the plot might, too. Certainly, in the wings there are numbers of new players, each demanding that in succeeding acts they too should have lines to speak—and dreaming, perhaps, of impossible things before breakfast.

NOTES

1. Paul Kennedy, *The Rise and Fall of the Great Powers: Economic Change and Military Conflict from 1500 to 2000* (New York: Random House, 1988).

2. *Foreign Affairs*, Summer 1988.

3. *The Wall Street Journal*, December 15, 1988.

4. *The Economist*, September 3, 1988.

5. *1992: The Impact on the Outside World*, London, July 12, 1988.

6. *1992: The External Dimension*. Group of Thirty, London and New York, Occasional Paper 25, 1989.

7. *Perestroika in the West: Progress, Limits and Implications*.

8. *GATT Information*, GATT/40/1, October 1987.

9. Raymond J. Waldmann, *Managed Trade: The New Competition between Nations* (Cambridge, Mass.: Ballinger, 1986).

10. *Financial Times*, January 28 1989.

11. In fact a task force that advised the USTR had recommended targeting only France. The serving of notice on the Commission marked Washington's recognition of the

Community as the competent authority. It had previously been U.S. policy to seek market access accords with individual member states.

12. "The High Cost of NATO," *Newsweek,* March 7, 1988.

13. *U.K. Statement on the Defence Estimates,* 1988.

14. "Exercises in Ally-Bashing: Designing a Cooperative Distribution of the Burden." *Armed Forces Journal International,* September 1988.

15. Interview in *Wirtschaftswoche,* November 25, 1988.

16. *Die Welt,* July 16, 1988.

17. Herr Scholz, was, in fact, a strong supporter of the modernisation of NATO's short-range nuclear weapons, which went down well in Washington and London, but his lack of tact and his arrogant manner won him few friends at home. When the West German chancellor reshuffled his cabinet in April 1989 he was dropped. His 11-month tenure made him the shortest-serving of the Federal Republic's nine defence ministers.

18. "If I think of Germany in the middle of the night, I can't sleep any more."

19. *Frankfurter Allgemeine Zeitung,* September 5, 1988.

20. Alain Minc, *La Grande Illusion* (Paris: Bernard Grasset, 1989).

21. *National Security Strategy of the United States,* January 1988.

22. *Joint Study of European Cooperative Measures for Aeronautical Research and Technology,* April 1988.

23. *The U.S. Aerospace Industry and the Trend Toward Internationalization* (Washington, D.C.: Aerospace Industries of America, Inc., March 1988).

24. See David C. Mowery, *Alliance Politics and Economics: Multinational Joint Ventures in Commercial Aircraft* (Cambridge, Mass.: Ballinger, 1987).

25. *Air & Cosmos,* March 18, 1989.

26. *Aeronautical Developments for the 21st Century.* 50th Wright Brothers Lecture in Aeronautics, St. Louis, Missouri, September 14, 1987.

27. Both parties, along with Aérospatiale, British Aerospace and McDonnell Douglas, were already members of the larger Supersonic Commercial Transport International Cooperation Study Group that was addressing technical, business and environmental issues.

28. *The Economist,* November 23, 1991.

29. *Financial Times,* February 25, 1992.

30. *Ibid.,* February 27, 1992.

31. Interview in Toulouse, February 1989.

32. *Current Market Outlook: World Market Demand and Airplane Supply Requirements* (Seattle: Boeing Commercial Airplane Group, February 1991).

33. Financial Times Conference on Asian-Pacific Aviation. See *Financial Times,* February 24, 1992. Boeing's orders also dropped sharply—from 543 new aircraft in 1990 to 252 in 1991.

34. Luigi Barzini, *The Impossible Europeans* (London: Weidenfeld and Nicolson, 1983).

35. Alizart, a British citizen, was born in Mauritius. Originally a journalist, he subsequently worked in Air France's PR department in London and later became Hilton International's Director of PR for Europe, Africa and the Middle East.

36. Interview in Toulouse, February 1989.

37. Some of the writing offers an insight into how the laws of cricket must seem to a follower of American football: "The case where the large country is playing Deadlock, and the small country the Stag Hunt–Chicken hybrid, is unlikely to lead to mutual cooperation unless the small country can credibly threaten to hurt itself. Even if it is so willing, the large country may continue to defect for reasons that have come to be known as the chain store paradox." Reinhard Selton, "The Chain Store Paradox," *Theory and Decision,* April

1978.

38. *White House Years* (Boston: Little, Brown and Company, 1979).

39. Interview in Seattle, February 1988.

40. Interview in Seattle, January 1989.

41. *The Wall Street Journal, Financial Times,* April 2, 1992; *Le Monde,* April 3, 1992.

42. *Newsweek,* April 13, 1992.

43. *The Economist,* April 4, 1992.

44. *Airbus update,* March/April 1992.

45. In the event, McDonnell Douglas were first out of the trap. They gave details at the beginning of May 1992 of their planned MD-12, which they hoped to build in collaboration with Taiwan—a four-engined, double-decker plane with 511 seats and a range of up to 9,000 miles

46. *Financial Times,* April 2, 1992.

Bibliography

Abelshauser, W. *Wirtschaftsgeschichte der Bundesrepublik Deutschland, 1945-80.* Frankfurt am Main: Suhrkamp Verlag, 1983.

Barzini, Luigi. *The Impossible Europeans.* London: Weidenfeld and Nicolson, 1983.

Benn, Tony. *Diaries, Vol. 1: Out of the Wilderness, 1963-67.* London: Hutchinson, 1987.

Benson, Lee. *The Concept of Jacksonian Democracy.* New Jersey: Princeton University Press, 1961.

Bogdan, Lew. *L'Epopée du Ciel Clair.* Paris: Hachette, 1988.

Boulton, David. *The Lockheed Papers.* London: Jonathan Cape, 1978.

Crossman, Richard. *The Diaries of a Cabinet Minister, Vol. III.* London: Hamish Hamilton and Jonathan Cape, 1977.

de Gaulle, Charles. *Mémoires d'Espoir: Le Renouveau, 1958-62.* Paris: Plon, 1970.

d'Estaing, Olivier Giscard. *Le Social-Capitalisme.* Paris: Fayard, 1977.

Erhard, Ludwig. *Germany's Comeback in the World Market.* London: Allen and Unwin, 1954.

Feldman, Elliot J. *Concorde and dissent. Explaining high technology project failures in Britain and France.* Cambridge: Cambridge University Press, 1985.

Franko, Lawrence G., and Stephenson, Sherry. *French Export Behavior in Third World Markets.* Washington D.C.: The Centre for Strategic and International Studies, Georgetown University, 1980.

Gunston, Bill. *Airbus, the European Triumph.* London: Osprey Publishing Company, 1988.

Harrison, Michael. *The Diplomacy of a Self-Assured Middle Power,* in *National Negotiating Styles,* ed. Hans Binnendijk. Washington, D.C.: U.S. Department of State Foreign Service Institute, 1987.

Hayward, Keith. *International Collaboration in Civil Aerospace.* London: Francis Pinter, 1986.

James, Henry. *A Little Tour in France.* Boston: Houghton Miflin and Co., 1884.

Kennedy, Paul. *The Rise and Fall of the Great Powers: Economic Change and Military Conflict from 1500 to 2000.* New York: Random House, 1988.

Kissinger, Henry. *White House Years.* Boston: Little, Brown and Company, 1979.

Langford, John S. *Federal Investment in Aeronautical R&D: Analyzing the NASA Experience.* Cambridge, Mass.: MIT Press, 1987.

Minc, Alain. *La Grande Illusion.* Paris: Bernard Grasset, 1989.

Mowery, David C. *Alliance Politics and Economics: Multinational Joint Ventures in*

Commercial Aircraft. Cambridge, Mass.: Ballinger Publishing Company, 1987.

Muller, Pierre. *Airbus. Du référentiel de l'arsenal au référentiel de marché.* Saint-Martin-d'Hères: CERAT, 1988.

Nelson, R. R. *Government and Technical Progress: A Cross-Industry Analysis.* New York: Pergamon Press, 1982.

Newhouse, John. *The Sporty Game.* New York: Alfred A. Knopf, 1982.

Plowden, Lord. *Report of the Committee of Enquiry into the Aircraft Industry appointed by the Minister of Aviation under the Chairmanship of Lord Plowden, 1964–65.* London: Her Majesty's Stationery Office, Cmnd. 2853, 1965.

Seitz, Frederick. *The Competitive Status of the U.S. Civil Aviation Manufacturing Industry.* Washington: National Academy Press, 1985.

Servan-Schreiber, J-J. *Le défi américain.* Paris: Denoel, 1967.

Shonfield, Andrew. *Modern Capitalism: The Changing Balance of Public and Private Power.* London: Royal Institute of International Affairs/Oxford University Press, 1965.

Strauss, F-J. *Challenge and Response. A programme for Europe.* London: Weidenfeld and Nicolson, 1969. Originally published as *Herausforderung und Antwort: Ein Programm für Europa.* Stuttgart: Seewald Verlag, 1968.

Tournoux, J-R. *Le mois de mai du Général,* Paris: Plon, 1969.

Waldmann, Raymond J. *Managed Trade: The New Competition between Nations.* Cambridge. Mass.: Ballinger Publishing Company, 1986.

Wilson, Harold. *The Labour Government 1964-70. A personal record.* London: Weidenfeld and Nicolson and Michael Joseph, 1971.

Yenne, Bill. *McDonnell Douglas: A Tale of Two Giants.* New York: Crescent Books, 1985.

Index

About the Author

IAN McINTYRE was educated at St. John's College, Cambridge, and the College of Europe in Bruges. He is well-known as a writer and broadcaster on politics and international affairs. He is a former associate editor of *The Times* of London and was for many years a senior executive of the British Broadcasting Corporation.

Lightning Source UK Ltd.
Milton Keynes UK
UKHW02n2035230218
318414UK00007B/52/P